Desert Islands

and Other Texts

1953–1974

Semiotext(e)
PO Box 629
South Pasadena, CA 91031
www.semiotexte.com

Distributed by The MIT Press, Cambridge, Mass. and London, England

Special thanks to fellow translators in this volume: Christopher Bush, Charles Stivale and Melissa McMahon, Alexander Hickox, Teal Eich. Other translations are indebted to David L. Sweet, Jarred Baker, and Jeanine Herman's versions previously published in Felix Guattari's *Chaosophy* (New York: Semiotext(e), 1995). Lysa Hochroth's first translations of Deleuze's articles on Hume, Kant, and Bergson, subsequently reviewed by Elie During, were also invaluable.

Special thanks to Giancarlo Ambrosino, Eric Eich, Teal Eich, Ames Hodges, Patricia Ferrell , Janet Metcalfe for their close reading and suggestions.

The Index was established by Giancarlo Ambrosino.

Cover Photo: Jean-Jacques Lebel.
© Jean-Jacques Lebel archive, Paris.

Design: Hedi El Kholti

ISBN: 978-1-58435-018-7
Printed in the United States of America

10 9 8 7

Desert Islands

and Other Texts

1953–1974

Gilles Deleuze

Edited by David Lapoujade

Translated by Michael Taormina

SEMIOTEXT(E) FOREIGN AGENTS SERIES

Contents

Introduction

This first volume gathers together almost all the texts which Gilles Deleuze published in France and abroad between 1953 and 1974, starting with *Empiricism and Subjectivity*, his first book, and ending with the debates following *Anti-Oedipus*, co-authored with Félix Guattari. This collection essentially contains articles, book reviews, prefaces, interviews, and conferences all previously published in French, but not found in any one work by Deleuze.

In order to avoid any bias as to order or emphasis, I have respected the strict chronology of publication (not of composition). A thematic organization would have jibed with the previous collection *Negotiations*, as well as the bibliographical project undertaken around 1989,[1] but it might have erroneously suggested that this collection constituted a book "by" Deleuze, or at least one he was planning.

The conditions for publication specified by Deleuze have been respected: no texts prior to 1953, and no previously unpublished or posthumous texts. Those texts published for the first time in this volume are all mentioned in the 1989 bibliography.

A second volume will collect texts published between 1975 and 1995: *Two Regimes of Madness and other texts* (*Deux régimes de fous et autres textes*).

—David Lapoujade

Desert Islands

Geographers say there are two kinds of islands. This is valuable information for the imagination because it confirms what the imagination already knew. Nor is it the only case where science makes mythology more concrete, and mythology makes science more vivid. *Continental islands* are accidental, derived islands. They are separated from a continent, born of disarticulation, erosion, fracture; they survive the absorption of what once contained them. *Oceanic islands* are originary, essential islands. Some are formed from coral reefs and display a genuine organism. Others emerge from underwater eruptions, bringing to the light of day a movement from the lowest depths. Some rise slowly; some disappear and then return, leaving us no time to annex them. These two kinds of islands, continental and originary, reveal a profound opposition between ocean and land. Continental islands serve as a reminder that the sea is on top of the earth, taking advantage of the slightest sagging in the highest structures; oceanic islands, that the earth is still there, under the sea, gathering its strength to punch through to the surface. We can assume that these elements are in constant strife, displaying a repulsion for one another. In this we find nothing to reassure us. Also, that an island is deserted must appear *philosophically* normal to us. Humans cannot live, nor live in security, unless they assume that the active struggle between earth and water is over, or at least contained. People like to call these two elements mother and father, assigning them gender roles according to the whim of their fancy. They must somehow persuade themselves that a struggle of this kind does not exist, or that it has somehow ended. In one way or another, the very existence of islands is the negation of this point of view, of this effort, this conviction. That England is populated will always come as a surprise; humans can live on an island only by forgetting what an island represents. Islands are either from before or for after humankind.

But everything that geography has told us about the two kinds of islands, the imagination knew already on its own and in another way. The *élan* that draws humans toward islands extends the double movement that produces islands in themselves. Dreaming of islands—whether with joy or in fear, it doesn't matter—is dreaming of pulling away, of being already separate, far from any continent, of being lost and alone—or it is dreaming of starting from scratch, recreating, beginning anew. Some islands drifted away from the continent, but the island is also that toward which one drifts; other islands originated in the ocean, but *the island is also the origin*, radical and absolute. Certainly, separating and creating are not mutually exclusive: one has to hold one's own when one is separated, and had better be separate to create anew; nevertheless, one of the two tendencies always predominates. In this way, the movement of the imagination of islands takes up the movement of their production, but they don't have the same objective. It is the same movement, but a different goal. It is no longer the island that is separated from the continent, it is humans who find themselves separated from the world when on an island. It is no longer the island that is created from the bowels of the earth through the liquid depths, it is humans who create the world anew from the island and on the waters. Humans thus take up for themselves both movements of the island and are able to do so on an island that, precisely, lacks one kind of movement: humans can drift toward an island that is nonetheless originary, and they can create on an island that has merely drifted away. On closer inspection, we find here a new reason for every island to be and remain in theory deserted.

An island doesn't stop being deserted simply because it is inhabited. While it is true that the movement of humans toward and on the island takes up the movement of the island prior to humankind, *some* people can occupy the island—it is still deserted, all the more so, provided they are sufficiently, that is, absolutely separate, and provided they are sufficient, absolute creators. Certainly, this is never the case in fact, though people who are shipwrecked approach such a condition. But for this to be the case, we need only extrapolate in imagination the movement they bring with them to the island. Only in appearance does such a movement put an end to the island's desertedness; in reality, it takes up and prolongs the *élan* that produced the island as deserted. Far from compromising it, humans bring the desertedness to its perfection and highest point. In certain conditions which attach them to the very movement of things, humans do not put an end to desertedness, they make it sacred. Those people who come to the island indeed occupy and populate it; but in reality, were they sufficiently separate, sufficiently creative, they would give the island only a dynamic image of itself, a consciousness of the movement which produced the island, such that through them the island would in the end become conscious of itself as deserted and unpeopled. The island would be only the dream of humans, and humans, the pure consciousness of the island.

For this to be the case, there is again but one condition: humans would have to reduce themselves to the movement that brings them to the island, the movement which prolongs and takes up the *élan* that produced the island. Then geography and the imagination would be one. To that question so dear to the old explorers—"which creatures live on deserted islands?"—one could only answer: human beings live there already, but uncommon humans, they are absolutely separate, absolute creators, in short, an Idea of humanity, a prototype, a man who would almost be a god, a woman who would be a goddess, a great Amnesiac, a pure Artist, a consciousness of Earth and Ocean, an enormous hurricane, a beautiful witch, a statue from the Easter Islands. There you have a human being who precedes itself. Such a creature on a deserted island would be the deserted island itself, insofar as it imagines and reflects itself in its first movement. A consciousness of the earth and ocean, such is the deserted island, ready to begin the world anew. But since human beings, even voluntarily, are not identical to the movement that puts them on the island, they are unable to join with the *élan* that produces the island; they always encounter it from the outside, and their presence in fact spoils its desertedness. The unity of the deserted island and its inhabitant is thus not actual, only imaginary, like the idea of looking behind the curtain when one is not behind it. More importantly, it is doubtful whether the individual imagination, unaided, could raise itself up to such an admirable identity; it would require the collective imagination, what is most profound in it, i.e. rites and mythology.

In the facts themselves we find at least a negative confirmation of all this, if we consider what a deserted island is in reality, that is, geographically. The island, and all the more so the deserted island, is an extremely poor or weak notion from the point of view of geography. This is to its credit. The range of islands has no objective unity, and deserted islands have even less. The deserted island may indeed have extremely poor soil. Deserted, the island may be a desert, but not necessarily. The real desert is uninhabited only insofar as it presents no conditions that by rights would make life possible, whether vegetable, animal, or human. On the contrary, the lack of inhabitants on the deserted island is a pure fact due to circumstance, in other words, the island's surroundings. The island is what the sea surrounds and what we travel around. It is like an egg. An egg of the sea, it is round. It is as though the island had pushed its desert outside. What is deserted is the ocean around it. It is by virtue of circumstance, for other reasons than the principle on which the island depends, that ships pass in the distance and never come ashore. The island is deserted more than it is a desert. So much so, that in itself the island may contain the liveliest of rivers, the most agile fauna, the brightest flora, the most amazing nourishment, the hardiest of savages, and the castaway as its most precious fruit, it may even contain, however momentarily, the ship that comes to take him away. For all that, it is not any less a deserted island. To change this situation, we would have to overhaul the general distribution of the continents, the state of the seas, and the lines of navigation.

This is to state once again that the essence of the deserted island is imaginary and not actual, mythological and not geographical. At the same time, its destiny is subject to those human conditions that make mythology possible. Mythology is not simply willed into existence, and the peoples of the earth quickly ensured they would no longer understand their own myths. It is at this very moment literature begins. Literature is the attempt to interpret, in an ingenious way, the myths we no longer understand, at the moment we no longer understand them, since we no longer know how to dream them or reproduce them. Literature is the competition of misinterpretations that consciousness naturally and necessarily produces on themes of the unconscious, and like every competition it has its prizes. One would have to show exactly how in this sense mythology fails and dies in two classic novels of the deserted island, Robinson and Suzanne. *Suzanne and the Pacific* emphasizes the separated aspect of islands, the separation of the young woman who finds herself there;[1] *Robinson Crusoe*, the creative aspect, the beginning anew. It is true that the way mythology fails is different in each case. In the case of Giraudoux's Suzanne, mythology dies the prettiest, most graceful death. In Robinson's case, its death is heavy indeed. One can hardly imagine a more boring novel, and it is sad to see children still reading it today. Robinson's vision of the world resides exclusively in property; never have we seen an owner more ready to preach. The mythical recreation of the world from the deserted island gives way to the reconstitution of everyday bourgeois life from a reserve of capital. Everything is taken from the ship. Nothing is invented. It is all painstakingly applied on the island. Time is nothing but the time necessary for capital to produce a benefit as the outcome of work. And the providential function of God is to guarantee a return. God knows his people, the hardworking honest type, by their beautiful properties, and the evil doers, by their poorly maintained, shabby property. Robinson's companion is not Eve, but Friday, docile towards work, happy to be a slave, and too easily disgusted by cannibalism. Any healthy reader would dream of seeing him eat Robinson. *Robinson Crusoe* represents the best illustration of that thesis which affirms the close ties between capitalism and Protestantism. The novel develops the failure and the death of mythology in Puritanism. Things are quite different with Suzanne. In her case, the deserted island is a depository of ready-made, luxurious objects. The island bears immediately what it has taken civilization centuries to produce, perfect, and ripen. But mythology still dies, though in Suzanne's case it dies in a particularly Parisian way. Suzanne has nothing to create anew. The deserted island provides her with the double of every object from the city, in the windows of the shops; it is a double without consistency, separated from the real, since it does not receive the solidity that objects ordinarily take on in human relations, amidst buying and selling, exchanges and presents. She is an insipid young woman. Her companions are not Adam, but young cadavers, and when she reenters the world of living men, she will love them in a uniform way, like a priest, as though love were the minimum threshold of her perception.

What must be recovered is the mythological life of the deserted island. However, in its very failure, Robinson gives us some indication: he first need-ed a reserve of capital. In Suzanne's case, she was first and foremost separate. And neither the one nor the other could be part of a couple. These three indi-cations must be restored to their mythological purity. We have to get back to the movement of the imagination that makes the deserted island a model, a prototype of the collective soul. First, it is true that from the deserted island it is not creation but re-creation, not the beginning but a re-beginning that takes place. The deserted island is the origin, but a second origin. From it everything begins anew. The island is the necessary minimum for this re-beginning, the material that survives the first origin, the radiating seed or egg that must be sufficient to re-produce everything. Clearly, this presupposes that the forma-tion of the world happens in two stages, in two periods of time, birth and re-birth, and that the second is just as necessary and essential as the first, and thus the first is necessarily compromised, born for renewal and already renounced in a catastrophe. It is not that there is a second birth because there has been a catastrophe, but the reverse, there is a catastrophe after the origin because there must be, from the beginning, a second birth. Within ourselves we can locate the source of such a theme: it is not the production of life that we look for when we judge it to be life, but its reproduction. The animal whose mode of reproduction remains unknown to us has not yet taken its place among living beings. It is not enough that everything begin, everything must begin again once the cycle of possible combinations has come to completion. The second moment does not succeed the first: it is the reappearance of the first when the cycle of the other moments has been completed. The second ori-gin is thus more essential than the first, since it gives us the law of repetition, the law of the series, whose first origin gave us only moments. But this theme, even more than in our fantasies, finds expression in every mythology. It is well known as the myth of the flood. The ark sets down on the one place on earth that remains uncovered by water, a circular and sacred place, from which the world begins anew. It is an island or a mountain, or both at once: the island is a mountain under water, and the mountain, an island that is still dry. Here we see original creation caught in a re-creation, which is concentrated in a holy land in the middle of the ocean. This second origin of the world is more important than the first: it is a sacred island. Many myths recount that what we find there is an egg, a cosmic egg. Since the island is a second origin, it is entrusted to man and not to the gods. It is separate, separated by the massive expanse of the flood. Ocean and water embody a principle of segregation such that, on sacred islands, exclusively female communities can come to be, such as the island of Circe or Calypso. After all, the beginning started from God and from a couple, but not the new beginning, the beginning again, which starts from an egg: mythological maternity is often a parthenogenesis. The idea of a second origin gives the deserted island its whole meaning, the survival of a sacred place in a world that is slow to re-begin. In the ideal of beginning anew there is something that precedes the beginning itself, that takes it up to deepen it and delay it in the passage of time. The desert island is the material of this something immemorial, this something most profound.

Jean Hyppolite's *Logic and Existence*[1]

Jean Hyppolite's earlier *Genesis and Structure of Hegel's 'Phenomenology of Spirit'* was a commentary on Hegel, preserving Hegel in its entirety.[2] The intention behind Hyppolite's new book is quite different.[3] Investigating Logic, Phenomenology, and the Encyclopedia, Hyppolite starts from a precise idea to make a precise point: *Philosophy must be ontology, it cannot be anything else; but there is no ontology of essence, there is only an ontology of sense.* Here we have, it seems, the thesis of this essential book, whose style alone is a tour de force. If Hyppolite's thesis 'philosophy is ontology' means one thing above all, it is that philosophy is not anthropology.

Anthropology aspires to be a discourse *on* humanity. As such, it presupposes the empirical discourse *of* humanity, in which the speaker and the object of his speech are separate. Reflection is on one side, while being is on the other. Seen in this light, understanding is a movement which is not a movement of the thing; it remains outside the object. Understanding is thus the power to abstract; and reflection is merely external and formal. It follows that empiricism ultimately sends us back to formalism, just as formalism refers back to empiricism. "Empirical consciousness is a consciousness directed at preexistent being, relegating reflection to subjectivity." Subjectivity will thus be treated as a fact, and anthropology will be set up as the science of this fact. Kant's legitimizing subjectivity does not change the essential point.

"Critical consciousness is a consciousness that reflects the knowing self, but which relegates being to the thing-in-itself." Kant indeed achieves the synthesis of the identity of subject and object—but only an object relative to the subject: the very identity is the synthesis of the imagination and is not posited in being itself. He goes beyond the psychological and the empirical, all the while remaining within the anthropological. So long as the determination is only subjective, we cannot get outside anthropology. Must we get outside it, and how do we do

15

so? These two questions are in fact one question: the way to get outside is also the necessity to do so. To his credit, Kant's insight is that thought is presupposed as given: thought is given because it thinks itself and reflects itself, and it is presupposed as given because the totality of objects presupposes thought as that which makes understanding possible. Thus, in Kant, thought and the thing are identical, but the thing identical to thought is only a relative thing, not the thing-as-being, not the thing-in-itself. Hegel, therefore, aspires to the veritable identity of what is given and what is presupposed, in other words, to the Absolute. In his Phenomenology, we are shown that the general difference between being and reflection, of being-in-itself and being-for-itself, of truth and certainty, develop in the concrete moments of a dialectic whose very movement abolishes this difference, or preserves it only as a necessary appearance. In this sense, the Phenomenology starts from human reflection to show that this human reflection and its consequences lead to the absolute knowledge which they presuppose. As Hyppolite remarks, it is a question of "reducing" anthropology, of "removing the obstacle" of a knowledge whose source is foreign. But it is not just at the finish, or at the beginning, that absolute knowledge *is*. Knowledge is already absolute in every moment: a figure of consciousness is a moment of the concept, only in a different guise; the external difference between being and reflection is, in a different guise, the internal difference of Being itself or, in other terms, Being which is identical to difference, to mediation. "Since the difference of consciousness has returned into the self, these moments are then presented as determined concepts and as their organic movement which is grounded in itself."

How "arrogant," someone will say, to act like God and grant yourself absolute knowledge. But we have to understand what being is with respect to the given. Being, according to Hyppolite, is not *essence* but *sense*. Saying that this world is sufficient not only means that it sufficient *for us*, but that it is sufficient *unto itself*, and that the world refers to being not as the essence beyond appearances, and not as a second world which would be the world of the Intelligible, but as the sense of this world. Certainly, we find this substitution of sense for essence already in Plato, when he shows us that the second world is itself the subject of a dialectic that makes it the sense of this world, not some other world. But the great agent of substitution is again Kant, because his critique replaces formal possibility with transcendental possibility, the being of the possible with the possibility of being, logical identity with the synthetic identity of recognition, the being of logic with the logical nature of being—in a word, the critique replaces essence with sense. According to Hyppolite, the great proposition of Hegel's Logic is that there is no second world, because such a proposition is at the same time the rationale for transforming metaphysics into logic, the logic of sense. 'There is no beyond' means there is no beyond to the world (because Being is only sense); and that there is in the world beyond to thought (because in thought it is being which thinks itself);

and finally, that there is in thought no beyond of language. Jean Hyppolite's book is a reflection on the conditions of an absolute discourse; and in this respect, those chapters on the ineffable and on poetry are crucial. The same people who chitchat are those who believe in the ineffable. But if Being is sense, true knowledge is not the knowledge of an Other, nor of some other thing. Absolute knowledge is what is closest, so to speak, what is most simple: it *is here*. "Behind the curtain there is nothing to see," or as Hyppolite says: "the secret is that there is no secret."

We see then the difficulty which the author emphatically underlines: if ontology is an ontology of sense and not essence, if there is no second world, how can absolute knowledge be distinguished from empirical knowledge? Do we not fall back into the simple anthropology which we just criticized? Absolute knowledge must at one and the same time include empirical knowledge and nothing else, since there is nothing else to include, and yet it has to include its own radical difference from empirical knowledge. Hyppolite's idea is this: essentialism, despite appearances, was not what preserved us from empiricism and allowed us to go beyond it. From the viewpoint of essence, reflection is no less exterior than it is in empiricism or pure critique. Empiricism posited determination as purely subjective; essentialism, by opposing determinations to one another and to the Absolute, leads only to the bottom of this limitation. Essentialism is on the same side as empiricism. On the other hand, however, the ontology of sense is total Thought that knows itself only in its determinations, which are moments of form. In the empirical and in the absolute, it is the same being and the same thought; but the empirical, external difference of thought and being has given way to the difference which is identical to Being, to the internal difference of Being that thinks itself. Thus absolute knowledge is in effect distinct from empirical knowledge, but only at the cost of denying the knowledge of non-different essence. In logic, therefore, there is no longer, as there is in the empirical realm, what I say on the one hand and the sense of what I say on the other—the pursuit of the one by the other being the dialectic of Phenomenology. On the contrary, my discourse is logically or properly philosophical when I speak the sense of what I say, and when Being thus speaks itself. Such discourse, which is the particular style of philosophy, cannot be other than circular. In this connection, we cannot fail to notice those pages Hyppolite devotes to the problem of beginning in philosophy, a problem which is not only logical, but pedagogical.

Hyppolite thus rises up against any anthropological or humanist interpretation of Hegel. Absolute knowledge is not a reflection of humanity, but a reflection of the Absolute in humanity. The Absolute is not a second world, and yet absolute knowledge is indeed distinct from empirical knowledge, just as philosophy is distinct from any anthropology. In this regard, however, if we must consider decisive the distinction Hyppolite makes between Logic and Phenomenology, does the philosophy of history not have a more ambiguous relation to Logic? Hyppolite says as much: the Absolute as sense is becoming; and it is certainly not an historical becoming. But what is the relation of Logic's becoming to history, if 'historical' in this instance designates anything but the simple character of a fact? The relation of ontology and empirical humanity is perfectly determined, but not the relation of ontology and historical humanity. And if as Hyppolite suggests finitude itself must be reintroduced into the Absolute, does this not risk the return of anthropologism in a new form? Hyppolite's conclusion remains open; it opens the way for an ontology. But I would only point out that the source of the difficulty, perhaps, was already in Logic itself. It is indeed thanks to Hyppolite that we now realize philosophy, if it means anything, can only be ontology and an ontology of sense. In the empirical realm and in the absolute, it is the same being and the same thought; but the difference between thought and being has been surpassed in the absolute by the positing of Being which is identical to difference, and which as such thinks itself and reflects itself in humanity. This absolute identity of being and difference is called sense. But there is one point in *all* this where Hyppolite shows his Hegelian bias: Being can be identical to difference only in so far as difference is taken to the absolute, in other words, all the way to contradiction. Speculative difference is self-contradictory Being. The thing contradicts itself because, distinguishing itself from all that is not, it finds its being in this very difference; it reflects itself only by reflecting itself in the other, since the other is *its* other. This is the theme Hyppolite develops when he analyzes the three moments of Logic: being, essence, and the concept. Hegel will reproach Plato and Leibniz both for not going *all the way* to contradiction: Plato remains at simple alterity; and Leibniz, at pure difference. This supposes in the very least not only that the moments of Phenomenology and the moments of Logic are not moments in the same sense, but also that there are two ways, phenomenological and logical, to contradict oneself. In the wake of this fruitful book by Jean Hyppolite, one might ask whether an ontology of difference couldn't be created that would not go all the way to contradiction, since contradiction would be less and not more than difference. Hyppolite says that an ontology of pure difference would restore us to a purely formal and exterior reflection, and would in the end reveal itself to be an ontology of essence. However, the same question could be asked in another way: is it the same thing to say that Being expresses itself and that Being contradicts itself? While it is true that the second and third parts of Hyppolite's book establish a theory of contradiction in Being, where contradiction itself is the absolute of difference, on the other hand, in the first part (the theory of language) and throughout the book (allusions to forgetting, remembering, lost meaning), does not Hyppolite establish a theory of expression, where difference is expression itself, and contradiction, that aspect which is only phenomenal?

Instincts and Institutions

What we call an instinct and what we call an institution essentially designate procedures of satisfaction. On the one hand, an organism reacts instinctively to external stimuli, extracting from the external world the elements which will satisfy its tendencies and needs; these elements comprise worlds that are specific to different animals. On the other hand, the subject institutes an original world between its tendencies and the external milieu, developing artificial means of satisfaction. These artificial means liberate an organism from nature though they subject it to something else, transforming tendencies by introducing them into a new milieu. So money will liberate you from hunger, provided you have money; and marriage will spare you from searching out a partner, though it subjects you to other tasks. In other words, every individual experience presupposes, as an *a priori*, the existence of a milieu in which that experience is conducted, a species-specific milieu or an institutional milieu. Instinct and institution are the two organized forms of a possible satisfaction.

There is no doubt that tendencies find satisfaction in the institution: sexuality finds it in marriage, and avarice in property. The example of an institution like the State, it will be objected, does not have a tendency to which it corresponds. But it is clear that such institutions are secondary: they already presuppose institutionalized behaviors, recalling a derived utility that is properly social. In the end, this utility locates the principle from which it is derived in the relation of tendencies to the social. The institution is always given as an organized system of means. It is here, moreover, that we find the difference between institution and law: law is a limitation of actions, institution a positive model for action. Contrary to theories of law which place the positive outside the social (natural rights), and the social in the negative (contractual limitation), the theory of the institution places the negative outside the social (needs), so as to present society as essentially positive and inventive (original means of satisfaction). Such a theory will afford us the following political criteria: tyranny is a regime in which there are many laws and few institutions; democracy is a regime in which there are many institutions, and few laws. Oppression becomes apparent when laws bear directly on people, and not on the prior institutions that protect them.

But if it is true that tendencies are satisfied by the institution, the institution is not explained by tendencies. The same sexual needs will never explain the multiple possible forms of marriage. Neither does the negative explain the positive, nor the general the particular. The "desire to whet your appetite" does not explain drinks before dinner, because there are a thousand other ways to whet your appetite. Brutality does not explain war in the least; and yet brutality discovers in war its best means. This is the paradox of society: we are always talking about institutions, but we are in fact confronted by procedures of satisfaction—and the tendencies satisfied by such procedures neither trigger nor determine the procedures. Tendencies are satisfied by means that do not depend on them. Therefore, no tendency exists which is not at the same time constrained or harassed, and thus transformed, sublimated—to such an extent that neurosis is possible. What is more, if needs find in the institution only a very indirect satisfaction, an "oblique" satisfaction, it is not enough to say "the institution is useful," one must still ask the question: useful for whom? For all those who have needs? Or just for a few (the privileged class)? Or only for those who control the institution (the bureaucracy)? One of the most profound sociological problems thus consists in seeking out the nature of this other instance, on which the social forms of the satisfaction of tendencies depend. The rituals of a civilization? The means of production? Whatever this other instance is, human utility is always something else than mere advantage. The institution sends us back to a social activity that is constitutive of models of which we are not conscious, and which are not explained either by tendencies or by utility, since human utility presupposes tendencies in the first place. In this sense, the priest, the man of ritual, always embodies the unconscious of the ritual's users.

How different is instinct? With instinct, nothing goes beyond utility, except beauty. Whereas tendencies were indirectly satisfied by the institution, they are directly satisfied by instinct. There are no instinctive prohibitions, or instinctive coercions; only repugnancies are instinctive. In this case, it is the tendencies themselves, in the form of internal psychological factors, that trigger certain behaviors. Undoubtedly, too, these internal factors will not explain how they, even if they were the self-same factors, trigger different behaviors in different species. In other words, instinct finds itself at the intersection of a double causality, that of individual psychological factors and that of the species itself—hormones and species-specificity. Thus, we ask ourselves only to what extent instinct can be reduced to the simple interest of the individual: in which case, if we take it to the limit, we should no longer speak of instinct, but rather of reflex, of tropism, of habit and intelligence. Or is it that instinct can be understood only within the framework of an advantage to the species, a good for the species, an ultimate biological cause? "Useful for whom?" is the question we rediscover here, but its meaning has changed. Instinct, seen from both angles, is given as a tendency launched in an organism at species-specific reactions.

The problem common to instinct and to institution is still this: how does the synthesis of tendencies and the object that satisfies them come about? Indeed, the water that I drink does not resemble at all the hydrates my organism lacks. The more perfect an instinct is in its domain, the more it belongs to the species, and the more it seems to constitute an original, irreducible power of synthesis. But the more perfectible instinct is, and thus imperfect, the more it is subjected to variation, to indecision, and the more it allows itself to be reduced to the mere play of internal individual factors and exterior circumstances—the more it gives way to intelligence. However, if we take this line of argument to its limit, how could such a synthesis, offering to the tendency a suitable object, be intelligent when such a synthesis, to be realized, implies a period of time too long for the individual to live, and experiments which it would not survive?

We are forced back on the idea that intelligence is something more social than individual, and that intelligence finds in the social its intermediate milieu, the third term that makes intelligence possible. What does the social mean with respect to tendencies? It means integrating circumstances into a system of anticipation, and internal factors into a system that regulates their appearance, thus replacing the species. This is indeed the case with the institution. It is night because we sleep; we eat because it is lunchtime. There are no social tendencies, but only those social means to satisfy tendencies, means which are original because they are social. Every institution imposes a series of models on our bodies, even in its involuntary structures, and offers our intelligence a sort of knowledge, a possibility of foresight as project. We come to the following conclusion: humans have no instincts, they builds institutions. The Human is an animal decimating its species. Therefore, instinct would translate the urgent needs of the animal, and the institution the demands of humanity: the urgency of hunger becomes in humanity the demand for bread. In the end, the problem of instinct and institution will be grasped most acutely not in animal "societies," but in relations of animal and humans, when the demands of men come to bear on the animal by integrating it into institutions (totemism and domestication), when the urgent needs of the animal encounters the human, either fleeing or attacking us, or patiently waiting for nourishment and protection.

Bergson, *1859–1941*[1]

A great philosopher creates new concepts: these concepts simultaneously surpass the dualities of ordinary thought and give things a new truth, a new distribution, a new way of dividing up the world. The name 'Bergson' remains associated with the notions of *duration, memory, élan vital,* and *intuition.* His influence and his genius are evaluated according to the way in which these concepts have been imposed and used, have entered and remained in the philosophical world. With *Time and Free Will* the original concept of duration was formed; in *Matter and memory,* a concept of memory; in *Creative Evolution,* that of *élan vital.* The relationship of these three neighboring notions can show us the development and the progress of Bergsonian philosophy. What, then, is this relationship?

To begin with, I will set out to examine intuition only, not because it is the essential notion, but because it can instruct us in the nature of Bergsonian problems. It is not by chance that, when speaking of intuition, Bergson shows us the importance, in the life of the mind, of an activity that sets up and organizes problems: there are false problems more than there are false solutions, more than there are false solutions for true problems.[2] Now, if a certain intuition is always at the heart of a philosopher's doctrine, one of the original things about Bergson is that in his own doctrine, he organized intuition itself as a true method, a method for eliminating false problems, for setting up problems truthfully, a method that sets them up, then, in terms of duration. "Questions related to the subject and to the object, to their distinction and their union, must be set up in terms of time rather than space."[3] No doubt it is duration that judges intuition, as Bergson recalls on numerous occasions, but it nonetheless remains the case that it is only intuition that can, when it has become conscious of itself as a method, seek duration in things, appeal to duration, invoke duration, precisely because it owes duration all that it is. If, therefore, intuition is not a simple pleasure, nor a presentiment, nor simply an affective process, we must first determine what its truly methodological character is.

The first characteristic of intuition is that in it and through it something is presented, is given in person, instead of being inferred from something else and concluded. Here, already, the general orientation of philosophy comes into question, for it is not enough to say that philosophy is at the origin of the sciences and that it was their mother; rather, now that they are grown up and well established, we must ask why there is still philosophy, in what respect science is not sufficient. Philosophy has only ever responded to such a question in two ways, doubtless because there are only two possible responses. One says that science gives us a knowledge of things, that it is therefore in a certain relation with them, and philosophy can renounce its rivalry with science, can leave things to science and present itself solely in a critical manner, as a reflection on this knowledge of things. On the contrary view, philosophy seeks to establish, or rather restore, *an other* relationship to things, and therefore *an other* knowledge, a knowledge and a relationship that precisely science hides from us, of which it deprives us, because it allows us only to conclude and to infer without ever presenting, giving to us the thing in itself. It is this second path that Bergson takes by repudiating critical philosophies when he shows us in science, in technical activity, intelligence, everyday language, social life, practical need and, most importantly, in space—the many forms and relations that separate us from things and from their interiority.

But intuition has a second characteristic: understood in this way, it presents itself as a return, because the philosophical relationship, which puts us in things instead of leaving us outside, is restored rather than established by philosophy, rediscovered rather than invented. We are separated from things; the immediate given is therefore not immediately given. But we cannot be separated by a simple accident, by a mediation that would come from us, that would concern only us. The movement that changes the nature of things must be founded in things themselves; things must begin by losing themselves in order for us to end up losing them; being must have a fundamental lapse of memory. Matter is precisely that in being which prepares and accompanies space, intelligence and science. Hence Bergson does something entirely different from psychology, because matter is more an ontological principle of intelligence than some mere intelligence is a psychological principle of matter itself or of space.[4] For the same reason, he refuses scientific knowledge nothing, not only telling us that it separates us from things and from their true nature, but also that it grasps at least one of the two halves of being, one of the two sides of the absolute, one of the two movements of nature, the one in which nature relaxes and places itself outside of itself.[5] Bergson will go even further, because under certain conditions science can be united with philosophy, that is to say, reach, together with it, a total comprehension.[6] Be that as it may, we can already say that there will not be in Bergson's work anything like a distinction between two worlds, one sensible, the other intelligible, but only two movements, or even just two directions of one and the same movement: the one is such that the movement tends to congeal in its product, in its result, that which interrupts it; and the other turns back and retraces its steps, rediscovers in the product the movement from which it resulted. The two directions are natural as well, each in its own way: the former occurs according to nature, though nature risks losing itself in it at each pause, at each breath; the latter occurs contrary to nature, but nature rediscovers itself in it, starts over again in the tension. The latter can only be found beneath the former, and it is always thus that it is rediscovered. We rediscover the immediate because we must return to find it. In philosophy the first time is already the second; such is the notion of foundation. No doubt it is the product that *is*, in a way, and the movement that is not, that is no longer. But it is not in these terms that the problem of being must be set up. At every instant, the movement is no more, but precisely because it is not made up of instants, because instants are only its real or virtual cessations, its product and the shadow of its product. Being is not made up of presents. In another way, then, it is the product that is not and the movement that *already was.* In one of Achilles' steps, the instants and the points are not divided up. Bergson shows us this in his most difficult book: it is not the present that is and the past that is no longer, rather the present is useful; being is the past, being used to be.[7] We will see that far from eliminating the unforeseeable and the contingent, such a thesis lays the foundation for them. In distinguishing the two worlds, Bergson replaced them by the distinction of two movements, two directions of one and the same movement, spirit and matter, two times in the same duration, the past and the present, which he knew how to conceive as coexistent precisely because they were in the same duration, the one *beneath* the other, and not the one *after* the other. We must simultaneously understand the necessary distinction as a difference of time, but also understand the different times, the present and the past, as contemporary with one another, and forming the same world. We will now see in what way.

Why is what we rediscover called the immediate? What is immediate? If science is a real knowledge of the thing, a knowledge of reality, what it loses or simply risks losing is not exactly the thing. What science risks losing, unless it is infiltrated by philosophy, is less the thing itself than the difference of the thing, that which makes its being, that which makes it this rather than that, this rather than something else. Bergson energetically denounces what seem to him false problems: why is there something rather than nothing, why order rather than disorder?[8] If such problems are false, badly set up, it is for two reasons. First because they make of being a generality, something immovable or undifferentiated that, in the immobile ensemble in which it is set, can only be distinguished from nothingness, from non-being. Subsequently, even if one tries to give a movement to the immovable being thus posited, this movement would only be contradiction:

order and disorder, being and nothingness, the singular and the multiple. But in fact, being cannot be composed with two contradictory points of view any more than movement is composed of points of space or of instants: the stitching would be too loose.[9] Being is a bad concept to the extent that it serves to oppose everything there is to nothingness, or the thing itself to everything that it is not. In both cases being has left, it has deserted things, and it is no more than an abstraction. The Bergsonian question is therefore not: why something rather than nothing, but: why this rather than something else? Why this tension of duration?[10] Why this speed rather than another?[11] Why this proportion?[12] And why will a perception evoke a given memory, or pick up certain frequencies rather than others?[13] In other words, being is difference and not the immovable or the undifferentiated, nor is it contradiction, which is merely false movement. Being is the difference itself of the thing, what Bergson often calls the *nuance*. "An empiricism worthy of the name . . . would measure out for the object a concept appropriate to only that object, a concept of which one could barely say that it was still a concept because it would apply only to that thing."[14] And there is an odd text in which Bergson attributes to Ravaisson the goal of opposing intellectual intuition to the general idea, like white light to the simple idea of color: "Instead of diluting his thought in the general, the philosopher should concentrate it on the individual . . . The object of metaphysics is to recapture in individual existences, and to follow to the source from which it emanates, the particular ray that, conferring upon each of them its own nuance, reattaches it thereby to the universal light."[15] The immediate is precisely the identity of the thing and its difference as philosophy rediscovers or "recaptures" it. Bergson denounces a common danger in science and in metaphysics: allowing difference to escape—because science conceives the thing as a product and a result, while metaphysics conceives being as something unmovable that serves as a principle. Both seek to attain being or to recompose it starting from resemblances and ever greater oppositions, but resemblance and opposition are almost always *practical*, not ontological, categories. Whence Bergson's insistence on showing us that for the sake of resemblance we risk putting extremely different things, things that differ in nature, under the same word.[16] Being in fact is on the side of difference, neither singular nor multiple. But what is nuance, the difference of the thing, what is the difference of a sugar cube? It is not simply its difference from another thing: there we would have only a purely exterior relation, leading us, in the final instance, back to space. Nor is it its difference with everything that it is not: we would be led back to a dialectic of contradiction. Plato already didn't want alterity and contradiction to be confounded. But for Bergson, alterity is still not enough to make it so that being rejoins things and really is the being of things. He replaces the Platonic concept of alterity with an Aristotelian concept of alteration, in order to make of it substance itself. Being is alteration, alteration is substance.[17] And that is what Bergson calls *duration*, because all the characteristics by which he defines it, after *Time and Free Will*, come back to this:

duration is that which differs or that which changes nature, quality, heterogeneity, what differs from itself. The being of the sugar cube will be defined by a duration, by a certain manner of persisting, by a certain relaxation or tension of duration.

How does duration have this power? Or put the question another way: if being is the difference of the thing, what results from this for the thing itself? We encounter a third characteristic of intuition, more profound than the preceding ones. Intuition as a method is a method that seeks difference. It presents itself as seeking and finding differences in nature, the "articulations of the real." Being is articulated; a false problem is one that does not respect these differences. Bergson loves to cite Plato's text comparing the philosopher to the good cook who cuts things up according to their natural articulations; he constantly reproaches science as well as metaphysics for having retained only differences of degree where there used to be something entirely different, of thus being part of a badly analyzed "composite." One of Bergson's most famous passages shows us that intensity in fact covers up differences of nature that intuition can rediscover.[18] But we know that science and even metaphysics do not invent their own errors or their illusions: something founds them in being. Indeed, to the extent that we find ourselves before products, to the extent that the things with which we are concerned are still results, we cannot grasp differences of nature for the simple reason that there aren't any there: between two things, between two products, there are only and there only could be differences of degree, of proportion. What differs in nature is never a thing, but a tendency. A difference of nature is never between two products or between two things, but *in one and the same thing* between the two tendencies that traverse it, in one and the same product between two tendencies that encounter one another in it.[19] Indeed, what is pure is never the thing; the thing is always a composite that must be dissociated; only the tendency is pure, which is to say that the true thing or the substance is the tendency itself. Intuition appears very much like a true method of division: it divides the mixed into two tendencies that differ in nature. Hence we see the meaning of the dualisms dear to Bergson: not only the titles of many of his works, but each of the chapters, and the heading that precedes each page, exhibit such a dualism. Quantity and quality, intelligence and instinct, geometric order and vital order, science and metaphysics, the closed and the open are its most known figures. We know that in the end they lead back to the always rediscovered distinction of matter and duration. Matter and duration are never distinguished as two things but as two movements, two tendencies, like relaxation and contraction. But we must go further: if the theme and the idea of purity have a great importance in the philosophy of Bergson, it is because in every case the two tendencies are not pure, or are not equally pure. Only one of the two is pure, or *simple*, the other playing, on the contrary, the role of an impurity that comes to compromise or to disturb it.[20] In the division of the composite there is always a right half; it is that which leads us back to duration. More than there ever really being a difference of nature between the two tendencies that divide the thing up, the difference itself of the thing was one of the two tendencies. And if we rise to the duality of matter and duration, we see quite clearly that duration shows us the very nature of difference, difference of self from self, whereas matter is only the undifferentiated, that which is repeated, or the simple degree, that which can no longer change its nature. Do we not at the same time see that dualism is a moment already surpassed in Bergson's philosophy? For if there is a privileged half in the division; it must be that this half contains in itself the secret of the other. If all the difference is on one side, it must be that this side comprehends its difference from the other and, in a certain way, the other itself or its possibility. Duration differs from matter, but it does so because it is first that which differs in itself and from itself, with the result that the matter from which it differs is still essentially of duration. As long as we remain within dualism, the thing is where two movements meet: duration, which by itself has no degrees, encounters matter as a contrary movement, as a certain obstacle, a certain impurity that mixes it up, that interrupts its impulse [*élan*], that gives it such and such a degree here, another one over there.[21] But more profoundly, duration is in itself susceptible to degrees because it is that which differs with itself, so that every thing is entirely defined in duration, including matter itself. From a still dualistic perspective, duration and matter were opposed as that which differs in nature and that which has only degrees; but more profoundly there are degrees of difference itself; matter is the lowest, the very point where precisely difference *is no longer anything but* a difference of degree.[22] If it is true that intelligence is on the side of matter according to the object on which it bears, we still cannot define it in itself except by showing in what way it persists, that which dominates its object. And if it is a question of finally defining matter itself, it will not be enough to present it as an obstacle and as an impurity; it will always be necessary to show how it persists, its vibration still occupying multiple instances. Thus any thing is completely defined from the right side, by a certain duration, by a certain degree of duration itself.

A composite breaks down into two tendencies, one of which is duration, simple and indivisible; but at the same time duration is differentiated in two directions, the other of which is matter. Space breaks down into matter and duration, but duration is differentiated into contraction and expansion, expansion being the principle of matter. Thus, if dualism is surpassed in favor of monism, monism gives us a new dualism, this time mastered, dominated. Because the composite does not break down in the same way that the simple is differentiated. Therefore the method of intuition has a fourth and final characteristic: it is not content to follow natural articulations when carving things up; it also follows up "lines of fact," lines of differentiation, in order to rediscover the simple as a convergence of probabilities; it not only carves up [*découpe*] but confirms [*recoupe*].[23] Differentiation is the power of what is simple, indivisible, of what persists. Here we see how duration itself is an *élan vital*. Bergson finds in biology, particularly in the evolution of species, the mark of a certain process essential to life, precisely that of differentiation as the production of real differences, a process whose concept and philosophical consequences he will pursue. The admirable pages he wrote in *Creative Evolution* and in *Two Sources* show us such a life activity, leading to plants and animals, or to instinct and intelligence, or to diverse forms of the same instinct. It seems to Bergson that differentiation is the mode of that which is realized, actualized, or made, in other words, that which gives rise to divergent series, lines of evolution, species. "The essence of a tendency is to be developed in the form of a sheaf, creating through the sole fact of its growth divergent directions."[24] *Elan vital* would therefore be duration itself to the extent it is actualized, is differentiated. *Elan vital* is difference to the extent that it passes into act. Hence differentiation does not come simply from matter's resistance, but more profoundly from a force that duration carries in itself: dichotomy is the law of life. And Bergson criticizes mechanism and finalism in biology, as he does the dialectic in philosophy, for always composing movement from points of view, as a relation between actual terms instead of seeing in it the actualization of something virtual. But if differentiation is thus the original and irreducible mode through which a virtuality is actualized, and if *élan vital* is duration differentiated, then duration itself is virtuality. *Creative Evolution* brings to *Time and Free Will* a necessary deepening as well as a necessary extension. Because, since *Time and Free Will*, duration was presented as the virtual or the subjective, because it was less that which cannot be divided than that which changes its nature by being divided.[25] We must understand that the virtual is not something actual but is for that no less a mode of being, and is, moreover, in a way, being itself; neither duration, nor life, nor movement is actual, but that in which all actuality, all reality is distinguished and comprehended and takes root. To be actualized is always the act of a whole that does not become entirely actual at the same time, in the same place, or in the same thing; consequently, it produces species that differ in nature, and it is itself this difference of nature among the species it has produced. Bergson constantly said that duration is a change of nature, of quality. "Between light and darkness, between colors, between nuances, difference is absolute. The passage from one to the other is itself also an absolutely real phenomenon."[26]

We therefore grasp duration and *élan vital*, the virtual and its actualization, as two extremes. Still, it must be said that duration is already *élan vital* because it is the essence of the virtual to be actualized; we therefore require a third aspect that shows it to us, one in some way intermediary to the two preceding. It is precisely under this third aspect that duration is called *memory*. Through all of its characteristics, duration is indeed a memory because it prolongs the past in the present, "whether the present distinctly encloses the ever-growing image of the past or whether it rather bears witness, through its continual changing of quality, of the ever-weightier burden one leads behind oneself as one grows older."[27] Let us recall that memory is always presented by Bergson in two ways: recollection-memory and contraction-memory, and that the second is the essential one.[28] Why these two figures, which will give to memory an entirely new philosophical status? The first returns us to something that has survived from the past. But among all the theses of Bergson, perhaps the most profound and least understood is the one according to which the past survives in itself.[29] Because this survival itself is duration, duration is in itself memory. Bergson shows us that recollection is not the representation of something that was; the past is that in which we put ourselves from the outset in order to recollect ourselves.[30] The past does not have to survive psychologically, nor physiologically in our brains, because it has not ceased to be, it has only ceased to be useful—it is; it survives in itself. And this being in itself of the past is but the immediate consequence of a good *setting up* of the problem: because if the past had to wait to be no more, if it were not immediately and henceforth past, "*past* in general," it would never be able to become what it is, it would never be *this* past. The past is therefore the in-itself, the unconscious or more precisely, as Bergson says, the *virtual*.[31] But in what sense is it virtual? It is here that we encounter the second figure of memory. The past is not constituted *after* it has been present; it *coexists with itself as present*. If we reflect upon it, we see that indeed the philosophical difficulty of the very notion of the past comes from the fact that it is in some way stuck between two presents: the present that it was and the current present in relation to which it is now past. The mistake of psychology, which badly sets up the *problem*, is to have retained the second present and therefore to have sought the past starting from something current, and finally, to have more or less situated it in the brain. But in fact, "memory does not at all consist of a regression from the present to the past."[32] What Bergson shows us is that if the past is not past at the same time that it is present, not only will it never be able to be constituted, but it could also never thereafter be reconstituted starting from a later present. This, then, is the sense in which the past coexists with itself as present: duration is but this coexistence itself, this coexistence of itself with itself. Thus the past and the present must be thought as two extreme degrees coexisting in duration, the one distinguished by its state of relaxation, the other by its state of contraction. A famous metaphor tells us that at each level of the cone there is the whole of our past, but to different degrees: the present is only the most contracted degree of the past. "The same psychic life would therefore be repeated an indefinite number of times, at successive stages of memory, and the same mental act could be played out on many different levels"; "everything happens as if our memories were repeated an indefinite number of times in these thousands and thousands of possible reductions of our past life"; everything is a change of energy, of tension, and nothing else.[33] At each degree everything is there, but everything coexists with everything, that is to say with the other degrees. We see therefore finally *what* is virtual: the coexistent degrees themselves and as such.[34] It is right to define duration as a succession, but wrong to insist on it; it is, in effect, a real succession only because it is *virtual coexistence*. As for intuition, Bergson writes: "Only the method of which we speak allows us to go beyond idealism as well as realism, to affirm the existence of objects inferior and superior to us, while at the same time in a certain sense interior to us, to make them coexist together without difficulty."[35] And in fact if we pursue the connections between *Matter and Memory* and *Creative Evolution*, we see that coexistent degrees are simultaneously what makes duration something virtual and what makes it so that duration nonetheless is actualized at every instant, because they delineate so many planes and levels that determine all the possible lines of differentiation. In short, actually divergent series give birth to, in duration, coexistent virtual degrees. Between intelligence and instinct there is a difference of nature because they arise from two divergent series; but what does this difference of nature finally express if not two degrees that coexist in duration, two different degrees of relaxation or of contraction? It is thus that each thing, each being is the whole, but the whole realized to a certain degree or another. In Bergson's first works, duration could appear an eminently psychological reality; but what is psychological is only *our* duration, that is to say, a certain well-determined degree. "If, instead of seeking to analyze duration (that is, at bottom, to synthesize it with concepts), one inhabits it initially through an effort of intuition, one has the feeling of a certain well-determined *tension*, whose determination itself appears as a choice among an infinity of possible durations. Thereafter, one perceives as many durations as one likes, all very different from one another . . ."[36] This is why the secret of Bergsonism is no doubt in *Matter and Memory*; Bergson tells us, moreover, that his work consisted of reflecting on the fact that not everything is given. But what does such a reality signify? Simultaneously that the given presupposes a movement that invents it or creates it, and that this movement must not be conceived in the image of the given.[37] What Bergson critiques in the idea of the *possible* is that it presents us a simple copy of the product, projected or rather retrojected onto the movement of production, onto invention.[38] But the virtual is not the same thing as the possible: the reality of time is finally the affirmation of a virtuality that is actualized, for which to be actualized is to invent. Because if everything [*tout*] is not given, it remains that the virtual is the whole [*le tout*]. Let us recall that the *élan vital* is finite: the whole is what is realized in species, which are not in its image any more than they are the image of one another. Each simultaneously corresponds to a certain degree of the whole and differs in nature from the others, such that the whole itself is presented at the same time as the difference of nature in reality, and as the coexistence of degrees in the mind.

If the past coexists with itself as present, if the present is the most contracted degree of the coexistent past, then this same present, because it is the precise point at which the past is cast toward the future, is defined as that which changes nature, the always new, the eternity of life.[39] It is understandable that a lyric theme runs through Bergson's work: a veritable hymn in praise of the new, the unforeseeable, of invention, of liberty. Therein lies not a renunciation of philosophy, but a profound and original attempt to discover the proper domain of philosophy, to attain the thing itself beyond the order of the possible, of causes and ends. Finality, causality, possibility are always in relation to the thing once it is complete, and always presuppose that "everything" is given. When Bergson critiques these notions, when he speaks to us of indeterminacy, he does not invite us to abandon reason but to reconnect with the true reason of the thing in the process of being made, the philosophical reason that is not determination but difference. We find the whole movement of Bergsonian thought concentrated in *Matter and Memory* in the triple form of difference of nature, coexistent degrees of difference, and differentiation. Bergson first shows us that there is a difference of nature between the past and the present, between recollection and perception, between duration and matter: psychologists and philosophers have been wrong by being in every case coming from a badly analyzed composite. He then shows us that it is still not enough to speak of a difference of nature between matter and duration, between the present and the past, because the whole question is precisely to know *what is* a difference of nature: he shows that duration itself is this difference, such that it comprehends matter as its lowest, most relaxed degree, as an *infinitely dilated past*, and comprehends itself in contracting itself as *an extremely narrow, tensed present*. Finally, he shows us that if degrees coexist in duration, duration is at each instant that which is differentiated, that it is differentiated into past and present, or, if you prefer, that the present is doubled in two directions, one toward the past, the other toward the future. These three times correspond, in the whole of the work, to the notions of duration, memory, and *élan vital*. The project we find in Bergson's work, that of reconnecting things by breaking with critical philosophies, was not absolutely new, even in France, because it defined a general conception of philosophy, and in many of its aspects participated in English empiricism. But the method was profoundly new, as well as the three essential concepts that gave it its meaning.

Bergson's Conception of Difference[1]

The notion of difference promises to throw light on the philosophy of Bergson, and inversely, Bergsonism promises to make an inestimable contribution to a philosophy of difference. Such a philosophy is always at work on two different planes: the one methodological, and the other ontological. On the one hand, we must determine the differences of nature between things: only in this way will we be able "to return" to the things themselves, to account for them without reducing them to something other than what they are, to grasp them in their being. On the other hand, if the being of things is somehow in their differences of nature, we can expect that difference itself is something, that it has a nature, that it will yield Being. These two problems, methodological and ontological, constantly echo one another: the problem of the differences of nature, the problem of the nature of difference. In Bergson's work, we encounter these two problems in their connection, surprising them in their passage back and forth.

Essentially, Bergson criticizes his predecessors for not having seen true differences of nature. The constant presence of this critique also signals the importance of the theme in Bergson's work: where there were differences of nature, others have found merely differences of degree. And certainly we find the opposite criticism: where there were only differences of degree, others have introduced differences of nature, for example, between the so-called perceptive faculty of the brain and the reflexive functions of the medulla, or the perception of matter and matter itself.[2] This second aspect of the same critique, however, has neither the frequency nor the importance of the first. To decide which is more important, we have to ask ourselves what is the aim of philosophy. If philosophy has a positive and direct relation to things, it is only insofar as philosophy claims to grasp the thing itself, according to what it is, in its difference from everything it is not, in other words, in its *internal difference*. Someone will object that internal difference makes no sense, such a notion is absurd; but then we would also have to deny

32

differences of nature between things of the same kind. If differences of nature do exist between individuals of the same kind, we must then recognize that difference itself is not simply spatio-temporal, that it is not generic or specific—in a word, difference is not exterior or superior to the thing. This is why, according to Bergson, it is important to show that general ideas, at least most of the time, present us with extremely different facts in a grouping that is merely utilitarian: "Suppose on examining those states grouped under the name of pleasure, we discover they share nothing in common, except being states that a person seeks out: humanity will have classified very different things as the same in kind, simply because humanity attributed the same practical interest to each and acted in the same way towards them."[3] In this sense, differences of nature are already the key: we must start from them, but first we must find them. Without prejudging the nature of difference as internal difference, we already know that internal difference exists, *given that there exist differences of nature between things of the same genus*. Therefore, either philosophy proposes for itself *this* means (differences of nature) and *this* end (to arrive at internal difference), or else it will have merely a negative or generic relation to things and will end up a part of criticism and mere generalities—in any case, it will run the risk of ending up in a merely external state of reflection. Opting for the first alternative, Bergson puts forward philosophy's ideal: to tailor "for the object a concept appropriate to that object alone, a concept that one can hardly still call a concept, since it applies only to that one thing."[4] This unity of the thing and the concept is internal difference, which one reaches through differences of nature.

Intuition is the joy of difference. But intuition is not just enjoying the result of the method, it *is* the method. As such, it is not a unique act. It offers us a plurality of acts, a plurality of efforts and directions.[5] Intuition in its first effort is the determination of the differences of nature. And since these differences are between things, we are dealing with a genuine distribution, a genuine problem of distribution. One must carve up reality according to its articulations,[6] and Bergson willingly cites Plato's famous text on carving and the good cook. But the difference of nature between two things is still not the internal difference of the thing itself. From *the articulations of the real* must be distinguished *factual lines* which define another effort of the intuition.[7] And while Bergsonian philosophy seems genuinely "empirical" where articulations of the real are concerned, when it comes to factual lines it will seem "positivist" and even probabilistic. The articulations of the real distribute things according to their differences of nature; they constitute differentiation. Factual lines are directions to be followed, each to its end, converging on one and the same thing; they define integration, each forming a line of probability. In *L'Énergie spirituelle*, Bergson shows us the nature of consciousness at the point where three factual lines converge.[8] In *Les Deux sources*, the immortality of the soul is situated at the convergence of two factual lines.[9] Intuition in this sense is not opposed to the hypothesis; rather, intuition encompasses it as hypothesis. In short, the articulations of the real correspond to dissection or cutting [*découpage*], and factual lines to intersection or cross-check-ing ["*recoupement*"].[10] The real is what at the same time can be dissected and cross-checked. To be sure, in both cases, the pathways are the same; what mat-ters is the direction one takes them in, toward divergence or convergence. There are always two aspects of difference that we intuit: the articulations of the real give us differences of nature between things; factual lines show us the thing itself identical to its difference, internal difference identical to something.

Neglecting differences of nature in favor of genres is like lying to philosophy. The differences of nature have been lost. We suddenly realize that science has substituted simple *differences of degree* in their place, and that metaphysics has prefered, more particularly, simple *differences of intensity*. The first question deals with science: how do we manage to see only differences of degree? "We dissolve qualitative differences into the space which underlies them."[11] As we know, Berg-son is referring to the conjugated operations of need, social life and language, intelligence and space, though space is what the intelligence makes of the matter that lends itself to intelligence. In a word, we substitute merely utilitarian modes of grouping for articulations of the real. However, this is not the most important point; utility cannot ground what makes it possible in the first place. Therefore, two other points must be emphasized. First, degrees do have effects in reality; and *in a non-spatial form*, they are in some way already included in the differ-ences of nature: "behind our qualitative distinctions" are usually numbers.[12] One of Bergson's more curious ideas is that difference itself has a number, a virtual number, a numbering number. Utility, then, only frees up and spreads out the degrees already included in difference, until difference is nothing more than a difference of degree. Second, if degrees can be freed up in this way and on their own form differences, we must look for the cause in the state of experience. What space presents to the understanding, and what understanding finds in space, are only things, i.e. products or results. However, between things (in the sense of results) there are never, and cannot ever be, anything but differences of propor-tion.[13] It is not things, nor the states of things, nor is it characteristics, that differ in nature; it is *tendencies*. This is why the conception of species-specific difference is unsatisfactory: we must closely follow not the presence of characteristics, but their tendency to develop. "The group will be defined no longer by the posses-sion of certain characteristics, but by its tendency to accentuate them."[14] Thus Bergson throughout his work shows that tendency is prior not only to its prod-uct, but also to the product's causes in time, since causes are always derived retroactively from the product itself: a thing in itself and in its true nature is the expression of a tendency prior to being the effect of a cause. In short, simple dif-ference of degree will be the correct status of things separated from their tendency and grasped in their elementary causes. Causes indeed fall within the scope of quantity. The human brain, for example, according to whether we grasp it in its product or its tendency, will present in comparison to the animal brain a simple difference of degree or a complete difference of nature.[15] Thus Bergson tells us that, *from a certain point of view*, differences of nature disappear or rather cannot appear. On static versus dynamic religion, he writes: "By adopting this point of view, one would perceive a series of transitions, something that looks like differences of degree, where in fact there are radical differences of nature."[16] Things, products, results are always *composite*. Space only ever presents, and the intelligence only ever discovers composites, e.g. the closed and the open, geometric order and vital order, perception and affection, perception and recollection, etc. And one must understand that a composite is undoubtedly a blending of tendencies that differ in nature, but as such is a state of things in which it is impossible to make out any differences of nature. A composite is what one sees from that point of view where nothing differs in nature from anything else. The homogeneous is by definition composite, because what is simple is always something that differs in nature: only tendencies are simple, pure. That which really differs, therefore, can be found only by rediscovering the tendency beyond its product. Since we have nothing else at our disposal, we have to use whatever such composites provide, differences of degree or proportion, but only as a mesure of tendency, to arrive at tendency as the sufficient reason of proportion. "Wherever this difference of proportion is met will be sufficient to define the group, if one can establish that such a difference is not accidental and that the group, as it evolved, tended more and more to accentuate these particular characteristics."[17]

Metaphysics, for its part, has retained hardly anything except differences of intensity. Bergson shows us this view of intensity as it informs Greek metaphysics: because this latter defines space and time as a simple relaxation, a lessening of being, it discovers among beings themselves only differences of intensity, situating them somewhere between the two extremes of perfection and nothingness.[18] We will have to examine how this illusion comes about, and what in turn grounds it in the differences of nature themselves. For the moment, suffice it to say that such an illusion depends less on composite ideas than on pseudo-ideas, such as disorder or nothingness. But these pseudo-ideas are themselves a kind of composite idea,[19] and the illusion of intensity at bottom depends on the illusion of space. In the end, there is only one kind of false problem, problems whose propositions fail to respect differences of nature. One of the roles intuition plays is to criticize the arbitrariness of such propositions.

To reach genuine differences, we have to attain that perspective from which whatever is composite can be divided. Tendencies that come in paired opposites differ in nature. Tendency is the subject here. A being is not the subject, but the expression of tendency; furthermore, a being is only the expression of tendency in as much as one tendency is opposed by another tendency. Thus intuition suggests itself as a method of difference or division: to divide whatever is composite into two tendencies. This method is something other than a spatial analysis, more than a description of experience, and less (so it seems) than a transcendental analysis. It reaches the conditions of the given, but these conditions are tendency-subjects, which are themselves given in a certain way: they are lived. What is more, they are at once the pure and the lived, the living and the lived, the absolute and the lived. What is essential here is that this ground is *experienced*, and we know how much Bergson insisted on the empirical character of the *élan vital*. Thus it is not the conditions of all possible experience that must be reached, but the conditions of real experience. Schelling had already proposed this aim and defined philosophy as a superior empiricism: this formulation also applies to Bergsonism. These conditions can and must be grasped in an intuition precisely because they are the conditions of real experience, because they are not broader than what is conditioned, because the concept they form is identical to its object. It will come as no surprise, then, that a kind of principle of sufficient reason, as well as indiscernibles, can be found in Bergson's work. What he rejects is a distribution that locates cause or reason in the genus and the category and abandons the individual to contingency, stranding him in space. Reason must reach all the way to the individual, the genuine concept all the way to the thing, and comprehension all the way to "this." Bergson always asks of difference: why "this" rather than "that"? Why will a perception call up one recollection rather than another?[20] Why will perception "gather" specific frequencies? Why these rather than others?[21] Why does duration exhibit such a tension?[22] In fact, the reason must be what Bergson calls *nuance*. There are no accidents in the life of the psyche:[23] its essence is nuance. As long as the concept that fits only the object itself has not been found, "the unique concept," we are satisfied with explaining the object by several concepts, general ideas "of which the object is supposed to partake."[24] What escapes then is that the object is *this* object rather than another of the same kind, and that the object in this genus has *these* proportions rather than some other proportions. Only tendency is the unity of the concept and its object, such that the object is no longer contingent, and the concept no longer general. These methodological clarifications, however, do not seem to avert the impasse where the method appears to be headed. Whatever is composite must be divided into two tendencies, but the differences of proportion in the mixture itself do not tell us how to find these tendencies, nor what is the rule of division. More importantly, given two tendencies, which is the right one? The two are not equivalent, they have different values: one tendency always predominates. Only the dominant tendency defines the true nature of whatever is composite; only the dominant tendency is the unique concept, it alone is pure, since it is the purity of the corresponding thing; the other tendency is the impurity that compromises the first and opposes it. So, animal behavior exhibits instinct as the dominant tendency, whereas in human behavior it is intelligence. In the composite of perception and affection, it is affection that plays the impure role and compromises pure perception.[25] In other words, there is a left-half to divide from a right-half. What rule or measure do we use to determine this? Here we rediscover a difficulty which Plato also encountered: how does one respond to Aristotle's remark that Plato's method of difference is just a feeble syllogism, unable to decide conclusively in which half of the divided genus resides the Idea being sought after, since the middle term is missing? And Plato seems better off than Bergson, because the Idea of a transcendent Good can effectively guide the choice of the right half. In general, however, Bergson refuses help from finality, as though he wanted the method of difference to be self-sufficient.

This difficulty may be illusory. We know that the articulations of the real do not define the essence and the aim of the method. Certainly, the difference of nature *between* two tendencies is an improvement over the difference of degree between things, as well as the difference of intensity between beings: and yet this difference remains external; it is still an external difference. At this point, Bergsonian intuition, to be complete, does not lack an external term which could serve as a rule; if anything, Bergsonian intuition still looks too external. Let's take an example: Bergson shows that abstract time is a composite of space and duration, and more profoundly, that space itself is a composite of matter and duration, matter and memory. So we see the composite divided into two tendencies: matter is a tendency, since it is defined as a relaxation; and duration is a tendency, since it is a contraction. However, if we examine all the definitions, descriptions, and characteristics of duration in Bergson's work, we will notice that the difference of nature, in the end, is not *between* these two tendencies. In the end, the difference of nature is itself *one* of these tendencies, and opposes the other. So, then, what is duration? Everything Bergson has to say about it comes down to this: duration is *what differs from itself.* Matter, on the other hand, is what does not differ from itself; it is what repeats itself. In *Données immédiates,* Bergson shows not only that intensity is a composite divided into two tendencies, but more importantly, that intensity is not a property of sensation; sensation is a pure quality, and a pure quality or sensation differs in nature from itself. Sensation is what changes in nature and not in magnitude.[26] The life of the psyche is therefore difference of nature itself: in the life of the psyche, there is always *otherness* without there being *number* or *several.*[27] Bergson distinguishes three sorts of movement: qualitative, evolutive, and extensive. But the essence of this movement, even pure transit like the race of Achilles, is alteration. Movement is qualitative change, and qualitative change is movement.[28] In a word, duration is what differs, and this is no longer what differs from other things, but what differs from itself. What differs has itself become a thing, a *substance.* Bergson's thesis could be summed up in this way: real time is alteration, and alteration is substance. Difference of nature is therefore no longer between two things or rather two tendencies; difference of nature is itself a thing, a tendency opposed to some other tendency. The decomposition of the composite does not just give us two tendencies that differ in nature; it gives us difference of nature as one of the two tendencies. And just as difference has become a substance, so movement is no longer the characteristic of something, but has itself acquired a substantial character. It presupposes nothing else, no body in motion.[29] Duration or tendency is the difference of self with itself; and what differs from itself is, in an *unmediated* way, the unity of substance and subject.

Now we know both how to divide the composite and how to choose the right tendency, since what differs from itself, namely duration, is always on the right side; duration is in each case revealed to us under an aspect, one of its "nuances." One cannot help notice, however, that in the case of what is composite, the same term can sometimes be on the right side, and sometimes on the left side. The division of animal behavior places intelligence on the left side because duration, the *élan vital*, is expressed as instincts through such behavior, whereas intelligence is on the right side for the analysis of human behavior. But intelligence cannot change sides without in turn revealing itself as an expression of duration, though in humanity now: if intelligence takes the form of matter, it has the sense of duration because intelligence is the organ that dominates matter: a sense uniquely present in humanity.[30] It should come as no surprise that duration thus exhibits several aspects which are its nuances, since duration is what differs from itself. And to see a final nuance of duration in matter, one has only to go farther, to go all the way. But to understand this crucial point, we must keep in mind what difference has become. Difference is no longer between two tendencies; difference is itself one of the tendencies and is always on the right side. External difference has become internal difference. *Difference of nature has itself become a nature*. More than that, it was so from the beginning. Thus it was that the articulations of the real and facutal lines were relayed back and forth: the articulations of the real sketched factual lines which at least revealed internal difference as the limit of their convergence, and conversely, factual lines gave us articulations of the real, e.g. the convergence of the three diverse lines, in *Matter and Memory*, leading to the true distribution of what belongs to the subject and what belongs to the object.[31] Difference of nature was external only in appearance. In this very appearance, difference of nature was already distinguished from the difference of degree, the difference of intensity, and species-specific difference. However, there are now other distinctions to be made in the state of internal difference: Duration can be presented as substance itself in so far as duration is simple, indivisible. Alteration must therefore maintain itself and achieve its status without allowing itself to be reduced to plurality, to contradiction, or even to alterity. Internal difference will have to distinguish itself from *contradiction, alterity*, and *negation*. This is precisely where Bergson's method and theory of difference are opposed to the other theory, the other method of difference called dialectic, whether it's Plato's dialectic of alterity or Hegel's dialectic of contradiction, each of which imply the presence and the power of the negative.

The originality of Bergson's conception resides in showing that internal difference does not go, and is not required to go as far as contradiction, alterity, and negativity, because these three notions are in fact less profound than itself, or they are viewpoints only from the outside. The real sense of Bergson's endeavor is thinking internal difference as such, as pure internal difference, and raising difference up to the absolute.

Duration is only one of two tendencies, one of two halves. So, if we accept that it differs from itself in all its being, does it not contain the secret of the other half? How could it still leave external to itself *that from which* it differs, namely the other tendency? If duration differs from itself, that from which it differs is still duration in a certain sense. It is not a question of dividing duration in the same way we divided what is composite: duration is simple, indivisible, pure. The simple is not divided, *it differentiates itself*. This is the essence of the simple, or the movement of difference. So, the composite divides into two tendencies, one of which is the indivisible, but the indivisible differentiates itself into two tendencies, the other of which is the principle of the divisible. Space is broken up into matter and duration, but duration differentiates itself into contraction and relaxation; and relaxation is the principle of matter. Organic form is broken up into matter and *élan vital*, but the *élan vital* differentiates itself into instinct and intelligence; and intelligence is the principle of the transformation of matter into space. Clearly, the composite is not broken up in the same way that the simple differentiates itself: the method of difference takes both these two movements together. But now this power of differentiation must be examined. It is this power which will lead us to the pure concept of internal difference. To determine such a concept, we will have to show *in what way* that which differs from duration, i.e. the other half, can still be duration.

In *Duration and Simultaneity*, Bergson attributes to duration a strange power, the ability to englobe itself, even while it splits itself up into fluxes and concentrates itself in a single current, according to the nature of attention we pay to it.[32] In *Données immédiates*, we find the fundamental idea of *virtuality*, which will subsequently be taken up and developed in *Matter and Memory*: duration, the indivisible is not exactly that which does not allow itself to be divided; it is what changes its nature when it divides, and what changes its nature defines the virtual or the subjective. But the necessary clarifications are to be found in *Creative Evolution*. Biology shows us the process of differentiation at work. We are looking for a concept of difference that does not allow itself to be reduced to degree or intensity, to alterity or contradiction: such a difference *is* vital, even if the concept itself is not biological. Life is the process of difference. In this instance, Bergson is thinking less of embryological differentiation than the differentiation of species, i.e. evolution. In his idea of evolution, Darwin helped associate the problem of difference with life, even though Darwin himself had a false conception of vital difference. Opposing a particular mechanism, Bergson shows that vital difference is an *internal* difference. Furthermore, he shows that internal difference cannot be conceived as a simple *determination*: a determination can be accidental, in any case it can get its being only from a cause, an end, or a coincidence; and this implies a subsisting exteriority; not to mention that the relation of several determinations is only one of association or addition.[33] Not only is vital difference not a determination, but it is very much the opposite: it is indetermination itself. Bergson always emphasizes the unforeseeable character of living forms: "they are indeterminate, by which I mean unforeseeable."[34] And in Bergson's work, the unforeseeable, the indeterminate, is not accidental; on the contrary, it is essential, the negation of accident. By making difference a simple determination, either it is surrendered to chance, or it becomes necessary with respect to something but only by making it accidental with respect to life. Where life is concerned, however, the tendency to change is not accidental.[35] Even more to the point, the changes themselves are not accidental, the *élan vital* "is the root cause of variations."[36] This is tantamount to saying that difference is not a determination but, in its essential relation to life, a differentiation. Differentiation certainly comes from the resistence life encounters from matter, but it comes first and foremost from the explosive internal force which life carries within itself. "The essence of a vital tendency is to develop itself in the form of a spray, creating by the sole power of its growth, the divergent directions its *élan* will pursue."[37] Virtuality exists in such a way that it actualizes itself as it dissociates itself; it must dissociate itself to actualize itself. Differentiation is the movement of a virtuality actualizing itself. Life differs from itself, so we are confronted by divergent lines of evolution and, on each line, orignal processes. Still, it is only with itself that life differs; consequently, also on each line, we are confronted by particular apparatuses, particular organ structures that are identical though obtained by different means.[38] Divergence of series, identity of particular apparatuses: this is the double movement of life as a whole. The notion of differentiation posits at once the *simplicity* of a virtual, the *divergence* of the series in which this virtual actualizes itself, and the *resemblence* of certain fundamental results produced in these series. Bergson explains just how important resemblence is as a biological category:[39] it is the identity of that which differs from itself; it proves that the same virtuality actualizes itself in the divergence of series; and it shows the *essence* subsisting in change, just as divergence shows the change itself at work in the essence. "What are the chances that two totally different evolutions, through two totally different series of accidents added together, end up with similar results?"[40]

In *Les Deux sources*, Bergson comes back to this process of differentiation: dichotomy is the law of life.[41] But something new appears: alongside biological differentiation, there now appears a properly historical differentiation. Biological differentiation certainly has its principle in life itself, but it is none the less bound up with matter, such that its products remain separate, external to one another.

"The materiality which they [the species] have given themselves, prevents them from fusing back together so as to reintroduce the original tendency, but stronger, more complex, and more evolved."[42] On the level of history, however, the tendencies constituted by dissociation evolve in the same individual or in the same society. From then on, these tendencies evolve successively but in the same being: humanity will go as far as it can in one direction, then turn around and go in the other direction.[43] This text is all the more important since it is one of the few in which Bergson accords a specificity to the historical with respect to the vital. What does this mean? It means that difference becomes conscious and achieves self-consciousness in humanity and only in humanity. If difference itself is biological, the consciousness of difference is historical. True, the function of this historical consciousness of difference should not be exaggerated. According to Bergson, more than providing something new, it liberates what is already there. Consciousness was already there, with and in difference. Duration is all by itself consciousness, life all by itself is consciousness—but it is so *by rights*.[44] If history is what reanimates consciousness, or is the place where consciousness is reanimated and posited in fact, it is only because this consciousness identical to life had fallen asleep, had grown numb in matter—a voided consciousness, not an absence of consciousness.[45] Consciousness is not the least bit historical in Bergson's work; history is simply that point where consciousness pops up again, once it has traversed matter. Consequently, there exists by rights an identity between difference itself and the consciousness of difference: history is never anything other than a matter of fact. This identity by rights between difference and the consciousness of difference is *memory*; and it is memory that will give us the nature of the pure concept.

Nevertheless, before we get there, we must examine how the process of differentiation is sufficient to distinguish Bergson's method from dialectic. The major similarity between Plato and Bergson is that they each created a philosophy of difference in which difference is thought as such; it is not reduced to contradiction and *does not go* as far as contradiction.[46] But the point where they part company (not the only point, but the most important) seems to be the necessary presence of a principle of finality in Plato: only the Good explains the difference of the thing and allows us to understand the thing in itself, as in the celebrated example of Socrates sitting in his prison cell. Therefore, in his dichotomy, Plato needs the Good as the rule to govern choice. There is no intuition in Plato, but there is inspiration by the Good. In this sense, at least one of Bergson's texts is Platonic: in *Les Deux sources*, he shows that one must examine functions if one hopes to uncover genuine articulations of the real. What is the function of each faculty? For example, what is the function of storytelling?[47] The thing gets its difference in this case from its use, its end, its purpose—from the Good. But we know that carving up reality, or the articulations of the real, is only a preliminary expression of the method. What governs the dissection of things is indeed their function, their end, such that they seem at this point to receive their very difference from outside themselves. Precisely, however, this is why Bergson both criticizes finality and does not restrict himself to the articulations of the real: the thing itself and its corresponding end are in fact one and the same thing, which on the one hand is seen as the composite it forms in space, and on the other, as difference and the simplicity of pure duration.[48] There is no longer any basis for speaking of finality: when difference has become the thing itself, there is no longer any basis for saying that the thing receives its difference from an end. Thus Bergson's conception of difference of nature allows him, unlike Plato, to avert any genuine recourse to finality. Similarly, using certain texts by Bergson, we can imagine the objections he would have had to a Hegelian-inspired dialectics, from which he is even more removed than Platonic dialectics. In Bergson, thanks to the notion of the virtual, the thing differs from itself *first, immediately*. According to Hegel, the thing differs from itself because it differs first from everything it is not, and thus difference goes as far as contradiction. The distinction between opposite and contradiction matter little in this context, since contradiction, like the opposite, is only the presentation of a whole. In both cases, difference has been replaced by the play of determination. "There is hardly any concrete reality on which one cannot hold two opposing views simultaneously; this reality, therefore, is subsumed under two antagonistic concepts."[49] The object is then reconstituted using these two points of view, or so it is claimed. For example, duration is supposedly the synthesis of unity and multiplicity. However, if Bergson could object that Platonism goes no farther than a conception of *difference as still external*, the objection he would address to a dialectic of contradiction is that it gets no farther than a conception of *difference as only abstract*. "This combination [of two contradictory concepts] cannot present either a diversity of degrees or a variety of forms: it is, or it is not."[50] Whatever entails neither degree nor nuance is an abstraction. Thus the dialectic of contradiction falls short of difference itself, which is the cause or reason of nuance. And in the end, contradiction is only one of the numerous retrospective illusions that Bergson denounces. What is differentiating itself in two divergent tendencies is a virtuality, and as such it is something absolutely simple that actualizes itself. We treat it as a real thing by composing it with the characteristic elements of two tendencies which, however, were created only in its very development. We *think* duration differs from itself because it is first the product of two contrary determinations, but we forget that it differentiated itself because it is *first* that which differs from itself. Everything comes back to Bergson's critique of the negative: his whole effort is aimed at a conception of difference without negation, a conception of difference that does not contain the negative. In his critique of disorder, as well as his critique of nothingness or contradiction, Bergson tries to show that the negation of one real term by the other is only the positive actualization of a virtuality that contains both terms at once. "Struggle, in this instance, is only the superficial aspect of progress."[51] It is our ignorance of the virtual that makes us believe in contradiction and negation. The opposition of two terms is only the actualization of a virtuality that contained them both: this is tantamount to saying that difference is more profound than negation or contradiction.

Whatever the importance of differentiation, it is not what is most profound. If it were, there would be no reason to speak of a concept of difference: differentiation is an action, an actualization. What differentiates itself is *first* that which differs from itself, in other words, the virtual. Differentiation is not the concept, but the production of objects that finds its cause or reason in the concept. Only, if we accept that what differs from itself must be such a concept, then the virtual must have a consistancy, an objective consistancy that enables it to differentiate itself, to produce such objects. In those crucial pages devoted to Ravaisson, Bergson explains that there are two ways of determining what colors have in common.[52] *Either* we extract the abstract and general idea of color, and we do so by "effacing from red what makes it red, from blue what makes it blue, and from green what makes it green": then we are left with a concept which is a genre, and many objects for one concept. The concept and the object are two things, and the relation of the object to the concept is one of subsumption. Thus we get no farther than spatial distinctions, a state of difference that is external to the thing. *Or* we send the colors through a convergent lense that concentrates them on the same point: what we have then is "pure white light," the very light that "makes the differences come out between the shades." So, the different colors are no longer objects *under* a concept, but nuances or degrees of the concept itself. Degrees of difference itself, and not differences of degree. The relation is no longer one of subsumption, but one of participation. White light is still a universal, but a concrete universal, which gives us an understanding of the particular because it is the far end of the particular. Because things have become nuances or degrees of the concept, the concept itself has become a thing. It is a universal thing, if you like, since the objects look like so many degrees, but a concrete thing, not a genus or a generality. Properly speaking, there is no longer many objects for one concept; the concept is identical to the thing itself. But it is not the resemblance of objects; the concept is the difference between them, to which they are related. This is internal difference: the concept which has become a concept of difference. To achieve this superior philosophical goal, what was required? We had to give up thinking in terms of space: the spatial distinction "does not entail degrees."[53] Spatial differences had to be replaced by temporal differences. And what properly belongs to internal difference is this: it makes the concept a concrete thing, because things are just nuances or degrees present within the concept. It is in this sense that Bergsonism has put difference, and the concept along with it, into time. "If the mind has a modest role to play by connecting the successive moments of the thing, and if the mind through this operation makes contact with matter, and if it is through matter that it is first distinguished, then an infinity of degrees between matter and a fully developed mind can be conceived."[54] The distinctions between subject and object, body and mind, are temporal and so a matter of degree—but they are not simple differences of degree.[55] Now we see how the virtual becomes the pure concept of difference, and what such a concept entails: *it is the possible coexistence of degrees or nuances.* If in spite of this apparent paradox, we label this possible coexistence *memory*, as Bergson himself does, we must conclude that the *élan vital* is less profound than duration. *Duration, memory, and élan vital are the three aspects of the concept that can be distinguished with precision.* Duration is difference from itself; memory is the coexistence of degrees of difference; the *élan vital* is the differentiation of difference. These three stages define a schematizism in Bergson's philosophy. The role of memory is to give the virtuality of duration itself an objective consistency which makes it a concrete universal, and enable it to actualize itself. When virtuality actualizes itself, that is to say, differentiates itself, it is through life and in a vital form. In this sense, it is true that difference *is* vital. But virtuality was able to differentiate itself using only the degrees that coexist within it. Differentiation is only the separation of what coexisted in duration. The differentiations of the *élan vital* are, in a more profound way, the degrees of difference itself. And the products of differentiation are objects in absolute conformity with the object, at least in their purity, because they are in fact nothing other than the complimentary position of the different degrees of the concept itself. It is in this sense again that the theory of differentiation is less profound than the theory of nuances or degrees.

The virtual now defines an absolutely positive mode of existence. Duration is the virtual; this degree of duration is real, to the extent that this degree differentiates itself. For example, duration is not in itself psychological, but the psychological represents a particular degree of duration that is actualized between other degrees as well as among them.[56] Certainly, the virtual is the mode of that which does not act, since it will act only by differentiating itself, by ceasing to be in itself, even as it keeps something of its origin. Precisely, however, it follows that the virtual is the mode of *what is*. This thesis of Bergson's is particularly famous: the virtual is a pure recollection, and pure recollection is difference. Pure recollection is virtual because it would be absurd to look for a mark of the past in something actual and already actualized.[57] Recollection is not the representation of something, it doesn't represent—it simply *is*. Or if we must speak of representation, a recollection "does not represent something which has been, but simply something that is…it is *a recollection of the present.*"[58] A recollection is not waiting to come about; it is not waiting to be formed; it is not waiting for the perception to disappear. Recollection is not posterior to perception. *The coexistence of the past with the present which has been is an essential theme of Bergsonism.* According to these characteristics, however, when we say that recollection thus defined is difference itself, we are saying two things at once. On the one hand, pure recollection is difference because no memory resembles any other memory, because each memory is immediately perfect, because it is all at once what it will always be: difference is the object of recollection, just as resemblance is the object of perception.[59] It is enough to dream to gain access to this world where nothing resembles anything else; a pure dreamer would never leave the particular, he would grasp only differences. On the other hand, recollection is difference in still another sense: it *contributes* difference; because if it is true that the demands of the present introduce some resemblance between our recollections, it is also true that recollection introduces difference into the present, in the sense that recollection constitutes, each subsequent moment, something new. Precisely because the past is preserved, "the subsequent moment always contains, in addition to the previous moment, the recollection which this previous moment has left behind."[60] "Internal duration is the continued life of memory prolonging the past in the present, whether the present directly contains the ceaselessly growing image of the past, or whether by virtue of its continual change in quality, the present bears witness to the increasingly heavy baggage one drags along as one grows older."[61] In a different way than Freud, though just as profound, Bergson saw that memory was a function of the future, that memory and will were the same function, that only a being capable of memory could turn away from its past, free itself from the past, not repeat it, and do something new. Thus the word "difference" at once designates *the particular that is* and *the new that is coming about*. Recollection is defined both in relation to the perception with which it is contemporaneous, and in relation to the subsequent moment in which it is prolonged. When we unite the two meanings, we get a strange impression: that of acting and being acted on at the same time.[62] But how can we avoid uniting them, since my perception is already the subsequent moment?

Let's begin with the second meaning. We know the importance Bergson attributes to this idea of *newness*, in his theory of the future and his theory of freedom. But we have to examine this notion more precisely, at the moment of its formation in the second chapter of the *Essai*. Saying that the past is preserved in itself and that it is prolonged in the present is tantamount to saying that the subsequent moment appears without the disappearance of the previous moment. This presupposes a *contraction*, and contraction defines duration.[63] What is opposed to contraction is pure repetition or matter: repetition is the mode of a present that appears only when the other present has disappeared—the present itself, or exteriority, vibration, relaxation. Contraction, on the other hand, designates difference because difference in its essence makes a repetition impossible, because it destroys the very condition of any possible repetition. In this sense, difference is the new, newness itself. But how does one define the appearance of something new *in general*? It is in the second chapter of the *Essai* that Bergson takes up this problem, which is most famously associated with Hume. Hume

45

posed the problem of causality by asking how a pure repetition, a repetition of similar cases which produce nothing new, can nevertheless produce something new in the mind looking on. This "something new" is the expectation the thousandth time around—there you have *difference*. Hume's response was that if repetition produces a difference in the the mind looking on, it is by virtue of the principles of human nature and especially the principle of habit. When Bergson analyzes the example of ticks of the clocks or the sounds of a hammer striking, he poses the problem in the same way as Hume, and resolves it similarly: anything new produced is not in the objects, but in the mind: it is a "fusion," an "interpenetration," an "organization," a preservation of the precedent, which has not disappeared when the subsequent appears. In a word, it is a contraction that occurs in the mind. The similarity between Hume and Bergson goes even farther: just as in Hume similar cases blend together in the imagination yet at the same time remain distinct in the understanding, so in Bergson states blend together in duration yet at the same time preserve something of the exteriority from which they come; it is with this last point that Bergson explains the construction of space. So, contraction initially happens *in* the mind, as it were; contraction is the origin of the mind; it gives birth to difference. Afterwards, but only afterwards, the mind appropriates it for its own use; the mind contracts and is contracted, as we see in Bergson's theory of freedom.[64] But it is enough for us to have grasped the notion in its origin.

Not only do duration and matter differ in nature, but what differs in this way is difference as well as repetition. We again encounter an old difficulty: at one and the same time, difference of nature was between two tendencies and, more profoundly, was one of the two tendencies. And these were not the only states of difference, there were still two others: the privileged tendency, the tendency on the right side was differentiated in two, and it was able to differentiate itself because, more profoundly, there are degrees in difference. What we must do now is regroup these four states: 1) *difference of nature*, 2) *internal difference*, 3) *differentiation*, and 4) *degress of difference*. The common thread is that (internal) difference differs (in nature) from repetition. Clearly, however, this does not add up: difference is said both to be internal and to differ externally. But if we are able to glimpse the outlines of a solution, it is only because Bergson is intent on showing us that difference is still a repetition, and repetition is already a difference. Repetition, or matter, is indeed a difference; the oscillations are clearly distinct in as much as "one disappears when the other appears." Bergson does not deny that science tries to attain difference itself and is able to succeed; he sees such an endeavor in infinitesimal analysis: a genuine science of difference.[65] More than that, when Bergson shows us the dreamer so immersed in the particular that he grasps only pure differences, he tells us that this region of the mind rejoins matter, that to dream is to be indifferent, to disinterest onself. It would thus be a mistake to confuse repetition with generality, because generality presupposes the contraction of the mind. Repetition creates nothing in the object; it lets the object persist, and even maintains it in its particularity. Repetition does indeed form objective genuses, but these genuses are not in themselves general ideas because they do not englobe a plurality of objects that resemble one another; they present to us only the particularity of an object that repeats itself identical to itself.[66] Repetition is thus a kind of difference; only, it's a difference always outside itself, a difference indifferent to itself. Conversely, *difference is in turn a repetition*. Indeed we saw that difference, in its very origin and in the act of this origin, was a contraction. But what is the effect of this contraction? It raises into coexistence what was elsewhere repeated. The mind, in its origin, is only the contraction of identical elements, and by virtue of this, it is memory. Whenever Bergson discusses memory, he presents two aspects of it, the second of which is the more profound: memory-recollection and memory-contraction.[67] By contracting itself, the element of repetition coexists with itself—one might say, multiplies itself and maintains itself. Thus the degrees of contraction are defined, each of which presents at its level the coexistence with itself of the element itself, in other words, the whole. There is no paradox in defining memory as coexistence itself, since all possible degrees of coexistence in turn coexist and constitute memory. The identical elements of material repetition blend together in a contraction; this contraction presents both something new, i.e. difference, and degrees which are the degrees of this difference itself. It is in this sense that difference is still a repetition. Bergson constantly comes back to this theme: "The same psychological life would thus be repeated an indefinite number of times, in the sucessive stages of memory, and the same act of the mind could be played out at many different levels";[68] the sections of the cone are "just so many repetitions of our whole past life";[69] "it is almost as if our memories were repeated an indefinite number of times in the thousands and thousands of possible reductions of our past life."[70] One sees the distinction left to be made between psychic repetition and material repetition: it is at the same moment that all our past life is indefinitely repeated; the repetition is virtual. What is more, the virtuality has no other consistancy than what it receives from this original repetition. "These planes are not presented...as ready-made things, superimposed on one another. Rather, they exist in a virtual way, having that existence proper to things of the mind."[71] At this point, we could almost say that for Bergson, matter is succession and duration is coexistence: "A sufficiently powerful attention to life, and sufficiently removed from any practical purpose, could embrace the entire past history of the conscious person in an undivided present."[72] But duration is a coexistence of a whole other kind: it is real coexistence, simultaneity. This is why the virtual coexistence that defines duration is at the same time a real succession, whereas matter in the end presents us less with a succession than the simple material of a simultaneity: real coexistence, juxtaposition. In a word, psychic degrees are just so many virtual planes of contraction or levels of tension. Bergson's philosophy comes to completion in a cosmology where everything is changes in tension, changes in energy, and nothing else.[73] Duration as it is given to intuition shows itself capable of thousands of possible tensions, an infinite diversity of relaxations and contractions. Bergson criticized the combination of antagonistic concepts for being able to give us a thing only in a monolithic aspect, without degrees or nuances. Intuition, on the other hand, gives us "a choice among an infinity of possible durations,"[74] "a continuity of durations that we must try to follow all the way to the bottom, or all the way to the top."[75]

Have the two senses of difference been rejoined: difference as particularity that is, and difference as personality, indetermination, newness that creates itself? Particularity is given as maximum relaxation, a spreading out, an expansion; in the sections of the cone, it's the base that carries memories in their individual form. "Memories take a more banal form when memory contracts, and they take a more personal form when memory expands."[76] The more the contraction relaxes, the more individual are the memories; they are more distinct from each other, too, and more localized."[77] The particular is located at the limit of relaxation or contraction, and its movement will be prolonged by the matter which it prepares. Matter and duration are the two extreme levels of relaxation and contraction, just as in duration itself, two extreme levels of relaxation and contraction are the pure past and the pure present, memory and perception. We see, then, the present is defined in its opposition to particularity, as resemblance or even universality. A being that lived in the pure present would evolve in the universal, "with habit being to action what generality is to thought."[78] But the two terms opposed in this way are only two extreme degrees that coexist. Opposition is always nothing but the virtual coexistence of two extreme degrees: a recollection coexists with that which it recalls, with its corresponding perception; the present is only the most contracted degree of memory, an *immediate past.*[79] Between these extremes, then, we will find all the intermediate degrees, which are the degrees of generality, or rather that which constitute the general idea. Now we see to what extent matter was not generality: true generality presupposes a perception of resemblances, a contraction. The general idea is a dynamic whole, an oscillation; "the essence of the general idea is to move constantly from the sphere of action to the sphere of pure memory," "it is the twofold current passing back and forth."[80] However, we know that the intermediate degrees between extremes are capable of recreating these extremes as the very products of a differentiation. We know that a theory of degrees is the basis for a theory of differentiation: in memory, two degrees only have to be opposed to one another for them to become at the same time the differentiation of an intermediary into two tendencies or movements that are distinct in nature. Because the present and the past are two inverse degrees, they are distinct in nature; they are the differentiation, the bifurcation of the whole. Every moment duration splits into two symmetrical streams, "one of which falls back toward the past, while the other is projected toward the future."[81] Saying that the present is the most contracted degree of the past is tantamount to saying that the present is in nature opposed to the past, that the present is an *imminent future*. Here is the second meaning of difference: something new. But what exactly is new here? The general idea is the whole which differentiates itself in particular images and bodily attitude, but this very differentiation is still the whole of the degrees going from one extreme to the next, inserting the one in the other.[82] The general idea places the recollection in the action, organizes recollections with acts, transforms recollection into perception—and more precisely, it makes the images which have issued from the past itself, "increasingly capable of being inserted into the driving schema."[83] The function of the general idea is this: to put the particular in the universal. What is new here, the newness, is precisely that the particular is in the universal. The new is clearly not the pure present: the pure present, as well as the particular memory, tend toward the state of matter, not by virtue of its spreading out, but its instantaneity. But when the particular descends into the universal, or recollection into movement, the automatic act leaves room for voluntary and free action. This new belongs to a being that, simultaneously, comes and goes from the universal to the particular, opposes them, and puts the particular in the universal. Such a being simultaneously thinks, desires, recollects. In short, it is the degrees of generality that unite and reunite the two meanings of difference.

Bergson can leave many readers with a certain impression of vagueness and incoherence: vagueness, because we learn in the end that difference is the unforeseeable, indetermination itself; and incoherence, because he seems to recycle for his own purposes the same notions he just finished criticizing. We see him attacking degrees, and here they come front and center in duration itself, to the point that Bergsonism seems a philosophy of degrees: "One moves by imperceptible degrees from recollections deposited throughout time to movements that outline nascent or possible action in space,"[84] "recollection is thus gradually transformed into perception";[85] "similarly, there are degrees of liberty."[86] Berson especially attacks intensity, and yet relaxation and contraction are invoked as fundamental principles of explanation; "between brute matter and the most reflective mind, are all the possible intensities of memory or, what amounts to the same thing, all the degrees of liberty."[87] Finally, Bergson attacks the negative and opposition, but they slip in the backdoor with inversion: geometrical order partakes of the negative, it comes from "the inversion of genuive positivity," "from an interruption";[88] and if we compare science and philosophy, we see that science is not relative, but "is about a reality of an inverse order."[89]

This impression of incoherence, however, I believe is unjustified. It is true that Bergson does come back to degrees, but not to differences of degree. His idea is this: there are no differences of degree in nature, only *degrees of difference itself*. Theories that rely on differences of degree mix everything up, because they fail to see differences of nature; they lose themselves in space and in the composites which space gives us. Furthermore, that which differs in nature is in the end that which differs in nature *from itself*; consequently, that from which it differs is only its lowest *degree*; this is duration, defined as difference of nature itself. When the difference of nature between two things has become one of the two things, the other of the two is only the *last* degree of the first. So it is that difference of nature, when it appears in person, is exactly the virtual coexistence of two *extreme* degrees. Since they are extremes, the twofold current passing between them forms intermediate degrees. These constitute the principle of composites and make us believe in differences of degree, but only if we examine them for themselves, forgetting that the extremities which they unite are two things that differ in nature. In fact, the extremities are degrees of difference itself. Therefore, that which differs is relaxation and contraction, matter and duration as the degrees, the intensities of difference. And in general, if Bergson does not thus simply fall back on differences of degree, neither does he come back to differences of intensity in particular. Relaxation and contraction are the degrees of difference itself only because they are opposed, in as much as they are opposed. As extremes, they are the *inverse* of each other. Bergson criticizes metaphysics for not having seen that relaxation and contraction are the inverse of each other; metaphysics believed they were only two more or less intense degrees in the degradation of the same immobile, stable, eternal Being.[90] In fact, just as degrees are explained by difference and not the reverse, so intensities are explained by inversion and presuppose it. There is no immobile and stable Being as principle; *the point of departure* is contraction itself; it is duration, whose relaxation is inversion. Bergson's concern with finding a genuine beginning, a genuine point of departure, shows up again and again, e.g. perception and affection: "we will begin with action instead of affection because nothing can be said of affection, since there is no reason for it to be what it is rather than something else."[91] But why is relaxation the inverse of contraction, and not contraction the inverse of relaxation? Because *philosophy precisely begins with difference*, and because difference of nature is that duration of which matter is only the lowest degree. Difference is the genuine beginning; it is in this respect that Bergson most diverges from Schelling, at least in appearance. By beginning with something else, on the other hand, some immobile and stable Being, indifference becomes posited as first principle, less is mistaken for more, and a simple view of intensities becomes inevitable. However, when Bergson makes inversion the basis for intensity, he seems to escape this view only to come back to negativity, to opposition. Again, in this instance, such an objection is not entirely exact. Ultimately, the opposition of the two terms that differ in nature is only the positive actualization of a virtuality that contained them both. The role of the intermediate degrees resides precisely in this actualization: they insert one in the other, the recollection in the movement. So, in my view, there is no incoherence in Bergson's philosophy, but there is a profound reconsideration of the concept of difference. Nor do I believe that indetermination is a vague concept. Indetermination, the unforeseeable, contingency, freedom—these all signify a certain independence with respect to causes: in this sense, Bergson honors the *élan vital* with many contingencies.[92] What he means is that the thing is in a certain way *prior* to causes; we must begin with the thing because the causes come after. Indetermination, however, always only means that the thing or the action could have been otherwise. "Could the act have been other?" That is a meaningless question. What Bergson demands of himself is to make us understand why a thing is itself rather than something else. What explains the thing itself is difference, not the causes of the thing. "Freedom must be sought in a particular nuance or quality of the action itself and not in a relation of this act with what it is not or what it could have been."[93] Bergsonism is a philosophy of difference, a philosophy of the actualization of difference: in it we meet difference in person, which actualizes itself as the new.

Jean-Jacques Rousseau: Precursor of Kafka, Céline, and Ponge[1]

There are two ways we risk misjudging a great writer: 1) by failing to recognize the profound logic or the systematic character of his work (we then talk of his "incoherencies" as though they gave us superior pleasure); and 2), by failing to recognize his comic genius and power, from which the work generally draws the greater part of its anti-conformist efficacy (we prefer to speak of his anguish and tragic aspect). In fact, whoever does not laugh out loud while reading Kafka does not truly admire Kafka. These two rules of thumb are especially invaluable for Rousseau.

In one of his most famous theses, Rousseau explains that humanity in the state of nature is good, or at least not mean. Such a proposition is neither from the heart nor a manifestation of optimism; it is a logical manifesto at its most precise. What Rousseau means is this: humanity, as supposed in a state of nature, cannot be mean, since the objective conditions that make human meanness and its exercise possible do not exist in nature itself. The state of nature is a state in which humanity has a relationship with things, not with one another (or only fleetingly). "Men, if you will, would attack one another in their encounters, but they encountered one another infrequently. There prevailed everywhere a state of war, and all the earth was at peace."[2] The state of nature is not only a state of independence, but a state of isolation. One of Rousseau's constant themes is that need is not a factor which brings people together: it does not unite, it isolates each of us. Being limited, our needs in a state of nature necessarily reach a kind of equilibrium with our powers and acquire a kind of self-sufficiency. Even sexuality in a state of nature engenders only fleeting encounters or leaves us in solitude. (Rousseau has much to say and says a great deal on this point, which is like the humorous flip-side of a profound theory.)

How could people be mean when the conditions are absent? The conditions which make meanness possible are those of any determined social state. There is no such thing as disinterested meanness, despite what imbeciles and mean people sometimes say. All meanness is profit or compensation. There is no human meanness that is not inscribed within relationships of oppression, in accordance with complex social interests. Rousseau is one of those writers who knew how to analyze the relations of oppression and the social structures they presuppose. We will have to wait for Engels to come along before this principle of an extreme logic will be called upon and renewed: viz., that violence or oppression does not constitute a primordial fact, but supposes a civil state, social situations, and economic determinations. If Robinson enslaves Friday, it is not due to Robinson's natural disposition, and it is not by the power of his fist; he does it with a small capital and the means of production which he saved from the depths, and he does it to subjugate Friday to social tasks, the ideas of which Robinson has not lost in his shipwreck.

Society constantly puts us in situations where it is in our interest to be mean. Our vanity would have us believe that we are naturally mean. But the truth is much worse: we become mean without knowing it, without even realizing it. It is difficult to be someone's heir without unconsciously wishing for their death now and then. "In such situations, however sincere a love of virtue we bring to them, we weaken sooner or later without noticing it, and we become unjust and mean in fact, without having ceased to be good and just in soul."[3] It seems, however, that the beautiful soul is strangely destined to be thrown again and again into the most ambiguous situations, from which it extirpates itself only with great pain. We see the beautiful soul play on its own tenderness and timidity to extract from the worst situations those elements that allow it nevertheless to keep its virtue intact. "From this continual opposition between my situation and my inclinations, we will witness the birth of enormous faults, unheard of misfortunes, and every virtue except power, that can be a credit to adversity."[4] To find oneself in impossible situations is the destiny of the beautiful soul. This extraordinary comedy of situations is the source of all Rousseau's gusto. If Rousseau's *Confessions* end up being a tragic and hallucinatory book, they begin as one of the most joyful books in literature. Even his vices manage to preserve Rousseau from the meanness into which they could have led him; and Rousseau excels at the analysis of these ambivalent and salutary mechanisms.

The beautiful soul is not content with the state of nature; it affectionately dreams of human relationships. These relationships, however, are realizable only in the most delicate situations. We know that Rousseau's love-dream is to discover the figures of a lost Trinity: either the woman whom he loves loves another man, who will be like a father or brother; or there are two women whom he loves, one of them a strict mother quick to punish, and the other a gentle mother who brings about rebirth. (Rousseau already pursues this quest for two mothers in one of his childhood loves.) But the actual situations that incarnate this revery are always ambiguous. They turn out badly: either we behave poorly, or we end up the odd man out, or both. Rousseau will not recognize this affectionate revery in Theresa and Theresa's mother, a greedy and disagreeable woman rather than a strict mother. Nor will he recognize it when Mme. de Warens wants Rousseau himself to play the role of big brother to her latest infatuation.

Rousseau often, and joyfully, explains that his ideas are slow and his feelings quick. But his slow-forming ideas emerge all of the sudden in his life, give him new directions, and inspire him to invent strange things. With poets and philosophers, we must love even those manias and bizarre behaviors which bear witness to combinations of idea and feeling. Thomas de Quincey developed a method meant to inspire us with love for great writers. In an article on Kant ("The Last Days of Emmanuel Kant," translated by Schwob),[5] Quincey describes the extremely complex device that Kant had invented to serve as a shoe-holder. The same goes for Rousseau's Armenian outfit when he used to live in Motiers and weave "braids" on his stoop while chatting with the women. —What we see in these examples are real ways of life; they are thinkers' anecdotes.

How do we avoid those situations in which it is in our interest to be mean? Certainly, by an act of will, a strong soul can affect the situation itself and modify it. For example, a legal heir can renounce his rights so as not to wish the death of his relative. Similarly, in *Julie, or the New Heloise*, Julie accepts the commitment not to marry Saint-Preux, even if her husband happens to die: this is how "she transforms the secret interest she had in her husband's demise into an interest in his preservation."[6] But Rousseau, by his own admission, is not a strong soul. He loves virtue more than he is virtuous. Except for matters of inheritance, he has too much imagination to embrace renunciation willingly in advance. He will therefore require subtle devices of another kind to avoid tempting situations or to get himself out of them. He plays on everything, including his bad health, to keep his virtuous aspirations intact. He himself explains how his bladder troubles were an essential factor in his great moral reform: fearing that he might not be able to contain himself in the presence of the king, he prefers instead to renounce his pension. Illness inspires him, like a sense of humor (Rousseau tells of his ear trouble with a gusto similar to Céline's much later). But humor is the flip-side of morality: he would sooner be a music-copyist than a pensioner of the king.

In *Julie, or the New Heloise*, Rousseau elaborates a profound method, perfect for averting dangerous situations. A situation does not tempt us uniquely of itself, but thanks to the full weight of a past that informs it. It is the search for the past in present situations, the repetition of the past that inspires our most violent passions and temptations. We always love in the past, and passions are first and foremost an illness proper to memory. To cure Saint-Preux and lead him back to virtue, M. de Wolmar uses a method by which he wards off the prestige of the past. He forces Julie and Saint-Preux to embrace in the same grove which witnessed their first moments of love: "Julie, there is no more reason to fear this sanctuary, it has just been profaned."[7] It is Saint-Preux's present interest that he wants to make virtuous: "it's not Julie de Wolmar that he loves, it's Julie d'Etange;

he doesn't hate me as the possessor of the woman he loves, but as the seducer of the woman he loved... He loves her in the past; there you have the key to the puzzle: take away his memory, and he will love no more."[8] It is in relation to objects, to places, e.g. a grove, that we learn the passing of time, and that we eventually know how to want in the future, instead of being passionate in the present.

The two poles of Rousseau's philosophical work are *Emile* and the *Social Contract*. The root of evil in modern society is that we are no longer either private individuals or public citizens: each of us has become "*homo oeconomicus*," in other words, "bourgeois," motivated by profit. Those situations which give us a stake in being mean always imply relationships of oppression, where one enters into a relationship with another: to command or to obey, master or slave. *Emile* is the reconstitution of the private individual; the *Social Contract*, that of the citizen. Rousseau's first pedagogical rule is the following: by restoring our natural relationship with things, we will manage to reeducate ourselves as private individuals, thus preserving us from those all too human, artificial relationships which from early childhood inculcate in us a dangerous tendency to command. (And the same tendency that makes us tyrants makes us slaves.) "Children, when they make it their right to be obeyed, leave behind the state of nature almost at birth."[9] True pedagogical rectification consists in subordinating human relations to the relation of human beings to things. The taste for things is a constant in Rousseau's work (Francis Ponge's studies have something Rousseau-like about them). Thus we have the famous rule from *Emile*, which demands only muscle: Never bring things to the child, bring the child to the things.

The private individual, by virtue of his relation to things, has already warded off the infantile situation that gives him a stake in being mean. But the citizen is one who enters into relationships with others, such that it is precisely in his interest to be virtuous. To create an objective, actual situation wherein justice and self-interest are reconciled is for Rousseau the proper task of politics. And virtue here again returns to its deepest meaning, which harks back to the public determination of the citizen. The *Social Contract* is surely one of the great books of political philosophy. Rousseau's birthday is but an occasion to read or reread it. In it the citizen learns about the mystification of the separation of powers, and how the Republic is defined by the existence of a sole power, the legislative. As it appears in Rousseau, the analysis of the concept of law will dominate philosophical reflection for a long time to come, and dominates it still.

The Idea of Genesis in Kant's Esthetics[1]

The difficulties of Kantian esthetics in the first part of the *Critique of Judgment* have to do with the diversity of points of view. On the one hand, Kant proposes an esthetics of the spectator, as in the theory of the judgment of taste; on the other, an esthetics or meta-esthetics of the creator, as in the theory of genius. Then again, he proposes an esthetics of the beautiful in nature, but also an esthetics of the beautiful in art. Sometimes it's a "classically" inspired esthetics of form, and sometimes a meta-esthetics of matter and Idea, which is closer to romanticism. The systematic unity of the *Critique of Judgment* can be established only by encompassing these various points of view and understanding the necessary transitions between them. Such a comprehension must explain the apparent organizational difficulties, in other words, both the place of the Analytic of the Sublime (sandwiched between the Analytic of the Beautiful and the deduction of the judgments of taste), and the place of the theory of art and genius (at the end of the deduction).

The judgment of taste—"this is beautiful"—expresses an agreement of two faculties in the spectator: the imagination and the understanding. The judgment of taste can be distinguished from the judgment of preference because the judgment of taste lays claim to a certain necessity, a certain *a priori* universality. It thus borrows understanding's legality. In this instance, however, the legality does not appear under determinate concepts. The universality of the judgment of taste is one of pleasure; the beautiful thing is singular and remains without concept. The understanding intercedes as the faculty of concepts in general, though any determinate concept has here been set aside. The imagination, on its side, has free reign since it is no longer constrained by any particular concept. When the imagination agrees with understanding in the judgment of taste, it means that a *free* imagination agrees with an *indeterminate* understanding. This expression of agreement, which is itself free and undetermined, between the imagination and the understanding, properly belongs to the judgment of taste. Consequently, esthetic pleasure is far from being prior to judgment; on the contrary, esthetic pleasure depends on judgment: the pleasure is the agreement of the faculties themselves, in as much as this agreement is achieved without concepts and so can only be felt. It can be said that the judgment of taste begins only with pleasure, but does not derive from it.

We have to consider this first point carefully: the theme of an agreement among several faculties. The idea of such an agreement is a constant of the Kantian Critique. Our faculties differ in nature and yet function harmoniously. In the *Critique of Pure Reason*, understanding, imagination and reason enter into a harmonious relationship, in accordance with a speculative purpose. Similarly, in the *Critique of Practical Reason*, reason and understanding enter into a harmonious relationship (I will leave aside examining the possible role of imagination for a practical aim). Still, in these cases, one of the faculties always predominates. "Predominant" in this context means three things: 1) determinate with respect to an aim; 2) determinative with respect to objects; 3) determinative with respect to the other faculties.[40] So, in the *Critique of Pure Reason*, the understanding disposes completely determinate *a priori* concepts for a speculative purpose; it applies its concepts to objects (phenomena) which are necessarily subject to it; and it induces the other faculties (imagination and reason) to carry out this or that function, with the aim of understanding, and in relation to the objects of understanding. In the *Critique of Practical Reason*, the Ideas of reason, and particularly the Idea of freedom, are determined by the moral law; with this law as intermediary, reason determines suprasensible objects which are necessarily subject to it; and finally, reason induces the understanding to a particualr function, in accordance with a practical purpose. In the first two Critiques, therefore, we cannot escape the principle of an agreement of the faculties among themselves. *But this agreement is always proportioned, constrained, and determinate*: there is always a determinative faculty that legislates, either the understanding for a speculative purpose, or reason for a practical purpose.

Let's come back to the example of the *Critique of Pure Reason*. It is widely acknowledged that schematizing is an original and irreducible act of the imagination: only the imagination can and knows how to schematize. Nevertheless, the imagination does not schematize of its own accord, simply because it is free to do so. It schematizes only to the extent that the understanding determines it, induces it to do so. It schematizes only for a speculative purpose, in accordance with the determinate concepts of the understanding, when the understanding itself plays the role of legislator. This is why it would be misguided to search the mystery of schematizing for the last word on the imagination in its essence or in its free spontaneity. Schematizing is indeed a secret, but not the deepest secret of the imagination. Left to its own devices, the imagination would do something else entirely than schematize. The same holds for reason: reasoning is an original act of reason, but reason reasons only for a speculative purpose, in so far as the understanding determines it to do so, that is, induces it to look for a middle term so it may attribute one of its concepts to the objects governed by the understanding. On its own, reason would do anything but reason; this is what we see in the *Critique of Practical Reason*.

For practical purpose, reason becomes the legislator. Reason, then, in turn determines the understanding in an original function for a new purpose. The understanding extracts, from the sensible natural law, a "type" for a suprasensible nature: the understanding alone can perform this task, but it could not without being determined to do so by reason for a practical purpose. So it is that the faculties enter into harmonious relations or proportions according to the faculty that legislates for this or that purpose. *Diverse proportions, or permutations in the relations of faculties, are therefore conceivable.* The understanding legislates for a speculative purpose; reason, for a practical purpose. In each case, an agreement obtains among the faculties, but this agreement is determined by the faculty that happens to be the legislator. Such a theory of permutations, however, should lead Kant to an ultimate problem. The faculties would never enter into an agreement that is fixed or determined by one of themselves if, to begin with, they were not in themselves and spontaneously capable of an indeterminate agreement, a free harmony, without any fixed proportion.[2] It is useless to appeal to the superiority of the practical over the speculative in this instance; the problem would not be resolved by that, it would only be put off and exacerbated. How could any faculty, which is legislative for a particular purpose, induce the other faculties to perform complementary, indispensable tasks, if all the faculties together were not, to begin with, capable of a free spontaneous agreement, without legislation, without purpose, without predominance?

This is tantamount to saying that the *Critique of Judgment*, in its esthetic part, does not simply exist to complete the other two Critiques: in fact, it provides them with a ground. The *Critique of Judgment* uncovers the *ground* presupposed by the other two Critiques: a free agreement of the faculties. Every determinate agreement can be traced back to the free indeterminate agreement which makes the others possible in general. But why precisely is it the esthetic judgment that reveals this ground, which was hidden in the previous Critiques? In the esthetic judgment, the imagination is liberated from both the domination of understanding and reason. Esthetic pleasure is itself disinterested pleasure: it is not only independent of any empirical purpose, but also any speculative or practical purpose. It follows that esthetic judgment does not legislate; it does not imply any faculty that legislates objects. Indeed how could it be otherwise, since there are only two sorts of objects, phenomena and things-in-themselves: the first are governed by the legislation of the understanding for a speculative purpose; and the second, by the legislation of reason for a practical purpose? Thus Kant has every right to say that the *Critique of Judgment*, contrary to the other two, has no "domain" proper to it; the judgment is not legislative or autonomous, but only heautomous (it legislates only itself).[3] The first two Critiques developed this common theme: the idea of a necessary submission to certain types of objects in relation to a dominant or determinative faculty. But there are no objects that are necessarily subject to esthetic judgment, nor to any faculty in the esthetic judgment. Beautiful things in Nature agree only in a contingent manner with our judgment, that is, with the faculties that function together in the esthetic judgment as such. Now we see what a mistake it would be to think of the *Critique of Judgment* as completing the other two Critiques. In esthetic judgment, the imagination cannot attain a role comparable to that played by the understanding in speculative judgment, or that played by reason in practical judgment. The imagination is liberated from the supervision of the understanding and reason. But it does not become a legislator in turn: on a deeper level, the signal it gives the other faculties is that each must become capable of free play on its own. In two respects, then, the *Critique of Judgment* releases us in a new element, which is something like a fundamental element: 1) a contigent agreement of sensible objects with all our faculties together, instead of a necessary submission to one of the faculties; 2) a free indeterminate harmony of the faculties among themselves, instead of a determinate harmony presided over by one of the faculties.

Kant also says that imagination, in esthetic judgment, "schematizes without concepts."[4] This is a brilliant formulation, though not quite exact. Schematizing is indeed an original act of the imagination, but always in respect to a determinate concept of the imagination. Without a concept from the understanding, the imagination does something else than schematize: it *reflects*. This is the true role of the imagination in esthetic judgment. It reflects the form of the object. By *form*, here, we should not understand form of intuition (sensibility), because forms of intuition still refer to existing objects that in themselves constitute sensible matter; they belong to the knowledge of objects. Esthetic form, however, merges with the reflection of the object in the imagination. It is indifferent to the existence of the reflected object; this is why esthetic pleasure is disinterested. Nor is it less indifferent to the sensible matter of the object; and Kant goes so far as to say that a color or a sound cannot be beautiful in itself, since they are too material, too deeply rooted in our senses to be freely reflected in the imagination. Only the design, the composition matter. These are the consitutive elements of esthetic form, while colors and sounds are only adjuncts.[5] In every respect, then, we must distinguish the intuitive form of sensibility from the reflected form of the imagination.

Every agreement of the faculties defines what Kant calls *common sense*. Kant criticizes empiricism for conceiving common sense as merely a particular empirical faculty, whereas it is the manifestation of an *a piori* agreement of the faculties together.[6] Thus the *Critique of Pure Reason* invokes a logical common sense, *"sensus communis logicus,"* without which knowledge would by rights be incommunicable. Similarly, the *Critique of Practical Reason* frequently invokes a properly moral common sense, which expresses the agreement of the faculties under the legislation of reason. But free harmony should lead Kant to recognize a third common sense, *"sensus communis aestheticus,"* which posits by rights the communicability of feeling or the universality of esthetic pleasure.[7] "This common sense cannot be grounded in experience, since it claims to authorize judgments that contain an obligation; it does not say that everyone will accept our judgment, but that everyone must accept it."[8] We don't hold it against someone for saying: I don't like lemonade, I don't like cheese. But we harshly judge someone who says: I don't like Bach, I prefer Massenet to Mozart. Thus esthetic judgment lays claim to a universality and a necessity by rights, and these are represented in common sense. This is where the real difficulty of the *Critique of Judgment* begins: what is the nature of this esthetic common sense?

This common sense cannot be affirmed by the categories. Such an affirmation would imply determinate concepts of the understanding, and they can enter the picture only in a logical sense. Nor do we fare any better if we *postulate* it: postulates imply knowledge that admits of being determined practically. It therefore seems that a purely esthetic common sense can only be *presumed, presupposed.*[9] But we see how unsatisfactory such a solution is. The free indeterminate agreement of the faculties is the ground, the condition of every other agreement; esthetic common sense is the ground, the condition of every other common sense. How could we be satisfied with supposing it, with giving it a merely hypothetical existence, if it must indeed serve as the foundation for all the other determinate relations among the faculties? How does one explain that while our faculties are different in nature, they still spontaneously enter into a harmonious relation? We cannot settle for presuming such an agreement. We must engender it in the soul. This is the only solution: to trace the genesis of the esthetic common sense, to show how the free agreement of the faculties is necessarily engendered.

If this interpretation is on target, the entire analytic of the beautiful has a precise objective: by analyzing the esthetic judgment of the spectator, Kant uncovers the free agreement of the imagination and the understanding as a ground of the soul, a ground which the other two Critiques presuppose. This ground of the soul shows up in the idea of a common sense that is more profound than any other. But is it enough to presume this ground, simply to "presuppose" it? The Analytic of the Beautiful can go no further. It can only end by making us feel how necessary is a genesis of the sense of the beautiful: is there a principle to give us a rule to *produce* in ourselves esthetic common sense? "Is taste a natural and primordial faculty, or only the idea of a faculty we must acquire?"[10] A genesis of the sense of the beautiful cannot belong to the exposition of the Analytic ("it is enough for now to resolve the faculty of taste in its parts and to reunite them in the idea of common sense"). The genesis can only be the object of a deduction: *the deduction of esthetic judgments*. In the *Critique of Pure Reason*, the deduction proposes to show us how objects are necessarily subject to a speculative purpose, and subject to the understanding which presides over this endeavor. In the judgment of taste, however, this necessary subjection is no longer the problem. Instead, the problem is now one of deducing the genesis of the agreement among faculties: this problem could not make its appearance as long as one of the faculties was considered legislative with respect to the others, binding them in a determinate relation.

Post-Kantians, especially Maïmon and Fichte, raised this fundamental objection: Kant neglected the demands of a genetic method. This objection has a subjective and an objective aspect: on the one hand, Kant relies on facts and is seeking only their conditions; on the other hand, Kant appeals to faculties that are ready-made, whose relation or proportion he seeks to determine, already supposing such faculties are capable of some harmony. If we recall that Maïmon's *Transcendental Philosophy* dates from 1790, we must admit that Kant anticipated, at least in part, the objections of his disciples. The first two Critiques indeed invoke facts, seek out the conditions for these facts, and find them in ready-made faculties. It follows that the first two Critiques point to a genesis which they are incapable of securing on their own. But in the esthetic *Critique of Judgment*, Kant poses the problem of a genesis of the faculties in their original free agreement. Thus he uncovers the ultimate ground still lacking in the other two Critiques. Kant's Critique in general ceases to be a simple *conditioning* to become a transcendental Education, a transcendental Culture, a transcendental Genesis.

The Analytic of the Beautiful left us with this question: whence originates the free indeterminate agreement among the faculties? What is the genesis of the faculties in this agreement? Precisely, the Analytic of the Beautiful stops because it does not have the means to answer the question; one notices, moreover, that the judgment—"this is beautiful"—brings into play only the understanding and the imagination (there is no place for reason). Following the Analytic of the Beautiful, the Analytic of the Sublime calls on reason. But what does Kant expect from this? How will this solve the genetic problem related to the beautiful?

The judgment—"this is sublime"—no longer expresses an agreement between the imagination and the understanding, but between the imagination and reason. But this harmony of the sublime is truly paradoxical. Reason and imagination agree or harmonize only from within a tension, a contradiction, a painful rending. There is agreement, but it is a discordant concord, a harmony in pain. And it is only pain that makes pleasure possible here. Kant emphasizes this point: the imagination undergoes violence; it seems even to lose its freedom. When the feeling of the sublime is experienced before the formless or the deformed in Nature (immensity or power), the imagination can no longer reflect the form of an object. Far from discovering another activity, however, the imagination realizes its very Passion. The imagination has two essential dimensions: successive apprehension, and simultaneous comprehension. If apprehension can reach infinity without trouble, comprehesion (an esthetic comprehension independent of any numerical concept) always has a maximum. So it is that the sublime confronts the imagination with this maximum, forces it to reach its limit, and come to grips with its boundaries. The imagination is pushed *to the limits of its power.*[11] But what pushes and constrains the imagination in this way? It is only in appearance, or by projection, that the sublime relates to sensible nature. In reality, reason alone obliges us to unite the infinity of the sensible world in a whole; reason alone forces the imagination to confront its limit. The imagination thus discovers the disproportion of reason, and it is forced to admit that its power is nothing compared to a rational Idea.[12]

And yet an agreement *is born* at the heart of this discord. Never was Kant closer to a dialectical conception of the faculties. Reason confronts the imagination with its own limits in the sensible world; conversely, however, the imagination awakens reason as the faculty able to conceive a supersensible substratum for the infinity of this sensible world. As it undergoes violence, the imagination seems to lose its freedom; but at the same time, the imagination is raised to a transcendental function, taking its own limit as object. Surpassed on every side, the imagination itself surpasses its limits—true, in a negative fashion only, by representing to itself the inaccessibility of the rational Idea, and by making this inaccessibility something present in sensible nature. "The imagination, with no place to take hold beyond the sensible, feels nonetheless unlimited thanks to the disappearance of its limits; and this abstraction is a presentation of the infinite which, for that very reason, can only be negative, but which still expands the soul."[13] Right when the imagination, suffering the violence of reason, thought it was losing its freedom, it frees itself from the constraints of the understanding and enters into an agreement with reason to discover what the understanding had kept hidden, namely the suprasensible destination of imagination, which is also like a transcendental origin. In its very Passion, the imagination discovers the origin and the destination of all its activities. This is the lesson of the Analytic of the Sublime: even the imagination has a suprasensible destination.[14] The agreement of the imagination and reason is engendered in discord. Pleasure is engendered in pain. What is more, the two faculties seem to enrich each other, discovering the principle of their genesis; the imagination discovers it in proximity to its limit; and reason, beyond the sensible—and together they discover it in a "point of concentration" that defines what is most profound in the soul: the suprasensible unity of all the faculties.

The Analytic of the Sublime gives us a result that the Analytic of the Beautiful could not even conceive: in the case of the sublime, the agreement of the concerned faculties is the object of a genuine genesis. This explains why Kant recognizes that the sense of the sublime, contrary to the sense of the beautiful, is inseparable from a cultured viewpoint: "in the trials of the forces of nature, in its devestation…the vulgar man sees only pain, danger, and misery."[15] The vulgar man remains in "discord." Not that the sublime involves some empirical and conventional culture; but the faculties which the sublime puts in play point to a genesis of their agreement within immediate discord. This is a transcendental genesis, and not an empirical culture. From this point on, the Analytic of the Sublime has a twofold significance. It stands on its own from the point of view of reason and imagination. But also it has value as a model: how can this discovery related to the sublime be extended or adapted to the sense of the beautiful? In other words, must not the agreement between the imagination and the understanding, which defines the beautiful, also be the object of a genesis, whose example was given by the Anaytic of the Sublime?

The problem of a transcendental deduction is always objective. For example, in the *Critique of Pure Reason*, once Kant has shown that the categories are *a priori* representations of the understanding, he asks how and why objects are necessarily subject to the categories, that is, subject to the understanding as legislator, or a speculative purpose. But when we examine the judgment of the sublime, we see no objective problem of deduction has been posed in this case. The sublime indeed relates to objects, but only by projecting our moods; and this projection is immediately possible, because whatever is formless or deformed in the object receives the projection.[16] However, at first blush, the same seems to be true of the judgment of taste or beauty: our pleasure is disinterested, we disregard the existence or even the matter of the object. There is no legislative faculty; there is no object necessarily subject to the judgment of taste. This is why Kant suggests that the problem of the judgment of taste is only subjective.[17]

And yet the major difference between the sublime and the beautiful is that the pleasure of the beautiful results from the form of an object: Kant says this characteristic is enough to ground the necessity of a "deduction" of the judgment of taste.[18] However indifferent we are to the existence of the object, there is nonetheless an object *concerning* which, *in the occurence* of which we experience the free harmony of our understanding and our imagination. In other words, nature has an aptitude for producing objects that are reflected formally in the imagination:

contrary to what occurs in the sublime, nature manifests in this case a positive property "which provides us with the occasion to grasp the internal finality of the relation of our mental faculties by means of the judgment brought to bear on certain examples of its productions."[19] So it is that the internal agreement of our faculties among themselves implies an external agreement between nature and these same faculties. This second agreement is quite special. It must not be confused with a necessary subjection of the objects of nature; but it must not be taken as a final or teleological agreement either. If there were a necessary subjection, then the judgment of taste would be autonomous and legislative; if there were a real objective finality, then the judgment of taste would no loger be heautonomous ("we would have to learn from nature what we should find beautiful, in which case judgment would be subject to empirical principles").[20] The agreement thus has no goal: nature is only obeying its mechanical laws, while our faculties are obeying their own specific laws. *"An agreement that presents itself without a goal, of itself, accidentally appropriated, as the judgment requires, with respect to nature and its forms."*[21] As Kant says, nature isn't doing us any favors; rather, we are organized in such a way that we can favorably receive nature.

Let's back up. The sense of the beautiful, as common sense, is defined by the supposed universality of esthetic pleasure. Esthetic pleasure itself results from the free agreement of the imagination and the understanding, and this free agreement can only be felt. But it is not sufficient to suppose in turn the universality and the necessity of the agreement, which must be engendered *a priori* in such a way that its claim is grounded. Here begins the real problem of the deduction: we must explain "why feeling in the judgment of taste is attributed to everyone, much like a duty."[22] But the judgment of taste, so it seemed, was connected to an objective determination. What we want to know is whether we cannot discover, *on the side of the determination*, a principle for the genesis of the agreement of the faculties in the judgment itself. Such a vantage point would have the advantage of explaining Kant's order of ideas: 1) the Analytic of the Beautiful uncovers a free agreement of the understanding and the imagination, but can posit it only as presupposed; 2) the Analytic of the Sublime uncovers a free agreement of the imagination and reason, but under internal conditions that also sketch their genesis; 3) the deduction of the judgment of taste uncovers an external principle according to which the understanding-imagination agreement is in turn engendered *a priori*; it thus uses the model furnished by the sublime, but with original means, since the sublime for its part does not require a deduction.

How does this genesis of the sense of the beautiful shape up? The *idea* of the agreement without goal between nature and our faculties defines a *purpose* for reason, a rational purpose connected with the beautiful. Clearly, this purpose is not a purpose for the beautiful as such, and clearly, it is very different from esthetic judgment. Otherwise, the entire *Critique of Judgment* would be contradictory. In fact, the pleasure of the beautiful is totally disinterested, and esthetic judgment expresses the agreement of the imagination and the understanding without the intervention of reason. The purpose in question is synthetically connected to judgment. It has no bearing on the beautiful as such, but on the aptitude of nature to produce beautiful things. It has to do with nature, in so far as nature presents an agreement with our faculties, but an agreement without a goal. Precisely, however, since this agreement is external to the agreement of the faculties among themselves, and since it defines only the occasion when our faculties do agree, the purpose connected with the beautiful is not part of esthetic judgment. From that point on, this agreement without goal can serve, without risking contradiction, as a genetic principle for the *a priori* agreement of the faculties in this judgment. In other words, *esthetic pleasure is disinterested, but we feel a rational purpose when the productions of nature agree with our disinterested pleasure.* "Because it is in the interest of reason that Ideas have an objective reality..., that is to say, that nature at least indicates by a trace or a sign that it contains a principle allowing a legitimate agreement between its productions and our satisfaction, *independent of any purpose...,* reason is necessarily interested in any natural manifestation of such an agreement."[23] It will come as no surprise, then, that the purpose connected with the beautiful has to do with determinations for which the sense of the beautiful remains indifferent. In the sense of the disinterested beautiful, the imagination reflects the form. Whatever has trouble being reflected—colors, sounds, matter—escapes it. On the other hand, the purpose connected with the beautiful has to do with sounds and colors, the color of flowers or the sounds of birds.[24] Again, there is no contradiction here. Purpose has to do with matter, because it is with matter that nature, in conformity with its mechanical laws, produces objects that happen to be apt for formal reflection. Kant even defines primal matter as it participates in the production of the beautiful: a fluid matter, part of which is separated out or evaporates, and the rest of which suddenly solidifies (crystal formation).[25]

This purpose connected with the beautiful, or the judgment of beauty, is described as meta-esthetic. How does this purpose of reason ensure the genesis of the understanding-imagination agreement in the judgment of beauty itself? Reason discovers the many presentations of its Ideas in sound, color, and free matter. For example, we are not satisfied with subsuming color under a concept of the understanding; we relate it still to a whole other concept (an Idea of reason) which, for its part, has no object of intuition, but does determine its object by analogy with the object of intuition that corresponds to the first concept. In this way, we transpose "the reflection on an object of intuition to a whole other concept to which, perhaps, an intuition may never directly correspond."[26] The white lily is no longer simply related to concepts of color and flower, but awakens the Idea of pure innocence, whose object, which is never given, is a reflexive analogue of white in the fleur-de-lis.[27] In this case, however, the meta-esthetic purpose of reason has two consequences: on the one hand, the concepts of the understanding are infinitely extended, in an unlimited way; on the other hand, the imagination is freed from the constraint of the determined concepts of the understanding, to which it was still subject in schematization. What the Analytic of the Beautiful in its exposition allowed us to say is only this: in the esthetic judgment, the imagination becomes free at the same time that the understanding becomes indeterminate. But how does the imagination become free? How does the understanding become indeterminate? Reason tell us, and thus secures the genesis of the free indeterminate agreement of the two faculties in judgment. The seduction of esthetic judgment explains what the Analytic of the Beautiful could not: it discovers in reason the principle of a transcendental genesis. But first it was necessary to go through the genetic model of the Sublime.

The theme of a presentation of Ideas in sensible nature is a fundamental theme in Kant's work. This is because there are several modes of presentation. The Sublime is the first mode: a direct presentation accomplished by *projection*, but it remains negative, having to do with the inaccessibility of the Idea. The second mode is defined by the rational purpose connected with the beautiful: this is an indirect but positive presentation, which is achieved through *symbol*. The third mode appears in Genius: a positive presentation, but it is secondary, accomplished through the *creation* of an "other" nature. Finally, the fourth mode is teleological: a positive presentation, primary as well as direct, which is achieved in the concepts of end and final agreement. This last mode does not concern us here. On the other hand, the mode of Genius does pose an essential problem in Kant's esthetics from the perspective developed in these pages.

The key to a genesis of an *a priori* agreement of faculties in the judgment of taste is rational purpose—but on what condition? On condition that we join to the particular experience of the beautiful, "the thought that nature produced this beauty."[28] In one respect, then, a disjunction appears: between the beautiful in nature and the beautiful in art. *Nothing in the exposition of the Analytic of the Beautiful authorized such a distinction*: the deduction introduces this distinction, i.e. the meta-esthetic vantage point of the purpose connected with the beautiful. This purpose concerns exclusively natural beauty; the genesis thus concerns the agreement between the imagination and the understanding, but only in as much as the agreement is produced in the soul of the spectator before nature. The agreement of the faculties before a work of art remains groundless, without a principle.

The final task of Kantian esthetics is to discover for art a principle analogous to the principle of the beautiful in nature. This principle is Genius. Just as rational purpose is the authority by which nature provides judgment with a rule, so genius is the subjective disposition by which nature provides art with rules (in this sense, it is a "gift of nature").[29] Just as rational purpose concerns the materials with which nature produces beautiful things, so Genius provides the materials with which the subject it inspires produces beautiful works of art: "genius essentially provides the fine arts with rich materials."[30] Genius is a meta-esthetic principle the same as rational purpose. That is, genius is defined as a presentation of Ideas. Of course, in this case, Kant is talking about esthetic Ideas, which he distinguishes from the Ideas of reason: Ideas of reason are concepts without intuitions, whereas esthetic Ideas are intuitions without concepts. But this is a false opposition; there are not two sorts of Ideas. The esthetic Idea goes beyond every concept because it produces the intuition of an *other nature* than the nature given to us: it creates a nature in which the phenomena are events of the spirit, in an unmediated way, and the events of the spirit are phenomena of nature. Thus invisible beings, the kingdom of the blessed, hell acquire a body; and love, death, acquire a dimension to make them adequate to their spiritual sense.[31] Now it occurs to one that the intuition of genius is the intuition which the Ideas of reason were lacking. The *intuition without concept* is precisely that which the *concept wihout intuition* was lacking. So, in the first formulation, it is the concepts of the understanding that are surpassed and disqualified; and in the second, the intuitions of sensibility. In genius, however, the creative intuition as intuition of an other nature, and the concepts of reason as rational Ideas, are adequately unified.[32] The rational Idea contains something inexpressible; but the esthetic Idea expresses the inexpressible, through the creation of an other nature. Therefore, the esthetic Idea is truly a mode of the presentation of Ideas, much like symbolism, though operating differently. And the esthetic Idea has an analogous effect: it "makes us think," it extends the concepts of the understanding in an unlimited way, and it frees the imagination from the constraints of the understanding. Genius "vitalizes." It "gives life." As a meta-esthetic principle, it makes possible, it engenders the esthetic agreement between the imagination and the understanding. It engenders each faculty in this agreement: the imagination as free, and the understanding as unlimited. The theory of Genius thus manages to bridge the gap that had opened up between the beautiful in nature and the beautiful in art, from a meta-esthetic point of view. Genius provides a genetic principle to the faculties in relation to a work of art. So, after paragraph 42 in the *Critique of Judgment* has separated out two kinds of the beautiful, paragraphs 58 and 59 restore their unity, through the idea of a genesis of the faculties which the two kinds have in common.

Nevertheless, the parallel between the purpose connected with the beautiful in nature, and genius as it relates to the beautiful, should not be pushed too far. Because genius entails a far more complex genesis. In the case of genius, we needed to engender the agreement of the imagination and the understanding, so we had to leave behind the spectator's point of view. Genius is the gift of the artistic creator. The imagination is liberated, and the understanding extended, *first in the artist*. We are faced with this difficulty: how can such a genesis have a universal implication if it is governed by the singularity of genius? It seems that we discover in genius not a universal subjectivity, but at most an exceptional intersubjectivity. Genius is always a calling out for other geniuses to be born. But vast deserts open up during which the call of genius goes unanswered. "Genius is the exemplary originality of a subject's natural gifts in the free use of the cognitive faculties. Thus the work of genius is an example, not to be imitated, but to bring about the birth of another genius in its wake, by awakening the sense of its own originality, and by spurring an exercise of its art independent of any and all rules…The genius is the darling of nature; its existence is rare."[33] However, this difficulty can be resolved if we consider the two activities of the genius. On the one hand, genius creates. That is to say, genius produces the *matter* of its art; by inventing an other nature adequate to Ideas, genius realizes the free creative function of the imagination. On the other hand, the artist *gives form*: by adjusting an imagination liberated from the indeterminate understanding, the artist gives to the work of art the form of an object of taste ("taste is sufficient to give this form to the work of art").[34] Precisely, what is inimitable in genius is the first aspect: the enormity of the Idea, the astonishing matter, the difformity of genius. But in its second aspect, the work of genius provides an example for everyone: it inspires imitators, gives rise to spectators, and engenders *everywhere* the free agreement of the imagination and the understanding, which agreement constitutes taste. So, we are not simply in the desert while the call of genius goes unanswered by another genius: men and women of taste, students, and aficionados fill up the space between two geniuses, and help pass the time.[35] Consequently, the genesis that originates in genius effectively acquires a universal value (the genius of the creator engenders the agreement of the faculties in the spectator): "Taste, like judgment in general, is the discipline of genius…Taste brings clarity and order to the mass of thoughts and gives Ideas their consistency, and therefore opens them up to a *lasting and universal* success, as examples for others, adapting themselves to a culture always in process."[36]

We thus have three parallel geneses in Kant's esthetics: the sublime, or a genesis of the reason-imagination agreement; purpose connected with the beautiful, or a genesis of the understanding-imagination agreement according to the beautiful in nature; and genius, or a genesis of the understanding-imagination agreement according to the beautiful in art. What is more is that, for each case, the faculties are engendered in their original free state and in reciprocal agreement. Thus the *Critique of Judgment* reveals a whole other domain from that of the other two Critiques. The previous two Critiques begin with ready-made faculties, and these enter determinate relations and take on organized tasks under the direction of one legislative faculty. The understanding legislates for a rational speculative purpose, and reason legislates for its own practical purpose. When Kant tries to articulate the originality of the *Critique of Judgment*, this is what he says: it ensures both the *passage* from a speculative to a practical purpose and the subordination of the first to the second.[37] For example, the sublime already shows how the suprasensible destination of our faculties can be explained only as the destiny of a moral being; the purpose connected with the beautiful in nature evidences a soul predestined to morality; and genius itself allows the artistic beautiful and the world of morality to be integrated, and thus to overcome the disjunction of the two kinds of the beautiful (the beautiful in art, no less than the beautiful in nature, is in the end declared a "symbol of morality").[38]

But if the *Critique of Judgment* opens up a *passage*, it is first and foremost because it unveils a *ground* that had remained hidden in the other two Critiques. Were this idea of a passage to be taken literally, the *Critique of Judgment* would be no more than a compliment, an adjustment: in fact, it constitutes the original ground from which derive the other two Critiques. Certainly, the *Critique of Judgment* does show how speculative purpose can be subordinated to practical purpose, how Nature can be in agreement with liberty, and how our destination is a moral destiny. But it does so only by attributing judgment, in the subject and beyond the subject, "to something which is *neither nature nor liberty*."[39] And the purpose connected with the beautiful is in itself neither moral nor speculative. And if we have the destiny of a moral being, it is because this destiny develops, explains a supra-sensible destination of our faculties; this destination remains none the less enveloped as the real heart of our being, as a principle more profound than any formal destiny. This is indeed the sense of the *Critique of Judgment*: beneath the determinate and conditioned relations of the faculties, it discovers free agreement, indeterminate and unconditional. No determinate relation of the faculties, a relation conditioned by one of them, would ever be possible if it were not first *made* possible by this free unconditioned agreement. Furthermore, the *Critique of Judgment* does not restrict itself to the perspective of conditions as it appeared in the other two Critiques: with the *Critique of Judgment*, we step into Genesis. The three geneses of the *Critique of Judgment* are not only parallel, they converge on the same discovery: what Kant calls the Soul, that is, the suprasensible unity of our faculties, "the point of concentration," the life-giving principle that "animates" each faculty, engendering both its free exercise and its free agreement with the other faculties.[40] A primeval free imagination that cannot be satisfied with schematizing under the constraints of the understanding; a primeval unlimited understanding that does not yet bend under the speculative weight of its determinate concepts, no more so than it is not already subjected to the ends of practical reason; a primeval reason that has not yet developed a taste for commanding, but which frees itself when it frees up the other faculties—these are the extreme discoveries of the *Critique of Judgment*: each faculty rediscovers the principle of its genesis as each converges on this focal point, "a point of concentration in the supra-sensible," whence our faculties derive both their force and their life.

Our problem was twofold. How does one explain that the analysis of the sublime interrupts the link between the exposition and the deduction of the judgment of beauty, when the sublime has no corresponding deduction? And how does one explain that the deduction of the judgment of beauty is extended to theories of purpose, art, and genius, which seem to address very different preoccupations? I believe the system of the *Critique of Judgment*, in its first part, can be reconstituted in the following manner:

1) The Analytic of the Beautiful, exposition: *this is the formal esthetics of the beautiful in general from the spectator's point of view*. The different moments of this Analytic show that the understanding and the imagination enter a free agreement, and that this free agreement is constitutive of the judgment of taste. This defines a spectator's esthetic point of view of the beautiful in general. Such a point of view is formal, since the spectator reflects the form of the object. But the last moment of the Analytic, i.e. modality, poses an essential problem. Free indeterminate agreement must be *a priori*. Moreover, it is what is most profound in the soul; every determinate proportion of the faculties presupposes the possibility of their free and spontaneous harmony. In this sense, the *Critique of Judgment* must be the genuine ground of the other two Critiques. Clearly, then, we cannot be satisfied with presuming the *a priori* agreement of the understanding and the imagination in the judgment of taste. This agreement must be the object of a transcendental genesis. But the Analytic of the Beautiful is unable to secure such a genesis: it points to the necessity, but it cannot on its own go beyond mere "presumption."

2) The Analytic of the Sublime, exposition and deduction: *this is the formless esthetics of the sublime from the spectator's point of view*. Taste did not call reason into play. The sublime, however, is explained by the free agreement of reason and the imagination. But this new "spontaneous" agreement occurs under very special conditions: pain, opposition, constraint, and discord. In the case of the sublime, freedom or spontaneity is experienced in boundary-areas, when faced with the formless or the deformed. In this way, however, the Analytic of the Sublime gives us a genetic principle for the agreement of the faculties, an agreement which the Analytic puts in play. It follows that it goes much farther than the Analytic of the Beautiful.

3) The Analytic of the Beautiful, deduction: *this is the material meta-esthetic of the beautiful in nature, from the spectator's point of view*. The judgment of taste

demands a particular deduction because it relates in the very least to the form of the object: furthermore, the judgment of taste in turn requires a genetic principle for the agreement of the faculties which it expresses, namely understanding and imagination. The Sublime furnishes us with a genetic model; the equivalent must be found for the beautiful, using other means. We are looking for a rule according to which we may by rights suppose the universality of esthetic pleasure. As long as we are satisfied to presume the agreement between the understanding and the imagination, the deduction is simple. What is more difficult is making the genesis of theis agreement *a priori*. However, precisely because reason does not intervene in the judgment of taste, it can furnish us with a principle according to which the agreement of the faculties in this judgment is engendered. There exists a rational purpose connected with the beautiful: this meta-esthetic purpose concerns the aptitude of nature for producing beautiful things, as well as the materials which nature uses for such "formations." Thanks to this purpose which is neither practical nor speculative, reason gives birth to itself, expands the understanding, and liberates the imagination. Reason secures the genesis of a free indeterminate agreement between the imagination and the understanding. The two aspects of the deduction are now joined: the objective reference to a nature capable of producing beautiful things, and the subjective reference to a principle capable of engendering the agreement of faculties.

4) Follow-up to the deduction in the theory of Genius: *this is an ideal meta-esthetic of the beautiful in art from the point of view of the creative artist*. The purpose connected with the beautiful secures a genesis only by excluding the case of the artistic beautiful. Genius thus intervenes as the meta-esthetic principle proper to the faculties being exercised in art. Genius has properties analogous to those of purpose: it furnishes a matter, it incarnates Ideas, it causes reason to give birth to itself, and it liberates the imagination and expands the understanding. But genius exercises all these faculties first and foremost from the vantage point of the creation of a work of art. Finally, without losing any of its singular and exceptional character, genius must give a universal value to the agreement which it engenders, and it must communicate to the faculties of the spectator something of its own life and force; thus Kant's esthetics forms a systematic whole, in which the three geneses are unified.

Raymond Roussel, or the Abhorrent Vacuum

The work of Raymond Roussel, which Pauvert has published in new editions, includes two sorts of books: poem-books that describe miniature objects in detail (for example, a complete spectacle on the label of an Evian water bottle) or objects that have doubles (actors, machines and Carnival masks); and those books known as "formula" books: starting explicitly or implicitly from a catalytic phrase (e.g. "the white letters on the legs of the old pool table"), the reader ends up rediscovering the same phrase, or almost ("the white fetters on the eggs of the old fool Able"); in the gap between them, however, a whole world of descriptions and catalogues have arisen, where the same words taken to mean different things lead two very different lives, or else they are dislocated to make way for other words ("I have some good tobacco" = "wave slum jude wacko").

This author who had a considerable influence on the Surrealists, and today on Robbe-Grillet, remains relatively unknown. But recently Michel Foucault has published a commentary of great poetic and philosophical power on the work of Roussel, and finds the keys to this work in an entirely different direction from what the Surrealists had indicated. It seems vital, moreover, to connect the reading of Foucault's book with that of Roussel himself. How does one explain the "formula"? According to Michel Foucault, there exists in language a kind of essential distance, a kind of displacement, dislocation, or breach. This is because words are less numerous than things, and so each word has several meanings. The literature of the absurd believed that meaning was deficient, but in fact there is a deficiency of signs.

Hence in a word a vacuum opens up: the repetition of a word leaves the difference of its meanings gaping. Is this the proof of an impossibility of repetition? No, this is where Roussel's enterprise comes into view: he tries to widen this gap to its maximum and thus determine and measure it, already filling it with a whole machinery, a whole phantasmagoria that binds the differences to, and integrates them with, repetition.

For example, the words "demoiselle à prétendant / gallant young woman" induces "demoiselle (hie) à reître en dents / a jackhammer with rough-neck teeth" and the problem, as an equation, becomes that of a jackhammer putting together a mosaic. The repetition must become paradoxical, poetic, and comprehensive. The repetition must encompass in itself difference instead of reducing it. The poverty of language must become its very source of wealth. Foucault writes: "Not the lateral repetition of things we repeat, but the radical repetition that has passed over and beyond non-language and that owes its poetry to the gap that has been crossed."

By what will the vacuum be filled and crossed? By extraordinary machines, by strange artisan-actors. Things and beings now follow language. Everything in the mechanisms and behaviors is imitation, reproduction, recitation. But the recitation of something singular, an unbelievable event, which is absolutely different from the recitation. As if Roussel's machines had grafted on themselves the technique of the formula: like the "job of daybreak," which itself sends us back to a profession that forces us to wake up early. Or the verse-worm that plays the zither by projecting drops of water along each string. Roussel elaborates multiple series of repetitions with the power to liberate: prisoners save their own lives through repetition and recitation, in the invention of corresponding machines.

These liberating repetitions are poetic precisely because they do not suppress difference; on the contrary, they experience difference and authenticate it by internalizing the Singular. As for those non-formula works, they can be explained in a similar fashion. In this case, things themselves are opened up thanks to a miniaturization, thanks to a doubling, a mask. And the vacuum is now crossed by language, which gives birth to a whole world in the interstice of these masks and doublings. Consequently, the non-formula works are like the flip-side of the formula itself. In both cases, the problem is to tell and show at the same time, to speak and set before the eyes.

This poorly states the wealth and depth of Foucault's book. This intertwining of difference and repetition is also about life, death, and madness. For it appears that the vacuum inside things and words are a sign of death, and what fills it is mad presence.

However, it is not the case that the personal madness of Raymond Roussel and his work have an element in common, positively speaking. On the contrary, we would have to speak of an element according to which the work and his madness mutually exclude one another. That element is common in one sense only; it is language. His personal madness and the poetic work, the delirium and the poem, represent two investments of language, on different levels, that are mutually exclusive.

From this point of view, Foucault in his last chapter sketches a whole interpretation of the work/madness relationship, which would apply and which he perhaps will apply to other poets (Artaud?). Michel Foucault's book is not only decisive with respect to Roussel; it also marks an important stage in its author's personal research on the relations of language, the gaze, death, and madness.

How Jarry's Pataphysics Opened the Way for Phenomenology

Major modern authors often surprise us with a thought that seems both a remark and a prophesy: metaphysics is and must be surpassed. In so far as its fate is conceived as metaphysics, philosophy makes room and must make room for other forms of thought, other forms of thinking.

This modern idea is seized on in various contexts, which dramatize it: 1) *God is dead* (it would be interesting to do an anthology of all the versions of the dead God, all the dramatizations of this death. For example, Jarry's bicycle race.[1] In Nietzsche alone, we could find a dozen versions, the first of which is not at all found in *The Gay Science*, but in *The Wanderer and His Shadow*, in the admirable text on the death of the prison-guard.[2] But whatever the case, the death of God for philosophy means the abolition of the cosmological distinction between two worlds, the metaphysical distinction between essence and appearance, the logical distinction between the true and the false. The death of God thus demands a new form of thought, a transmutation of values.)

2) *The Human dies also* (finished is the belief in the substitution of humanity for God, the belief in the Human-God who would replace God-the Human. For in changing places, nothing has changed, the old values remain in place. Nihilism must go all the way, to the end of itself, in the human being who wants to perish, the last human, the men and women of the atomic age foretold by Nietzsche.)

3) This something "other" is conceived as a force already at work in human subjectivity, but hiding in it, and also destroying it. (cf. Rimbaud's "Something thinks me.") The action of this force follows two paths: the path of actual history and the development of technology, and the path of poetry and the poetic creation of fantastic imaginary machines. This conception demands a new thinker (a new subject of thought, "death to the Cogito"), new concepts (a new object to be thought), and new forms of thought (which integrate the old poetic unconscious and today's powerful machines, e.g. Heraclitus and cybernetics).

In a certain way, this attempt to surpass metaphysics is already well known. We find it in different degrees in Nietzsche, Marx, and Heidegger. The only general name that befits it was coined by Jarry: *pataphysics*. Pataphysics must be defined: "An epiphenomenon is that which is added on to a phenomenon. Pataphysics ... is the science of that which is added on to metaphysics, either from within, or outside it, extending as far beyond metaphysics as metaphyics extends beyond physics. E.g. since the epiphenomenon is often equated with the accident, pataphysics will be above all the science of the particular, even though it is said that science deals only with the general."[3] In the jargon of specialists: Being is the epiphenomenon of all *beings* [*étants*] and must be thought by the new thinker, who is an epiphenomenon of humankind.

In that proportion of black humor and white seriousness, so difficult to keep separate, but demanded by the new thinking, Kostas Axelos has brought out a book: *Vers la pensée planétaire* (Les Editions de Minuit).[4] Previously, he wrote *Alienation, Praxis, and Techne in the Thought of Karl Marx* and *Héraclite et la philosophie*. It is fitting that the publishing house which welcomed the *nouveau roman* [Les Editions de Minuit] should also attest a new philosophy. Kostas Axelos, director of the series 'Arguments,' has been trained both as a Marxist and a Heideggerian. What is more, he possesses the force and inspiration of a Greek, both clever and learned. He reproaches his mentors for not haiving sufficiently broken with metaphysics, for not having sufficiently conceived of the powers of a technology both real and imaginary, for having remained prisoners of the perspectives which they themselves denounce. In his notion of *planetary*, he discovers the motive and the condition, the object and the subject, the positive and the negative of the new thinking. And following this path, he writes an astonishing book—in my opinion, the culmination of pataphysics.

Axelos's method procedes by an enumeration of senses. This enumeration is not a juxtaposition, since each meaning participates in the others. Not according to *Rules* which would refer back to the old metaphysics, but according to a *Game* which includes within it all possible rules, which thus has no other internal rule than to affirm all that 'can' be affirmed (including chance and nonsense), and to deny all that 'can' be denied (including God and man). Hence the fundamental list of the senses of the word *planetary*: global, itinerant, errancy, planning, platitude, gears and wheels. "The play of thought and the planetary era is thus *global, erratic, itinerant, organizing, planning and flattening, caught up in gears and wheels*" (p. 46).

Giving an extreme mobility to each of its senses [in ref. to. *Logic of Senses.* SL], his planetarism is presented in the following way: find the *fragment* represented by each object in such a way that thought makes up the always open sum (and subtraction) of all the other fragments subsisting as such. Axelos opens an irreducible dialogue between the fragment and the whole. No other totality than that of Dionysos, but Dionysos dismembered. In this new pluralism, the

One can be said only of the multiple and must be said of the multiple; Being is said only of becoming and time; Necessity, only of chance; and the Whole, only of fragments. Axelos develops the power of what Jarry used to call "l'epiphe-nomenon"—but Axelos launches an entirely different term, and a different idea: "being in the process of becoming the fragmentary and fragmented totality."

Two fundamental notions will be remarked: *Game*, which must be substi-tuted for the metaphysical relation of the relative and the absolute; and *Errancy*, which must surpass the metaphysical opposition of true and false, error and truth. Axelos writes his most brilliant pages on errancy. Similarly, his commen-taries on Pascal, Rimbaud, and Freud are truly profound (the text on Rimbaud is extremely beautiful). Still this brilliant and strange book is only an introduc-tion. Axelos will have to invent his own new forms of expression, his own versions of the death of God, his own real fantastic machines. All the way to the great synthesis, which must unite the two sides of a true "pataphysics"—the ubuesque side, and the doctoral or Faustrollian side. As Axelos says, in one of his strangely polite phrases: "with and without joy and sadness...." But never with indifference. Planatarism or pataphysics.

"He Was my Teacher"[1]

The sadness of generations without "teachers." Our teachers are not just public professors, though we badly need professors. Our teachers, once we reach adulthood, are those who bring us something radical and new, who know how to invent an artistic or literary technique, finding those ways of thinking that correspond to our *modernity*, that is, our difficulties as well as our vague enthusiasms. We know there is only one value for art, and even for truth: the "first-hand," the authentic newness of something said, and the "unheard music" with which it is said. That's what Sartre was for us (for us twenty-year-olds during the Liberation). In those days, who except Sartre knew how to say anything new? Who taught us new ways to think? As brilliant and profound as the work of Merleau-Ponty was, it was professorial and depended in many respects on Sartre's work. (Sartre readily likened the existence of human beings to the non-being of a "hole" in the world: little lakes of nothingness, he called them. But Merleau-Ponty took them to be folds, simple folds and pleats. In this way, one can distinguish a tough, penetrating existentialism from a more tender and reserved existentialism.) As for Camus—alas! Either it was inflated heroism, or it was second-hand absurdity; Camus claimed descent from a line of cursed thinkers, but his whole philosophy just led us back to Lalande and Meyerson, writers well-known to any undergraduate. The new themes, a particular new style, a new aggressive and polemical way of posing problems—these came from Sartre. In the disorder and the hope of the Liberation, we discovered, we re-discovered everything: Kafka, the American novel, Husserl and Heidegger, incessant renegotiations with Marxism, enthusiasm for a *nouveau roman*... It was all channeled through Sartre, not only because he was a philosopher and had a genius for totalization, but because he knew how to invent something new. The first performances of *The Flies*, the publication of *Being and Nothingness; An Essay in Phenomenological Ontology*, his conference *Existentialism and Humanism*—these were events: they were how we learned, after long nights, the identity of thought and liberty.

"Private thinkers" are in a way opposed to "public professors." Even the Sorbonne needs an anti-Sorbonne, and the students don't really listen to their professors except when they have other teachers also. Nietzsche in his day had ceased to be a professor to become a private thinker: Sartre did the same, in another context, and with another outcome. Private thinkers have a double character: a kind of solitude that remains their own in every situation; but also a particular agitation, a particular disorder of the world in which they rise up and speak. Hence they speak only in their own name, without "representing" anything; and they solicit those raw presences, those naked powers in the world which are hardly more "representable." Already in *What is Literature?*, Sartre sketched the ideal writer: "The writer takes up the world as is, totally raw, stinking, and quotidian, and presents it to free people on a foundation of freedom... It is not enough to grant the writer the freedom to say whatever he pleases! He must address a public that has the freedom to change everything, which implies, beyond the suppression of social classes, the abolition of all dictatorship, the perpetual renewal of categories, and the continual reversal of every order, as soon as it starts to ossify. In a word, literature is essentially the subjectivity of a society in permanent revolution."[2] From the beginning, Sartre conceived the writer as a being like any other, addressing others from the sole point of view of their freedom. His whole philosophy was part of a speculative movement that contested the notion of *representation*, the *order* itself of representation: philosophy was changing its arena, leaving the sphere of judgment, to establish itself in the more vivid world of the "pre-judgmental," the "sub-representational." Sartre has just refused the Nobel prize: this is the practical continuation of the same attitude; it shows his revulsion at the idea of representing something in a practical manner, even spiritual values, or as Sartre himself says, his revulsion at the idea of being institutionalized.

The private thinker requires a world that contains a certain minimum disorder, even if only revolutionary hope, a seed of permanent revolution. In Sartre, we find almost a fixation with the Liberation, with the disappointments of the day. It took the Algerian War to recover something of the necessary political struggle or liberating agitation, and then, the conditions were all the more complex, since we were no longer the oppressed, but those who would turn on one another. Ah, youth. All that is left is Cuba and the Venezuelan maquis. But greater still than the solitude of the private thinker is the solitude of those looking for a teacher, who would like a teacher, and would not have come to him except in an agitated world. The moral order, the "representational" order has closed in on us. Even atomic fear has taken on the appearance of a bourgeois fear. Today, young people are schooled in thought with Teilhard de Chardin for a teacher. You get what you deserve. After Sartre, not only Simone Weil, but Simone Weil's monkey. Not that profoundly new things in contemporary literature are lacking. Take a few random examples: the *nouveau roman*,

Gombrowicz's books, Klossowski's stories, Lévi-Strauss's sociology, Genet's theatre, Gatti's theatre, the philosophy of "unreason" that Foucault is working on... But what is missing today, what Sartre knew how to bring together and incarnate for the previous generation, were the conditions of *totalization*: a totalization in which politics, the imagination, sexuality, the unconscious, and the will are all united in the rights of human totality. We continue to live on like so many scattered limbs. Speaking of Kafka, Sartre said: his work is "a free and unitary reaction to the Judeo-Christian world of Central Europe; his novels are the synthetic overcoming of his situation as a man, a Jew, a Tchec, a recalcitrant fiancé, a TB patient, etc."[3] But what about Sartre himself: his work is a reaction to the bourgeois world as exposed by communism. His work expresses the overcoming of his own situation as a bourgeois intellectual, as a graduate of the *Ecole Normale*, as a free fiancé, as an ugly man (Sartre often presented himself as such), etc.: all those things which are reflected and echoed in the movement of his books.

We speak of Sartre as though he belonged to a bygone era. Alas, we are the ones who in today's conformist moral order are bygone. At least Sartre allows us to await some vague future moment, a return, when thought will form again and make its totalities anew, like a power that is at once collective and private. This is why Sartre remains my teacher. Sartre's last book, *Critique of Dialectical Reason, Theory of Practical Ensembles*, is one of the most beautiful books to have come out in recent years. It provides *Being and Nothingness* with its necessary complement, in the sense that collective demands now complete the subjectivity of the person. And when we think back on *Being and Nothingness*, we rediscover the initial astonishment we felt for Sartre's renewal of philosophy. We know better today that the relation of Sartre to Heidegger, his debt to Heidegger, was a false problem, based on a misunderstanding. It was the uniquely Sartrian that struck me in *Being and Nothingness*, it was the measure of his contribution: his theory of *bad faith*, where consciousness, from within itself, plays on its dual power not to be what it is and to be what it is not; his theory of the *Other*, where the gaze of the other is enough to make the world vacillate, "stealing" the world from me; his theory of *liberty*, where liberty limits itself by constituting *situations*; *existential psychoanalysis*, where one discovers the foundational *choices* of an individual at the heart of his concrete life. And every time, essence and example would enter complex relationships that gave a new style to philosophy. The café waiter, the girl in love, the ugly man, and above all my friend-Pierre-who-was-never-there: these comprised real novels in the philosophical work and set the essences going to the rhythm of existential examples. A violent syntax of breaks and stretches were everywhere dazzling evidence, recalling the twin Sartrian obsessions: the lakes of non-being, and the viscosity of matter.

His refusal of the Nobel prize is good news. Finally someone is not trying to explain what a delicious paradox it is for a writer, for a private thinker, to accept honors and public representations. The clever few are already trying to make Sartre contradict himself: they attribute to him feelings of vexation at having the prize come too late; they object that, in any case, he represents something; they remind him that, at any rate, his success was and remains bourgeois; they suggest that his refusal is neither reasonable nor grown-up; they point to the example of those who accepted-while-refusing, determined to put the money to good works. We shouldn't get too involved. Sartre is a formidable polemicist... There is no genius without self-parody. But which is the better parody? To become a polite old man, a coquettish spiritual authority? Or rather to wish oneself the half-wit of the Liberation? To watch yourself be elected to the Academy, or dream of being a Venezuelan maquis? Who fails to see the qualitative difference, the difference of genius, the vital difference between these two choices, these two parodies? To what is Sartre faithful? Ever and always to the friend Pierre-who-is-never-there. It is his peculiar destiny to circulate pure air when he speaks, even if this pure air, the air of absences, is difficult to breathe.

The Philosophy of Crime Novels[1]

La Série Noire is celebrating a momentous occasion—its release of #1000. The coherence, the idea of this collection owes everything to its editor. Of course everyone knew something about cops, criminals, and their relationship, even if it was only from reading the papers, or the knowledge of special reports. But literature is like consciousness, it always lags behind. These things had not yet found their contemporary literary expression, or they hadn't attained the status of common-place in literature. The credit for closing this gap at a particularly favorable moment goes to Marcel Duhamel.[2] Malraux had this insight to offer in his preface to the translation of *Sanctuary*: "Faulkner knows very well that detectives don't exist; that police power stems neither from psychology nor from clarity of vision, but from informants; and that it's not Moustachu or Tapinois, the modest thinkers of the Quai des Orfèvres, who bring about the apprehension of the murderer on the loose, but rank-and-file cops".... *La Série Noire* was above all an adaptation of *Sanctuary* for a mass market (look at Chase's *No Orchids for Miss Blandish*), and a generalization of Malraux's preface.

In the old conception of the detective novel, we would be shown a genius detective devoting the whole power of his mind to the search and discovery of the truth. The idea of truth in the classic detective novel was totally philosophical, that is, it was the product of the effort and the operations of the mind. So it is that police investigation modeled itself on philosophical inquiry, and conversely, gave to philosophy an unusual object to elucidate: crime.

There were two schools of truth: 1) the French school (Descartes), where truth is a question of some fundamental intellectual intuition, from which the rest is rigorously deduced; and 2) the English school (Hobbes), according to which truth is always induced from something else, interpreted from sensory indices. In a word, deduction and induction. The detective novel reproduced this duality, though in a movement which was proper to the literary genre, and has produced famous examples of each. The English school: Conan Doyle gave us Sherlock Holmes, the masterful interpreter of signs, the inductive genius. The French school: Gaboriau gave us Tabaret and Lecoq; and Gaston Leroux, Rouletabille, who with "a circle between the two lobes of his forehead," is always invoking "the right track of reason" and explicitly opposing his theory of certainty to the inductive method, the Anglo-Saxon theory of signs.

The criminal side of the affair can also be quite interesting. By a metaphysical law of reflection, the cop is no more extraordinary than the criminal—he, too, professes allegiance to justice and truth and the powers of deduction and induction. And so you have the possibility of two series of novels: the hero of the first is the detective, and the hero of the second is the criminal. With Rouletabille and Chéri-Bibi, Leroux brought each series to its perfection. But never the twain shall meet: they are the motors for two different series (they could never meet without one of them looking ridiculous; cf. Leblanc's attempt to put Arsène Lupin together with Sherlock Holmes).[3] Rouletabille and Chéri-Bibi: Each is the double of the other, they have the same destiny, the same pain, the same quest for the truth. This is the destiny and quest of Oedipus (Rouletabille is destined to kill his father; Chéri-Bibi attends a performance of Oedipus and shouts: "He's just like me!"). After philosophy, Greek tragedy.

Still we mustn't be too surprised that the crime novel so faithfully reproduces Greek tragedy, since Oedipus is always called on to indicate any such coincidence. While it is the only Greek tragedy that already has this detective structure, we should marvel that Sophocles's Oedipus is a detective, and not that the detective novel has remained Oedipal. We should give credit where credit is due: to Leroux, a phenomenal novelist in French literature, who had a genius for striking phrases: "not the hands, not the hands," "the ugliest of men," "Fatalitas," "men who open doors and men who shut traps," "a circle between two lobes," etc.

But the birth of *La Série Noire* has been the death of the detective novel, properly speaking. To be sure, the great majority of novels in the collection have been content to change the detective's way of doing things (he drinks, he's in love, he's restless) but keep the same structure: the surprise ending that brings all the characters together for the final explanation that fingers one of them as the guilty party. Nothing new there.

What the new literary use and exploitation of cops and criminals taught us is that police activity has nothing to do with a metaphysical or scientific search for the truth. Police work no more resembles scientific inquiry than a telephone call from an informant, inter-police relations, or mechanisms of torture resemble metaphysics. As a general rule, there are two distinct cases: 1) the professional murder, where the police know immediately more or less who is responsible; and 2) the sexual murder, where the guilty party could be anyone. But in either case the problem is not framed in terms of truth. It is rather an astonishing compensation of error. The suspect, known to the cops but never charged, is either nabbed in some other domain than his usual sphere of criminal activity (whence the American schema of the untouchable gangster, who is arrested and deported for tax fraud); or he is provoked, forced to show himself, as they lie in wait for him.

With *La Série Noire*, we've become accustomed to the sort of cop who dives right in, come what may, regardless of the errors he may commit, but confident that something will emerge. At the other extreme, we've been allowed to watch the meticulous preparation of a sting operation, and the domino effect of little errors that loom ever larger as the moment of reckoning approaches (it's in this sense that *La Série Noire* influenced cinema). The totally innocent reader is shocked in the end by so many errors committed on both sides. Even when the cops themselves are hatching a nasty plot, they make so many blunders, they defy belief.

This is because the truth is in no way the ambient element of the investigation: not for a moment does one believe that this compensation of errors aims for the discovery of the truth as its final objective. On the contrary, this compensation has its own dimension, its own sufficiency, a kind of equilibrium or the reestablishment of it, a process of restitution that allows a society, at the limits of cynicism, to hide what it wants to hide, reveal what it wants to reveal, deny all evidence, and champion the improbable. The killer still at large may be killed for his own errors, and the police may have to sacrifice one of their own for still other errors, and so it is that these compensations have no other object than to perpetuate an equilibrium that represents a society in its entirety *at the heights of its power of falsehood.*

This same process of restitution, equilibrium or compensation also appears in Greek tragedy (Aeschylus, for example). The greatest novel of this kind, and the most admirable in every respect, is not part of *La Série Noire*: it's Robbe-Grillet's *Les Gommes*, which develops an incredible compensation of errors whose keynotes are an Aeschylean equilibrium and an Oedipal quest.

From a literary point of view, *La Série Noire* made the power of falsehood the primary detective element. And this entails another consequence: clearly, the relation between cop and criminal is no longer one of metaphysical reflection. The interpenetration is real, and the complicity deep and compensatory. Fair's fair, *quid pro quo*, they exchange favors and no less frequently betrayals on the one side and the other. We are always led back to the great trinity of falsehood: informant-corruption-torture. But it goes without saying that the cops do not of their own accord initiate this disquieting complicity. The metaphysical reflection of the old detective novel has given way to a mirroring of the other. A society indeed reflects itself to itself in its police and its criminals, even while it protects itself from them by means of a fundamental deep complicity between them.

We know that a capitalist society more willingly pardons rape, murder, or kidnapping than a bounced check, which is its only theological crime, the crime against spirit. We know very well that important political dealings entail any number of scandals and real crimes; conversely, we know that crime is organized in business-like fashion, with structures as precise as a board of directors or managers. *La Série Noire* introduced us to a politics-crime combo that, despite the evidence of History past and present, had not been given a contemporary literary expression.

The Kefauver report,[4] and especially the book by Turkus, *Société anonyme pour assassinats*, were the source of inspiration for many of the texts in *La Série Noire*. Many writers did little more than plagiarize them, or rather they turned them into popular novels. Whether it's the Trujillo regime, or Battista, or Hitler, or Franco—what will be next when everyone is talking about Ben Barka—that begets a hybrid that is properly Série Noire; whether it's Asturias writing a novel of genius: *M. le Président*;[5] or whether it's people sitting around trying to figure out the secret of this unity of the grotesque and the terrifying, the terrible and the clownish, which binds together political power, economic power, crime and police activity—it's all already in Suetonius, Shakespeare, Jarry, Asturias: *La Série Noire* has recycled it all. Have we really made any progress in understanding this hybrid of the grotesque and terrifying which, under the right circumstances, could determine the fate of us all?

So it is that *La Série Noire* has transformed our imaginings, our evaluations of the police. It was high time. Was it good for us to participate as "active readers" in the old detective novel, and thereby lose our grip on reality and thus our power of indignation? Indignation wells up in us because of reality, or because of masterful works of art. *La Série Noire* indeed seems to have pastiched every great novelist: imitation Faulkner, but also imitation Steinbeck, imitation Caldwell, imitation Asturias. And it followed the trends: first American, then it rediscovered French crime.

True, *La Série Noire* is full of stereotypes: the puerile presentation of sexuality, or what about the eyes of the killers (only Chase managed to lend a particular cold life to his killers, who are headstrong and non-conformist). But its greatness belongs to Duhamel's idea, which remains the driving force behind recent releases: a reorganization of the vision of the world that every honest person has concerning cops and criminals.

Clearly, a new realism is insufficient to make good literature. In bad literature, the real as such is the object of stereotypes, puerile notions, and cheap fantasies, worse than any imaginative imbecile could dream up. But more profound than either the real or the imaginary is parody. *La Série Noire* may have suffered from an over-abundant production, but it has kept a unity, a tendency, which periodically found expression in a beautiful work (the contemporary success of James Bond, who was never integrated into *La Série Noire*, seems to represent a serious literary regression, though compensated for by the cinema, a return to a rosy conception of the secret agent).

The most beautiful works of *La Série Noire* are those in which the real finds its proper parody, such that in its turn the parody shows us directions in the real which we would not have found otherwise. These are some of the great works of parody, though in different modes: Chase's *Miss Shumway Waves a Wand*; Williams's *The Diamond Bikini*; or Hime's negro novels, which always have extraordinary moments. Parody is a category that goes beyond real and imaginary. And let's not forget #50: James Gunn's *Deadlier than the Male*.

The trend in those days was American: it was said that certain novelists were writing under American pseudonyms. *Deadlier than the Male* is a marvelous work: the power of falsehood at its height, an old woman pursuing an assassin by smell, a murder attempt in the dunes—what a parody, you would have to read it—or reread it—to believe it. Who is James Gunn anyway? Only a single work in *La Série Noire* appeared under his name. So now that *La Série Noire* is celebrating the release of #1000, and is re-releasing many older works, and as a tribute to Marcel Duhamel, I humbly request the re-release of my personal favorite: #50.

On Gilbert Simondon[1]

The principle of individuation is by all accounts a respectable, even venerable notion. Until quite recently, however, it seems modern philosophy has been wary of adopting the problem as its own. The accepted wisdom of physics, biology, and psychology has led thinkers to attenuate the principle, but not to reinterpret it. But Gilbert Simondon makes no small display of intellectual power with a profoundly original theory of individuation implying a whole philosophy. Simondon begins from two critical remarks: 1) Traditionally, the principle of individuation is modeled on a completed individual, one who is already formed. The question being asked is merely what constitutes the individuality of this being, that is to say, what characterizes an already individuated-being. And because we put the individual after the individuation, in the same breath we put the principle of individuation *before* the process of becoming an individual, beyond the individuation itself. 2) From that point on, individuation is perceived to be everywhere. We make it a characteristic coextensive with being, at least with concrete being (even if it were divine). We remake all being in its image, as well as the first moment of being beyond the concept. This mistake is related to the previous one. In reality, the individual can only be contemporaneous with its individuation, and individuation, contemporaneous with the principle: the principle must be truly genetic, and not simply a principle of reflection. Also, the individual is not just a result, but an *environment* of individuation. However, on this view, individuation is no longer coextensive with being; it must represent a moment, which is neither all of being nor its first moment. We must be able to localize individuation, to determine it with respect to being, in a movement that will cause a passage from the pre-individual to the individual.

The prior condition of individuation, according to Simondon, is the existence of a metastable system. By not recognizing the existence of such systems, philosophy arrived at the two previous aporias. But what essentially defines a metastable system is the existence of a "disparation," the existence of at least two different dimensions, two disparate levels of reality, between which there is not yet any interactive communication. A metastable system thus implies a fundamental *difference*, like a state of dissymmetry. It is nonetheless a system insofar as the difference therein is like *potential energy*, like a *difference of potential* distributed within certain limits. Simondon's conception, it seems to me, can in this respect be assimilated to a theory of intensive quanta, since each intensive quantum in itself is difference. An intensive quantum includes difference within itself, contains factors of the E-E' type, *ad infinitum*, and establishes itself first and foremost between disparate levels, between heterogeneous orders that enter into communication only much later, when extended. Like the metastable system, an intensive quantum is the structure (not yet the synthesis) of heterogeneity.

The importance of Simondon's thesis is now apparent. By discovering the prior condition of individuation, he rigorously distinguishes singularity and individuality. Indeed the metastable, defined as *pre-individual* being, is perfectly well endowed with singularities that correspond to the existence and the distribution of potentials. (Is this not the same as in the theory of differential equations, where the existence and the distribution of "singularities" are of another nature than the "individual" forms of the integral curves in their neighborhood?) Singular without being individual: that is the state of pre-individual being. It is difference, disparity, "disparation." And the finest pages in the book are those where Simondon shows how disparity, as in the first moment of being, a singular moment, is in fact presupposed by all other states, whether unification, integration, tension, opposition, resolution of oppositions, etc. Most notably, against Lewin's *Gestaltheorie*, Simondon holds that the idea of "disparation" is more profound than the idea of opposition, and the idea of potential energy more profound than the idea of a field of forces: "Prior to odo-logical space, there is an overlapping of perspectives which does not allow one to grasp the determined object, because there are no dimensions with respect to which the unique whole could be ordered; the *fluctatio animi*, which precedes any resolute action, is not a hesitation between several paths, but a mobile overlapping of incompatible wholes, almost similar, and yet disparate" (p. 233). An overlapping world of discrete singularities, which overlaps all the more given that the discrete singularities do not yet communicate, or are not yet taken up in an individuality: such is the first moment of being.

So how will individuation arise from this condition? Clearly, it must establish an interactive communication between dimensions or disparate realities; it must actualize the potential energy or integrate the singularities; it needs to *resolve the problem* which disparate realities pose, by organizing a new dimension in which they form a unique whole at a higher level (analogous to the perception of depth that emerges from retinal images). This category of problem acquires in Simondon's thought tremendous importance insofar as the category is endowed with an objective sense: it no longer designates a provisional state of our knowledge, an undetermined subjective concept, but a moment of being, the first pre-individual moment. And in Simondon's dialectic, the problematic replaces the negative. Individuation is thus the organization of a solution, the organization of a "resolution" for a system that is objectively problematic. This resolution must be conceived in two complementary ways: on the one hand, as *internal resonance*, which is "the most primitive mode of communication between realities of different orders" (and in my opinion, Simondon has succeeded in making 'internal resonance' an extremely productive concept, open to all sorts of applications, especially in psychology, in the area of affectivity); on the other hand, as *information*, which in its turn establishes communication between two disparate levels, one of them defined by a *form* already contained in the receiver, and the other by the signal brought in from the outside (here we encounter Simondon's preoccupations with cybernetics, and a whole theory of signification in the relations of the individual). In any event, individuation appears as the advent of a new moment of Being, the moment of phase-locked being, coupled to itself: "Individuation creates the phase-locking, because the phases are but the development of being, on the one side and the other, of itself ... Pre-individual being is phaseless, whereas being after individuation is phase-locked. Such a conception identifies, or at least connects the individuation and the becoming of being" (p. 276).

To this point I have indicated only the very general principles of the book. In its detail, the analysis is organized around two centers. First, a study of the different domains of individuation; in particular, the differences between physical and vital individuation receive a profound exposition. The economy of internal resonance looks different in each case; the physical individual is content to receive information only once, and reiterate an initial singularity, whereas the living being receives several contributions of information in succession and balances several singularities; and most importantly, the physical individual creates and prolongs itself to the limit of the body—for example, crystal—whereas the living being grows from the interior and the exterior, with the whole content of its interior in contact "topologically" with the content of interior space (on this point Simondon writes an admirable chapter, "topology and ontogenesis"). It may be surprising that Simondon did not avail himself of the research conducted by the Child school in the domain of biology, dealing with the gradients and resolution systems in egg development, since their work suggests the idea of individuation by intensity, an intensive field of individuation, which would confirm Simondon's theses in several respects. But certainly this is due to Simondon's desire not to restrict himself to a biological determination of the individual, but to specify increasingly complex levels. We therefore find a properly psychic individuation emerging precisely when the vital functions no longer suffice to resolve the problems encountered by the living being, and when a new dose of pre-individual reality is mobilized in a new problematic, in a new process of problem solving (cf. his very interesting theory of affectivity). In turn, the psyche opens up to a "trans-individual collective."

Now we see the second center of Simondon's analyses: his moral vision of the world. The fundamental idea is that the pre-individual, a "source of future metastable states," must remain associated with the individual. *Estheticism* is therefore condemned as that act by which an individual cuts him or herself off from the pre-individual reality from which he or she emerged. As a result, the individual is closed in on a singularity, refusing to communicate, and provoking a loss of information. "*Ethics* exists to the extent that there is information, in other words, signification overcoming a disparation of the elements of being, such that what is interior is also exterior" (p. 297). Ethics thus follows a kind of movement running from the pre-individual to the trans-individual via individuation. (The reader may indeed ask whether, in his ethics, Simondon has not reintroduced the form of the Self which he had averted with his theory of disparity, i.e. his theory of the individual conceived as dephased and multiphased being.)

In any event, few books can impress a reader as much as this one can: it demonstrates the extent to which a philosopher can both find his inspiration in contemporary science and at the same time connect with the major problems of classical philosophy—even as he transforms and renews those problems. The new concepts established by Simondon seem to me extremely important; their wealth and originality are striking, when they're not outright inspiring. What Simondon elaborates here is a whole ontology, according to which Being is never One. As pre-individual, being is more than one— metastable, superposed, simultaneous with itself. As individuated, it is still multiple, because it is "multiphased," "a phase of becoming that will lead to new processes."

Humans: A Dubious Existence[1]

Foucault's book begins with a detailed description of Velazquez's *Maids of Honor*—or rather a description of the painting's space: we see the painter, but in the process of looking; we see the canvas he is painting, but only from the back; we see the people converging on a point just in front of the painted surface; and the true model, the king, reflected only in a mirror in the background, is contemplating all those contemplating him, thereby forming the great absence and yet also the extrinsic center of the work. As we read these fine pages by Michel Foucault, we see both the elements and the moments of what is called a *representation* emerge: its system of identity, difference, doubling and reflection, a space all its own, down to to the essential emptiness designating the personage for whom the representation exists, who is himself represented in the representation, and who yet is not present in person—this is "the king's place."

Foucault defines the Classical Age, which falls between the Renaissance and our modernity, by the notion of representation. The Renaissance still understood its knowledge as an "interpretation of signs"; the relation of the sign to what it signifies was covered by the rich domain of "similitudes." Once again, Foucault's analysis from the outset is so masterful, and the tone he strikes so new, that the reader senses a new form of thought being born in this apparent reflection on history. According to Foucault, every thought unfolds in a "characteristic" space. However, in the seventeenth-century, *the space of signs* is tending toward dissolution, giving way to the space of representation which reflects significations and decomposes similitudes, causing a new order of identities and differences to emerge. (*Don Quixote* is precisely the first great work to acknowledge the bankruptcy of signs in favor of a world of representation.) This Order, this form of representation, will be completed by positive orders founded on empirical results: "Natural History," "Theory of Money and Value," "General Grammar." These three orders will produce all kinds of resonances among themselves, due to their common membership in the space of representation: "character" is the representation of the individual of nature; "money," the representation of the objects of need; the "name," the representation of language itself.

In vain, however, does one search for *the human sciences*, allegedly created in the eighteenth-century. The preceding analysis in fact shows that *the human does not exist and cannot exist* in this classical space of representation. Again, it's the king's place: "human nature" is certainly represented, in a doubling of representation that attributes this human nature to *Nature*, but the Human does not yet exist in its proper nature or its sub-representative domain. The Human does not exist "as an opaque first reality, as a difficult object, the sovereign subject of all possible knowledge."[2] It is in this sense that Foucault subtitles his book: "An Archeology of the Human Sciences." What were the conditions of possibility of the human sciences, or what is humanity's true date of birth?

There is a precise answer: the Human can exist in the space of knowledge only once the "classical" world of representation itself has collapsed under the pressure of non-representable and non-representative forces. This is the emergence of something obscure, or a dimension of depth. Before the Human can exist, *biology* must first be born, and *political economy* and *philology*: the living organism's conditions of possibility are sought in life itself (Cuvier), the conditions of exchange and profit are sought in the depths of labor (Ricardo), and the possibility of discourse and grammar is sought in the historical depth of languages, in its system of inflexions, in the series of its endings and the modifications of its radicals (Grimm, Bopp). "Once living organisms have left the space of representation to lodge themselves in the specific depth of life; and wealth, in the progressive development of the forms of production; and words, in the becoming of language;" then natural history gives way to biology, the theory of money to political economy, and general grammar to philology.

At the same time, humanity discovers itself in two different ways: *on the one hand*, as dominated by labor, life, and language; henceforth as an object of new positive sciences, which will model themselves on biology or political economy or philology; *on the other hand*, humanity sees itself as founding this new positivity on the category of his own finitude: the metaphysics of the infinite will be replaced by an analytic of the finite that uncovers "transcendental" structures in life, labor, and language. Humanity thus comes to have a double being. What has collapsed is the sovereignty of identity in representation. The Human is traversed by an essential disparity, almost an *alienation by rights*, separated from itself by its words, by its works, and by its desires. And in this revolution that explodes representation, it is no longer difference that must be subordinated to the same, but the same that must be said of the Different: the Nietzchean revolution.

Foucault indeed undertakes to provide the human sciences with a foundation, but it is a poisonous foundation, an archeology that smashes its idols, a malicious gift. Let's try to sum up Foucault's thesis: the human sciences did not come about when humanity took itself to be the object of representation, nor even when humanity discovered its history. On the contrary, they came about when humanity became "dehistoricized," when things (words, living organisms, productions) received their own history that liberated them from humanity and its representation. Then the human sciences were constituted by *mimicking* the new positive sciences of biology, political economy, and philology. To affirm their specificity, the human sciences restored the order of representation, though they load it down with the resources of the unconscious.

This false equilibrium already shows that the human sciences are not sciences. They aspired to occupy the empty place in representation, but this place of the king cannot and must not be occupied: anthropology is a mystification. From the Classical Age to Modernity, we move from a state where the Human does not yet exist to a state where it has already disappeared. "Today we no longer think but in the emptiness which the Human has left. Because the emptiness does not create a lack: it does not prescribe a lacuna to be filled. It is nothing more, and nothing less than the unfolding of a space in which it is finally once again possible to think."[3] Indeed, this analytic of finitude invites us not to create a human science, but to set up a new *image of thought*: a thinking that no longer opposes itself as from the outside to the unthinkable or the unthought, but which would lodge the unthinkable, the unthought within itself as thought, and which would be in an essential relationship to it (desire is "what remains always unthought at the heart of thought"); a thinking that would of itself be in relation to the obscure, and which by rights would be traversed by a sort of fissure, without which thought could no longer operate. The fissure cannot be filled in, because it is the highest object of thought: the Human does not fill it in or glue it back together; the fissure in humanity is the end of the Human or the origin of thought. A Cogito for a self underneath... Of those disciplines that treat of humanity, only ethnology, psychoanalysis, and linguistics effectively surpass the Human, providing the three major axes of the analytic of the finite.

Now we see how this book continues Foucault's reflections on madness, on the transformation of the concept of madness from the Classical Age to Modernity. Above all, it is crystal clear that Foucault's three major works—*Madness and Civilization: A History of Insanity in the Age of Reason*, *The birth of the Clinic: An Archaeology of Medical Perception*, and *The Order of Things: An Archaeology of the Human Sciences*—form a chain in a radically new project for philosophy as well as the history of sciences. Foucault himself describes his method as archeological. What should be understood by archeology is a study of the "substratum," the "ground" on which thought operates, and into which it reaches to form its concepts. What Foucault shows us is the very different strata in this ground, even the mutations, the topographical upheavals, the organization of new spaces: for example, the mutation that makes the classic image of thought possible, or the one which prepares the modern image of thought. To be sure, one can assign sociological or even psychological causes to this "history"; but in reality the causalities at work already unfold in spaces that presuppose an image of thought. We must try to imagine events of pure thought, radical or transcendental events that determine a space of knowledge for any one era.

Instead of an historical study of opinions (a point of view that still governs the traditional conception of the history of philosophy), we find a synchronic study of knowledge and its conditions: not conditions that make knowledge possible in general, but those that make it real and determine it at any one moment.

Such a method has at least two paradoxical results: it displaces the importance of concepts, and also the importance of authors. Accordingly, what is important in defining the Classical Age is not mechanics or mathematics, but an upheaval in the economy of signs, which cease to be a figure of the world and slip into representation: it is only this that makes possible both *mathesis* and mechanics. Similarly, what is important to know is not that Cuvier is "fixist," but how in reaction against the point of view of natural history that still imprisons Lamarck, Cuvier establishes a biology that makes possible both evolutionism and discussions on evolutionism. As a general rule, and this book abounds in decisive examples, the major polemics involving different opinions are less important than the space of knowledge that makes them possible; and those authors who occupy a central place in a more visible history are not necessarily the same in archeology. Foucault says: "...I saw it more clearly in Cuvier, in Bopp, in Ricardo than in Kant or Hegel," and nowhere does Foucault more resemble a great philosopher than when he rejects the major lineages for a more secret, subterranean genealogy.

A new image of thought—a new conception of what thinking means is the task of philosophy today. This is where philosophy, no less than the sciences and the arts, can demonstrate its capacity for mutations and new "spaces." To the question, What's new in philosophy? Foucault's books all by themselves provide a profound answer, one of the most lively and most penetrating. In my opinion, *The Order of Things* is a great book, brimming with new thoughts.

The Method of Dramatization[1]

Gilles Deleuze, university professor of Letters and Human Sciences in Lyon, proposes to develop before the members of the French Society of Philosophy the following arguments:

It is not certain that the question *what is this?* is a good question for discovering the essence or the Idea. It may be that questions such as *who? how much? how? where? when?* are better—as much for discovering the essence as for determining something more important about the Idea.

Spatio-temporal dynamisms have several different properties: 1) they create particular spaces and times; 2) they provide a rule of specification for concepts, which without these dynamisms would remain unable to receive their logical articulations; 3) they determine the double aspect of *differentiation*, qualitative and quantitative (qualities and extensions, species and parts); 4) they entail or designate a subject, though a "larval" or "embryonic" subject; 5) they constitute a special theatre; 6) they express Ideas. —It is through all these different aspects that spatio-temporal dynamisms figure the movement of dramatization.

Through dramatization, the Idea is incarnated or actualized, *it differentiates itself*. Nevertheless, the Idea in its proper content must already present characteristics that correspond with the two aspects of its differentiation. The Idea is in itself a system of *differential* relations and the result of a distribution of remarkable or singular points (ideal events). In other words, the Idea is fully differential in itself, before even *differentiating* itself in the actual. This status of the Idea explains its logical value, which is not the clear and distinct, but rather as Leibniz sensed, the distinct-obscure. The method of dramatization as a whole is represented in the complex concept of differentiation (differential / differentiation), which gives an orientation to the questions from which I began.

TRANSCRIPT OF THE SESSION

The session began at 4:30 pm at the Sorbonne, in the Michelet Amphitheatre, with President of the Society Mr. Jean Wahl presiding.

Jean Wahl: Mr. Gilles Deleuze needs no introduction: you are no doubt familiar with his work on Hume as well as Nietzsche and Proust, and I'm sure you are all familiar with his extraordinary talent. So without further ado, I give you Gilles Deleuze.

Gilles Deleuze: The Idea, the discovery of the Idea, is inseparable from a certain type of question. The Idea is first and foremost an "objectality" that corresponds, as such, to a certain way of asking questions. The Idea responds only to the call of certain questions. Platonism has determined the Idea's form of question as *what is X?* This noble question is supposed to concern the essence and is opposed to vulgar questions which point merely to the example or the accident. So, we do not ask *who or what* is beautiful, but *what* is the Beautiful. It is not *where* and *when* does justice exist, but what is the Just. Not *how* we obtain "two," but what is the dyad. Not *how much*, but what... Platonism in its entirety seems to oppose a major question, which is always taken up and repeated by Socrates as that of the essence or the Idea, to the minor questions of opinion which express only sloppy thinking, whether by old men and not so clever children, or by all too clever sophists and rhetoricians.

And yet the privilege accorded the question *What is this?* reveals itself to be confused and doubtful, even in Plato and the Platonic tradition. Because the question *What is this?* is in the end the driving force behind those dialogues known as aporetic. Is it possible that the question of the essence is the question of contradiction, that it leads us into inextricable contradictions? But when the Platonic dialectic becomes something serious and positive, it takes other forms: who? in the *Republic*; how much? in *Philebus*; where and when? in the *Sophist*; and in which case? in *Parmenides*. It is almost as if the Idea were not positively determinable except according to a typology, a topology, a posology, a casuistry—all transcendental. Plato criticizes the sophists in this instance less for using inferior forms of questions than for not knowing how to determine the conditions in which questions acquire their ideal import and sense. And when we examine the history of philosophy as a whole, we will have a tough time discovering any philosopher whose research was guided by the question *What is this?* Aristotle? Definitely not Aristotle. Maybe Hegel, maybe there is only Hegel who did so, precisely because his dialectic, that of the empty and abstract essence, is inseparable from the movement of contradiction. The question *What is this?* prematurely judges the Idea as simplicity of the essence; from then on, it is inevitable that the simple essence includes the inessential, and includes it *in essence*, and thus contradicts itself. Another way of going about it (as in the philosophy of Leibniz), and this must be completely distinguished from contradiction, is to have the inessential include the essential. But the inessential includes the essential only *in case*. This subsumption under "the case" constitutes an original language of properties and events. This procedure is totally different from that of contra-diction and can be called *vice-diction*. It is a way of approaching the Idea as a multiplicity. It is no longer a question of knowing whether the Idea is one or multiple, or even both at once; "multiplicity," when used as a substantive, designates a domain where the Idea, of itself, is much closer to the accident than to the abstract essence, and can be determined only with the questions *who? how? how much? where and when? in which case?*—forms that sketch the genuine spatio-temporal coordinates of the Idea.

First I want to ask: what is the characteristic or distinctive trait of a thing in general? Such a trait is twofold: the quality or qualities which it possesses, the extension which it occupies. Even when we cannot distinguish actual divisible parts, we still single out remarkable regions or points; and it is not only the internal extension that must be examined, but also the way in which the thing determines and differentiates a whole external space, as in the hunting grounds of an animal. In a word, each thing is at the intersection of a twofold synthesis: a synthesis of qualification or specification, and of partition, composition, or organization. There is no quality without an extension underlying it, and in which the quality is diffused, no species without organic parts or points. These are the two correlative aspects of *differentiation*: species and parts, specification and organization. These constitute the conditions of the representation of things in general.

But if differentiation thus has two complimentary forms, what is the agent of this distinction and this complimentarity? Beneath organization and specification, we discover nothing more than spatio-temporal dynamisms: that is to say, agitations of space, holes of time, pure syntheses of space, direction, and rhythms. The most general characteristics of branching, order, and class, right on up to generic and specific characteristics, already depend on such dynamisms or such directions of development. And simultaneously, beneath the partitioning phenomena of cellular division, we again find instances of dynamism: cellular migrations, foldings, invaginations, stretchings; these constitute a "dynamics of the egg." In this sense, the whole world is an egg. No concept could receive a logical division in representation, if this division were not determined already by sub-representational dynamisms; we see this in the Platonic process of division which works only in two directions: left and right, and—to take an example from fishing—with the help of determinations such as "surround and strike," "strike from top to bottom, bottom to top."

These dynamisms always presuppose a field in which they are produced, outside of which they would not be produced. This field is intensive, that is, it implies differences of intensity distributed at different depths. Though experience always shows us intensities already developed in extensions, already covered over by qualities, we must conceive, precisely as a condition of experience, of pure intensities enveloped in a depth, in an intensive *spatium* that preexists every quality and every extension. Depth is the power of pure unextended *spatium*; intensity is only the power of differentiation or the unequal in itself, and each intensity is already difference, of the type E - E', where E in turn refers to e - e', and e, to e - e', etc. Such an intensive field constitutes an environment of individuation. This explains the insufficiency of any reminder that individuation functions neither through prolonged specification (*species infima*) nor through composition or division of parts (*pars ultima*). It is not enough to discover a difference of nature between individuation on the one hand, and specification or partition on the other. Because individuation is the prior condition under which specification, and partition or composition, function in a system. Individuation is intensive, and it is presupposed by all qualities and species, by all extensions and parts that happen to fill up or develop the system.

Nevertheless, since intensity is difference, differences of intensity must enter into communication. Something like a "difference operator" is required, to relate difference to difference. This role is filled by what is called an *obscure precursor*. A lightning bolt flashes between different intensities, but it is preceded by an *obscure precursor*, invisible, imperceptible, which determines in advance the inverted path as in negative relief, because this path is first the agent of communication between series of differences. If it is true that every system is an intensive field of individuation constructed on a series of heterogeneous or disparate boundaries, then when the series come into communication thanks to the action of the obscure precursor, this communication induces certain phenomena: *coupling* between series, *internal resonance* within the system, and *inevitable movement* in the form of an amplitude that goes beyond the most basic series themselves. It is under these conditions that a system fills up with qualities and develops in extension. Because a quality is always a sign or an event that rises from the depths, that flashes between different intensities, and that lasts as long as it takes for its constitutive difference to be nullified. And most importantly, these conditions taken together determine spatio-temporal dynamisms, which themselves are responsible for generating qualities and extensions.

Dynamisms are not absolutely subjectless, though the subjects they sustain are still only rough drafts, not yet qualified or composed, rather patients than agents, only able to endure the pressure of an internal resonance or the amplitude of an inevitable movement. A composed, qualified adult would perish in such an environment. The truth of embryology is that there are movements which the embryo alone can endure: in this instance, the only subject is larval. The nightmare is perhaps one of these movements which neither someone awake, *nor even the dreamer*, can endure—but only the deep-sleeper in a dream-less sleep. And thought itself, considered as a dynamism proper to the philosophical system, is perhaps in its turn one of these terrifying movements that are irreconcilable with a formed, qualified, and composed subject, such as the subject of the *cogito* in representation. "Regression" will be misunderstood as long as we fail to see in it the activation of a larval subject, the only patient able to endure the demands of a systematic dynamism.

These determinations as a whole: field of individuation, series of intensive differences, obscure precursor, coupling, resonance and inevitable movement, larval subject, spatio-temporal dynamisms—these sketch out the multiple coordinates which correspond to the questions *how much? who? how? where? and when?*, and which gives such questions their transcendent consequences, beyond empirical examples. These determinations as a whole indeed are not connected with any particular example borrowed from a physical or biological system, but articulate the categories of every system in general. A physical experiment, no less than psychic experiments of the Proustian variety, imply the communication of disparate series, the intervention of an obscure precursor, as well as the resonances and inevitable movements that result. It happens all the time that dynamisms which are qualified in a certain way in one domain, are then taken up in an entirely different mode in another domain. The geographical dynamism of the island (island as rupture with the continent, and island as an eruption from the deep) is taken up in the mythical dynamism of mankind on the deserted island (a derived rupture and an original rebeginning). Ferenczi has shown how, in sexual life, the physical dynamism of cellular elements is taken up in the biological dynamism of organs and even in the psychic dynamism of people.

Dynamisms, and all that exists simultaneously with them, are at work in every form and every qualified extension of representation; they constitute not so much a picture as a group of abstract lines coming from the unextended and formless depth. This is a strange theatre comprised of pure determinations, agitating time and space, directly affecting the soul, whose actors are larva—Artaud's name for this theatre was "cruelty." These abstract lines constitute a drama which corresponds to this or that concept, and which also directs its specification and division. Scientific knowledge, the dream, as well as things in themselves—these all dramatize. Given any concept, we can always discover its drama, and *the concept would never be divided or specified* in the world of representation *without the dramatic dynamisms* that thus determine it in a material system beneath all possible representation. Take the concept of truth; it is not enough to ask the question: "what is the true?" As soon as we ask *who wants the true, when and where, how and how much?*, we have the task of assigning larval subjects (the jealous man, for example) and pure spatio-temporal dynamisms (sometimes we cause the very "thing" to emerge, at a certain time, in a certain place; sometimes we accumulate indexes and signs from moment to moment, following a path that never ends). Then when we learn that the concept of truth in representation is divided in two directions—the first according to which the true emerges in an intuition and as itself, the second according to which the true is always concluded from indices or inferred from something else as that which is not there—we have no trouble discovering beneath *these traditional theories of intuition and induction*, the dynamisms of inquisition or admission, accusation or inquiry, silently and dramatically at work, in such a way as to determine the theoretical division of the concept.

What I am calling a drama particularly resembles the Kantian schema. The schema, according to Kant, is indeed an *a priori* determination of space and time corresponding to a concept: *the shortest* schema is the drama (dream or nightmare) of the straight line. It is precisely dynamism that divides the concept of line into straight and curved, and more importantly, in the Archimedian conception of limits, that allows the curve to be measured according to the straight. Still, what remains rather mysterious is the way in which the schema has this power in relation to the concept. In a certain way, all the post-Kantians have tried to elucidate the mystery of this hidden art, according to which dynamic spatio-temporal determinations genuinely have the power to dramatize a concept, although they have a nature totally different from the concept.

The answer perhaps lies in a direction that certain post-Kantians have indicated: pure spatio-temporal dynamisms have the power to dramatize *concepts*, because first they actualize, incarnate *Ideas*. We have at our disposal a point of departure to test this hypothesis: if it is true that dynamisms control the two inseparable aspects of differentiation—specification and partition, the qualification of a species and the organization of an extension—the Idea in turn should present two aspects, from which those of differentiation somehow derive. So, we have to ask ourselves about the nature of the Idea, about its difference of nature from the concept.

An Idea has two principal characteristics. On the one hand, it consists of a group of differential relations among elements stripped of all sensible form and function, existing only through their reciprocal determination. Such relations are of the $\frac{dx}{dy}$ type (even though the question of the infinitely small will not come up here). In the most diverse cases, we can ask whether we are indeed confronted by *ideal elements*, that is to say, without figure or function, though reciprocally determinable in a network of differential relations: do phonemes fall under this case? And what about physical particles? Or biological genes? In each case, we have to continue the search till we obtain these differentials, which exist and are determined only in respect to one another. So you see I am invoking this principle, called reciprocal determination, as the first aspect of sufficient reason. On the other hand, distributions of singularities, distributions of remarkable and ordinary points, correspond to these differential relations, such that a remarkable point can engender a series capable of being prolonged along every ordinary point, all the way to the vicinity of another singularity. Singularities are *ideal events*. It is possible that notions such as singular and regular, or remarkable and ordinary, have a greater epistemological and ontological importance for philosophy than do the notions of true and false, because *sense* depends on the distinction and distribution of these brilliant points in the Idea. In this way, we see how a complete determination of the Idea, or of the thing in Idea, proceeds. This constitutes the second aspect of sufficient reason. The Idea thus appears as a multiplicity which must be traversed in two directions: from the point of view of the variation of differential relations, and from the point of view of the distribution of singularities corresponding to particular values of those relations. What I previously called the operation of *vice-diction* merges with this twofold determination or twofold approach, which is reciprocal and complete.

This has several consequences. In the first place, the Idea defined in this way has no actuality. It is virtual, it is pure virtuality. All the differential relations, by virtue of reciprocal determination, and all the distributions of singularities, by virtue of complete determination, coexist in the virtual multiplicity of Ideas. The Idea is actualized precisely only insofar as its differential relations are incarnated in species or separate qualities, and insofar as the concomitant singularities are incarnated in an extension that corresponds to this quality. A species is made up of differential relations among genes, just as organic parts are made up of incarnated singularities (cf. "*loci*"). However, we must emphasize the absolute condition of non-resemblance: the species or the quality does not resemble the differential relations that it incarnates, no more so than the singularities resemble the organized extension which actualizes them.

If it is true that qualification and partition constitute the two aspects of differentiation, it follows that the Idea actualizes itself through differentiation. When the Idea actualizes itself, it differentiates itself. In itself and in its virtuality, the Idea is completely *undifferentiated*. However, it is not at all indeterminate. We must absolutely underline the difference between the two operations, whose *distinctive trait* is this: $\frac{1}{n}$, differential (l) / differentiation (n). The Idea in itself, or the thing in Idea, is not at all *differentiated*, since it lacks the necessary qualities and parts. But it is fully and completely *differential*, since it has at its disposal the relations and singularities that will be actualized, without resemblance, in the qualities and parts. It seems, then, that each thing has two "halves"—uneven, dissimilar, and unsymmetrical—each of which is itself divided into two: an *ideal half*, which reaches into the virtual and is constituted both by differential relations and by concomitant singularities; and an actual half, constituted both by the qualities that incarnate those relations and by the parts that incarnate those singularities. The question of the "*ens omni modo determinatum*" must be posed in the following way: a thing in Idea can be completely determined (*differential*), and yet lack the determinations that constitute actual existence (*the thing is undifferentiated*). If we characterize the state of the fully differential Idea as *dis-*

tinct, and the state of the actualized, i.e. differentiated, Idea as *clear*, then the proportion that governs the clear and distinct must be abandoned: the Idea in itself is not clear and distinct; on the contrary, it is *distinct and obscure*. In this same sense, the Idea is Dionysian: that zone of obscure distinction which it preserves within itself, that undifferentiation which is no less perfectly determined—this is its drunkenness.

I should make clear under what conditions the word "virtual" can be rigorously used (in the way Bergson, for example, uses it when he distinguishes virtual and actual multiplicities, or the way in which Mr. Ruyer[2] uses it). The virtual is not opposed to the real; it is the real that is opposed to the possible. Virtual is opposed to actual, and therefore, possesses a full reality. We saw that this reality of the virtual is constituted by the differential relations and the distributions of singularities. In every respect, the virtual echoes the formulation which Proust gave to his states of experience: "real without being actual, ideal without being abstract."[3] The virtual and the possible are opposed in several ways. On the one hand, the possible is such that the real is constructed as its resemblance. It is even because of this defect that the possible looks suspiciously retrospective or retroactive; it is suspected of being constructed after the fact, in resemblance to the real which it is supposed to precede. This is why, too, when someone asks what *more* is found in the real, there is nothing to point out except "the same" thing as posited outside representation. The possible is just the concept as principle of the representation of the thing, under the following categories: the identity of *what is representing*, and the resemblance of *what is being represented*. On the other hand, the virtual belongs to the Idea and does not resemble the actual, no more than the actual resembles the virtual. The Idea is an image without resemblance; the virtual actualizes itself not through resemblance, but through divergence and differentiation. Differentiation or actualization is always creative with respect to what it actualizes, whereas realization is always reproductive or limiting. The difference between the virtual and the actual is no longer the difference of the Same insofar as the Same is posited once in representation, and once again outside representation. Rather, it is the difference of the Other, insofar as the Other appears once in the Idea, and once again, though in a totally different manner, in the process of actualizing the Idea.

The extraordinary world of Leibniz puts us in touch with an *ideal continuum*. This continuity, according to Leibniz, is defined not at all by homogeneity, but by the coexistence of all the variations of differential relations, and of the distributions of singularities that correspond to them. The state of this world is beautifully expressed by the image of murmuring, or the ocean, or a water mill, or vanishing, or even drunkenness: they all bespeak a Dionysian depth rumbling beneath this apparently Apollonian philosophy. It has often been asked what the notions "compossible" and "incompossible" consist of, and how exactly they differ from the possible and the impossible. It is difficult to give an answer, perhaps because Leibniz's philosophy as a whole exhibits a certain hesitation between a clear conception of the possible and the obscure conception of the virtual. In fact, the incompossible and the compossible have nothing whatsoever to do with the contradictory and the non-contradictory. It has to do with something else: divergence and convergence. What defines the compossibility of a world is the convergence of those series which are each constructed in the vicinity of a singularity, all the way to the vicinity of another singularity. The incompossibility of worlds, on the other hand, arises at that moment when the generated series diverge. The best of all possible worlds therefore encompasses a maximum of relations and singularities, under the condition of continuity, in other words, a maximum convergence of series. Now we see how, in such a world, individual essences or monads are formed. Leibniz says both that the world does not exist outside the monads that express it, and that God created the world rather than the monads (God did not create Adam the sinner, but the world in which Adam sinned). The singularities of the world serve as principles for the constitution of individualities: each individual envelops a certain number of singularities and clearly expresses their relations *with respect to* his own body. Consequently, the expressed world virtually preexists the expressive individualities, but does not exist actually outside the individualities which express it little by little. The process of individuation determines the relations and singularities of the ideal world to be incarnated in the qualities and extensions filling up the intervals between individuals. This approach toward a "depth" populated by relations and singularities, the resulting formation of individual essences, and the consequent determination of qualities and extensions, are the elements that constitute a method of *vice-diction*, which itself constitutes a theory of multiplicities, always subsuming each thing under its "case."

The notion of differential / differentiation ($\frac{1}{n}$) expresses not only a mathematico-biological complex, but the very condition of any cosmology, as the two halves of the object. The differential (1) expresses the nature of a pre-individual depth, which is in no way reducible to an abstract universal, but which entails relations and singularities characterizing virtual multiplicities or Ideas. Differentiation (n) expresses the actualization of these relations and singularities in qualities and extensions, species and parts, as objects of representation. The two aspects of differentiation thus correspond to the two aspects of the differential, but they do not resemble them: we need a third thing which determines the Idea to actualize itself, to incarnate itself in a particular way. I tried to show how this role was filled by the intensive fields of individuation, with their precursors to put them in a state of activity, with their larval subjects formed around singularities, and with their dynamisms filling up the system. The complete notion is this: (in)differential / (in)differentiation. It is the spatio-temporal dynamisms within the fields of individuation that determine the Ideas to actualize themselves in the differentiated aspects of the object. Though a subject is given in representation, we still know nothing. We learn only insofar as we discover the Idea operating underneath the concept, the field or fields of individuation, the system or systems that envelop the Idea, the dynamisms that determine the Idea to incarnate itself; it is only in such conditions that we can lift the veil of mystery concerning the division of the concept. All these conditions define dramatization, and its attendant questions: *in what case? who? how? how much?* The shortest schema is the concept of the straight line only because it is first the drama of the Idea of line, the differential of the straight and the curve, the dynamism that operates in silence. The clear and distinct is the claim of the concept in the Apollonian world of representation; but beneath representation there is always the Idea and its distinct-obscure depth, a drama beneath every logos.

DISCUSSION

Jean Wahl:[4] Let me thank you on everyone's behalf for your talk. Rarely have we ever witnessed such a—well, I'm not going to say system, but an attempt to peer through the lens of differentiation, understood as twofold, giving us a world understood perhaps as fourfold. But let me stop here, since my role as President is to open up the floor to questions.

Pierre-Maxime Schuhl:[5] I would like to ask Deleuze something. I would like to know how, from his perspective, the opposition between the natural and the artificial would look, since it is not spontaneously dynamic, but becomes dynamic through auto-regulation.

Gilles Deleuze: Is it not because the artificial entails its own dynamisms which have no equivalent in nature? You have indeed shown the importance of the categories 'natural' and 'artificial' particularly in Greek thought. Precisely, however, are these categories not differentiated according to dynamisms, according to approaches, places, and directions? But in systems of nature as well as artifice, we find intensive organizations, precursors, larval subjects, every sort of vitality, a vital character, even though in another mode…

Pierre-Maxime Schuhl: This is beginning to sound like the poet Nerval.

Gilles Deleuze: Well, I should hope so.

Pierre-Maxime Schuhl: In *Phelibos*, 64 b, Socrates says that creation has been completed by an abstract order that will have the power to animate itself. In the domain of the spirit, this happens all by itself. So what's left over is the immense domain of matter…

Gilles Deleuze: We would have to classify the different systems of intensity. From this perspective, the regulatory operations you alluded to a moment ago would have a decisive importance.

Pierre-Maxime Schuhl: I would just like to add a simple anecdote, concerning the allusions Deleuze made to the different ways of thinking about fishing in the *Sophist*. A few years ago, Leroi-Gourhan published a book on technology that revamps exactly these Platonic distinctions. I asked him if he had the *Sophist* in mind, and he said he had never thought about it. This confirms the permanence of certain divisions that were underlined.

Noël Mouloud:[6] I won't follow Mr. Deleuze into the ontological depths of his conception of the Idea. His way of posing the problem goes beyond my usual habits of thought. What I found most interesting in Mr. Deleuze's talk is this conception of art; clearly, the artist takes up a non-serial temporality, which is not yet organized, or a multiplicity of lived and precategorical spacialities, and through his art or artifice, he brings these to a particular language, and a particular syntax. The artist's style or personal recreation consists in imposing as objective, structures which have been borrowed from a non-objective stage. And there you have a good part of the dynamism of art.

I would like to ask a few questions about certain points I find troublesome. For example, how does one apply this conception of a priority of spatiality or temporality to science? In one sense, we can think of space, time, and dynamism as the opposite of the concept, I mean, as that which introduces variety in a concept that tends toward stability. In another sense, however, space and time, at least as they are accessible to our intuition, also tend toward a certain stability, a certain immobility. Early physics and early chemistry began with a mechanics that relied heavily on the idea of spatial continuities or the composition of elements in a compound. Early biology began with a kind of intuition of duration, becoming, a continuous unfolding that tied apparent forms together and went beyond their separations. And mathematization, for its part, seems to have introduced a second dramatization. In this case, the dramatization comes from the concept, and not so much from intuition. So, when chemistry arrives at the stage of electronic analysis, there are no more genuine substances, genuine valences; there are only linking functions that are created as the process develops and are understood one after the other. We have a process that is analyzable only by the mathematics of the electron. And as chemistry becomes quantic, or undulatory, a combination can absolutely not be conceived as a simple and necessary transition. It's a probability that results from a calculation with an energetic basis, in which one must keep in mind, for example, the symmetrical or unsymmetrical spin of electrons, or the overlapping fields of two waves that create a particular energy, etc. The energetic inventory can be taken only by the algebrist, and not by the geometer. In a similar sort of way, modern biology began with the combinatorial analysis of genetic elements, or when the chemical or radioactive effects on genes was studied—how they affected genetic developments or created mutations. So, the first intuition of biologists, who believed in a continuous evolution, was destroyed and reformulated in a way by a more mathematical and operational science. I just wanted to emphasize that I have the feeling the more dramatic aspects, or if you prefer, the more dialectical aspects of conception are contributed not by the imagination, but by the work of rationalization.

In general, I don't see how the development of concepts, in the mathematical sciences, can be compared to a biological unfolding, to the "growth of an egg." The development is more accurately dialectical: systems are constructed in a coherent manner, and it does happen that they must be smashed from time to time in order to be rebuilt. But I've already spoken too long.

Gilles Deleuze: I won't disagree with you. I think our differences amount mostly to terminology. Concepts, it seems to me, bring about dramatization less than they endure it. Concepts are differentiated through operations that are not exactly conceptual and point to Ideas. One of the notions you alluded to, "a non-localizable liason," goes beyond the field of representation and the localization of concepts in this field. They are "ideal" liasons.

Noël Mouloud: I don't really want to have to defend the notion of concept, which is ambiguous at best, over-saturated with philosophical traditions: for example, the Aristotelian concept is a model of stability. But I would define the scientific concept by the work of an essentially mathematical thought. Mathematical thought ceaselessly smashes the preestablished orders of our intuition. And I would point out, too, the ambiguous use that could be made of the term *idea*, if one were to associate it too closely, as Bergson in fact did, with some organizing schema, whose foundations are in a profound, almost biological intuition. The sciences, and even the biological sciences, have not developed in the direction these schemas indicated. Or if they indeed began in that direction, mathematical and experimental models quickly overturned the schemas in question.

Jean Wahl: In this case again, I see possible agreement and a difference of language rather than a difference of conception.

Ferdinand Alquié:[7] I very much admired the talk our good friend Deleuze just gave. The question I'd like to ask him is simple, and concerns the beginning of his speech. Deleuze condemned, right at the start, the question *What is this?* and then never came back to it. I can accept what came after that, and I acknowledge the extraordinary wealth procured by the other questions he wants to ask. But I can't accept his hasty rejection of the question *What is this?*, nor can I accept what he said, a little intimidatingly, when he claimed that no other philosopher than Plato had ever asked such a question, except for Hegel. I confess I'm a little shocked: because I can think of numerous philosophers who have asked this question. Leibniz himself asked: "what is a subject?" and "what is a monad?" Berkeley, too, asked: "what is being?" and "what is the essence and the signification of the word being?" Kant also asked: "what is an object?" I could cite many more examples, so many that no one would contest my point, I hope. It seems to me, then, that Deleuze went on to orient philosophy toward other problems, problems which are perhaps not specific to his work—or rather, he seems to have criticized classical philosophy—justifiably so—for not providing us with concepts sufficiently adaptable to science, or psychological analysis, or even historical analysis. This seems perfectly true to me, and in that respect, I can't praise him enough. However, what struck me was that all the examples he uses are not properly philosophical examples. He spoke about the straight line, which is a mathematical example, about the egg, which is a physiological example, about genes, which is a biological example. When he arrived at the question of truth, then I said: OK, now we have a philosophical example. But it soon went astray, because Deleuze says we should ask: who wants the truth? why does one want the truth? only the jealous man?, etc. These are all certainly interesting questions, but they don't touch on the very essence of truth, and they are perhaps not strictly philosophical questions. They are questions turned instead toward problems that are psychological, psychoanalytic, etc. So, I myself would like to ask a simple question. I understand that Mr. Deleuze criticizes philosophy for making the Idea a conception that is not adaptable, as he would like, to scientific, psychological, and historical problems. But I think that alongside these problems there remain classical philosophical problems, namely problems having to do with essence. In any event, I don't believe, as Deleuze does, that the great philosophers have never posed such questions.

Gilles Deleuze: It is certainly true that numerous philosophers have asked the question: *What is this?* But is this not, in their case, just a convenient way of talking? Kant indeed asks what is an object, but he asks this question within the framework of a more profound question, a *how* question, which took on new meaning: "How is this possible?" What seems most important to me is the new way in which Kant interprets the question *how?* As for Leibniz, when he allows himself to ask *what is this?*, does he not get definitions which he himself labels nominal? But when he attains real definitions, is it not thanks to questions such as *how? from what perspective? in which case?* In Leibniz we find a whole topology, a whole casuistry, that finds expression primarily in his interest in law. But in any event, I was too hasty.

It's your other criticism that hits home more forcefully. Because I do believe in the specificity of philosophy, and furthermore, this belief of mine derives from you yourself. You say that the method I describe borrows its applications from all over, from different sciences, but hardly at all from philosophy. And that the only philosophical example I used, the problem of truth, went astray because it consisted in dissolving the concept of truth into psychological or psychoanalytic determinations. If this is the case, then I have failed. Because the Idea, as real-virtual, must not be described in uniquely scientific terms, even if science necessarily comes into play in its actualization. Even concepts such as singular and regular, or remarkable and ordinary, are not exhausted by mathematics. I want to call on Lautman's theses: a theory of systems must show how the movement of scientific concepts participates in a dialectic that surpasses them. Nor are dynamisms reducible to psychological determinations (and when I cited the jealous man as the "type" of the seeker of truth, it was not as a psychological character, but as a complex of space and time, as a "figure" belonging to the very *notion* of truth). It seems to me not only that the theory of systems is philosophical, but that this theory forms a system of a very particular type—the philosophical system, with its own dynamisms, precursors, larval subjects, specific to it. At any rate, it is on this condition alone that the dramatic method would make sense.

Maurice de Gandillac:[8] Behind your suggestive and poetic vocabulary, I sense profound and solid thinking, as always, but I confess I would like additional clarification as to dramatization, which is in your title, and which you defined as though it were a well-known concept that needs little commentary. Usually when we use the word *dramatic* or *dramatization*, we use it in a pejorative sense to reproach someone for turning some minor incident into a theatrical production (like when we say: "Quit being so dramatic!"). Etymologically, a drama is an action but staged, stylized, presented before a public. But I have difficulty imagining a situation of this kind arising in connection with the fantasmic subjects you just spoke about: the embryos, larvae, undifferentiated differentiations which are also dynamic schemas, because the terms you chose are pretty vague, they're used to mean just about anything depending on the context. More precisely, whereas you refuse the question *ti* (inasmuch as it concerns an *ousia*), you seem to accept *tis* as the subject of a doing or making (*tis poiei ti*). But can we really speak of a subject doing something at the larval level?

My second question is about the relation between the dramatic and the tragic. Does the drama you have in mind, like tragedy, refer to an irresolvable conflict between two uneven halves, in a subtle disharmonious harmony? Your allusion to Artaud and his theatre of cruelty sufficiently demonstrates that you are not an optimist philosopher, or if you are, it's in the way Leibiz is, whose vision of the world is, all things considered, one of the most cruel imaginable. Is your dramatization a *Theodicy*, this time situated not in the celestial palaces to which the famous apologists for Sextus alludes, but rather with the lemurs from the second *Faust*?

Gilles Deleuze: I will try to define dramatization more rigorously: what I have in mind are dynamisms, dynamic spatio-temporal determinations, that are pre-qualitative and pre-extensive, taking "place" in intensive systems where differences are distributed at different depths, whose "patients" are larval subjects and whose "function" is to actualize Ideas…

Maurice de Gandillac: But why do you use the term *dramatization* to translate all that (which I find a little obscure)?

Gilles Deleuze: When you assign such a system of spatio-temporal determination to a concept, in my view you're replacing a logos with a "drama," you're setting up the drama of this logos. For example, you used to say: we dramatize when we're with our family. It's true that everyday life is full of dramatizations. Some psychoanalysts use the word, I believe, to designate the movement by which logical thought is dissolved in pure spatio-temporal determinations, as in falling asleep. And this is not so far removed from the famous experiments of the Wurtzbourg school. Take the case of an obsessive compulsive, where the subject keeps shrinking: handkerchiefs and towels are perpetually cut, first in two, then the halves are cut again; the cord for the bell in the dining room is regularly shortened, and the bell gets closer to the ceiling; everything is gnawed at, miniaturized, put into boxes. This is indeed a drama, in the sense that the patient organizes a space, agitates it, while in this space he expresses an Idea of the unconscious. An angry fit is a dramatization that stages larval subjects. You asked me whether dramatization in general is related to the tragic. I don't see there being any privileged relation between them. The tragic and the comic are still categories of representation, whereas there is a more fundamental relation between dramatization and a certain mode of terror, which can entail a maximum of clownishness as well as grotesque… You said yourself that the world of Leibniz, in the end, is the most cruel of all worlds.

Maurice de Gandillac: Clownishness, the grotesque, and snickering all belong to the region of the tragic, I believe. Your conclusion alluded to Nietzschean themes, all told more Dionysian than Apollonian.

Jean Wahl: I think Deleuze could have answered you with the question *when?*, because there are times when it all becomes tragic and there are times when it becomes…

Gilles Deleuze: Indeed I could have.

Michel Souriau:[9] I'd like to ask for clarification as to a reference. Mr. Deleuze cited several philosophers, not many, but certain ones; I thought I may have detected a reference to Malebranche, though he wasn't cited. There are several things in Malebranche that would be completely out of place in your work, for example, his vision in God: whereas for yourself it is more a question of a "vision in Mephistopheles." But we can't forget the Malebranche of *intelligible extension*; when you refer to the at first obscure and in every case dynamic becoming of ideas, and then to this extension which is not quite space, but tends to become space, it really does sound like Malebranche's *intelligible extension*.

Gilles Deleuze: It didn't occur to me until now, but there is indeed a kind of pure, pre-extensive *spatium* in intelligible extension. The same goes for the distinction Leibniz makes between *spatium* and *extensio*.

Lucy Prenant:[10] My question is along the same lines as Mr. Souriau's. What you call obscure and distinct, wouldn't Leibniz call it intelligible and un-imaginable? Un-imaginable corresponds to obscure—to what you're calling the obscure. For Leibniz, the obscure is thought not being able to determine its object, as in the *Meditationes*, for example: a fleeting memory of an image. On the other hand, the knowledge that metal workers have of gold is converted into a law of a series of properties; this is not available for the senses, and it does not take the form of an image, and consequently, I think Leibniz would translate it as obscure, as opposed to clear. And this can even apply to what Leibniz called blind thought—not under just any conditions, because blind thought can lead to verbalism and error, as he points out in his critique of the ontological proof. But this can correspond to certain forms of blind thought; for example, to characteristics—to forms that are rigorously constructed.

Precisely, however, must not these "distinct and blind" ideas of Leibniz be based on "distinct visions"? Leibniz sees that a straight line can be extended to infinity because he sees the reason: the similitude of the segments. Thus we have recourse to "primitive notions" which "are the proper marks of themselves," to the alphabet of human thought. In other words, I don't believe that thought can remain fully "obscure," in Mr. Deleuze's sense of the word, throughout its course. Thought must at least "see a reason," grasp a law.

Gilles Deleuze: I am struck by your remarks on the rigor of Leibniz's terminology. But is it not true, Ms. Prenant, that "distinct" has many senses in Leibniz? His texts on the sea emphasize that there are elements in perception, i.e. remarkable points, that in combination with other remarkable points of our body, determine a threshold of conscious perception. This conscious perception is clear and confused (non-distinct), but the differential elements that it actualizes are themselves distinct and obscure. It is true that we are dealing with a depth, which perhaps in a certain way exceeds sufficient reason itself...

Lucy Prenant: Furthermore, when a simple substance "expresses" the universe, I don't think it always does so through an image; it is certainly expressed through some quality—conscious or not (at most partially conscious for the finite activity of a created substance), and this quality corresponds to a system of variable relations from some "point of view." God alone can reflect on the totality of these virtualities with perfect distinction—which for him eliminates any need for a calculus of probabilities…

But I wanted to ask you a second question. Doesn't this virtuality that claims to correspond to existence not pose a problem for the researcher on the look-out for a tidy classification, who finds only "messy" examples, which then obligate her to readjust her species? In other words, is this virtuality anything other than a progressive and mobile expression?

Gilles Deleuze: I don't think virtuality can ever correspond to the actual in the way essence does to an existence. This would be to confuse the virtual with the possible. In any event, the virtual and the actual correspond but do not resemble one another. This is why the search for actual concepts can be infinite, there is always an excess of virtual Ideas animating them.

Jean Ullmo:[11] I am a little overwhelmed by such a purely philosophical exposé, and I very much admired it, first for its form and its poetic value, but also for the feeling—but is it a feeling?—I had while listening to it, that despite my ignorance, philosophically speaking, and my naiveté with respect to the concepts, methods, and references you used, I felt like I could follow you, or rather at every moment I could translate you into a more humble language, the language of epistemology, from which I have elaborated a scientific reflection which has been going on for a few years now and encompasses more than a few experiments. Of course, these two disciplines do not exactly overlap, and from time to time I lost my footing. But thanks to the questions that were raised, now I understand why I lost my footing, since there were precise allusions to philosophical issues I am not familiar with. Having said that, I think everything you said can be translated into the language of modern epistemology, and I believe that the project you have undertaken—giving philosophical concepts a genetic and evolutive extension, the kind of internal differentiation that allows them to be adapted to the disciplines of science and history, as well as biology, since we agree that the field of biology is more evolved than the physical sciences—I think this project is extremely interesting and that you have made tremendous progress.

Georges Bouligand:[12] I would just like to comment on the "messy" examples that Ms. Prenant brought up. For the mathematician, such "messy" examples are always counter-examples. A researcher who, in good faith, examines a theme derives a prospective view from it, in conformity with such examples as "lead" him toward the desired "theorem." But a friend whom he meets soon puts this theorem to the test with a counter-example. Then our researcher undergoes this "psychological shock," which can be severe, but which is quickly dominated by evaluating as "strange" the case which was "practically" excluded from the start. This is a frequent phenomenon, too. This is what happens when you take a point h of a surface S—with a normal vertical for h—and try to justify a "minimum height" for h using this hypotheses: every vertical meets S in a single point; for every line of S obtained as the intersection of S and an arbitrary vertical plane containing the vertical of h, the minimum would be produced for h. The return to a clear vision of things can be rather difficult: having started with more or less subjective impressions, we would have to rediscover full agreement with rigorous logic.

Jacques Merleau-Ponty:[13] Several times you spoke about spatio-temporal dynamisms, which clearly have an important role to play, and I think I more or less understood what you meant by them in your talk. However, and this is certainly feasible, there may be reason to divide the spatial from the temporal in these dynamisms. A comparison of two images you used makes me think it could be important to clarify this point. You used the image of lightning; I don't know if you found it in Leibniz or if you found it all by yourself, it doesn't matter. But clearly, what we're dealing with in this case is what you call the intensive, and in particular, potential. We're dealing with an instantaneous dispersion that is purely spatial, such as the movement of charges, or sound waves, etc. Then you used the image of the embryo; in this case, however, the temporal aspect is clearly tied to the spatial aspect, since the differentiation is as rigorously controlled in time as it is in space. So I would like to know if you have any clarifications on this point, because this is what I'm thinking: I thought I detected, and this is no surprise, a certain echo of Bergson in your talk; precisely, however, the lightning bolt is not at all Bergsonian, because in Bergson there is never a rupture of time, or at least I don't see it that way.

Gilles Deleuze: Your question is a good one. We would have to distinguish what belongs to space and what to time in these dynamisms, and in each case, the particular space-time combination. Whenever an Idea is actualized, there is a space and a time of actualization. The combinations are clearly variable. On the one hand, if it is true that an Idea has two aspects, differential relations and singular points, the time of actualization relates to the first, whereas the space of actualization relates to the second. On the other hand, if we examine the two aspects of actualization, qualities and extensions, the qualities result for the most part from the time of actualization: what properly belongs to qualities is duration, lasting as long as an intensive system maintains and communicates its constitutive differences. And the extensions, for their part, result from the space of actualization or from the movement by which these singularities are incarnated. We see very well in biology how differential rhythms determine the organization of the body and its temporal specification.

Jacques Merleau-Ponty: Regarding the same question, I'm thinking of an image you didn't use in your talk, the image of lineage. In the talk you gave on Proust a few years ago, you spoke about lineage, e.g. the two lineages that arise from the great hermaphrodite, etc. Wouldn't that image be suitable in your talk today?

Gilles Deleuze: Yes, dynamisms indeed determine "lineages." Today I spoke about abstract lines, and the depth from which these lines emerge.

Jean Beaufret:[14] I would like to ask a question, but not concerning the talk itself. It's about the last answer Deleuze gave to Mr. de Gandillac. At the end of your exchange, Apollo and Dionysus were evoked, and everything was summed up: the opposition is insurmountable. Am I on track?

Gilles Deleuze: Yes, I believe so.

Jean Beaufret: Then I would ask you this: by whom? how far? how? where? when? By whom can this opposition be overcome? I feel like...

Gilles Deleuze: By whom could it be overcome? Certainly not by Dionysus, who has no reason to do so. Dionysus wants what is distinct to remain obscure. He sees no reason and no advantage in it. The idea of a reconciliation is unbearable to Dionysus. The clear and distinct is just as unbearable. He has taken on the distinct and wants it to remain obscure. I suppose it's just his particular will... But who wants to overcome this opposition? I can tell that the dream of a reconciliation between the clear and the distinct can only be explained by the clear. Apollo wants to overcome this opposition. He elicits the reconciliation of the clear and distinct, and he inspires the artisan with this reconciliation: the tragic artist. Let me come back to the theme M. de Gandillac touched on a few moments ago. The tragic is the effort at reconciliation, which necessarily comes from Apollo. But in Dionysus there is always something that withdraws and turns away, something that wants to maintain the distinct obscure...

Jean Beaufret: I think we've accepted the Apollo-Dionysus distinction a little too quickly, though the distinction is indeed sharply drawn in *The Birth of Tragedy*. More and more, however, I get the feeling there is a third character that shows up in Nietzsche, and which he tends to call Halcyon. I don't know what it does, but what strikes me is this *Alkyonische*, which is, as Nietzsche says, the sky of Nice, like a dimension that doesn't correspond to either the Apollonian or the Dionysian dimension. At the end of *Beyond Good and Evil*, Nietzsche discusses his encounter with Dionysus and says that the god replied with "his halcyon smile." I asked myself what this halcyon smile could mean. In any case, this is why I think Nietzsche is more reticent than you have been. I think it's a late discovery.

Gilles Deleuze: Certainly, the signification of Halcyon remains a real problem in Nietzsche's later work.

Stanislas Breton:[15] The question *what is this?* indeed hardly gets me anywhere in the discovery of the essence or the Idea. But it does seem to have an indispensable *regulative function*. It opens up a region of inquiry which only the *heuristic questions who? how?*, etc., are able to fill. Far from replacing the question *what is this?*, these other questions thus appear to require it. They form an indispensable mediation. It is in order to answer the question *what is this?* that I ask the other questions. The two types of questions are therefore heterogeneous and complimentary.

Furthermore, these other questions appear founded on a prior idea of the "thing," an idea that is already a response, in a global way, to the question *what is this?* They presuppose a "larval" subject that unfolds in an *interval of actualization*, which the spatio-temporal dynamisms make concrete.

It follows that, by virtue of what has been called the conversion of substance into the subject, the essence is less *what is* already there than *to ti ev einai* (what is about to be). Hegel also speaks of a *Bestimmtheit* that becomes a *Bestimmung*. The determination of the thing would be the past of its "dramatization." *Esse sequitur operari* (rather than *operari sequitur esse*). Traditional ontology would thus be only an approximation of an onto-genius, whose center is the *causa sui* or the *authupostaton* that Proclus discusses.

By situating your reflections within this ontological horizon, I'm not trying to diminish their implications or their importance. I want to understand them better. But there is nevertheless one question that comes first: what exactly is the application of your method? Within which horizon of reality exactly do you pose your "topical" questions *quis? quomodo?*, etc. Don't these questions only make sense in the world of mankind? Or can they be applied to the "things" of common or scientific experience? Spatio-temporal dynamisms are objects of inquiry in dynamic psychology and microphysics. What relations of analogy are there between these very different spatio-temporal dynamisms? Can we imagine a process of differentiation that relates them?

Gilles Deleuze: I'm not sure that the two kinds of questions can be reconciled. You say that the question *what is this?* precedes and directs the inquiry of the other questions. And that these other questions allow us to answer *what is this?* However, is there not every reason to fear that, if we begin with *what is this?*, we will never even get to the other questions. The question *what is this?* biases the results of the inquiry, it presupposes the answer as the simplicity of an essence, even if the essence is properly multiple, contradictory, etc. This is just abstract movement, and we will never be able to reconnect with real movement, that which traverses a multiplicity as such. In my view, the two kinds of questions imply irreconcilable methods. For example, when Nietzsche asks *who*, or *from what perspective*, instead of *what*, he is not trying to complete the question *what is this?*, he is criticizing the form of this question and all its possible responses. When I ask *what is this?*, I assume there is an essence behind appearances, or at least something ultimate behind the masks. The other kind of question, however, always discovers other masks behind the mask, displacements behind every place, other "cases" stacked up in a case.

You indicate the profound presence of a temporal operation *in to ti en enai*. But it seems to me that this operation in Aristotle does not depend on the question *what is this?*, but rather on the question *who?*, which Aristotle uses to express his anti-Platonism: *to ti a*, or "who is" (or rather, "who, being").

And you would like to know what is the scope of this dramatization. Is it exclusively psychological or anthropological? I don't see it as privileging mankind in any way. In any event, what is dramatized is the unconscious. All kinds of repetitions and resonances intervene among physical, biological, and psychic dynamisms. Perhaps the differences between dynamisms primarily derives from the *order* of the Idea being actualized. The various orders of Ideas would have to be determined.

Alexis Philonenko:[16] I would like a clarification from Mr. Deleuze. You affirmed that in the movement of actualization, the differential elements had no sensible figure, no function, no conceptual signification (which seems totally anti-Leibniz, so to speak, since Leibniz assigns a conceptual signification to the differential precisely because the differential has no "figure;" but that's not my question). To introduce your thesis, you alluded to the post-Kantians. For me, that implied not only a reference to Hegel, but also to Maïmon, Fichte, Schelling, even Schopenhauer. Maybe even Nietzsche, if you like... I would like you to clarify which post-Kantians in particular you had in mind.

Gilles Deleuze: You're asking me who I had in mind: obviously Maïmon and certain aspects of Novalis.

Alexis Philonenko: And you were thinking of the differential of consciousness?

Gilles Deleuze: That's right...

Alexis Philonenko: Well, parts of your talk seemed inspired by the work of Maïmon. This clarification is important because the notion of the differential of consciousness in Maïmon is crucial, and in many respects, the spatio-temporal dynamisms you described are remarkably reminiscent of Maïmon's differential of consciousness. Let me explain. At the level of representation we have something like integrations; but there is a sub-representative level, as you

yourself tried to show, and at this level the differential has a genetic signification, at least in Maïmon's view. I was asking for clarification to set up the
discussion. What, to my way of thinking, is so interesting is that for Maïmon,
*the notion of the differential, which is associated with the transcendental imagina-
tion, is a skeptical principle*, a principle which leads us to judge the real as
illusory. Insofar as the root of spatio-temporal dynamisms is sub-representational, we have according to Maïmon, no criterion. And this means two things:
in the first place, we cannot discern what we produce and what the object produces; in the second place, we cannot discern what is produced logically and
what is not. All there remains is the results of the sub-representational genesis
of the transcendental imagination. So, according to Maïmon, a dialectic of the
transcendental imagination must be developed, or if you prefer, *a dialectic of
synthesis*. This could be associated with Leibniz, but just a little. So this is what
I want to know: what part does illusion (or the illusory) have in the movement
of differential elements?

Gilles Deleuze: For me, none.

Alexis Philonenko: And what allows you to say that?

Gilles Deleuze: You say to me: for Maïmon there is an illusion. I follow you, but
I wasn't trying to explicate Maïmon. If what you're trying to ask me is: what part
does illusion have in the schema you're proposing? My answer is: none. It seems
to me we have the means to penetrate the sub-representational, to reach all the
way to the roots of spatio-temporal dynamisms, and all the way to the Ideas actualized in them: the elements and ideal events, the relations and singularities are
perfectly determinable. The illusion only comes afterward, from the direction of
constituted extensions and the qualities that fill out these extensions.

Alexis Philonenko: So illusion appears only in what is constituted?

Gilles Deleuze: That's right. To sum things up, I don't have the same conception
of the unconscious as Leibniz or Maïmon. Freud already went down that road.
So illusion has been displaced...

Alexis Philonenko: Well, I mean to stay on the level of logic and even transcendental logic, without getting into psychology—but if you push illusion
over to the side of what is constituted, without accepting illusion in genesis, in
constitution, are you not in the end just coming back to Plato (when in fact
you would like to avoid such a thing), for whom precisely constitution, understood as proceeding from the Idea, in as much as it can be understood, is
always veracious, truthful?

Gilles Deleuze: Yes, maybe.

Alexis Philonenko: So, as far as specification and multiplicity are concerned, we would experience the same truth as Plato, and we would have the same idea of the true, i.e. the simplicity of the true always equal to itself in the totality of its production?

Gilles Deleuze: That's not the Plato I have in mind. If we think of the Plato from the later dialectic, where the Ideas are something like multiplicities that must be traversed by questions such as *how? how much? in which case?*, then yes, everything I've said has something Platonic about it. If you're thinking of the Plato who favors a simplicity of the essence or a ipseity of the Idea, then no.

Jean Wahl: If no one else wants to ask a question, then I will conclude by thanking Mr. Deleuze and all those who participated in the discussion.

Conclusions on the Will to Power and the Eternal Return[1]

If we were to take away only one lesson from this colloquium,[2] it would be how many things in Nietzsche are hidden, masked. And this for several reasons.

First for reasons concerning the *editions* of Nietzsche's work. It's not so much a question of falsifications: his sister was indeed one of those abusive relatives that figure in the procession of cursed thinkers, but her principal faults did not consist in falsifying texts. The extent editions suffer more from bad readings or displacements, and especially arbitrary selections taken from the mass of posthumous notes. *The Will to Power* is the most famous example. We can further say that none of the extent editions, even the most recent, meet normal scientific and critical demands. This is why the project by Mr. Colli and Mr. Montinari is in my opinion so important: the complete posthumous notes will at last be edited, observing the most rigorous chronology possible, according to the periods corresponding to the books Nietzsche published. The succession of one mode of thinking for 1872 and another for 1884 will thus come to an end. Mr. Colli and Mr. Montinari were gracious enough to update us on the progress of their work and its imminent completion; and I am happy to announce that their edition will also appear in French.

But things are hidden in Nietzsche for still other reasons—of a pathological nature. His work is unfinished, interrupted by madness. We must not forget that the Eternal Return and the Will to Power, the two most fundamental concepts in the Nietzschean corpus, are hardly introduced at all. They never did receive the extended treatment Nietzsche intended. In particular, you will recall that Zarathoustra cannot be said to have articulated or formulated the eternal return, which is on the contrary hidden in the four books of *Thus Spoke Zarathustra: A Book for All and None*. What little is articulated in *Thus Spoke Zarathustra* is not formulated by Zarathoustra himself, but either by the "dwarf" or by the eagle and the serpent.[3] This is a simple introduction, which can even entail voluntary disguises. And Nietzsche's notes, in this case, do not permit us to anticipate how he would have organized any future essays concerning it. We have every right to believe that madness brutally interrupted Nietzsche's work before he was able to write what seemed to him most fundamental.—In what sense madness belongs to the work is a complex question. For my part, I don't see the least madness in *Ecce Homo*, unless one sees also great mastery in it. I feel that the mad letters of 1888 and 1889 do belong to the work, even while they interrupt it and cause its termination (the great letter to Burkhardt is in any case unforgettable).

Mr. Klossowski said that the death of God, the dead God, deprives the Self of its only guarantee of identity, its substantial basis of unity: with God dead, the self dissolves or evaporates, but in a certain way, opens itself up to all the other selves, roles, and characters which must be run through in a series like so many fortuitous events. "I am Chambige, I am Badinguet, I am Prado, I am essentially every name in history." Mr. Wahl had already given us a picture of this brilliant wastefulness prior to Nietzsche's sickness—this power of metamorphosis at the heart of Nietzsche's pluralism. Indeed Nietzsche's whole psychology, not only his personal psychology but also the one he is inventing, is a psychology of the mask, a typology of masks; and behind every mask there lies still another mask.

But the most general reason why there are so many hidden things in Nietzsche and his work is *methodological* in nature. A thing never has only one sense. Each thing has several senses that express the forces and the becoming of forces at work in it. Still more to the point, there is no "thing," but only interpretations hidden in one another, like masks layered one on the other, or languages that include each other. As Mr. Foucault has shown us, Nietzsche invents a new conception and new methods of interpretation: first by changing the space in which signs are distributed, by discovering a new "depth" in relation to which the old depth flattens out and is no longer anything; second, and most importantly, by replacing the simple relation of sign and sense with a complex of senses, such that every interpretation is already the interpretation of an interpretation *ad infinitum*. Not that every interpretation therefore has the same value and occupies the same plane—on the contrary, they are stacked or layered in the new depth. But they no longer have the true and the false as criteria. The noble and the vile, the high and the low, become the immanent principles of interpretations and evaluations. Logic is replaced by a topology and a typology: there are some interpretations that presuppose a base or vile way of thinking, feeling, and even existing, and there are others that exhibit nobility, generosity, creativity…, such that interpretations say something about the "type" of interpreter, and renounce the question "what is it?" in favor of "who is it?"

This is how the notion of value allows the truth to be "stamped out," so to speak, and a more profound force to be discovered behind the true and the false. Does this notion of value commit Nietzsche to a Platonic-Cartesian metaphysics, or does it open up a new philosophy, even a new ontology? This second theme of our colloquium is the problem that Mr. Beaufret tackled. The question is this: if everything is a mask, if everything is interpretation and evaluation, is there some ultimate court of appeal, since there are no things to interpret or evaluate, no things to mask? Ultimately, there is nothing except the will to power, which is the power to metamorphose, to shape masks, to interpret and evaluate. Mr. Vattimo showed us one approach: he argued that the two principle aspects of Nietzsche's philosophy, the critique of all current values and the creation of new values, demystification and transvaluation, could not be understood and would amount to nothing but simple propositional states of consciousness, should we fail to refer these two aspects to an original, ontological depth—"a cave behind every cave," "an abyss under every ocean floor."

This original depth, Zarathoustra's celebrated height-depth, must be named the will to power. Of course, Mr. Birault figured out how we must understand the term "will to power." It's not wanting to live, because how could whatever life is want to live? It's not a desire for domination either, because how could whatever it is that dominates desire to dominate? Zarathoustra says: "The desire to dominate: now who would call that a desire?" The will to power, then, is not a will that wants power or wants to dominate.

Such an interpretation would indeed have two disadvantages. If the will to power meant wanting power, it would clearly depend on long established values, such as honor, money, or social influence, since these values determine the attribution and recognition of power as an object of desire and will. And this power which the will desired could be obtained only by throwing itself into the struggle or fight. More to the point, we ask: *who* wants such power? *who* wants to dominate? Precisely those whom Nietzsche calls slaves and the weak. Wanting power is the image of the will to power which the impotent invent for themselves. Nietzsche always saw in struggle, in fighting, a means of selection that worked in reverse, turning to the advantage of slaves and herds. This is one of Nietzsche's great observations: "The strong must be defended just like the weak." Certainly, in the desire to dominate, in the image of the will to power which the impotent invent for themselves, we discover a will to power: but at its lowest level. The will to power has its highest level in an intense or intensive form, which is neither coveting nor taking, but giving, creating. Its true name, says Zarathoustra, is the virtue that gives.[4] And the mask is the most beautiful gift, showing the will to power as a plastic force, as the highest power of art. Power is not what the will wants, but that which wants in will, that is to say, Dionysos.

This is why, as Mr. Birault remarked, Nietzsche's perspectivism changes everything, depending whether you look at things from above or from below. From above, the will to power is affirmation, an affirmation of difference, play, pleasure and gift, the creation of difference. But from below, everything is reversed. Affirmation is reflected into negation, and difference into opposition; it is only things-from-below that originally need to oppose whatever they are not. Mr. Birault and Mr. Foucault agree on this point. Mr. Foucault showed us that good movements, in Nietzsche, originate from above, beginning with the movement of interpretation. Whatever is good, whatever is noble, participates in the eagle's flight: hovering and descent. And the depths are interpreted only when they are excavated, in other words, traversed, turned upside down, and repossessed by a movement which comes from above.

This leads us to the third theme of the colloquium, which often came up in our discussions, concerning the relation of affirmation and negation in Nietzsche's work. Mr. Löwith, in a masterful presentation whose repercussions echoed throughout our colloquium, analyzed the nature of nihilism and showed how going beyond nihilism leads Nietzsche to a real recuperation of the world, a new alliance, an affirmation of the earth and body. This idea of the "recuperation of the world" sums up Mr. Löwith's interpretation of Nietzsche. He relied in particular on a text from *The Gay Science*: "Suppress your venerations, or else suppress yourselves!"[5] And I think we were all impressed by Mr. Gabriel Marcel, when he evoked the same text to clarify his own position with respect to nihilism, to Nietzsche, and eventual disciples of Nietzsche.

Indeed, the respective role of Yes and No, of affirmation and negation, in Nietzsche's work raises many problems. In Mr. Wahl's opinion, and as he demonstrated, there are so many significations of Yes and No, they coexist only at the cost of tensions, lived contradictions, contradictions in thought, some of which are unthinkable. And Mr. Wahl multiplied question on question, beautifully wielding the method of perspectives which he takes from Nietzsche, and which he knows how to make new.

Let's take an example. There is no doubt that the Mule in Zarathoustra is an animal that says Yes, I-A, I-A. But his Yes is not the Yes of Zarathoustra. Not to mention the Mule's No, which is not like Zarathoustra's either. This is because when the Mule says Yes, when he affirms or believes he is affirming, he does nothing but shoulder a burden; he measures the value of his affirmations by the burden he bears. As Mr. Gueroult reminded us at the start of this colloquium, the Mule (or the Camel) bears first the values of Christianity; then, when God is dead, he bears the burden of humanist values—human, all too human; and finally the burden of the real, when there are no longer any values at all. We here recognize the three stages of Nietzschean nihilism: God, humanity, and the last human—the burden we ourselves hoist on our own shoulders, and when we have nothing else to bear, the burden of our own fatigue.[6] Hence the Mule in fact says No, because he says Yes to all the products of nihilism, even as he exhausts each of its stages. Consequently, affirmation here is only the phantom of affirmation; the negative is the only reality.

Zarathoustra's Yes is quite different. Zarathoustra knows that affirmation does not mean shouldering a burden. Only the clown, the monkey of Zarathoustra has himself carried. On the contrary, Zarathoustra knows that affirmation means unburdening life, making it light, dancing and creating.[7] That's why for Zarathoustra affirmation comes first, whereas negation is only a consequence that serves affirmation, like a surplus of pleasure. Nietzsche-Zarathoustra contrasts his small, round, labyrinthine ears with the Mule's long, pointed ears: Zarathoustra's Yes is indeed the affirmation of the dancer, whereas the Mule's Yes is the affirmation of the beast of burden; Zarathoustra's No is pure aggression, whereas the Mule's No is merely resentment. Zarathoustra's movement, coming from above, thus brings us back to the legitimacy of a Nietzchean typology, and even topology. The Mule's movement reverses the depth, inverting the Yes and the No.

But only the fourth theme of our colloquium could address the fundamental sense which the Dionysian Yes discovers in the eternal return. Once again, there were many questions put forward. In the first place: How does one explain that the eternal return is an ancient idea, dating from the pre-Socratics, and yet Nietzsche's great innovation, or what he presents as his own discovery? And how does one explain that there is something new in the idea that nothing is new? The eternal return is most certainly not the negation or suppression of time, an atemporal eternity. But how does one explain that it is both cycle and moment: on the one hand continuation; and on the other, iteration? On the one hand, a continuation of the process of becoming which is the World; and on the other, repetition, lightning flash, a mystical view on this process or this becoming? On the one hand, the continual rebeginning of what has been; and on the other, the instantaneous return to a kind of intense focal point, to a "zero" moment of the will? And in the second place: How does one explain that the eternal return is the most devastating thought, eliciting the "Greatest Disgust," and yet is the greatest consolation, the great thought of convalescence, which provokes the super-human? All these problems were constantly present in our discussions; and little by little, divisions and distinctions made themselves felt.

At least one thing is clear: the eternal return, as the ancients understood it, does not have either the simplicity or the dogmatism often attributed to it; it is in no way a constant of the archaic psychology. On this point, we were reminded that the eternal return in ancient thought was never pure, but always accompanied by other themes such as the transmigration of souls. Nor was it conceived in a uniform way, but depending on the civilization and the school, it could be conceived in any number of ways. Also, the return was perhaps not total or eternal, consisting rather in partial cycles that were incommensurate. Strictly speaking, we cannot even categorically affirm that the eternal return was an ancient doctrine; and the theme of the Great Year is sufficiently complex for us to be cautious in our interpretations.[8] Nietzsche knew this, unwilling as he was to acknowledge any precursors here, neither Heraclitus, nor the venerable Zoroaster. Even if we do suppose that an eternal return was explicitly professed by the Ancients, we must then recognize that it is either a "qualitative" or an "extensive" eternal return. In other words, either it is the cyclical transformation of qualitative elements, each in the other, that determines the return of each thing, including celestial bodies. Or on the other hand, it is the local circular movement of qualities and things in the sublunar world. We here vacillate between a physical and an astronomical interpretation.

But neither the one nor the other corresponds to Nietzsche's thought. And if Nietzsche considers his thought so absolutely new, it is certainly not due to any lack of familiarity with the Ancients. He knows that what he calls the eternal return is taking us into a dimension as yet unexplored: neither extensive quantity nor local movement, nor physical quality, but a domain of pure intensities. Mr. de Schloezer made a rather important observation: there is indeed an assignable difference between one time and a hundred or a thousand times, but not between one time and an infinite number of times. This implies that infinity is in this case like the "nth" power of 1, or like that developed intensity which corresponds to 1. Mr. Beaufret, moreover, asked a fundamental question: is Being a predicate? Is it not something more and something less, and is it not itself above all *a more and a less*? This more and this less, which must be understood as a difference of intensity in being, and of being, as a difference of levels, is one of the fundamental problems Nietzsche is working on. Nietzsche's taste for the physical sciences and energetics has occasioned much surprise. In fact, Nietzsche was interested in physics as a science of intensive quantities, and ultimately he was aiming at the will to power as an "intensive" principle, as a principle of pure intensity—because the will to power does not mean wanting power; on the contrary, whatever one desires, it means raising this to its ultimate power, to the *nth* power. In a word, it means extracting *the superior form* of everything that is (the form of intensity).

It is in this sense that Mr. Klossowski wanted to show us a world of intense fluctuations in the Will to power, where identities are lost, and where each one cannot want itself without wanting all the other possibilities, without becoming innumerable "others," without apprehending itself as a fortuitous moment, whose very chance implies the necessity of the whole series. In Mr. Klossowski's formulation, it is a world of signs and sense; the signs are established in a difference of intensity, and become "sense" insofar as they aim at other differences included in the first difference, coming back at themselves through these others. It is Mr. Klossowski's particular strength to have uncovered the link that exists in Nietzsche between the death of God and the dissolution of the self, the loss of personal identity. God is the only guarantee of the self: the first cannot perish without the second evaporating. And the will to power follows from this, as the principle of these fluctuations or intensities that interpenetrate and flow into one another. And the eternal return also follows from this, as the principle of these fluctuations or intensities that come back and flow back through all their modifications. In short, the world of the eternal return is a world of differences, an intensive world, which presupposes neither the One nor the Same, but whose edifice is built both on the tomb of the one God and on the ruins of the identical self. The eternal return is itself the only unity of this world, which has none at all except as it comes back; it is the only identity of a world which has no "same" at all except through repetition.

In the texts which Nietzsche published, the eternal return does not figure as the object of any formal or "definitive" essay. It is only announced, intimated, in horror or ecstasy. And if we examine the two principal texts from *Thus Spoke Zarathustra* that deal with it, "On the Vision and the Riddle" and "The Convalescent," we see how the announcement, the intimation is always performed under dramatic conditions, but expresses nothing of the profound content of this "supreme thought." In one case in particular, Zarathoustra challenges the Dwarf, the Clown—his proper caricature. But what Zarathoustra says about the eternal return is already enough to make him sick, giving rise to the unbearable vision of an uncoiled serpent slithering from the mouth of a shepherd, as though the eternal return undid itself to the extent Zarathoustra spoke of it. And in the second text, the eternal return is the object of a conversation among animals, the eagle and the serpent. Zarathoustra says nothing this time, and their conversation is enough to put the convalescent Zarathoustra to sleep. But he had just enough time to tell them: "You've already turned it into the same old song!" You've turned the eternal return into "the same old song," that is to say, a mechanical or natural repetition, when in fact it is something else entirely... (Similarly, in the first text, responding to the Dwarf who had said "All truth is slanted, time itself is a circle," Zarathoustra said: "You blockhead, don't oversimplify things so much.")

We have every right to believe that Nietzsche in his published works had only prepared the revelation of the eternal return, but that he did not reveal it, indeed did not have the time to do so. Everything suggests that his projected work, on the eve of the crisis of 1888, would have gone much farther in this direction. But already the texts from *Thus Spoke Zarathustra* on the one hand, and the notes from 1881–1882 on the other, at least tell us what the eternal return is *not* according to Nietzsche. It is not a cycle. It does not presuppose the One, the Same, the Equal or equilibrium. It is not the return of All. It is not the return of the Same. It thus has nothing in common with what is presumed to be ancient doctrine, the idea of a cycle that causes everything to come back, passing through a point of equilibrium, bringing the All back to the One, amounting to the Same. There you have "the same old song" or the "over-simplification": the eternal return as a physical transformation or an astronomical movement—the eternal return lived as though it were a natural animal certainty (such as the Clown or as Zarathoustra's animal sees it). We are all too familiar with the critique that Nietzsche, in all his work, brings to bear on the general notions of One, Same, Equal, and All. Still more to the point, the notes from 1881-1882 explicitly oppose the cyclical hypothesis; they exclude the presupposition of any state of equilibrium. These notes proclaim that All does not come back, because the eternal return is essentially *selective*, indeed selective par excellence. Furthermore, what happened in Zarathoustra's two moments, between the time when he was sick and when he was recovering? Why did the eternal return first inspire him with unbearable disgust and fear, which then disappear when he feels better? Are we to believe that Zarathoustra takes it on himself to shoulder what he could not bear a moment before? Obviously not; the change is not simply psychological. It's a "dramatic" progression in the very comprehension of the eternal return. What sickened Zarathoustra was the idea that the eternal return was in the end, in spite of everything, linked to a cycle; that it would cause everything to come back; that everything would come back, even humanity, "little humanity"... "The great disgust for the Human is what suffocated me and got stuck in my throat, and also what the seer predicted: All is equal... And the eternal return, of even the littlest thing, was the cause of my lassitude with all of existence."[9] If Zarathoustra feels better, it's because he understands that the eternal return is not that at all. He finally understands the unequal and the selection in the eternal return.

Essentially, the unequal, the different is the true rationale for the eternal return. It is because nothing is equal, or the same, that "it" comes back. In other words, the eternal return is predicated only of becoming and the multiple. It is the law of a world without being, without unity, without identity. Far from *presupposing* the One or the Same, the eternal return constitutes the only unity of the multiple as such, the only identity of what differs: coming back is the only "being" of becoming. Consequently, the function of the eternal return as Being is never to identify, but to authenticate. This explains why, each in his own way, Mr. Löwith, Wahl and Klossowski alluded to the selective signification of the eternal return.

This signification is double. First, the eternal return is selective of thought, because it eliminates "half-desires." A rule that is valid beyond good and evil. The eternal return gives us a parody of the Kantian imperative. Whatever you will, will it in such a way that you also will its eternal return...What falls away, what is annihilated as a result, is everything I feel, do or desire provided that it happen "once, only once." Imagine laziness that willed its eternal return and stopped saying: "tomorrow I will get to work"—or cowardice, or abjection that willed its eternal return: clearly, we would find ourselves faced with forms as yet unknown and unexplored. These would no longer be what we usually call laziness or cowardice. And the fact that we have no idea of what they would be means only that extreme forms do not *preexist* the ordeal of the eternal return. The eternal return is indeed the category of the ordeal, and we must understand, as such, of events, of everything that happens. Misfortune, sickness, madness, even the approach of death have two aspects: in one sense, they separate me from my power; in another sense, they endow me with a strange power, as though I possessed a dangerous means of exploration, which is also a terrifying realm to explore. The function of the eternal return, in every case, is to separate the superior from the moderate means, the torrid or glacial zones from the temperate ones, the extreme powers from the middle states. The words "separate" or "extract" are not even adequate, since the eternal return *creates* the superior forms. It is in this sense that the eternal return is the instrument and the expression of the will to power: it raises each thing to its superior form, that is, its *nth* power.

This creative selection does not happen only in the thought of the eternal return. It happens in being: being is selective, being is selection. There is no way to believe that the eternal return causes everything to come back, and back to the same, since it eliminates everything that cannot withstand the ordeal: not only the "half-desires" in thought, but the half-powers in being. "Little humanity" will not come back…nothing that denies the eternal return will be able to come back. If we insist on thinking of the eternal return as the movement of a wheel, we must nevertheless endow it with a centrifugal movement, by means of which it expulses everything which is too weak, too moderate, to withstand the ordeal. What the eternal return produces, and causes to come back in correspondence with the will to power, is the Superman, defined as "the superior form of everything that *is*." The superman very much resembles the poet as Rimbaud defines it: one who is "loaded with humanity, even with animals," and who in every case has retained only the superior form, and the extreme power. Everywhere, the eternal return undertakes to authenticate: not to identify the same, but to authenticate desires, masks and roles, forms and powers.

Mr. Birault was therefore right to remind us that according to Nietzsche, there is a difference of nature between extreme and middle forms. The same goes for the Nietzschean distinction between the creation of values and the recognition of current values. This distinction would make no sense if we interpreted it from the perspectives offered by historical relativism: those values currently recognized would have been new values in their day; and the new values would have been called on in turn to become current. Such an interpretation would miss what is most essential. We already saw it in the will to power: there exists a difference of nature between "attributing current values to oneself" and "creating new values." This difference between them is the very difference of the eternal return, that which constitutes the essence of the eternal return: viz., "new" values are precisely those superior forms of everything that is. Some values, then, are born current and appear only by soliciting an order of recognition, even if they must await favorable historical conditions to be, in effect, recognized. On the other hand, some values are eternally new, forever untimely, always contemporary with their creation, and these, even when they seem established, apparently assimilated by a society, in fact address themselves to other forces, soliciting from within that society anarchic forces of another nature. Such values alone are trans-historical, supra-historical, and bear witness to a congenial chaos, a creative disorder that is irreducible to any order whatsoever. It is this chaos of which Nietzsche spoke when he said it was not the contrary of the eternal return, but the eternal return in person. The great creations depart from this supra-historical stratum, this "untimely" chaos, at the extreme limit of what is livable.

This is why Mr. Beaufret questioned the notion of value, asking himself to what extent value was apt to manifest this stratum without which there is no ontology. This is also why Mr. Vattimo underlined the existence of a chaotic depth in Nietzsche, without which the creation of values would lose their sense. But concrete examples had to be provided, we wanted to show how artists and thinkers come together in this dimension. Hence the fifth theme of our colloquium. Certainly, in this respect, when Nietzsche was confronted by other authors, he must have been influenced by some of them. But there was always something else at stake. So, when Mr. Foucault confronted Nietzsche with Freud and Marx, independently of any influence, he was careful not to choose a theme such as the commonly shared "recognition" of the unconscious by the three authors; on the contrary, he considered that the discovery of an unconscious depends on something more profound, on a fundamental change in interpretive demands, a change that itself implies a particular evaluation of the "madness" of the world and men. Mr. de Schloezer spoke of Nietzsche and Dostoïevsky; Mr. Gaede, of French literature; Mr. Reichert, of German literature and Hermann Hesse; Mr. Grlic, of art and poetry. What we saw in every case, regardless of any actual influence, was how one thinker could encounter another, meet up with another in a dimension that is no longer that of chronology or history (much less the dimension of eternity; Nietzsche would call it the dimension of the untimely).

A special thanks to Mr. Goldbeck, and to Ms. de Sabran, who played the *Manfred* score, and to ORTF for letting us hear the melodies of Nietzsche;

thanks to them we experienced an aspect of Nietzsche little known in France: Nietzsche-as-musician. In different ways, Mr. Goldbeck, Gabriel Marcel, and Boris de Schloezer explained to us what seemed moving or interesting in this music. And the question occurred to us: what sort of mask was "Nietzsche-as-musician"? I hope you won't mind me formulating one last hypothesis: Nietzsche is perhaps deeply theatrical. He not only wrote a philosophy of the-atre (Dionysos), he also brought theatre into philosophy itself. And with it, he brought new means of expression to transform philosophy. How many apho-risms must be understood as the principles and evaluations of a *director*? Nietzsche conceives Zarathoustra completely in philosophy, but also com-pletely for the stage. He dreams of putting Zarathoustra to Bizet's music, as a form of derisive Wagnerian theatre. He dreams of a music, as he does of a mask, for "his own" philosophical theatre, which is already a theatre of cruel-ty, a theatre of the will to power and the eternal return.

Nietzsche's Burst of Laughter[1]

[How was the new edition of Nietzsche's *Complete Philosophical Works* established?][2]

Gilles Deleuze: The problem was to reclassify the posthumous notes—the *Nachlass*—in accordance with the dates Nietzsche had written them, and to place them after the works with which they were contemporaneous. Some of them had been used in an abusive way after Nietzsche's death to compose *The Will to Power*. So it was essential to reestablish the exact chronology. This explains why the first volume, *The Gay Science*, is more than half composed of previously unpublished fragments dating from 1881–1882. Our conception of Nietzsche's thought as well as his creative process may be profoundly altered as a result. The new edition will appear simultaneously in Italy, Germany, and France. But we owe the texts to the work of two Italians, Colli and Montinari.

Guy Dumur: How do you explain that Italians rather than Germans did the job?

Gilles Deleuze: Maybe the Germans were not in a good position to do it. They already had numerous editions, which they were fond of, despite the arbitrary organization of the notes. Also, Nietzsche's manuscripts were in Weimar, East Germany—where the Italians were better received than any West German could have hoped to be. Finally, the Germans were undoubtedly embarrassed at having accepted the edition of *The Will to Power* created by Nietzsche's sister. Elizabeth Forster-Nietzsche put together an extremely harmful work that privileges many Nazi interpretations. She didn't falsify the texts, but we know well enough that there are other ways to distort an author's thinking, even if it is merely an arbitrary selection from among his papers. Nietzschean concepts like those of "force" or "master" are complex enough to be betrayed by a selection such as hers.

Guy Dumur: Will the translations be new?

Gilles Deleuze: Completely new. This is especially important for those writings toward the end (there have been some poor readings, for which Elizabeth Nietzsche and Peter Gast are responsible). The first two volumes to be published, *The Gay Science* and *Human, All Too Human*, have been translated by Pierre Klossowski and Robert Rovini. This doesn't mean that the prior translations by Henri Albert, and by Geneviève Bianquis, were bad—not at all. But if they were determined to publish Nietzsche's notes with his works, they had to begin from scratch and unify the terminology. On that note, interestingly enough, Nietzsche was first introduced in France not by the "right," but by Charles Andler and Henri Albert, who represented a whole socialist tradition with anarchical colorings.

Guy Dumur: Do you think a "return to Nietzsche" is taking place in France today? And if so, why is it?

Gilles Deleuze: It's difficult to say. Maybe there has been a change, or maybe the change is taking place now, with respect to the modes of thought which have been so familiar to us since the Liberation. We were used to thinking dialectically, historically. Today it seems the tide has turned from dialectical thinking toward structuralism, for example, as well as other systems of thought.

Foucault insists on the importance of the techniques of interpretation. It's possible that in the actual idea of interpretation is something which goes beyond the dialectical opposition between "knowing" and "transforming" the world. Freud is the great interpreter, so is Nietzsche, but in a different way. Nietzsche's idea is that things and actions are already interpretations. So to interpret is to interpret interpretations, and thus to change things, "to change life." What is clear for Nietzsche is that society cannot be an ultimate authority. The ultimate authority is creation, it is art: or rather, art represents the absence and the impossibility of an ultimate authority. From the very beginning of his work, Nietzsche posits that there exist ends "just a little higher" than those of the State, than those of society. He inserts his entire corpus in a dimension which is neither historical, even understood dialectically, nor eternal. What he calls this new dimension which operates both in time and against time is *the untimely*. It is in this that life as interpretation finds its source. Maybe the reason for the "return to Nietzsche" is a rediscovery of the untimely, that dimension which is distinct both from classical philosophy in its "timeless" enterprise and from dialectical philosophy in its understanding of history: a singular element of upheaval.

Guy Dumur: Could we then say this is a return to individualism?

Gilles Deleuze: Yes, but a bizarre individualism, in which modern consciousness undoubtedly recognizes itself to some degree. Because in Nietzsche, this individualism is accompanied by a lively critique of the notions of "self" and "I." For Nietzsche there is a kind of dissolution of the self. The reaction against oppressive structures is no longer done, for him, in the name of a "self" or an "I." On the contrary, it is as though the "self" and the "I" were accomplices of those structures.

Must we say that the return to Nietzsche implies a kind of estheticism, a renunciation of politics, an "individualism" as depersonalized as it is depoliticized? Maybe not. Politics, too, is in the business of interpretation. *The untimely*, which we just discussed, is never reducible to the political-historical element. But it happens from time to time that, at certain great moments, they coincide. When people die of hunger in India, such a disaster is political-historical. But when the people struggle for their liberation, there is always a coincidence of poetic acts and historical events or political actions, the glorious incarnation of something sublime or untimely. Such great coincidences are Nasser's burst of laughter when he nationalized Suez, or Castro's gestures, and that other burst of laughter, Giap's television interview. Here we have something that reminds us of Rimbaud's or Nietzsche's imperatives and which puts one over on Marx—an artistic joy that comes to coincide with historical struggle. There are creators in politics, and creative movements, that are poised for a moment in history. Hitler, on the contrary, lacked to a singular degree any Nietzschean element. Hitler is not Zarathoustra. Nor is Trujillo. They represented what Nietzsche calls "the monkey of Zarathoustra." As Nietzsche said, if one wants to be "a master," it is not enough to come to power. More often than not it is the "slaves" who come to power, and who keep it, and who remain slaves while they keep it.

The masters according to Nietzsche are *the untimely*, those who create, who destroy in order to create, not to preserve. Nietzsche says that under the huge earth-shattering events are tiny silent events, which he likens to the creation of new worlds: there once again you see the presence of the poetic under the historical. In France, for instance, there are no earth-shattering events right now. They are far away, and horrible, in Vietnam. But we still have tiny imperceptible events, which maybe announce an exodus from today's desert. Maybe the return to Nietzsche is one of those "tiny events" and already a reinterpretation of the world.

Mysticism and Masochism[1]

Madeleine Chapsal: How did you come to be interested in Sacher-Masoch?

Gilles Deleuze: I always felt Masoch was a great novelist. I was struck by the injustice of reading so much Sade, but never Masoch: people make him out to be a pathetic, reverse Sade.

Madeleine Chapsal: His work is hardly translated...

Gilles Deleuze: No, no, it was very much translated toward the end of the nine-teenth-century and was well-known, but for political and folkloric reasons rather than sexual ones. His work is connected to the political and national movements of central Europe, to pan-Slavism. Masoch is as inseparable from the revolutions of '48 in the Austrian Empire, as Sade from the French Revolution. The types of sexual minorities that Masoch imagines refer in a rather complex way to the national minorities of the Austrian Empire—just as the libertine minorities in Sade refer to pre-Revolutionary lodges and sects.

Madeleine Chapsal: When someone says Masoch, you say Sade...

Gilles Deleuze: Necessarily, because I want to dissociate their pseudo-identity! There are values that belong specifically to Masoch, even if these were only on the level of literary technique. There are specifically masochistic processes inde-pendent of any reversal or turning by sadism. But, interestingly, the sado-masochistic unity goes without saying, whereas in my view they have entire-ly different esthetic and pathological mechanisms. Even Freud himself invents nothing new here: his genius set about inventing the passageways of transforma-tion from the one to the other, but never questioned the unity itself. In any event, perversion is the least studied domain in psychiatry: it's not a therapeutic concept.

Madeleine Chapsal: How do you explain that it is not psychiatrists but writers, Sade and Masoch, who are the experts in the domain of perversion?

Gilles Deleuze: Perhaps there are three different medical acts: symptomology, or the study of signs; etiology, or the search for causes; and therapeutics, or the search for and application of a treatment. Whereas etiology and therapeutics are integral parts of medicine, symptomology appeals to a kind of neutral point, a limit that is premedical or sub-medical, belonging as much to art as to medicine: it's all about drawing a "portrait." The work of art exhibits symptoms, as do the body or the soul, albeit in a very different way. In this sense, the artist or writer can be a great symptomologist, just like the best doctor: so it is with Sade or Masoch.

Madeleine Chapsal: Why only them?

Gilles Deleuze: Not only them. There are of course others whose work hasn't yet been recognized as a creative symptomology, as in the case of Masoch. Samuel Beckett's work is an extraordinary portrait of symptoms: it's not just about identifying an illness, but about the world as symptom, and the artist as symptomologist.

Madeleine Chapsal: Now that you mention it, we might say the same thing about Kafka's work or the work of Marguerite Duras...

Gilles Deleuze: Absolutely.

Madeleine Chapsal: Not to mention that Jacques Lacan expressed his appreciation of *The Ravishing of Lol Stein* and told Marguerite Duras that he saw in it the exact, troubling description of particular manias found in the clinic... But certainly that is not the case with the work of every writer.

Gilles Deleuze: No, of course not. What properly belongs to Sade, Masoch and a few others (for example, Robbe-Grillet or Klossowski) is making the phantasm itself the object of their work, whereas usually it is only the origin of the work. What literary creation and the constitution of symptoms have in common is the phantasm. Masoch calls it "the figure" and in fact says "one must go beyond the living figure to the problem." If the phantasm for most writers is the source of the work, for those writers who interests me it is precisely the phantasm that is at stake in the work and has the last word, as if the whole work reflected its origin.

Madeleine Chapsal: Do you think we may one day speak of kafkaism or beckettism the way we speak of sadism or masochism?

Gilles Deleuze: I suppose so... But just like Sade and Masoch, these writers will not lose one bit of their esthetic "universality" for it.

Madeleine Chapsal: How do you see the kind of work you did in your *Présentation de Sacher-Masoch*? What I mean is, what was your particular objective: literary criticism, psychiatry?

Gilles Deleuze: What I would like to do (and this book would be only a preliminary study) is articulate a relation between literature and clinical psychology. There is an urgent need for clinical psychology to keep away from sweeping unities accomplished through "reversals" and "transformations": the idea of a sado-masochism is simply a prejudice. (There is a sadism of the masochist, but this sadism is well within masochism and is not true sadism: the same goes for the masochism of the sadist). This prejudice results from hasty symptomology, such that we no longer attempt *to see* what is there, but seek instead to justify our prior idea. Freud himself experienced this difficulty, for example, in his admirable *A Child is Being Beaten*,[2] and yet he still didn't seek to question the theme of sado-masochistic unity. So it does happen that a writer can go farther in symptomology, that the work of art gives him a new means—perhaps also because the writer is less concerned with causes.

Madeleine Chapsal: Freud nonetheless respected the clinical genius of writers, often looking to literary works to confirm his psychoanalytic theories...

Gilles Deleuze: Very much so, but he didn't do it for Sade or Masoch. All too often the writer is still considered as one more case added to clinical psychology, when the important thing is what the writer himself, as a creator, brings to clinical psychology. The difference between literature and clinical psychology, and this makes an illness not the same thing as a work of art, is the kind of *work* done on the phantasm. In each case, the source is the same: it's the phantasm. But from there the work is quite different, even incommensurate, between the work of the artist and the work of pathology. Very often the writer goes farther than the clinician and even the patient. Masoch, for example, is the first and only person to say and to show that the essence of masochism is the contract, a special contractual relation.

Madeleine Chapsal: The only person?

Gilles Deleuze: I've never seen this symptom—the need to establish a contract—counted as an element of masochism. In this instance, Masoch went farther than the clinicians, who afterwards failed to take account of his discovery. Masochism can be considered from three different points of view: 1) as an alliance between pleasure and pain, 2) as a way to act out humiliation and slavery, and 3) as slavery instituted within a contractual relation. This third characteristic is perhaps the most profound, and so it should account for the others.

Madeleine Chapsal: You're not a psychoanalyst, you're a philosopher. Do you have reservations about venturing out on psychoanalytic terrain?

Gilles Deleuze: Sure I do, it's a delicate matter. I would never have allowed myself to talk about psychoanalysis and psychiatry if this were not a question of symptomology. Precisely, symptomology is located almost outside medicine, at a neutral point, a zero point, where artists and philosophers and doctors and patients can come together.

Madeleine Chapsal: How did you settle on *Venus in Furs* for your book?

Gilles Deleuze: Masoch has written three especially beautiful books: *La Mère de Dieu*, *Pêcheuse d'âmes*, and *Venus in Furs*. I had to choose, and I thought the book best able to introduce someone to Masoch's work would be *Venus*, since its themes are purest and simplest. In the other two, mystical sects are mixed up with exercises that are properly masochist. But new editions of these works would be much welcomed.[3]

Madeleine Chapsal: One other thing concerning Masoch, something that you wrote in your previous work, *Proust and Signs*: you say that the essence of any great work of art is comic, and that it is a misreading to be satisfied with tragic first impressions. Specifically, on Kafka, you write: *"This pseudo-sense of the tragic make us stupid. How many authors we deface by substituting a puerile, tragic feeling for the aggressive, comic power of the thought which animates their work."*

Gilles Deleuze: Yes, the essence of art is a kind of joy, and this is the very point of art. There can be no tragic work because there is a necessary joy in creation: art is necessarily a liberation that explodes everything, first and foremost the tragic. No, there is no unhappy creation, it is always a *vis comica*. Nietzsche said: "the tragic hero is happy." So is the masochist hero, in his own way, which is inseparable from Masoch's own literary techniques.

On Nietzsche and the Image of Thought[1]

Jean-Noël Vuarnet: Gallimard's reedition of Nietzsche's complete works has started to appear on the shelves. You and Foucault have been credited with "responsibility" for the first volume.[2] What exactly was your role?

Gilles Deleuze: We played a small role. You are no doubt well aware that the whole point of this edition is to publish all posthumous notes, many of which have never seen the light of day, by distributing them chronologically in the order of the books that Nietzsche himself published. Accordingly, *The Gay Science*, translated by Klossowski, includes the posthumous notes of 1881-1882. The authors of this edition are, on the one hand, Colli and Montinari, to whom we are indebted for the texts, and on the other, the translators, for whom Nietzsche's style and techniques have posed enormous problems. We were responsible only for grouping the texts in order.

Jean-Noël Vuarnet: In *Nietzsche and Philosophy*, you write that his project in the most general sense is to bring the concepts of sense and value into philosophy, and that *"it goes without saying that modern philosophy has for the most part lived off and still lives off Nietzsche."* How should we interpret these declarations?

Gilles Deleuze: They have to be understood in two ways: negatively as well as positively.

But first there is this fact: Nietzsche questions the concept of truth, he denies that the true can be an element of language. What he is contesting is the very notions of true and false. Not because he wants to "relativize" them like an ordinary skeptic. In their place he substitutes sense and value as rigorous notions: the sense of what one says, and the evaluation of the one saying it. You always get the truth you deserve according to the sense of what you say, and according to the values *to which you give voice*. This presupposes a radically new conception of thought and language, because sense and value, signification and evaluation, bring into play mechanisms of the unconscious. It thus goes without saying that Nietzsche leads philosophy and thought in general into a new element. What is more, this element implies not only new ways of thinking and "judging," but also new ways of writing, and maybe acting.

In this respect, modern philosophy has been and is clearly Nietzschean, because it never tires of discussing sense and value. Of course, other very different and no less essential influences must be added here: the Marxist conception of value, the Freudian conception of sense—they turned everything upside down. But the fact that modern philosophy has found the source of its renewal in the Nietzsche-Marx-Freud trinity is indeed rather ambiguous and equivocal. Because it can be interpreted positively as well as negatively. For example, after the war, philosophies of value were in vogue. Everyone was talking about values, and they wanted "axiology" to replace both ontology and the theory of knowledge…But it wasn't the least bit Nietzschean or Marxist in inspiration. On the contrary, no one talked about Nietzsche or Marx at all, no one knew them, and they didn't want to know them. What they made of "value" was a place to resurrect the most traditional, abstract spiritualism imaginable: they called on values in order to inspire a new conformity which they believed was better suited to the modern world, you know, the respect for values, etc. For Nietzsche, as well as for Marx, the notion of value is strictly inseparable 1) from a radical and total critique of society and the world (look at the theme of the "fetish" in Marx, or the theme of "idols" in Nietzsche), and 2) from a creation no less radical: Nietzsche's trans-valuation, and Marx's revolutionary action. So, in the post-war context, everyone was all for using a concept of value, but they had completely neutralized it; they had subtracted all critical or creative sense from it. What they made of it was an instrument of established values. It was pure anti-Nietzsche—even worse, it was Nietzsche hijacked, annihilated, suppressed, it was Nietzsche brought back to Sunday mass.

But such misappropriations cannot last for long, since there is something in the Nietzschean notion of value to explode all recognized, established values, something to create, in a state of permanent creation, new things that escape all recognition and every establishment. There you have a positive getting back to Nietzsche, how to philosophize with a hammer: never what is known, but a great destruction of the known, for the creation of the unknown.

Jean-Noël Vuarnet: If I follow you, you're saying that the notions of sense and value come to us from Nietzsche, Marx, and Freud, though they are always in danger of being hijacked by serving the rebirth of a spiritualism that they were supposed to destroy—and that they are once again finding their way back, coming into their own today by energizing works that are both critical and creative. So much for the notion of value, can the same thing be said of sense?

Gilles Deleuze: Absolutely, even more so. The notion of sense can also be the refuge of a renascent spiritualism: what is sometimes called "hermeneutics" (interpretation) has taken up the slack of what was called "axiology" (evaluation) after the war. The Nietzschean or, in this case, Freudian notion of sense is just as much in danger of being misappropriated. You hear everyone talking about "sense": original sense, forgotten sense, erased sense, veiled sense, reemployed sense, etc. All the old mirages are just rebaptized under the category of sense; Essence is being revived, with all its sacred and religious values. In Nietzsche and Freud, it's the exact opposite; the notion of sense is an instrument of absolute contestation, absolute critique, and also specific creation: sense is not a reservoir, not a principle or an origin, not even an end, it's an "effect," an effect *produced*, whose laws of production must be uncovered. Look at the preface which J.-P. Osier just did for the book by Feuerbach he translated:[3] Osier indeed distinguishes between these two conceptions of sense and has a real boundary, from the point of view of philosophy, pass between them. This is one of structuralism's essential ideas, unifying authors as different as Lévi-Strauss, Lacan, Foucault, and Althusser: the idea of sense as an effect produced by a specific machinery, a physical, optic, sonorous effect, etc. (And this is not the same thing as an appearance.) Well, an aphorism by Nietzsche is a sense-producing machine, in that order specific to thought. Of course, there are other orders, other machineries—for example, those which Freud discovered, and others still that are political or practical in nature. But we must become machinists, "operators."

Jean-Noël Vuarnet: How would you define the problems of contemporary philosophy?

Gilles Deleuze: Perhaps in the way I just described it, using the notions of sense and value. Many things are happening in philosophy right now, it's a confused and rich period. No one believes any more in the I, the Self, in characters or persons. This is quite clear in literature. But it goes even deeper: what I mean is, many people have spontaneously stopped thinking in terms of I and Self. For a long time philosophy offered you a particular alternative: God or man—or in philosophical jargon: infinite substance or the finite subject. None of that is very important any more: the death of God, the possibility of replacing God with humanity, all the God-Human permutations, etc. It's like Foucault said, we are no more human than God, the one dies with the other. Nor can we remain satisfied with the opposition between a pure universal and particularities enclosed within persons, individuals, or Selves. We can't let ourselves be satisfied with that, especially if the two terms are to be reconciled, or completed by one another. What we're uncovering right now, in my opinion, is a world packed with *impersonal individuations*, or even *pre-individual singularities* (that's what Nietzsche means when he says: "neither God nor man," it's anarchy triumphant).

137

The new novelists talk of nothing else: they give voice to these non-personal individuations, these non-individual singularities.

But most importantly, all this corresponds to something happening in the contemporary world. Individuation is no longer enclosed in a word. Singularity is no longer enclosed in an individual. This is really important, especially politically; it's like the "fish dissolved in water"; it's the revolutionary struggle, the struggle for liberation… And in our wealthy societies, the many and various forms of non-integration, the different forms of refusal by young people today, are perhaps manifestations of it. You see, the forces of repression always need a Self that can be assigned, they need determinate individuals on which to exercise their power. When we become the least bit fluid, when we slip away from the assignable Self, when there is no longer any person on whom God can exercise his power or by whom He can be replaced, the police lose it. This is not theory. All the stuff going on as we speak is what matters. We can't dismiss the upheavals troubling the younger generation just by saying: oh, they'll grow out of it. It's difficult, of course, sometimes worrisome, but it's also really joyful, because they're creating something, accompanied by the confusion and suffering that attends any practical creation, I think.

Well then, philosophy, too, must create worlds of thought, a whole new conception of thought, of "what it means to think," and it must be adequate to what is happening around us. It must adopt as its own those revolutions going on elsewhere, in other domains, or those that are being prepared. Philosophy is inseparable from "critique." Only, there are two ways of going about it. On the one hand, you criticize "false applications": false morality, false knowledge, false religions, etc. This is how Kant, for instance, thinks of his famous "Critique": ideal knowledge, true morality, and faith come out perfectly intact. On the other hand, you have this other family of philosophers who subject true morality, true faith, and ideal knowledge to comprehensive criticism, in the pursuit of something else, as a function of a new image of thought. As long as we're content with criticizing the "false," we're not bothering anyone (true critique is the criticism of true forms, not false contents. You don't criticize capitalism or imperialism by denouncing their "mistakes"). This other family of philosophers includes Lucretius, Spinoza, Nietzsche—an incredible lineage in philosophy, a broken line, explosive, totally volcanic.

Jean-Noël Vuarnet: You've written books on Hume, Nietzsche, Kant, Bergson, Proust, Masoch. Can you explain these successive choices, do they somehow converge? And don't you have a particular interest in Nietzsche?

Gilles Deleuze: Oh yes, for reasons that I have been trying to explain: Nietzsche is not at all the inventor of the famous phrase "God is dead." On the contrary, he is the first to believe this phrase to have no importance whatsoever as long as the human occupies the place of God. Nietzsche was trying to uncover something that was neither God nor Human, trying to give voice to these impersonal individuations and these pre-individual singularities…that's what he calls Dionysos, or also the super-man. It is his particular philosophical and literary genius to have found the techniques to give them voice. Nietzsche says of the super-man: it's the superior kind of everything that is, including animals—like Rimbaud says, "he is loaded with humanity, even animals…."[4] Consequently, Nietzsche reinvents that total critique which is at the same time a creation, total positivity.

The other books I've done for different reasons. Kant, for example, is the perfect incarnation of false critique: that's why he fascinates me. But when you're facing such a work of genius, there's no point saying you disagree. First you have to know how to admire; you have to rediscover the problems *he* poses, his particular machinery. It is through admiration that you will come to genuine critique. The mania of people today is not knowing how to admire anything: either they're "against," or they situate everything at their own level while they chit-chat and scrutinize. That's no way to go about it. You have to work your way back to those problems which an author of genius has posed, all the way back to that which he does not say *in* what he says, in order to extract something that still belongs to him, though you also turn it against him. You have to be inspired, visited by the geniuses you denounce.

Jules Vallès says that a revolutionary must first know how to admire and respect: this is an extraordinary remark, practically speaking. Look at cinema, for example. When Jerry Lewis or Tati "criticize" modern life, they don't have the complacency, the vulgarity to show us ugly things. What they criticize, they show as *beautiful*, as *magnificent*: they love what they criticize and give it a new beauty. Their critique is only the more forceful. In every modernity and every novelty, you find conformity and creativity; an insipid conformity, but also "a little new music"; something in conformity with the time, but also something untimely—separating the one from the other is the task of those who know how to love, the real destroyers and creators of our day. Good destruction requires love.

Hume, Bergson, and Proust interest me so much because in their work can be found profound elements for a new image of thought. There's something extraordinary in the way they tell us: thinking means something else than what you believe. We live with a particular image of thought, that is to say, before we begin to think, we have a vague idea of what it means to think, its means and ends. And then someone comes along and proposes another idea, a whole other image. Proust, for example, has the idea that every thought is an aggression, appearing under the constraint of a sign, and that we think only when we are forced and constrained to think. From then on, thought is no longer carried on by a voluntary self, but by involuntary forces, the "effects" of machines…Still, you have to be able to love the insignificant, to love what goes beyond persons and individuals; you have to open yourself to encounters and find a language in the singularities that exceed individuals, a language in the individuations that exceed persons. Yes, what we're looking for these days is a new image of the act of thought, its functioning, its genesis in thought itself.

Jean-Noël Vuarnet: Would this quote taken from your book on Proust sum up your thinking here: *"There is no logos, there are only hieroglyphs"*? Elsewhere, speaking of Masoch, you said the artist was *"a symptomologist,"* indicating that *"etiology, the scientific or experimental part of medicine, must make room for symptomology, which is the literary or artistic part."* Is this the same problem in each case?

Gilles Deleuze: It's the same problem: hieroglyphs vs. the logos, symptoms vs. essences (symptom here means events, drops, encounters, aggressions). The artist is a symptomologist. In the sense that characters from Shakespeare say: how *goes* it with the world? With all the psychological and political implications such a question entails. Nazism is a recent disease on this earth. And what the Americans are doing in Vietnam is yet another disease. The world can be treated as a symptom and searched for signs of disease, signs of life, signs of a cure, signs of health. And sometimes a violent reaction is a sign of a robust health returning. Nietzsche thought of the philosopher as the physician of civilization. Henry Miller was an extraordinary diagnostician. The artist in general must treat the world as a symptom, and build his work not like a therapeutic, but in every case like a clinic. The artist is not outside the symptoms, but makes a work of art from them, which sometimes serves to precipitate them, and sometimes to transform them.

Jean-Noël Vuarnet: Here is something you wrote somewhere: *"The physiologist, the physician is an interpreter, one who considers phenomena as symptoms and speaks in aphorisms. The artist evaluates, both considering and creating perspectives, and speaks in poems. The philosopher of the future is both artist and physician—in a word, a legislator...."* It has always struck me that most of those philosophers inspired by Nietzsche's thought, paradoxically, write in an almost traditional form. It seems to me that the structure of some of your books (which one could perhaps qualify as a mosaic structure) is moving toward inventing a new language for philosophy today. How should we interpret the clear interest you have in literature?

Gilles Deleuze: As you are no doubt aware, the problem of formal renewal can be posed only when the content is new. Sometimes, even, the formal renewal comes after. It is what one has to say, what one thinks one has to say, that imposes new forms. Now philosophy, it's true, is nothing spectacular. Philosophy has not at all undergone similar revolutions or experiments as those produced in science, painting, sculpture, music, or literature. Plato, Kant, and the rest—they remain fundamental, and that's fine. I mean, non-Euclidean geometries don't keep Euclid from being fundamental to geometry. Schoenberg doesn't nullify Mozart. Similarly, the search for modes of expression (both a new image of thought and new techniques) must be essential for philosophy. Beckett's complaint: "Ah, the old style!" takes on its full significance here. We get the feeling that we can't go on writing philosophy books in the old style much longer; they no longer interest the students, they don't even interest their authors. So, I think everyone is on the look-out for something new. Nietzsche discovered extraordinary methods, but you can't do it over again. You really have to be an impudent bastard to write *Fruits of the Earth* after *Thus Spoke Zarathustra*.

The novel discovered its own renewal. It matters little that some people reproach the *nouveau roman* for being experimental or laboratory work. Those "books written against something" have never amounted to much (against the *nouveau roman*, against structuralism, etc.). It is only in the name of new creation that you can oppose, and then you have other things to think about. Let's take an example from cinema: Godard transforms cinema by introducing thought into it. He didn't have thoughts *on* cinema, he doesn't put more or less valid thought *into* cinema; he starts cinema thinking, and for the first time, if I'm not mistaken. Theoretically, Godard would be capable of filming Kant's *Critique* or Spinoza's *Ethics*, and it wouldn't be abstract cinema or a cinematographic application. Godard knew how to find both a new means and a new "image"—which necessarily presupposes a revolutionary content. So, in philosophy, we're all experiencing this problem of formal renewal. It's certainly possible. It begins with little things. For example, using the history of philosophy as a "collage" (already an old technique in painting) would not in the least diminish the great philosophers of the past—making a collage at the heart of a properly philosophical picture. That would be better than "selections," but it would require particular techniques. You would need some Max Ernsts in philosophy… Also, the medium in philosophy is the concept (like sound for the musician or color for the painter), the philosopher creates concepts. He executes his creation in a conceptual "continuum" just like the musician does in a sonorous continuum. What's important here is this: where do concepts come from? What is the creation of concepts? A concept exists no less than characters do. In my opinion, what we need is a massive expenditure of concepts, an excess of concepts. You have to present concepts in philosophy as though you were writing a good detective novel: they must have a zone of presence, resolve a local situation, be in contact with the "dramas," and bring a certain cruelty with them. They must exhibit a certain coherence but get it from somewhere else. Samuel Butler coined a fabulous word to designate those stories that seem to come from elsewhere: EREWHON, it's both 'no-where,' the nowhere of origins, and 'now-here,' the here and now turned upside down, displaced, disguised. This is the genius of empiricism, which is so poorly understood: the creation of concepts in the wild, speaking in the name of a coherence which is not their own, nor that of God, nor that of the Self, but a coherence always on the way, always in disequilibrium with itself. What philosophy lacks is empiricism.

Jean-Noël Vuarnet: They say you're now working on a book centered around the concept of repetition. How does this concept affect the human sciences, literature, or philosophy?

Gilles Deleuze: Yes, I finished the book—on repetition and difference (they're the same thing) as the actual categories of our thought. It's the problem of repetitions and constants, but also the problem of masks, disguises, displacements, and variations in repetition. These themes must mean something to our time if philosophers and novelists keep circling around them. People usually think about these themes quite independently of one another. But there's nothing quite so festive as a popular tune, is there? It's also one of my themes, rather involuntarily, just something that preoccupies me. Without trying to, I've been looking for it in all the writers I've loved. There are many recent excellent studies on the concepts of difference and repetition. So why not join in? Why not like so many others ask the question: What are we doing in philosophy? We're looking for "vitality." Even psychoanalysis needs to address a certain "vitality" in the patient, which the patient has lost, but which the analyst has lost, too. Philosophical vitality is not far off, nor is political vitality. Many things, many decisive repetitions and many changes are not far off.

Gilles Deleuze Talks Philosophy[1]

Jeanette Colombel: You just published two books, *Difference and Repetition* and *Spinoza and the Problem of Expression*. And a still more recent work, *The Logic of Sense*, will come out very soon. Who speaks in these books?

Gilles Deleuze: Whenever we write, we speak as someone else. And it is a particular form that speaks through us. In the classical world, for example, what speaks is the individual. The classical world is entirely founded on the form of individuality; the individual is coextensive with being (we see this in God's position as the individuated sovereign being). In the romantic world, it is persons who speak, and this is quite different: the person is defined as coextensive with representation. These were new values in language and life. Spontaneity today perhaps escapes the individual as much as the person, and not simply because of anonymous powers. For a long time we were stuck with the alternative: either you are persons or individuals, or you sink back into an undifferentiated sea of anonymity. Today, however, we are uncovering a world of pre-individual, impersonal singularities. They are not reducible to individuals or persons, nor to a sea without difference. These singularities are mobile, they break in, thieving and stealing away, alternating back and forth, like anarchy crowned, inhabiting a nomad space. There is a big difference between partitioning a fixed space among sedentary individuals according to boundaries or enclosures, and distributing singularities in an open space without enclosures or properties. The poet Ferlinghetti talks about the fourth person singular: it is that to which we try to give voice.

Jeanette Colombel: Is that how you see the philosophers you interpret, as singularities in an open space? To this day, I have always wanted to compare what you do to what a stage director does when he illuminates the written dramatic text. In *Difference and Repetition*, however, the comparison has been displaced: you're no longer an interpreter, you're a creator. Is this comparison still valid? Or is the role of the history of philosophy different? Is the history of philosophy the "collage" you are after, the "collage" that renews the landscape, or is it the "citation" integrated into the text?

Gilles Deleuze: Yes, philosophers often have a difficult time with the history of philosophy; it's horrible, it's not easy to put behind you. Perhaps a good way of dealing with the problem is, as you say, to substitute a kind of staging for it. Staging means that the written text is going to be illuminated by other values, non-textual values (at least in the ordinary sense): it is indeed possible to substitute for the history of philosophy a theatre of philosophy. You say I have sought another technique, closer to collage than to theatre, for my conception of difference. The kind of collage technique or even the genesis of series (repetition with slight variations) which you see in Pop Art. But you also thought I wasn't entirely successful. I believe I go farther in my book on the logic of sense.

Jeanette Colombel: What strikes me especially is the friendship you have for the authors you write about. Sometimes your reception seems too favorable even: for example, when you silence the conservative aspects of Bergson's thought. On the other hand, you are merciless with Hegel. Why is that?

Gilles Deleuze: If you don't admire something, if you don't love it, you have no reason to write a word about it. Spinoza or Nietzsche are philosophers whose critical and destructive powers are without equal, but this power always springs from affirmation, from joy, from a cult of affirmation and joy, from the exigency of life against those who would mutilate and mortify it. For me, that is philosophy itself. But you're asking me about two other philosophers. Precisely, by virtue of those criteria of staging or collage we just discussed, it seems admissible to extract from a philosophy considered conservative as a whole those singularities which are not really singularities: that is what I did for Bergsonism and its image of life, its image of liberty or mental illness. Why not Hegel? Well, somebody has to play the role of traitor. What is philosophically incarnated in Hegel is the enterprise to "burden" life, to overwhelm it with every burden, to reconcile life with the State and religion, to inscribe death in life—the monstrous enterprise to submit life to negativity, the enterprise of resentment and unhappy consciousness. Naturally, with this dialectic of negativity and contradiction, Hegel has inspired every language of betrayal, on the right as well as on the left (theology, spiritualism, technocracy, bureaucracy, etc.).

Jeanette Colombel: Your hatred of negativity leads you to show difference and contradiction as antagonistic. Certainly the symmetrical opposition of contraries in the Hegelian dialectic confirms your point, but is this relation the same for Marx? Why do you address this only in an allusive way? Your analysis, which is so fruitful, of the conflict-differences relation in Freud unmasks false symmetries: sadism/masochism, death instinct/death drive—couldn't one do the same for Marx?

Gilles Deleuze: You're right, but this liberation of Marx from Hegel, this reappropriation of Marx, this uncovering of differential and affirmative mechanisms in Marx, isn't this what Althusser is accomplishing so admirably? In any case, under the false opinions, under the false oppositions, you discover much more explosive systems, unsymmetrical wholes in disequilibrium (fetishes, for example, both economic and psychoanalytic).

Jeanette Colombel: One last question in connection with the "un-spoken" in Marx: I clearly see the link between your philosophy and play, and I understand its relationship to contestation. But can it have a political dimension and contribute to a revolutionary practice?

Gilles Deleuze: That's a tough question, I don't know. In the first place, there are relations of friendship or love that do not wait for the revolution, that do not prefigure it, although they are revolutionary on their own account: they have in them a contesting force which is proper to the poetic life, the beatniks for instance. They have more to do with Zen Buddhism than Marxism, but there are effective, explosive things in Zen. As for social relations, let's suppose that the task of philosophy in this or that era is to have a particular instance speak through it: the individual in the classical world, the person in the romantic world, or singularities in the modern world. Philosophy does not bring about the existence of these instances: it gives them voice through itself. But they do exist and are produced in history and themselves depend on social relations. Well then! Revolution would be the transformation of those relations corresponding to the development of this or that instance (such as the bourgeois individual in the "classical" revolution of 1789). The real problem of revolution, a revolution without bureaucracy, would be the problem of new social relations, where singularities come into play, active minorities in nomad space without property or enclosure.

Gueroult's General Method
for Spinoza[1]

M. Geuroult has published the first volume of his *Spinoza*, which focuses on Book I of the *Ethics*. It is too bad that the publisher has its own reasons for keeping the second volume, which is finished, from being released at this time, since the second volume promises to follow up the direct consequences of the first. One can nevertheless appreciate the importance of this first volume, from the perspective of Spinozism as well as the perspective of the general method developed by Gueroult.

Gueroult renewed the history of philosophy through a genetic-structural method which he had developed well before structuralism became fashionable in other disciplines. In Gueroult's method, a structure is defined by an *order of reasons*. Reasons are the differential and generative elements of the corresponding system; they are genuine philosophemes that exist only in relation to one another. Reasons are nonetheless quite different according to whether they are simple reasons of knowledge or genuine reasons of being—in other words, according to whether their order is analytic or synthetic, an order of knowledge vs. an order of production. It is only in the second case that the genesis of the system is also a genesis of things through and in the system. But we must be careful not to oppose the two systems in too summarily a fashion. When the reasons are reasons of knowledge, it is true that the method of invention is essentially analytical; synthesis, however, is integrated within it, either as a method of exposition, or more profoundly, because reasons of being are encountered in the order of reasons, but precisely that place assigned to them by the relation among elements of knowledge (e.g., Descartes's ontological proof). Conversely, in the other type of system, when the reasons are determined as reasons of being, it is true that the synthetic method becomes the real method of invention; however, since regressive analysis is destined to lead *as quickly as possible* to the determination of those elements which are reasons of being, it takes on meaning or sense at the very

146

point where it is relayed and even absorbed by progressive synthesis. The two types of systems can thus be distinguished structurally, that is to say, more profoundly than just by a simple opposition.

Gueroult demonstrated this already concerning Fichte's method, which is opposed to Kant's analytic method. The opposition is not comprised of a radical duality, but a particular reversal: the analytic process is not ignored or rejected by Fichte, but works to suppress itself. "As the principle tends to absorb it completely, the analytic process takes on an ever larger scale… At every moment, [*The Doctrine of Science*] affirms that, since the principle must stand alone, the analytic method must not pursue any end other than its own suppression. This means that the constructive method alone should be effective."[2] The deep Spinozism of Fichte leads us to think that an analogous problem may be posed concerning Spinoza himself, but in opposition to Descartes. Because it is literally false that Spinoza begins with the idea of God, in a synthetic process which is assumed to be ready-made. The *Treatise on the Reform of the Intellect* invites us to raise ourselves, beginning from any idea at all, *as quickly as possible* to the idea of God, where all fiction ceases, and where progressive genesis relays and in a way wards off, but does not suppress, the preliminary analysis. Nor does the *Ethics* begin with the idea of God; in the order of definitions, it comes in sixth place, and in the order of propositions, ninth and tenth place. Consequently, one of the fundamental problems of Gueroult's book can be formulated in this way: what exactly is going on in the first eight propositions?

The order of reasons is in no case a hidden order. It does not refer to a latent content, to something left unsaid; rather, the order of reasons is always on the same plane as the system (e.g. the order of reasons of knowledge in Descartes's *Meditationes*, or the order of reasons of being in Spinoza's *Ethics*). According to Gueroult, this is why the historian of philosophy is not an interpreter.[3] Structure is never something left unsaid which must be discovered beneath what is said; the structure can be discovered only by following the explicit order of the author. And yet, though always explicit and manifest, the structure is the most difficult thing to see: it goes unnoticed, neglected by the historian of ideas or other subjects. This is because structure is identical to the fact of saying, a pure philosophical given (*factum*), but which is constantly twisted by what one says, both the material treated and the ideas brought together. Seeing structure or the order of reasons is thus following the path along which the material is dissociated according to the demands of the order, and the ideas decomposed according to their generative differential elements, along which also the elements or reasons are organized into "series"; one must follow the chains to where independent series form a "*nexus*," the intersection of problems or solutions.[4]

Just as he followed Descartes's analytic geometric order step by step in the *Meditationes*, so Gueroult follows Spinoza's synthetic geometric order step by step in the *Ethics*: definitions, axioms, propositions, demonstrations, corollaries, scolia… And this procedure no longer has a simply didactic application, as it does in Lewis Robinson's commentary.[5] The reader has every right to expect: 1) the emergence of the structure of the Spinozist system, that is, the determination of the generative elements and kinds of relations they exhibit, the series into which they fall, and the "nexuses" between series (structure as *spritual automaton*); 2) the reasons why Spinoza's geometric method is strictly adequate to this structure, that is, how the structure effectively frees the geometric construction from the limits that affect it as long as it is applied to figures (beings of reason or imagination), and causes it to impact real beings by assigning the conditions of such an extension;[6] finally, and this is hardly a detail, 3) the reasons why a demonstration shows up in one particular place, is accompanied when necessary by other demonstrations to double it, and refers to this or that previous demonstration (when the impatient reader could imagine other filiations).[7] These last two aspects, concerning the proper method and the proper formalism of the system, derive directly from the structure.

Let's add a final theme: since the structure of the system is defined by an order or a space of coexistent reasons, we can ask what the proper history of the system, its internal evolution become. If Gueroult more often than not relegates such a study to appendices, it is not at all because it is negligible, nor because his book is meant to be a commentary on the *Ethics* as "masterpiece." Rather, an evolution—unless it is purely imaginary, arbitrarily fixed by the historian of ideas—can be deduced only from a rigorous comparison of the structural states of the system. Only the structural state of the *Ethics* enables one to decide, for example, whether the *Short Treatise* exhibits some other structure or simply another state less resonant with the same structure, and what is the importance of the revisions from the perspective of the generative elements and their relations. In general, a system evolves inasmuch as certain pieces change their position, in such a way that they cover a larger space than before, even while they more tightly control this space. However, it can happen that a system includes enough points of indetermination for several possible orders to coexist within it: Gueroult brilliantly showed this for Malebranche.[8] But in the case of systems that are particularly saturated or tight-knit, an evolution is necessary for particular reasons to change their positions and thus produce a new effect. Concerning Fichte, Gueroult already discusses "internal surges of the system" which determine new dissociations, displacements, and relations.[9] Gueroult raises the question of such internal surges in Spinozism on several occasions in the appendices of his book: concerning the essence of God, the proofs of the existence of God, and the demonstration of absolute determinism, but most importantly, in two extremely dense and exhaustive pages, concerning the definitions of substance and attribute.[10]

In effect, it seems that the *Short Treatise* is above all preoccupied with identifying God and Nature: thus attributes can be unconditionally identified with

substances, and substances defined as attributes. So we find a particular valorization of Nature, since God is defined as Being which presents only every attribute
or substance, and a devalorization of substances or attributes, which are not yet
self-caused but only self-conceived. On the other hand, the *Ethics* is concerned
to identify God and substance itself: so we find a valorization of substance which
is genuinely constituted by every attribute or qualified substance, each fully
enjoying the property of being self-caused, and each being a constitutive element
and no longer a simple presence; we also find a particular displacement of
Nature, whose identity with God must be established, and so from that point on,
such a displacement aptly expresses the mutual immanence of created nature and
creative nature. Suddenly, we realize that it is less a question of another structure
than of another state of the same structure. Thus the study of the internal evolution completes the study of the method proper as well as the study of the
characteristic formalism, all three of which become clear once the structure of the
system has been determined.

What exactly is going on in the first eight propositions, when Spinoza
demonstrates that there is one substance per attribute, and thus that there are just
as many qualified substances as there are attributes, each qualified substance
enjoying the properties of being unique in its kind, self-caused, and infinite?
Critics have often acted like Spinoza's reasoning had adopted a hypothesis that
was not his own and then ascended to the unity of substance as an ahypotheical
principle which nullifies his initial hypothesis. This problem is crucial for several reasons. First, this ahypothetical procedure attributed to Spinoza can be
corroborated by a corresponding element in the *Treatise on the Reform of the
Intellect*: here Spinoza's point of departure is any true idea, ideas of geometrical
beings which can still be impregnated with fiction, in order to reach as quickly
as possible the idea of God, where all fiction ceases. Secondly, from the perspective of the *Ethics*, the practical evaluation of the role of the first eight propositions
becomes decisive for the theoretical comprehension of the nature of attributes;
certainly, moreover, it is only insofar as the first eight propositions are accorded
merely a hypothetical sense that we get two misreadings of the attribute: 1) the
Kantian illusion that makes attributes forms or concepts of the understanding,
and 2) the neo-Platonic vertigo that makes attributes already degraded emana-
tions or manifestations.[11] Finally, it is clear that something in the first eight
propositions is merely provisional and conditioned, so the real question is what,
and whether we can say that it is the first eight propositions as a whole which are
provisional and conditioned.

Gueroult's answer is that the first eight propositions are perfectly categorical.
If they weren't, then we could not understand how these propositions confer on
each qualified substance positive and apodictic properties, and especially the
property of being self-caused (qualified substances did not yet have this proper-

ty in the *Short Treatise*). That there is one substance per attribute, and one only, is tantamount to saying that attributes, and only attributes, are in reality distinct; this affirmation from the *Ethics*, moreover, has nothing hypothetical about it.[12] It is only by ignoring the nature of real distinction according to Spinoza, and thus the whole logic of distinction, that commentators have conferred a merely hypothetical sense on the first eight propositions. In fact, it is because real distinction *cannot* be numerical that qualified substances or attributes which are in reality distinct constitute one and the same substance. More than that, in all rigor, *one* as a number is no more adequate to substance than 2, 3, 4...are adequate to attributes as qualified substances; and throughout his commentary, Gueroult emphasizes a devaluation of number in general, since it does not adequately express the nature of mode.[13] Saying that attributes are in reality distinct is tantamount to saying that each is conceived of itself, without negation or in opposition to another, and that they are all therefore affirmed of the same substance. Far from being an obstacle, their real distinction is the condition for constituting a being all the more rich for having attributes.[14] The logic of real distinction is a logic of purely affirmative difference and without negation. Attributes indeed constitute an irreducible *multiplicity*, but the whole question is what type of multiplicity. The problem is erased if the substantive 'multiplicity' is transformed into two opposed adjectives (*multiple* attributes and *one* substance). Attributes are a formal or qualitative multiplicity, "a concrete plurality which, because it implies the intrinsic difference and reciprocal heterogeneity of the beings that comprise it, has nothing in common with the plurality of number literally understood."[15] On two occasions, moreover, Gueroult uses the term "motley" [*bigarré*]: God is simple insofar as he is not composed of parts, but no less complex insofar as he is constituted by "*prima elementa*" which alone are absolutely simple; "God is thus a motley *ens realissimum*, not a pure, ineffable and unqualifiable *ens simplicissimum* in which all differences would disappear;" "God is motley, but unfragmentable, constituted of heterogeneous but inseparable attributes."[16]

Keeping in mind the inadequacy of numerical language, we can say that attributes are quiddities or substantial forms of absolutely one substance: constitutive elements, which are irreducible, of a substance that is ontologically constituted as one; structural elements, which are multiple, of the systematic unity of the substance; differential elements of a substance that neither juxtaposes nor grounds them, but integrates them.[17] In other words, we find in Spinozism not only a genesis of modes from the substance, but *a genealogy of the substance itself*, and the sense of the first eight propositions precisely establishes this genealogy. Certainly, the genesis of the modes is not the same as the genealogy of the substance, since the first concerns the determinations or the parts of one same reality, and the second deals with the diverse realities of one same being; the first concerns physical composition, the second deals with logical constitution; or to borrow an expression from Hobbes which inspired Spinoza: the first is a "*descriptio generati*," whereas the second is a "*descriptio generationis*."[18] Nevertheless, both the genesis and the genealogy can be spoken of *in one and the same sense* (God as the cause of all things having the same sense as being self-caused) precisely because the genesis of modes comes about in the attributes, and this could not occur immanently if the attributes themselves were not the genealogical elements of the substance. What emerges from this is the method-ological unity of Spinozism as a genetic philosophy.

This genetic or constructive philosophy is inseparable from a synthetic method, in which attributes are determined as genuine reasons of being. These reasons are constitutive elements: there is thus no ascension from attributes to substance, from "attributive substances" to absolutely infinite substance; the absolutely infinite substance contains no other reality than these attributive sub-stances, although the absolutely infinite substance is their integration and not their sum (a sum would yet presuppose number and numerical distinction). But as we saw earlier, Gueroult has shown that the synthetic method cannot be sim-ply opposed to an analytic and regressive process. And in the *Treatise on the Reform of the Intellect*, the point of departure is any true idea whatsoever, even if it is still impregnated with fiction and nothing in nature corresponds to it, in order then to ascend as quickly as possible to the idea of God, where all fiction ceases, and where things as well as ideas are engendered starting from God. In the *Ethics*, to be sure, we do not ascend from attribute-substances to the absolute-ly infinite substance; but we attain attribute-substances as real constitutive elements through a regressive analytic process, such that the attribute-substances are not objects of a genetic construction, and they must not be; rather, they are objects of a *demonstration from absurdity* (essentially, the modes of substance are "toppled" to show that each attribute can only designate an incommensurable substance, unique in its kind, existing for itself, and necessarily infinite). And what is abolished or overcome after that is not the result of the regressive process, since the attributes exist exactly as they are perceived, but the process itself which, as soon as the attributes are perceived as constitutive elements, gives way to the process of genetic construction. Thus genetic construction integrates the analytic process and its *self-suppression*. In this sense, then, we are sure to attain reasons of being and not simple reasons of knowledge. In this sense, too, the geo-metric method surmounts what was still fictional when it was applied to simple figures, revealing itself adequate to the constructability of the real.[19] In short, what is provisional is not the content of the first eight propositions, nor is it any of the properties conferred on the attribute-substances, it is only the analytic pos-sibility for these substances to form separate existences, a possibility that was not effected at all in the first eight propositions.[20]

Now we see that the construction of the unique substance occurs at the inter-section of two series and precisely forms a *nexus* (because commentators were

151

unaware of this, they acted like there was an "ascent" from the attributes to the substance, according to a single hypothetical series, or like the attributes were only reasons of knowledge, according to a problematic series). In fact, the first eight propositions represent a first series through which we ascend to the differential constitutive elements; then the 9th, 10th, and 11th represent another series through which the idea of God integrates these elements and makes clear it can be constituted only by all these elements together. This is why Spinoza expressly states that the first eight propositions can have no impact if we do not "simultaneously" keep in mind the definition of God. Spinoza is never satisfied with drawing a conclusion, according to one series only, about the unicity of the constituted substance from the unity of constitutive substances. On the contrary, he invokes the infinite power of an *Ens realissimum*, and its necessary unicity as substance, to draw a conclusion about the unity of the substances that constitute it without losing any of their previous properties.[21] Thus we distinguish the structural elements that are in reality distinct from the condition under which they compose a structure that functions as a whole, where everything works in pairs, and where real distinction will be a guarantee of formal correspondence and ontological identity.

The "nexus" between the two series is apparent in the notion of self-cause, with the central role it plays in genesis. *Causa sui* is first and foremost a property of each qualified substance. And the apparent vicious circle according to which it derives itself from the infinite, even as it grounds the infinite, can be undone in the following way: it derives itself from infinitude as the full perfection of *essence*, but grounds infinitude as the absolute affirmation of *existence*. The same goes for God or the unique substance: its existence is proved first by the infinity of its essence, then by self-causation as the genetic reason of the infinitude of existence, "namely the infinitely infinite power of the *Ens realissimum*, by which this being, necessarily causing itself, absolutely posits its existence in all its extension and plenitude, without limitation or fault."[22] On the one hand, it follows that the genetic construction as a whole is inseparable from a deduction of its distinctive features, whose *causa sui* is paramount. The deduction of distinctive features is interwoven, intertwined with the genetic construction: "If we discovered that the thing causes itself after having proceded to the *genesis of its essence*...it is no less certain that the *genesis of the thing* was obtained only by the knowledge of this distinctive feature that accounts for its existence. And from this fact, we have made real progress also in the knowledge of essence, since with its truth being rigorously demonstrated, it becomes rigorously clear that it is in reality an essence. And what holds for the *causa sui* holds, in varying degrees, for all the other distinctive features: eternity, infinitude, indivisibility, unicity, etc., because these are nothing more than the *causa sui* itself from different points of view."[23] On the other hand, the *causa sui* appears at the "nexus" of the two series of genesis, because it is the identity of the attributes, as to the cause or causal act, that explains the unicity of a single substance existing of itself, despite the difference of its attributes as to its essence: the attributes are diverse and incommensurable realities, integrated into an indivisible being "only by the identity of the causal act through which they give themselves existence and produce their modes."[24]

The *causa sui* animates the whole theme of power. However, we risk a misreading as we evaluate the intertwining of notions, if we attribute to this power an independence which it does not have, and to the distinctive features, an autonomy which they do not have in relation to the essence. Power itself, the *causa sui*, is only a distinctive feature; and if it is true that it is displaced from qualified substances to the unique substance, it is only insofar as this substance, because of *its* essence, made use *a fortiori* of the characters of the substantial attributes, because of *their* essence. In conformity with the difference between distinctive feature and essence, the substance would not be unique without power, but it is not by virtue of power that the substance is unique, it is by virtue of its essence: "If by the unicity of power (i.e. the power of the attributes), we understand *how it is possible* that the attributes are one despite the diversity of their proper essences, *the reason that grounds* their union in one substance alone is nothing other than the infinite constitutive perfection of the essence of God."[25] This explains why it is so misleading to invert Spinoza's formulation and claim that the essence of God is power, especially when Spinoza himself says: "the power of God is his very essence."[26] In other words, power is the inseparable distinctive feature of essence, and it expresses at once how the essence is the cause of the existence of substance and the cause of the other things that derive from it. So, "power is nothing other than essence" means two things: 1) God has no other power than the power of his essence; he acts and produces only through his essence, and not through an understanding or a will: he is thus the cause of every thing in the same sense that he is self-caused, since the notion of power expresses precisely the identity of the cause of every thing with the self-caused; 2) the products or effects of God are *properties* which derive from essence, but which are necessarily *produced* in the constitutive attributes of this essence; they are thus *modes*, whose unity in the different attributes is in turn explained by the theme of power, that is, the identity of the causal act which posits the properties in each of the modes (whence you have the assimilation: real effects = properties = modes; plus the formulation "God produces an infinity of things in an infinity of modes," where *thing* refers to the singular cause acting in all the attributes at once, and *modes*, to the essences dependent on the respective attributes).[27]

The rigorous interweaving of essence and power precludes essences from being models in a creative understanding, and power from being raw force in a creative will. The conception of possibles is excluded from God, just as is the realization of contingents: the understanding as well as the will can only be a finite or infinite mode. We must take a moment to appreciate this devaluation of the understanding. Because when understanding in the essence of God is established, the word 'understanding' becomes ambiguous; clearly, the infinite understanding can only be related to our own by analogy, and clearly, the perfections generally belonging to God cannot have the same form as those belonging to his creatures. On the contrary, when we say that divine understanding is no less a mode than finite or human understanding is, we not only establish the adequation of the human understanding as part, to the divine understanding as whole, we also establish the adequation of all understanding to the forms which it includes, since *modes envelope the perfections on which they depend in the same form as the perfections which constitute the essence of substance.* Mode is an effect; but if the effect differs from the cause in essence and existence, it at least has in common with cause the forms that it envelopes only in its essence, whereas the forms constitute the essence of the substance.[28] Thus, the reduction of the infinite understanding to the state of a mode is inseparable from two other theses, which ensure at once the most rigorous distinction of essence and existence between substance and its products, and yet the most perfect commonality of form (univocity). Conversely, the confusion of infinite understanding with the essence of substance leads to a distortion of the forms which God possesses only in his incomprehensible manner, i.e. eminently, but also a confusion of essence between substance and its creatures, since the perfections of humankind are complacently attributed to God by raising them to the infinite.[29]

This formal status of the understanding explains the possibility of the geometric, synthetic, and genetic method. Whence we have Gueroult's insistence on the nature of the Spinozist understanding, the opposition between Descartes and Spinoza as to this problem, not to mention Spinozism's most radical thesis: absolute rationalism, based on the adequation of our understanding to absolute knowledge. "By affirming the total intelligibility for humankind of the essence of God and things, Spinoza is consciously opposing Descartes… Absolute rationalism, imposing the total intelligibility of God, the key of the total intelligibility of things, is thus for Spinozism the first article of faith. Through God alone is the soul purged from the multiple superstitions, for which an incomprehensible God serves as the ultimate refuge, and through him does the soul accomplish this perfect union of God and humanity that conditions salvation."[30] There would be no genetic and synthetic method if what is engendered were not in a way equal to what engenders (thus the modes are neither more nor less than the substance),[31] and if what engenders were not itself the object of a genealogy that grounds the genesis of what is engendered (thus the attributes are the genealogical elements of substance, and the genetic principles of the modes). Gueroult analyzes this structure of Spinozism in every detail. And because a structure is defined by its effect as a whole, no less than by its elements, relations, *nexuses and intertwinings*, we sometimes witness a change in tone, as though Gueroult were unveiling or suddenly revealing the functioning effect of the structure as a whole, which he will develop in the volumes to follow: such as the *effect of knowledge* (how does humankind manage to "situate itself" in God, that is, to occupy in the structure that place which the knowledge of the true assigns to God, and which also ensures true knowledge and true freedom); or also, the *effect of life* (how does power, as essence, constitute the "life" of God which is communicated to humankind, and how does it in reality ground the identity of humankind's independence in God and of its independence from God).[32] The importance of this admirable book by Gueroult is twofold: from the standpoint of the general method he establishes, and from the standpoint of Spinozism, of which the method does not represent merely one application among others, but indeed embodies, coming as it does at the end of a series of studies on Descartes, Malebranche and Leibniz, the most adequate, the most saturated, and the most exhaustive object for such a method. Gueroult's book establishes the genuinely scientific study of Spinozism.

The Fissure of Anaxagoras and the Local Fires of Heraclitus

Kostas Axelos, in search of planetary thought, defines it in these terms: "Planetary certainly means planet earth, the terrestrial globe, and its relationship to the other planets. It is the *global*. But the extension of this concept remains too great... Planetary means whatever is *itinerant* and *errant*, wandering as it follows a trajectory in space-time and performing a rotational movement. Planetary indicates the era of global planning, in which the subjects and the objects of the will to organize and foresee are swept up motionless on an itinerary that surpasses both subject and object. Planetary names the reign of *platitude* as it spreads and flattens everything, which is also more errant than aberrant. As a noun, moreover, and according to dictionaries, the planetary designates a kind of *technological mechanism*, or *gears and wheels*. Therefore, the play of thought and the planetary is *global, erratic, itinerant, organizing, planning and flattening, caught up in gears and wheels*."[2] The history of the world is marked by the great figures of errancy: Odysseus, Don Quixote, the Wandering Jew, Bouvard and Péchuet, Bloom, Malone—who in the words of Ezra Pound are average sensual types hoping and praying for "the most general generalization." The great figures of errancy are indeed thinkers. Bouvard and Péchuet are the first planetary couple. But we have perfected errancy, as though we no longer needed to move. Planetary thought includes the sanitized philosophy of technician-generals who dream of precision-guided bombs, and whose cosmology rivals that of Teilhard, as well as the meager reflections of those who are going to the moon, but also the thought recorded in the instruments that propel them into space, and finally the thoughts of us all as we watch, glued to the television, motionless and schizoid: average, sensual, "compact and fissured."[3] There is no reason to privilege one aspect over the other: planning over globalization, or errancy over platitude. We have achieved what was foretold: the absence of any goal. Errancy has ceased being a return to the origin; it is no longer even ab-erration, which would still presuppose a fixed point; it is as far from error as it is from truth. Errancy has conquered autonomy in a kind of catatonic immobility.

Attention has been turned to the means Axelos uses to express the magma which planetary thought ought to be, and which it is indeed, but which poses considerable technical problems of registration, translation, and poeticization, with one filter placed on another, and one fragment lodged in another. Axelos pulls up short of Plato, tending toward the pre-Socratics; and he goes beyond Marx, moving toward post-Marxism. In his work we find: a turning of aphorisms borrowed from what survives of Heraclitus, a posing of theses borrowed from the militant Marx, zen-like anecdotes, projects, refrains, tracts, and plans reminiscent of the utopian socialists. But one feels, too, that Axelos would like to have audio-visual means at his disposal, that he is dreaming of a Heraclitus at the head of a post-Marxist group of commandos, seizing a radio station to broadcast short aphoristic messages or round-tables of eternal return. In his work, Heideggerian terminology is retuned and takes on new meaning, even as it is converted from the country to the city. Axelos tries to reevaluate the possibilities of cinema as an expression of the modern forms of errancy.[4] But his assiduous study of the pre-Socratics is no more a return to origins than post-Marxism is itself a goal: it is rather about grasping an absence of origin as the "planetary becoming" that appeared in Greece, and that now appears to us, as we deviate with respect to every goal.

Le Jeu du monde is written in aphorisms. The object proper to the aphorism is the partial object, the fragment, the part. Today we are familiar with what Maurice Blanchot has taught us about the conditions of a thought and a "language of fragment": speaking and thinking the partial object not as presupposing any anterior totality from which it would derive, nor any posterior whole which would derive from the fragment, but quite the opposite: letting the fragment evolve for itself and for other fragments. This is accomplished by making the distance, the divergence, and the decentering which separate the fragments, but which also mix them up, into an affirmation such as "a new relation with the Outside," and which cannot be reduced to unity. Each aphorism must be conceived as endowed with a propulsive mechanism; and projections, introjections, as well as fixations, regressions, and sublimations, are not simply psychological processes but cosmo-anthropological mechanisms. In a sense, humankind renews its ties with a destiny that can be read in the planets and stars.[5] Planetary thought is not unifying: it implies hidden depths in space, an extension of deep universes, incommensurate distances and proximities, non-exact numbers, an essential opening of our system, a whole fiction-philosophy. This is why the planetary is not the same thing as the world, even in Heideggerian terms: Heidegger's world is dislocated, "the world and the cosmos are not identical."[6] Nor are the affective overtones of planetary being the same as those of being-in-the-world. Charles Koechlin, inquiring into the expressive sentimental possibilities of modern music, claims that modern music has renounced classical "affirmations" and romantic "effusions," but that it is rather apt for expressing "a particular disarray, a particular disequilibrium, even a particular indifference," and also "a strange joy almost like happiness." This triple 'particular'—disarray, disequilibrium, indifference—defines planetary music, the pathos of planetary thought, which is bitter, but joyful by dint of a particular strangeness (strangeness, rather than alienation, as the determination of errancy).[7]

To this pathos there corresponds a logic, a logos. The aphorism's "small form" must not be reminiscence or archaicism, a collection of pieces surviving a past whole, but a means adapted to exploring the contemporary world, its holes and constellations. The logic here is one of probability, referring not to properties or classes but to cases. Whence the importance of an ambiguous sign (*and/or*) that must indicate all at once conjunction (*and*), disjunction (*or*), and exclusion (*nor*). When Axelos accumulates expressions such as "metaphysically anti-metaphysical," "discordant concord," "to marvel but without astonishment," "one crab devouring another is devoured by a third," "what does the manipulating is manipulated," etc., they are not so much facile dialectical transformations, the monotone identity of opposites, as sequences of random cases in which conjunction and disjunction, disjunction or conjunction replace the form of the judgment of existence and attribution which was still the basis of dialectical thinking (*is, is not*). "What if the *there is* and the *is* no longer tyrannized us, what if the *there is not* and the *is not* did not appear as simple privation...."[8] The Hegelian, as well as Marxist dialectic, which is perhaps Heideggarian, too, evolves in the categories of being, non-being, and the One-All. And what can the All do except totalize nothingness, and nihilize nothingness no less than being? "Nihilism nihilizes nothingness, because it leaves *nothingness unthought*."[9] This *nothing* can drive us mad, cause us anguish, even be imagined, but it nonetheless remains unthought in nihilism. Nihilism is indeed the universal determination of modernity, just as platitude is the movement of errancy. As Axelos keeps saying and showing: "it's not about stopping the process," whether fighting against platitude or overcoming nihilism.[10] But this *nothing* in nihilism is precisely what remains unthought as total universal conflagration or end of the world, and it is also what detotalizes and disperses its own movement, kindling here and there the local fires of these fragments in which nihilism is already self-overcome and self-foreseen—which causes Axelos to remark: "ever to begin again and again. Till the final and fatal explosion, which will come *much later* than we think." Planetary thought can have no other logic: it wills itself, it presents itself as politics, strategy. Some of the books Axelos has published in his "Arguments" series he likes to think of as unstable states of that planetary thought of which he dreams.[11] One of the first books in the series was Clausewitz's *On War*. Beyond Clausewitz, the modern identity of strategy and politics from the perspective of thermonuclear nihilism has been recently shown to produce "detotalized and dispersed war: wars and/or limited agreements."[12] The revolutionary response to American world politics, invoking game theory, is four or five Vietnams. Heraclitus as strategist, combat philosopher: Heraclitus says that all things become fire, but is precisely not thinking of a universal conflagration, which he leaves unthought as the nothing of nihilism, showing nihilism necessarily self-overcome or overcome by what is unthought in it, in the local fires that unite the peoples of the earth.[13] Physics, metaphysics, psychology and sociology are no more in planetary thought; there is nothing left but a generalized strategy.

This is our difference from Clausewitz, but also Hegel, Marx, Heidegger, and even still from Heraclitus… Because we think without origin, and without destination, difference becomes the highest thought, but we cannot think it *between* two things, between a point of departure and a point of arrival, not even between Being [*l'être*] and being [*l'étant*]. Difference cannot be affirmed as such without devouring the two terms that cease to contain it, though it does not itself cease from passing through assignable terms. Difference is the true logos, but logos is the errancy that does away with fixed points; indifference is its pathos. Difference emerges from and re-enters a fissure that swallows up all things and beings. Where does difference go? asks Axelos, with one near-sighted, and one far-sighted eye. "What line separates the horizon of the visible from the invisible harmony?" Where does the rhythm alternate? "In the great encompassing space and not in one specific place?" Axelos traces a commentary by Anaxagoras, which keeps asking the question: where is the fissure? Where does it lie? "Is there on one side an autonomous pure *Noûs*, and on the other a chaos of preexisting beings, and in a third place, a chaos transformed into a cosmos by the *Noûs*? Where does the fissure lie? In the chaos? Between the chaos and the cosmos? In the cosmos? In the *Noûs* and its position? In its action? In the composition of the world? In the exposition of Anaxagoras? In our comprehension?…We are struck by the fragmentation and dispersion that go hand in hand with differences; we grow nostalgic, crushed by and under the pressure of indifference; we mix everything up, yet we come from this mixture…we are obsessed by our time, yet how can we communicate with ancient time and with the play of time?"[14] Axelos occupies that point where difference ceaselessly communicates—where the difference between mixture and separation is also the difference in the mixture and/or in the separation, and the difference "in" Anaxagoras is also our difference "from" Anaxagoras, at once origin and destination. Therefore, it would be imprecise to present Axelos as a critic of totality, retaining only a world of fragments. It is true that the whole is never conceived as totalization: neither the way Plato does, as the action of a unity principle ordering chaos, nor the way Hegel and Marx do, as the process of a becoming that gathers and surpasses its moments. Once again, here we see Axelos, who with his "Arguments"—both the journal and the series—did all he could to disseminate Lukàcs and the Frankfurt School in

France, marking off "his" own difference with respect to a conception of the Whole.[15] All totalization, including first and foremost the totalization of the "process of social and historical experience praxis," is nihilism to Axelos, and leads to the *nothing* which remains unthought in nihilism. Totalization seems to him the movement of bureaucratic platitude. But if it is true that nihilism is self-overcome in the sense that the *nothing* is thought, it must be thought as a Whole—but a whole that does not totalize or unify, whose parts do not presuppose it as a lost unity nor even as a fragmented totality, and which is not formed or prefigured by the parts in the course of a logical development or organic evolution. A whole that no longer counts on existence and attribution, but thrives on conjunction and disjunction, in mixture or separation, being but one with the unforeseen course of the fissure in every direction, a river carrying partial objects and varying their distances, constituting in Blanchot's words a new relation with the Outside, which is the object of thought today. In this sense, the keynote of all Axelos's books is "being in the process of becoming a fragmentary totality"; and writing in aphorisms, he can say that the aphorism and the system are the same thing, the Whole-Fragment always outside itself, which throws itself both in the fissure of Anaxagoras and in the local fires of Heraclitus.[16]

Axelos's *Le Jeu du monde* is a planetary history. The elementary forces of work and strife, language and thought, love and death comprise the great powers of myths and religions, poetry and art, science and philosophy. But the technology at work in all these powers brings about a generalized planning that ushers in their crisis, and it raises the question of their planetary destiny. It is as if at one and the same time a single code persists, the code of technology, and yet there is no longer any code capable of covering the whole of the social field. In planetary being, the earth has become flat again. However, this leveling of dimensions previously filled by such powers, this flattening that reduces things and beings to the *unidimensional*—in a word, this nihilism, has the most bizarre effect: it revitalizes the elementary forces in the raw play of all their dimensions; *it liberates the unthought nothing in a counter-power which is multidimensional play*. Of the most unfortunate souls, one no longer says that they are alienated or tortured by the powers, but rather that they are played by forces. Even the planetary politics of the Unites States, in its role as aggressive policeman, is systematized and fragmented in game theory. And the efforts of the revolution can respond to it only by local strategies, giving as good as it gets, inventing parades, initiatives, and new stratagems. From the outset, Axelos's work has taken this concept of play to its highest point. With Fink, Axelos was one of the first to go beyond the traditional conception of the game: which was a circumscribed and specific human activity defined in opposition to other powers and other forces (reality, utility, work, the sacred…). In this connection, Jacques Ehrmann has recently analyzed all the postulates of this traditional conception that tries to define the game in isolation from reality, culture, and seriousness.[17] To this compartmentalization is opposed Fink's attempt: he shows how the Game spreads through the universe, interferes with it, and to the extent that one moves away from the metaphysical interpretation that devalues and isolates games and toward the mythical interpretation of the game as a relation with the world, one finally reaches the Game as being, totally of the world and without a player.[18] Axelos undoubtedly accepts this distinction between games played, play in the world, and the games of the world. But Axelos gives it the turn that he does to all Heideggerian concepts, where the world gives way to the planetary, the "rational" to strategy, being and truth to errancy. Axelos is to Heidegger what a kind of zen is to the Buddha. Axelos does not start from the game of humanity (phenomenologically) to see humanity able to symbolize the game of the world (ontologically). He starts from a dialogue, from a game called planetary that already connects play of humanity and play of the world. Axelos gives full force to this phrase: *It plays, without players*. With Axelos, the overcoming of metaphysics rediscovers the sense that Jarry had given it in accordance with the etymology, pataphysics, the planetary gesture of Dr. Faustroll, from where the salvation of philosophy can now come.

Hume[1]

The Significance of Empiricism

The history of philosophy has pretty much absorbed and digested empiricism, which has been traditionally defined as the reverse of rationalism: yes or no, is there within ideas something not in the senses or sense-data? The history of philosophy has made empiricism a critique of the *a priori* and innate ideas. But empiricism has always held other secrets. And it is these which Hume brings to light and develops to the utmost in his extremely subtle and difficult work. Thus Hume has a peculiar place in the history of philosophy. His empiricism is, so to speak, a kind of universe of science fiction: as in science fiction, the world seems fictional, strange, foreign, experienced by other creatures; but we get the feeling that this world is our own, and we are the creatures. At the same time, science or theory undergoes a conversion: theory becomes *inquiry* (this conception originates with Bacon; recalling this conception, Kant will transform and rationalize it when he conceives of theory as a tribunal). Science or theory is an inquiry, in other words, a practice: a practice of the apparently fictitious world described by empiricism, a study of the conditions of legitimacy of the practices in this our empirical world. This is the great conversion of theory into practice. History of philosophy manuals will misunderstand what they call "associationism" when they see in it a theory, in the ordinary sense of the word, and something like rationalism stood on its head. Hume asks some bizarre questions which seem somehow familiar to us: to take possession of an abandoned city, is it enough to throw one's spear against the gate, or do you have to touch it with your hand? Just how far can we possess the seas? Why in a system of justice is the soil more important than the surface? But then why is the paint more important than the canvas? Only here does the problem of association take on its full implications.

What is called the theory of association locates its destination and its truth in a casuistry of relations, in a practice of law, politics, and economy, which completely changes the nature of philosophical reflection.

The Nature of Relation

Hume's originality, one aspect of his originality, derives from the force with which he affirms: *relations are exterior to their terms.* Such a thesis can be understood only in opposition to the tireless effort by rationalist philosophers to resolve the paradox of relations: either a means is found to make the relation internal to the terms, or a more profound and inclusive term is discovered to which the relation is already internal. Peter is smaller than Paul: how does one make this relation internal to Peter or Paul? Or to their concept? Or to the whole they compose? Or to the Idea in which they participate? How does one overcome the irreducible exteriority of their relation? Certainly empiricism had always militated for the exteriority of relations, but in a certain way, its position on this topic was occluded by the problem of the origin of knowledge or ideas: everything had to have its origin in sense-data, and in the operations of the mind on these sense-data. Hume effects an inversion that will take empiricism to a higher power: if ideas contain nothing else, and nothing more, than what there is in sense impressions, this is precisely because the relations are heterogeneous and exterior to their terms, impressions, or ideas. The difference, therefore, is not between ideas *and* impressions, but between two kinds of impressions or ideas: the impressions or ideas of terms *and* the impressions or ideas of relations. Now the empiricist world can for the first time truly unfold in all its extension: a world of exteriority, a world where thought itself is in a fundamental relation to the Outside, a world where terms exist like veritable atoms, and relations like veritable external bridges—a world where the conjunction "and" dethrones the interiority of the verb "is," a Harlequin world of colored patterns and non-totalizable fragments, where one communicates via external relations. Hume's thought is founded on a dual register: *atomism*, which explains how ideas or sense impressions refer to discrete minima that produce space and time; *associationism*, which explains how relations are established between these terms, relations which are always external to them and depend on other principles. On the one hand, a physics of the mind; on the other, a logic of relations. Hume deserves the credit for breaking the bonds imposed by the form of the judgment of attribution, for making possible an autonomous logic of relations, and discovering a conjunctive world of atoms and relations, whose ulterior development can be seen in Russell and modern logic—relations are, after all, conjunctions themselves.

Human Nature

What is a relation? It is what allows a passage from a given impression or idea to the idea of something not presently given. For example, I think of something "similar"... When I see Peter's portrait, I think of Peter who is absent. In vain would we search in the given term for the rationale of the passage. Relation is itself the effect of so-called principles of association: contiguity, resemblance, and causality, which indeed constitute *human nature*. Human nature means that which is universal or constant in the human mind. It is never this or that idea as a term, but merely ways of proceeding from one particular idea to another. In this sense, Hume will engage in the concerted destruction of three great limit-ideas in metaphysics: the Self, the World, and God. At first blush, however, Hume's thesis looks disappointing: what is the advantage of explaining relations by principles of human nature, principles of association that appear to be just another name to designate such relations? But we are disappointed only to the extent that we misunderstand the problem. The problem is not one of causes, but the functioning of relations as the effects of these causes, and the practical conditions of this functioning.

Let's look at a special relation in this regard: the relation of cause. This relation is special because it not only allows the passage from a given term to the idea of something that is not presently given; but causality also allows the passage from something given to what has never been given, even something unable to be given in experience. For example, given signs in a book, I believe that Caesar lived. Watching the sun come up, I say that it will come up again tomorrow; having observed that water boils at 100° C, I say that it will necessarily do so at 100° C. But expressions such as "always," "tomorrow," or "necessarily" express something unable to be given in experience: tomorrow is not given without becoming today, without ceasing to be tomorrow, and every experience is of a contingent particular. In other words, causality is a relation according to which I go beyond what is given, I say more than what is given or able to be given—in short, *I infer and I believe*, I await, I expect... What is essential here is this initial displacement which Hume effects, positing belief as the basis and principle of knowledge. This functioning of causal relation is explained in the following way: similar observable cases (every time I have seen A followed or accompanied by B) are fused in the imagination, whereas they remain separate and distinct from one another in the understanding. This property of fusion in the imagination constitutes habit (I expect), while the distinction in the understanding calculates belief in proportion to those cases that have been observed (probability as a calculation of the degrees of belief). The principle of habit, as fusion of similar cases in the imagination, and the principle of experience, as observation of distinct cases in the understanding, thus combine to produce both relation and the inference following on relation (belief), according to which causality functions.

Fiction

Fiction and nature have a particular distribution in the empiricist world. Left to itself, the mind does not lack the power to pass from one idea to another, but indeed does so haphazardly, in a delirium that goes through the universe dreaming up fire-breathing dragons, winged horses, giants, and other monstrosities. On the other hand, the principles of human nature impose on this delirium unchanging rules as laws of passage, transition, and inference, in accordance with Nature itself. From this point on, however, a strange battle ensues. Because if it is true that the principles of association determine the mind by imposing on it a nature to discipline its delirium or fictions of the imagination, conversely the imagination uses these same principles to pass off its fictions and fantasies as real, lending them a surety they would not otherwise have. In this sense, what is proper to fiction is feigning the relations themselves, inducing fictive relations, and making us believe in tales of madness. We see this not only in the imagination's gift for doubling present relations with other relations that do not exist in a particular case, but especially where causality is concerned; the imagination forges fictive causal chains, illegitimate rules, simulacra of belief. Either it confuses the accidental with the essential, or it uses the properties of language (i.e. surpassing experience) to substitute for the repetition of similar cases that have been actually observed, a simple verbal repetition that mimics the effect. The liar comes in this way to believe his lies by repeating them. And education, superstition, eloquence, and poetry all work in the same way. It is no longer on the path of science that we go beyond experience, confirmed by Nature itself and a corresponding calculation; we go beyond it always and everywhere in our delirium, which dreams up a counter-nature and ensures the fusion of anything whatsoever. The imagination uses the principles of association to redirect these principles themselves, giving them an illegitimate extension. Hume is here effecting a second major displacement in philosophy: for the traditional concept of error he substitutes the concept of illusion or delirium, according to which there are not false but illegitimate beliefs, illegitimate operations of the faculties, and illegitimate functionings of relations. In this respect, Kant once again owes something essential to Hume. We're not threatened by error. It's much worse: we're swimming in delirium.

Still, it's not so bad that the fictions of the imagination turn the principles of human nature against themselves, as long as it's under conditions that can always be corrected: so in the case of causality, an unforgiving calculation of probabilities can expose feigned relations or delirious fantasies that go beyond experience. But the illusion is particularly more serious when it belongs to human nature, that is, when the illegitimate operation or belief is incorrigible, inseparable from legitimate beliefs, and indispensable to their organization. Now the fanciful use of the principles of human nature become themselves a principle. Delirium and fiction come over to the side of human nature. This is what Hume will demonstrate in his most subtle, most difficult analyses of ideas of the Self, the World, and God: how positing a distinct and continuous existence of bodies, and how positing an identity of the self introduce all kinds of fictive functionings of relations, especially a fictive causality, under conditions where no fiction may be corrected, driving us rather from one fiction to another, all of which belong to human nature. Hume, in the posthumous *Dialogues concerning Natural Religion*, which may be his masterpiece, applies the same critical method not only to revealed religion, but to so-called natural religion and the teleological arguments on which it is based. Never has Hume's sense of humor reached such heights: the more illegitimate these beliefs are from the point of view of the principles of human nature, the more completely they belong to our nature. Certainly now we're in a position to understand the complex notion of modern skepticism as Hume practices it. Contrary to ancient skepticism, founded on the variety of sensory appearances and the errors of the senses, modern skepticism is founded on the status of relations and their exteriority. The first act of modern skepticism is discovering belief at the basis of knowledge, that is, naturalizing belief (positivism). From then on, the second act is exposing illegitimate beliefs as those which do not obey rules effectively productive of knowledge (probabilism, the calculation of probabilities). The third act gives it a final touch: the illegitimate beliefs in the World, the Self, and God appear as the horizon of every possible legitimate belief, or as the lowest degree of belief. Because if everything is belief, everything is a question of the degrees of belief, even the delirium of non-understanding. The virtue of Hume's modern skepticism is humor—as against irony, the ancient dogmatic virtue of Socrates and Plato.

The Imagination

Now if the inquiry into the understanding has skepticism as its principle and result, and if it leads to an inextricable mixture of fiction and human nature, this is perhaps because it is only part of the inquiry, not even its principal part. The principles of association indeed make sense only in relation to the passions. Not only do affective circumstances direct the association of ideas, but the relations themselves are assigned a sense, a direction, an irreversibility, and an exclusivity according to the passions. In a word, what constitutes human nature, and what gives the mind its nature or consistency are not only the principles of association whence derive relations, but also the principles of passion whence derive our "inclinations." We have to keep two things in mind here: on the one hand, the passions do not determine the mind, do not impart a nature to the mind in the same way the principles of association do; and on the other hand, the essence of the mind as delirium or fiction does not react to the passions in the same way it reacts to relations.

We saw how the principles of association, especially causality, compel the mind to go beyond what is given, inspiring it with beliefs or fanciful notions not all of which are legitimate. The effect of the passions, however, is to restrict the range of the mind and attach it to privileged ideas and objects. In fact, the essence of passion is not egoism—it's worse: *partiality*. We have strong feelings about our parents, siblings, and friends (restricted causality, contiguity, and resemblance). And this is much worse than if we were governed by egoism. To make society possible, egoism would only have to be limited. In this sense, the celebrated theories of the contract, from the sixteenth- to the eighteenth-century, have posed the social problem ideally as the limitation of natural rights, or even a renunciation of them, whence arises the contractual society. But when Hume says that humans are not naturally egoist, but naturally partial, we mustn't see this as a simple nuance of wording. It is a radical change in the practical positing of the social problem. The problem is no longer: how do we limit egoism and its corresponding natural rights? The problem is now: how do we go beyond partiality? How do we go from "limited sympathy" to an "extended generosity"? How do we extend the passions, give them an extension that they do not have of themselves? Society is no longer conceived as a system of legal and contractual limitations, but as an institutional invention: How do we *invent artifices*, create institutions that force the passions to go beyond their partiality, producing moral, juridical, and political feelings (for example, the feeling of justice)? Whence you have the opposition that Hume establishes between the contract and the convention or artifice. Hume is certainly the first to break with the restrictive model of contract and law that still dominates the sociology of the eighteenth-century. He proposes instead the positive model of artifice and institution. Consequently, the whole problem of humanity has been displaced: it is no longer a question, as it is in understanding, of the complex relationship between fiction and human nature, but between human nature and artifice (humankind as an inventive species).

The Passions

In the understanding, the principles of human nature themselves established the rules for extending or going beyond the given, which the imagination used to pass off simulacra of belief as legitimate: consequently, a calculation was constantly necessary as a correction, to distinguish the legitimate from the illegitimate. With the passions, however, the problem is different: how can we invent the artificial extension that goes beyond the partiality of human nature? Here fiction or fantasy takes on a new sense. As Hume says, the mind or the imagination does not function, in relation to the passions, like a wind instrument, but like a percussion instrument "where after each stroke the vibrations still retain some sound, which gradually and insensibly decays."[2] In short, what is proper to the imagination is reflecting the passions, making them resonate, and causing them to go beyond the limits of their natural partiality and presentness. Hume shows how esthetic and moral feelings come about: the passions reflected in the imagination become those of the imagination. By reflecting the passions, the imagination liberates them, stretches them very thin, and projects them beyond their natural limits. In one respect, however, the percussion metaphor must be revised: as they resonate in the imagination, the passions are not content to become gradually less present and less intense; they completely change their color and their tone, much the same way the sadness of a represented passion in tragedy changes into the pleasure of an almost infinite play of the imagination. The passions acquire a new nature and are attended by a new kind of belief. Thus the will "seems to move easily every way, and casts a shadow or image of itself even to that side on which it did not settle." [3]

What constitutes the world of artifice or culture is precisely this resonance, this reflection of the passions in the imagination, and it is what make culture at once the most frivolous and most serious of worlds. But there are two defects to be avoided in these cultural formations: on the one hand, extended passions that are less intense than actual passions, even if they are of another nature; and on the other, passions that are indeterminate, projecting their fainter images in every direction independently of any rule. The first defect finds its solution in the governing bodies of social power, in the apparatuses of permission, reward and punishment, which lend to amplified feelings or reflected passions a supplementary degree of intensity or belief: primarily the governement, but also more subterranean and implicit authorities such as custom and taste—once again, we see Hume is one of the first to have posed the problem of power and government in terms of credibility, not representivity.

As for the second defect, it also involves the way in which Hume's philosophy forms a general system. Because if the passions are reflected in the imagination, it is not in some bare imagination, but an imagination as it is already determined or naturalized by the principles of association. Resemblance, contiguity, and causality—in a word, any and all relations that are the object of understanding or calculation—furnish general rules to determine reflected feelings, beyond the immediate and restricted use that the non-reflected passions make of them. So the esthetic feelings discover genuine rules of taste in the principles of association. Most importantly, Hume explains in detail how the passions of possession, being reflected in the imagination, find in the principles of association the means to determine general rules that constitute the factors at work in property or the world of law. There is a whole study of the variations of relations, a whole calculus of relations, that allows a response in each case to the question: does there exist between this person and that object such a relation as to make us believe (to make the imagination believe) that one belongs to the other? "A person who has hunted a hare to the last degree of weariness would look upon it as an injustice for another to rush in before him and seize his prey. But the same person, advancing to pluck an apple that hangs within his reach, has no reason to complain if another, more alert, passes him and takes possession. What is the reason of this difference, but that immobility, not being natural to the hare, but the effect of industry, forms in that case a strong relation with the hunter, which is wanting in the other?"[4] Does a spear thrown against the gate suffice to ensure ownership of an abandoned city, or do you have to touch it with your hand to establish a sufficient relation? Why in civil law does the soil have priority over the surface, but the paint over the canvas, whereas the paper has it over writing? The principles of association find their true sense in a casuistry of relations that determine the last detail of the world of culture and law. And this is indeed the genuine object of Hume's philosophy: relations as the means of an activity, a practice at once juridical, economic, and political.

A Philosophy both Popular and Scientific

Hume is a rather precocious philosopher: he was about twenty-five years old when he wrote his masterpiece *A Treatise of Human Nature* (published in 1739–1740). A new tone in philosophy, an extraordinary simplicity and concreteness, emerges from a great complexity of arguments, which simultaneously bring in the use of fictions, the science of human nature, and the practice of artifices. A kind of philosophy that is popular and scientific: a pop-philosophy. Its ideal? A decisive clarity, which is not the clarity of ideas, but that which comes from relations and operations. It is clarity that he will attempt to work more and more into his later books, even though it means giving up some of the complexity, and renouncing what was thought too difficult in his *Treatise*: *Essays, Moral and Political* (1742), *An Enquiry concerning Human Understanding* (1748), *An Enquiry concerning the Principles of Morals* (1751) and *Political Discourses* (1752). Then he will try his hand at *The History of Great Britain* (1754–1762). The admirable *Dialogues concerning Natural Religion*, appearing after Hume's death in 1779, find him again more complex and more clear. This is perhaps the only example of a genuine dialogue in philosophy because there are not only two, but three characters. And they don't have univocal roles: they form provisional alliances, break them off, seek reconciliation, etc. Demea is the advocate of revealed religion; Cleanthes, of natural religion; and Philon is the skeptic. The sense of humor of Hume-Philon is not only a way of getting everyone to agree, in the name of a skepticism that assigns "degrees" of belief, but it is already a rupture, breaking with the dominant currents of the eighteenth-century, to prefigure a future philosophy.

How Do We Recognize Structuralism?[1]

Not long ago we used to ask: What is existentialism? Now we ask: What is structuralism? These questions are of keen interest, provided they are timely and have some bearing on work actually in progress. *This is 1967.* Thus we cannot invoke the unfinished character of such work to avoid a reply, for it is that character alone which gives the question its significance. So, the question *What is structuralism?* must undergo certain transformations. In the first place, *who* is a structuralist? In the current climate, rightly or wrongly, it is customary to name names [*désigner*], to provide 'samples' [échantillonner]: a linguist like Roman Jakobson; a sociologist like Claude Lévi-Strauss; a psychoanalyst like Jacques Lacan; a philosopher like Michel Foucault, renewing epistemology; a Marxist philosopher like Louis Althusser, once again taking up the problem of the interpretation of Marxism; a literary critic like Roland Barthes; writers like those from *Tel Quel*... Of these, some do not reject the word "structuralism," and use "structure," "structural." Others prefer the Saussurean term "system." These are all very different kinds of thinkers, and from different generations, and some have exercised a real influence on their contemporaries. But more import is the extreme diversity of the domains they explore. Each of them discovers problems, methods, solutions that are analogically related, as if sharing in a free atmosphere or spirit of the time, but one that distributes itself into singular creations and discoveries in each of these domains.—*Ism* words, in this sense, are perfectly justified.

There is good reason to ascribe the origin of structuralism to linguistics: not only Saussure, but the Moscow and Prague schools. And if structuralism then migrates to other domains, this occurs without it being a question of analogy, nor merely in order to establish methods "equivalent" to those that first succeeded for the analysis of language. In fact, language is the only thing that can properly be said to have structure, be it an esoteric or even non-verbal language. There is a structure of the unconscious only to the extent that the unconscious speaks and is language. There is a structure of bodies only to the extent that bodies are supposed to speak with a language which is one of the symptoms. Even things possess a structure only in so far as they maintain a silent discourse, which is the language of signs. So the question *What is structuralism?* is further transformed—it is better to ask: What do we recognize in those that we call structuralists? And what do they themselves recognize?—since one does not recognize people, in a visible manner, except by the invisible and imperceptible things they themselves recognize in their own way. How do the structuralists go about recognizing a language in something, the language proper to a domain? What do they discover in this domain? We thus propose only to discern certain formal criteria of recognition, the simplest ones, by invoking in each case the example of cited authors, whatever the diversity of their works and projects.

I. First Criterion: The Symbolic

We are used to, almost conditioned to a certain distinction or correlation between the real and the imaginary. All of our thought maintains a dialectical play between these two notions. Even when classical philosophy speaks of pure intelligence or understanding, it is still a matter of a faculty defined by its aptitude to grasp the depths of the real (*le réel en son fond*), the real "in truth," the real as such, in opposition to, but also in relation to the power of imagination. Let us cite some creative movements that are quite different: Romanticism, Symbolism, Surrealism... In doing so, we invoke at once the transcendent point where the real and the imaginary interpenetrate and unite, and their sharp border, like the cutting edge of their difference. In any case, we get no farther than the opposition and complementarity of the imaginary and the real—at least in the traditional interpretation of Romanticism, Symbolism, etc. Even Freudianism is interpreted from the perspective of two principles: the reality principle with its power to disappoint, the pleasure principle with its hallucinatory power of satisfaction. With all the more reason, methods like those of Jung and Bachelard are wholly inscribed within the real and the imaginary, within the frame of their complex relations, transcendent unity and liminary tension, fusion and cutting edge.

The first criterion of structuralism, however, is the discovery and recognition of a third order, a third regime: that of the symbolic. The refusal to confuse the symbolic with the imaginary, as much as with the real, constitutes the first dimension of structuralism. In this case again, everything began with linguistics: beyond the word in its reality and its resonant parts, beyond images and concepts associated with words, the structuralist linguist discovers an element of quite another nature, a structural object. And perhaps it is in this symbolic element that the novelists of *Tel Quel* wish to locate themselves, in order to renew the resonant realities as well as the associated narratives. Beyond the history of men, and the history of ideas, Michel Foucault discovers a deeper, subterranean ground that forms the object of what he calls the archaeology of thought. Behind real men and their real relations, behind ideologies and their imaginary relations, Louis Althusser discovers a deeper domain as object of science and of philosophy.

We already had many fathers in psychoanalysis: first of all, a real father, but also father-images. And all our dramas occurred in the strained relations of the real and the imaginary. Jacques Lacan discovers a third, more fundamental father, a symbolic father or Name-of-the-Father. Not just the real and the imaginary, but their relations, and the disturbances of these relations, must be thought as the limit of a process in which they constitute themselves in relation to the symbolic. In Lacan's work, in the work of other structuralists as well, the symbolic as element of the structure constitutes the principle of a genesis: structure is incarnated in realities and images according to determinable series. Moreover, the structure constitutes series by incarnating itself, but is not derived from them since it is deeper, being the substratum both for the strata of the real and for the heights [*ciels*] of imagination. Conversely, catastrophes that are proper to the symbolic structural order take into account the apparent disturbances of the real and the imaginary: thus, in the case of *The Wolf Man* as Lacan interprets it, the theme of castration reappears in the real since it remains non-symbolized ("foreclosure"), in the hallucinatory form of the cut finger.[2]

We can enumerate the real, the imaginary, and the symbolic: 1, 2, 3. But perhaps these numerals have as much an ordinal as a cardinal value. For the real in itself is not separable from a certain ideal of unification or of totalization: the real tends towards one, it is one in its "truth." As soon as we see two in "one," as soon as we make doubles [*dédoublons*], the imaginary appears in person, even if it is in the real that its action is carried out. For example, the real father is one, or wants to be according to his law; but the image of the father is always double in itself, cleaved according to a law of the dual or duel. It is projected onto two persons at least, one assuming the role of the play-father, the father-buffoon, and the other, the role of the working and ideal father: like the Prince of Wales in Shakespeare, who passes from one father image to the other, from Falstaff to the Crown. The imaginary is defined by games of mirroring, of duplication, of reversed identification and projection, always in the mode of the double.[3] But perhaps, in turn, the symbolic is three, and not merely the third beyond the real and the imaginary. There is always a third to be sought in the symbolic itself; structure is at least triadic, without which it would not "circulate"—a third at once unreal, and yet not imaginable.

We will see why later; but already the first criterion consists of this: the positing of a symbolic order, irreducible to the orders of the real and the imaginary, and deeper than they are. We do not yet know what this symbolic element consists of. We can say at least that the corresponding structure has no relationship with a sensible form, nor with a figure of the imagination, nor with an intelligible essence. It has nothing to do with a *form*: for structure is not at all defined by an autonomy of the whole, by a preeminence [*pregnance*] of the whole over its parts, by a *Gestalt* which would operate in the real and in perception. Structure is defined, on the contrary, by the nature of certain atomic elements which claim to account both for the formation of wholes and for the variation of their parts. It has nothing to do with *figures* of the imagination, although structuralism is riddled with reflections on rhetoric, metaphor and metonymy, for these figures themselves imply structural displacements which must account for both the literal and the figurative. Nor has it has anything to do with an *essence*: it is more a combinatory formula [*une combinatoire*] supporting formal elements which by themselves have neither form, nor signification, nor representation, nor content, nor given empirical reality, nor hypothetical functional model, nor intelligibility behind appearances. No one has better determined the status of the structure as identical to the "Theory" itself than Louis Althusser—and the symbolic must be understood as the production of the original and specific theoretical object.

Sometimes structuralism is aggressive, as when it denounces the general misunderstanding of this ultimate symbolic category, beyond the imaginary and the real. Sometimes it is interpretative, as when it renews our interpretation of works in relation to this category, and claims to discover an original point at which language is constituted, in which works elaborate themselves, and where ideas and actions are bound together. Romanticism and Symbolism, but also Freudianism and Marxism, thus become the objects of profound reinterpretations. Not to mention the mythical, poetic, philosophical, or practical works which themselves are subjected to structural interpretation. But this reinterpretation only has value to the extent that it animates new works which are those of today, as if the symbolic were the source, inseparably, of living interpretation and creation.

II. Second Criterion: Local or Positional

What does the symbolic element of the structure consist of? We sense the need to go slowly, to state repeatedly, first of all, what it is not. Distinct from the real and the imaginary, the symbolic cannot be defined either by pre-existing realities to which it would refer and which it would designate, or by the imaginary or conceptual contents which it would implicate, and which would give it a signification. The elements of a structure have neither extrinsic designation, nor intrinsic signification. Then what is left? As Lévi-Strauss recalls rigorously, they have nothing other than a *sense* [*sens* = meaning and direction]: a sense which is necessarily and uniquely "positional."[4]

It is not a matter of a location in a real spatial expanse, nor of sites in imaginary extensions, but rather of places and sites in a properly structural space, that is, a topological space. Space is what is structural, but an unextended, pre-extensive space, pure *spatium* constituted bit by bit as an order of proximity, in which the notion of proximity first of all has precisely an ordinal sense and not a signification in extension.[5] Or take genetic biology: the genes are part of a structure to the extent that they are inseparable from "loci," sites capable of changing their relation within the chromosome. In short, places in a purely structural space are primary in relation to the things and real beings which come to occupy them, primary also in relation to the always somewhat imaginary roles and events which necessarily appear when they are occupied.

The scientific ambition of structuralism is not quantitative, but topological and relational, a principal that Lévi-Strauss constantly reaffirms. And when Althusser speaks of economic structure, he specifies that the true "subjects" there are not those who come to occupy the places, i.e. concrete individuals or real human beings—no more than the true objects are the roles that they fulfill and the events that are produced. Rather, these "subjects" are above all the places in a topological and structural space defined by relations of production.[6] When Foucault defines determinations such as death, desire, work, or play, he does not consider them as dimensions of empirical human existence, but above all as the qualifications of places and positions which will render those who come to occupy them mortal and dying, or desiring, or workman-like, or playful. These, however, only come to occupy the places and positions secondarily, fulfilling their roles according to an order of proximity that is an order of the structure itself. That is why Foucault can propose a new distribution of the empirical and the transcendental, the latter finding itself defined by an order of places independently of those who occupy them empirically.[7] Structuralism cannot be separated from a new transcendental philosophy, in which the sites prevail over whatever occupies them. Father, mother, etc., are first of all sites in a structure; and if we are mortal, it is by moving into the line, by coming to a particular site, marked in the structure following this topological order of proximities (even when we do so ahead of our turn).

"It is not only the subject," says Lacan, "but subjects grasped in their intersubjectivity, who line up... and who model their very being on the moment of the signifying chain which traverses them... The displacement of the signifier determines subjects in their acts, in their destiny, in their refusals, in their blindnesses, in their conquests and in their fate, their innate gifts and social acquisition notwithstanding, without regard for character or sex..."[8] One could not say more clearly that empirical psychology is not only founded, but determined by a transcendental topology.

174

Several consequences follow from this local or positional criterion. First of all, if the symbolic elements have no extrinsic designation nor intrinsic signification, but only a positional sense, it follows necessarily and by rights that *sense always results from the combination of elements which are not themselves signifying*.[9] As Lévi-Strauss says in his discussion with Paul Ricoeur, sense is always a result, an effect: not merely an effect like a product, but an optical effect, a language effect, a positional effect. There is, profoundly, a nonsense of sense, from which sense itself results. Not that we return in this way to what was once called a philosophy of the absurd since, for such a philosophy, sense itself is lacking, essentially. For structuralism, on the other hand, there is always too much sense, an overproduction, an over-determination of sense, always produced in excess by the combination of places in the structure. (Hence the importance, in Althusser's work for example, of the concept of *over-determination*.)[10] Nonsense is not at all the absurd or the opposite of sense, but rather that which gives value to sense and produces it by circulating in the structure. Structuralism owes nothing to Albert Camus, but much to Lewis Carroll.[11]

The second consequence is structuralism's inclination for certain games and a certain kind of theatre, for certain play and theatrical spaces. It is no accident that Lévi-Strauss often refers to the theory of games, and accords such importance to playing cards. As does Lacan to his game metaphors which are more than metaphors: not only the moving object [*le furet*, literally the ferret; or, moving token in the *jeu de furet*, the game of hunt-the-slipper] which darts around the structure, but also the dummy-hand [*la place du mort*] that circulates in bridge. The noblest games such as chess are those that organize a combinatory system of places in a pure *spatium* infinitely deeper than the real extension of the chessboard and the imaginary extension of each piece. Or when Althusser interrupts his commentary on Marx to talk about theatre, but a theatre that is neither of reality nor of ideas, a pure theatre of places and positions, the principle of which he sees in Brecht,[12] and that would today perhaps find its most extreme expression in Armand Gatti's work. In short, the very manifesto of structuralism must be sought in the famous formula, eminently poetic and theatrical: to think is to cast a throw of the dice [*penser, c'est émettre un coup de dés*].[13]

The third consequence is that structuralism is inseparable from a new materialism, a new atheism, a new anti-humanism. For if the place is primary in relation to whatever occupies it, it certainly will not do to replace God with man in order to change the structure. And if this place is the dummy-hand [*la place du mort*, i.e. the dead man's place], the death of God surely means the death of man as well, in favor, we hope, of something yet to come, but which could only come within the structure and through its mutation. This is how we understand the imaginary character of man for Foucault or the ideological character of humanism for Althusser.

175

III. Third Criterion: The Differential and the Singular

What then do these symbolic elements or units of position finally consist of? Let us return to the linguistic model. What is distinct both from the voiced elements, and the associated concepts and images, is called a phoneme, the smallest linguistic unit capable of differentiating two words of diverse meanings: for example, "*b*illard" [billiard] and "*p*illard" [pillager]. It is clear that the phoneme is embodied in letters, syllables and sounds, but that it is not reducible to them. Moreover, letters, syllables and sounds give it an independence, whereas in itself, the phoneme is inseparable from the phonemic relation which unites it to other phonemes: b / p. Phonemes do not exist independently of the relations into which they enter and through which they reciprocally determine each other.[14]

We can distinguish three types of relation. A first type is established between elements which enjoy independence or autonomy: for example, 3 + 2, or even 2 / 3. The elements are real, and these relations must themselves be said to be real. A second type of relationship, for example, $x2 + y2 - R2 = 0$, is established between terms for which the value is not specified, but which in each case, however, must have a determined value. Such relations can be called imaginary. But the third type is established between elements which have no determined value themselves, and which nevertheless determine each other reciprocally in the relation: thus $ydy + xdx = 0$, or $dy-/ dx = - x/y$. Such relationships are symbolic, and the corresponding elements are held in a differential relationship. Dy is totally undetermined in relation to y, and dx is totally undetermined in relation to x: each one has neither existence, nor value, nor signification. And yet the relation dy/dx is totally determined, the two elements determining each other reciprocally in the relation.[15] This process of a reciprocal determination is at the heart of a relationship that allows one to define the symbolic nature. Sometimes the origins of structuralism are sought in the area of axiomatics, and it is true that Bourbaki, for example, uses the word "structure." But this use, it seems to me, is in a very different sense, that of relations between non-specified elements, not even qualitatively specified, whereas in structuralism, elements specify each other reciprocally in relations. In this sense, axiomatics would still be imaginary, not symbolic properly speaking. The mathematical origin of structuralism must be sought rather in the domain of differential calculus, specifically in the interpretation which Weierstrass and Russell gave to it, a *static and ordinal* interpretation, which definitively liberates calculus from all reference to the infinitely small, and integrates it into a pure logic of relations.

Corresponding to the determination of differential relations are singularities, distributions of singular points which characterize curves or figures (a triangle for example has three singular points). In this way, the determination of phonemic relations proper to a given language ascribes singularities in proximity to which the vocalizations and significations of the language are constituted. *The recipro-*

cal determination of symbolic elements continues henceforth into *the complete determination* of singular points that constitute a space corresponding to these elements. The crucial notion of singularity, taken literally, seems to belong to all the domains in which there is structure. The general formula, "to think is to cast a throw of the dice," itself refers to the singularities represented by the sharply outlined points on the dice. Every structure presents the following two aspects: a system of differential relations according to which the symbolic elements determine themselves reciprocally, and a system of singularities corresponding to these relations and tracing the space of the structure. Every structure is a multiplicity. The question, "Is there structure in any domain whatsoever?," must be specified in the following way: in a given domain, can one uncover symbolic elements, differential relations and singular points which are proper to it? Symbolic elements are incarnated in the real beings and objects of the domain considered; the differential relations are actualized in real relations between these beings; the singularities are so many places in the structure, which distributes the imaginary attitudes or roles of the beings or objects that come to occupy them.[16]

It is not a matter of mathematical metaphors. In each domain, one must find elements, relationships and points. When Lévi-Strauss undertakes the study of elementary kinship structures, he not only considers the real fathers in a society, nor only the father-images that run through the myths of that society. He claims to discover real kinship phonemes, that is, *kin-emes* [*parentèmes*], positional units which do not exist independently of the differential relations into which they enter and that determine each other reciprocally. It is in this way that the four relations—brother / sister, husband / wife, father / son, maternal uncle / sister's son—form the simplest structure. And to this combinatory system of "kinship names" correspond in a complex way, but without resembling them, the "kinship attitudes" that realize the singularities determined in the system. One could just as well proceed in the opposite manner: start from singularities in order to determine the differential relations between ultimate symbolic elements. Thus, taking the example of the Oedipus myth, Lévi-Strauss starts from the singularities of the story (Oedipus marries his mother, kills his father, immolates the Sphinx, is named club-foot, etc.) in order to infer from them the differential relations between "mythemes" which are determined reciprocally (overestimation of kinship relations, underestimation of kinship relations, negation of aboriginality, persistence of aboriginality).[17] In any case, the symbolic elements and their relations always determine the nature of the beings and objects which come to realize them, while the singularities form an order of positions that simultaneously determines the roles and the attitudes of these beings in so far as they occupy them. The determination of the structure is therefore completed in a theory of attitudes which explains its functioning.

Singularities correspond with the symbolic elements and their relations, but do not resemble them. One could say, rather, that singularities "symbolize" with them, derive from them, since every determination of differential relations entails a distribution of singular points. Yet, for example: the values of differential relations are incarnated in species, whereas singularities are incarnated in the organic parts corresponding to each species. The former constitute variables, the latter constitute functions. The former constitute within a structure the domain of *appellations*, the latter the domain of *attitudes*.[18] Lévi-Strauss insisted on this double aspect—derived, yet irreducible—of attitudes in relation to appellations.[19] A disciple of Lacan, Serge Leclaire, shows in another field how the symbolic elements of the unconscious necessarily refer to "libidinal movements" of the body, incarnating the singularities of the structure in such and such a place.[20] In this sense, every structure is psychosomatic, or rather represents a category-attitude complex.

Let us consider the interpretation of Marxism by Althusser and his collaborators: above all, the relations of production are determined as differential relations that are established, not between real men or concrete individuals, but between objects and agents which, first of all, have a symbolic value (object of production, instrument of production, labor force, immediate workers, immediate non-workers, such as they are held in relations of property and appropriation).[21] Each mode of production is thus characterized by singularities corresponding to the values of the relations. And if it is obvious that concrete men come to occupy the places and carry forth the elements of the structure, this happens by fulfilling the role that the structural place assigns to them (for example the "capitalist"), and by serving as supports for the structural relations. This occurs to such an extent that "the true subjects are not these occupants and functionaries... but the definition and distribution of these places and these functions." The true subject is the structure itself: the differential and the singular, the differential relations and the singular points, the reciprocal determination and the complete determination.

IV. Fourth Criterion: The Differenciator, Differenciation

Structures are necessarily unconscious, by virtue of the elements, relations and points that compose them. Every structure is an infrastructure, a micro-structure. In a certain way, they are not actual. What is actual is that in which the structure is incarnated or rather what the structure constitutes when it is incarnated. But in itself, it is neither actual nor fictional, neither real, nor possible. Jakobson poses the problem of the status of the phoneme, which is not to be confused with any actual letter, syllable or sound, no more than it is a fiction, or an associated image.[22] Perhaps the word virtuality would precisely designate the mode of the structure or the object of theory, on the condition that we eliminate any vagueness about the word. For the virtual has a reality which is proper to it, but which does not merge with any actual reality, any present or past actuality.

The virtual has an ideality that is proper to it, but which does not merge with any possible image, any abstract idea. We will say of structure: *real without being actual, ideal without being abstract.*[23] This is why Lévi-Strauss often presents the structure as a sort of ideal reservoir or repertoire, in which everything coexists virtually, but where the actualization is necessarily carried out according to exclusive rules, always implicating partial combinations and unconscious choices. To discern the structure of a domain is to determine an entire virtuality of coexistence which pre-exists the beings, objects and works of this domain. Every structure is a multiplicity of virtual coexistence. Louis Althusser, for example, shows in this sense that the originality of Marx (his anti-Hegelianism) resides in the manner in which the social system is defined by a coexistence of elements and economic relations, without one being able to engender them successively according to the illusion of a false dialectic.[24]

What is it that coexists in the structure? All the elements, the relations and relational values, all the singularities proper to the domain considered. Such a coexistence does not imply any confusion, nor any indetermination for the relationships and differential elements coexist in a completely and perfectly determined whole. Except that this whole is not actualized as such. What is actualized, here and now, are particular relations, relational values, and distributions of singularities; others are actualized elsewhere or at other times. There is no total language [*langue*], embodying all the possible phonemes and phonemic relations. But the virtual totality of the language system [*langage*] is actualized following exclusive rules in diverse, specific languages, of which each embodies certain relationships, relational values, and singularities. There is no total society, but each social form embodies certain elements, relationships, and production values (for example "capitalism"). We must therefore distinguish between the total structure of a domain as an ensemble of virtual coexistence, and the sub-structures that correspond to diverse actualizations in the domain. Of the structure as virtuality, we must say that it is still undifferentiated (c), even though it is totally and completely differential (t). Of structures which are embodied in a particular actual form (present or past), we must say that they are differentiated, and that for them to be actualized is precisely to be differentiated. The structure is inseparable from this double aspect, or from this complex that one can designate under the name of differential (t) / differentiation (c), where t / c constitutes the universally determined phonemic relationship.[25]

All differentiation, all actualization is carried out along two paths: species and parts. The differential relations are incarnated in qualitatively distinct species, while the corresponding singularities are incarnated in the parts and extended figures which characterize each species: hence, the language species, and the parts of each one in the vicinity of the singularities of the linguistic structure; the specifically defined social modes of production and the organized parts corresponding to each one of these modes, etc. One will notice that the process of

179

actualization always implies an internal temporality, variable according to what is actualized. Not only does each type of social production have a global internal temporality, but its organized parts have particular rhythms. As regards time, the position of structuralism is thus quite clear: time is always a time of actualization, according to which the elements of virtual coexistence are carried out at diverse rhythms. Time goes from the virtual to the actual, that is, from structure to its actualizations, and not from one actual form to another. Or at least time conceived as a relation of succession of two actual forms makes do with expressing abstractly the internal times of the structure or structures that are realized at different depths in these two forms, and the differential relations between these times. And precisely because the structure is not actualized without being differentiated in space and time, hence without differentiating the species and the parts which carry it out, we must say in this sense that structure *produces* these species and these parts themselves. It produces them as differentiated species and parts, such that one can no more oppose the genetic to the structural than time to structure. Genesis, like time, goes from the virtual to the actual, from the structure to its actualization; the two notions of multiple internal time and static ordinal genesis are in this sense inseparable from the play of structures.[26]

We must insist on this differenciating role. Structure is in itself a system of elements and of differential relations, but it also differentiates the species and parts, the beings and functions in which the structure is actualized. It is differential in itself, and differentiating in its effect. Commenting on Lévi-Strauss's work, Jean Pouillon defined the problem of structuralism: can one elaborate "a system of differences which leads neither to their simple juxtaposition, nor to their artificial erasure?"[27] In this regard, the work of Georges Dumézil is exemplary, even from the point of view of structuralism: no one has better analyzed the generic and specific differences between religions, and also the differences in parts and functions between the gods of a particular, single religion. For the gods of a religion, for example, Jupiter, Mars, Quirinus, incarnate elements and differential relations, at the same time as they find their attitudes and functions in proximity to the singularities of the system or "parts of the society" considered. They are thus essentially differentiated by the structure which is actualized or carried out in them, and which produces them by being actualized. It is true that each of them, considered solely in its actuality, attracts and reflects the function of the others, such that one risks no longer discovering anything of this originary differenciation which produces them from the virtual to the actual. But it is precisely here that the border passes between the imaginary and the symbolic: the imaginary tends to reflect and to resituate around each term the total effect of a wholistic mechanism, whereas the symbolic structure assures the differential of terms and the differentiation of effects. Hence the hostility of structuralism toward the methods of the imaginary: Lacan's critique of Jung, and the critique of Bachelard by proponents of "New Criticism." The imagination duplicates and reflects, it projects and identifies, loses itself in a play of mirrors, but the distinctions that it makes, like the assimilations that it carries out, are surface effects that hide the otherwise subtle differential mechanisms of symbolic thought. Commenting on Dumézil, Edmond Ortigues has this to say: "When one approaches the material imagination, the differential function diminishes, one tends towards equivalences; when one approaches the formative elements of society, the differential function increases, one tends towards distinctive values [valences]."[28]

Structures are unconscious, necessarily overlaid by their products or effects. An economic structure never exists in a pure form, but is covered over by the juridical, political and ideological relations in which it is incarnated. One can only read, find, retrieve the structures through these effects. The terms and relations which actualize them, the species and parts that realize them, are as much forms of interference [brouillage] as forms of expression. This is why one of Lacan's disciples, J.-A. Miller, develops the concept of a "metonymic causality," or Althusser, the concept of a properly structural causality, in order to account for the very particular presence of a structure in its effects, and for the way in which it differenciates these effects, at the same time as these latter assimilate and integrate it.[29] The unconscious of the structure is a differential unconscious. One might believe then that structuralism goes back to a pre-Freudian conception: doesn't Freud understand the unconscious as a mode of the conflict of forces or of the opposition of desires, whereas Leibnizian metaphysics already proposed the idea of a differential unconscious of little perceptions? But even in Freud's writing, there is a whole problem of the origin of the unconscious, of its constitution as "language," which goes beyond the level of desire, of associated images and relations of opposition. Conversely, the differential unconscious is not constituted by little perceptions of the real and by passages to the limit, but rather of variations of differential relations in a symbolic system as functions of distributions of singularities. Lévi-Strauss is right to say that the unconscious is made neither of desires nor of representations, that it is "always empty," consisting solely in the structural laws that it imposes on representations and on desires.[30]

For the unconscious is always a problem, though not in the sense that would call its existence into question. Rather, the unconscious by itself forms the problems and questions that are resolved only to the extent that the corresponding structure is instantiated [s'effectue] and always according to the way that it is instantiated. For a problem always gains the solution that it deserves based on the manner in which it is posed, and on the symbolic field used to pose it. Althusser can present the economic structure of a society as the field of problems that the society poses for itself, that it is determined to pose for itself, and that it resolves according to its own means, that is, according to the lines of differentiation along which the structure is actualized (taking into account the absurdities, ignominies and cruelties that these "solutions" involve by reason of the structure). Similarly, Serge Leclaire, following Lacan, can distinguish psychoses and neuroses, and different kinds of neuroses, less by types of conflict than by modes of questions that always find the answer that they deserve as a function of the symbolic field in which they are posed: thus the hysterical question is not that of the obsessive.[31] In all of this, problems and questions do not designate a provisional and subjective moment in the elaboration of our knowledge, but on the contrary, designate a perfectly objective category, full and complete "objectalities" [*objectités*][32] which are the structure's own. The structural unconscious is at once differential, problematizing and questioning. And, as we shall see, it is finally serial.

V. Fifth Criterion: Serial

All of the preceding, however, still seems incapable of functioning, for we have only been able to define half of the structure. A structure only starts to move, and become animated, if we restore its other half. Indeed, the symbolic elements that we have previously defined, taken in their differential relations, are organized necessarily in series. But so organized, they relate to another series, constituted by other symbolic elements and other relations: this reference to a second series is easily explained by recalling that singularities derive from the terms and relations of the first, but are not limited simply to reproducing or reflecting them. They thus organize themselves in another series capable of an autonomous development, or at least they necessarily relate the first to this other series. So it is for phonemes and morphemes; or for the economic and other social series; or for Foucault's triple series, linguistic, economic and biological, etc. The question of knowing if the first series forms a basis and in which sense, if it is signifying, the others only being signified, is a complex question the nature of which we cannot yet assess. One must state simply that every structure is serial, multi-serial, and would not function without this condition.

When Lévi-Strauss again takes up the study of totemism, he shows the extent to which the phenomenon is poorly understood as long as it is interpreted in terms of imagination. For according to its law, the *imagination* necessarily conceives totemism as the operation by which a man or a group are identified with an animal. But *symbolically*, it is quite a different matter, not the imaginary identification of one term with another, but the structural homology of two series of terms: on the one hand, a series of animal species taken as elements of differential relations; on the other, a series of social positions themselves caught symbolically in their own relations. This confrontation occurs "between these two systems of differences," these two series of elements and relations.[33]

The unconscious, according to Lacan, is neither individual nor collective, but intersubjective, which is to say that it implies a development in terms of series: not only the signifier and the signified, but the two series at a minimum organize themselves in quite a variable manner according to the domain under consideration.[34] In one of Lacan's most famous texts, he comments on "The Purloined Letter" by Edgar Allen Poe, showing how the "structure" puts into play two series, the places of which are occupied by variable subjects. First series: the king who does not see the letter, the queen who is thrilled at having so cleverly hidden it by leaving it out in the open, the minister who sees everything and takes possession of the letter.[35] Second series: the police who find nothing at the minister's hotel; the minister who is thrilled at having so cleverly hidden the letter by leaving it out in the open; Dupin who sees everything and takes back possession of the letter. Already in a previous text, Lacan examined the case of *The Rat Man* on the basis of a double series, paternal and filial, in which each put into play four relational terms according to an order of places: debt / friend, rich woman / poor woman.[36]

It goes without saying that the organization of the constitutive series of a structure supposes a veritable *mise en scène* and, in each case, requires precise evaluations and interpretations. There is no general rule at all; we touch here on the point at which structuralism implies, from one perspective, a true creation, and from another, an initiative and a discovery that is not without its risks. The determination of a structure occurs not only through a choice of basic symbolic elements and the differential relations into which they enter, nor merely through a distribution of the singular points which correspond to them. The determination also occurs through the constitution of a second series, at least, that maintains complex relations with the first. And if the structure defines a problematic field, a field of problems, it is in the sense that the nature of the problem reveals its proper objectivity in this serial constitution, which sometimes makes structuralism seem close to music. Phillipe Sollers writes a novel, *Drame*, punctuated [*rhythmé*] by the expressions "Problem" and "Missing" [*Manqué*], in the course of which tentative series are elaborated ("a chain of maritime memories passes through his right arm... the left leg, on the other contrary, seemed to be riddled with mineral groupings").[37] Or Jean-Pierre Faye's attempt in *Analogues*, concerning a serial co-existence of narrative modes.[38]

But what keeps the two series from simply reflecting one another, and henceforth, identifying each of their terms one to one? The whole of the structure would then fall back into the state of a figure of imagination. The factor that allays such a threat is seemingly quite strange. Indeed, the terms of each series are in themselves inseparable from the slippages [*décalages*] or displacements that they undergo in relation to the terms of the other. They are thus inseparable from the variation of differential relations. In the case of the purloined letter, the minister in the second series comes to the place that the queen had occupied in the first one. In the filial series of *The Rat Man*, the poor woman comes to occupy the friend's place in relation to the debt.[39] Or again, in the double series of birds and twins cited by Lévi-Strauss, the twins are the "people from on high" in relation to the people from below, necessarily coming to occupy the place of the "birds from below," not of the birds from on high.[40] This relative displacement of the two series is not at all secondary; it does not come to affect a term from the outside and secondarily, as if giving it an imaginary disguise. On the contrary, the displacement is properly structural or symbolic: it belongs essentially to the places in the space of the structure, and thus regulates all the imaginary disguises of beings and objects that come secondarily to occupy these places. This is why structuralism brings so much attention to bear on metaphor and metonymy. These are not in any way figures of the imagination, but are, above all, structural factors. They are even *the* two structural factors, in the sense that they express the two degrees of freedom of displacement, from one series to another and within the same series. Far from being imaginary, they prevent the series that they animate from confusing or duplicating their terms in imaginary fashion. But what are these relative displacements then, if they belong absolutely to places in the structure?

VI. Sixth Criterion: The Empty Square [La Case Vide]

It appears that the structure envelops a wholly paradoxical object or element. Let us consider the case of the letter, in Edgar Allen Poe's story, as examined by Lacan; or the case of the debt, in *The Rat Man*. It is obvious that this object is eminently symbolic, but we say "eminently" because it belongs to no series in particular: the letter is nevertheless present in both of Poe's series; the debt is present in both *Rat Man* series. Such an object is always present in the corresponding series, it traverses them and moves with them, it never ceases to circulate in them, and from one to the other, with an extraordinary agility. One might say that it is *its own* metaphor, and *its own* metonymy. The series in each case are constituted by symbolic terms and differential relations, but this object seems to be of another nature. In fact, it is in relation to the object that the variety of terms and the variation of differential relations are determined in each case. The two series of a structure are always divergent (by virtue of the laws of differenciation), but this singular object is the convergence point of the divergent series as such. It is "eminently" symbolic, but precisely because it is immanent to the two series at once. What else would we call it, if not Object = x, the riddle Object or the great Mobile element? We can nevertheless remain a bit doubtful: what Jacques Lacan invites us to discover in two cases, the particular role played by a letter or a debt—is it an artifice, strictly applicable to these cases, or rather is it a truly general method, valid for all the structurable domains, a criterion for every structure, as if a structure were not defined without assigning an object = x that ceaselessly traverses the series? As if the literary work, for example, or the work of art, but other *oeuvres* as well, those of society, those of illness, those of life in general, enveloped this very special object which assumes control over their structure. And as if it were always a matter of finding who is H,[41] or of discovering an x shrouded within the work. Such is the case with songs: the refrain encompasses an object = x, while the verses form the divergent series through which this object circulates. It is for this reason that songs truly present an elementary structure.[42]

A disciple of Lacan, André Green, signals the existence of the handkerchief that circulates in *Othello*, traversing all the series of the play.[43] We also spoke of the two series of the Prince of Wales, Falstaff or the father-buffoon, Henry IV or the royal father, the two images of the father. The crown is the object = x that traverses the two series, with different terms and under different relations. The moment when the prince tries on the crown, his father not yet dead, marks the passage from one series to the other, the change in symbolic terms and the variation of differential relations. The old dying king is angered, and believes that his son wants to identify with him prematurely. Yet responding quite capably in a splendid speech, the prince shows that the crown is not the object of an imaginary identification, but on the contrary, is the eminently symbolic term that traverses all the series, the infamous series of Falstaff and the great royal series, and that permits the passage from one to the other at the heart of the same structure. As we saw, there was a first difference between the imaginary and the symbolic; the differentiating role of the symbolic, in opposition to the assimilating and reflecting role, doubling and duplicating, of the imaginary. But the second dividing line appears more clearly here: against the dual character of the imagination, the Third which essentially intervenes in the symbolic system, which distributes series, displaces them relatively, makes them communicate with each other, all the while preventing the one from imaginarily falling back on the other.

Debt, the letter, the handkerchief or the crown, the nature of this object is specified by Lacan: it is always displaced in relation to itself. Its peculiar property is not to be where one looks for it, and conversely, also to be found where it is not. One would say that it "is missing from its place" [*il manque à sa place*] (and, in this, is not something real); furthermore, that it does not coincide with its own resemblance (and, in this, is not an image); and that it does not coincide with its own identity (and, in this, is not a concept). "What is hidden is never what is *missing from its place*, as the call slip puts it when speaking of a volume lost in the library. And even if the book be on an adjacent shelf or in the next slot, it would be hidden there, however visible it may appear. For only something that can change its place can *literally* be said to be missing from it: i.e., the symbolic. For the real, whatever upheaval we subject it to, is always in its place; it carries it glued to its heel, ignorant of what might exile it from it."[44] If the series that the object = x traverses necessarily present relative displacements in relation to each other, this is so because the *relative* places of their terms in the structure depend first on the *absolute* place of each, at each moment, in relation to the object = x that is always circulating, always displaced in relation to itself.[45] It is in this sense that the displacement, and more generally all the forms of exchange, does not constitute a characteristic added from the outside, but the fundamental property that allows the structure to be defined as an order of places subject to the variation of relations. The whole structure is driven by this originary Third, but that also fails to coincide with its own origin. Distributing the differences through the entire structure, making the differential relations vary with its displacements, the object = x constitutes the differenciating element of difference itself.

Games need the empty square, without which nothing would move forward or function. The object = x is not distinguishable from its place, but it is characteristic of this place that it constantly displaces itself, just as it is characteristic of the empty square to jump ceaselessly.[46] Lacan invokes the *dummy-hand* in bridge, and in the admirable opening pages of *The Order of Things*, where he describes a painting by Velasquez, Foucault invokes the place of the king, in relation to which everything is displaced and slides, God, then man, without ever filling it.[47] No structuralism is possible without this degree zero. Phillipe Sollers and Jean-Pierre Faye like to invoke the *blind spot* [*tache aveugle*], so designating this always mobile point which entails a certain blindness, but in relation to which writing becomes possible, because series organize themselves therein as genuine "literemes" [*littérèmes*].[48] In his effort to elaborate a concept of structural or metonymic causality, J.-A. Miller borrows from Frege the position of a *zero*, defined as lacking its own identity, and which conditions the serial constitution of numbers.[49] And even Lévi-Strauss, who in certain respects is the most positivist among the structuralists, the least romantic, the least inclined to welcome an elusive element, recognized in the "mana" or its equivalents the existence of a "floating signifier," with a symbolic zero value circulating in the structure.[50] In so doing, he connects with Jakobson's zero phoneme which does not by itself entail any differential character or phonetic value, but in relation to which all the phonemes are situated in their own differential relations.

If it is true that structural criticism has as its object the determination of "virtualities" in language which pre-exist the work, the work is itself structural when it sets out to express its own virtualities. Lewis Carroll, Joyce, invented "portmanteau" words, or more generally, esoteric words, to ensure the coincidence of verbal sound series and the simultaneity of associated story series.[51] In *Finnegan's Wake*, it is again a *letter* which is Cosmos, and which reunites all the series of the world. In Lewis Carroll's works, the portmanteau word connotes at least two basic series (speaking and eating, verbal series and alimentary series) that can themselves be subdivided, such as the Snark. It is incorrect to say that such a word has two meanings; in fact, it is of another order than words possessing a sense. It is the nonsense which animates at least the two series, but which provides them with sense by circulating through them. It is this nonsense, in its ubiquity, in its perpetual displacement, that produces sense in each series, and from one series to another, and that ceaselessly dislocates [*décaler*] the series in relation to each other. This word is the word = *x* in so far as it designates the object = *x*, the *problematic* object. As word = *x*, it traverses a series determined as that of the signifier; but at the same time, as object = *x*, it traverses the other series determined as that of the signified.[52] It never ceases at once to hollow out and to fill in the gap between the two series. Lévi-Strauss shows this in relation to the "mana," that he assimilates to the words "thingamajig" [*truc*] or "thingie" [*machin*]. As we have seen, this is how nonsense is not the absence of signification but, on the contrary, the excess of sense, or that which provides the signifier and signified with sense. Sense here emerges as the effect of the structure's functioning, in the animation of its component series. And no doubt, portmanteau-words are only one device among others that ensure this circulation. The techniques of Raymond Roussel, as Foucault has analyzed them, are of another nature, founded on differential phonemic relations, or on even more complex relations.[53] In Mallarmé's works, we find systems of relations between series, and the moving parts which animate them, of yet another type. Our purpose is not to analyze the whole set of devices which have constituted and are still constituting modern literature, making use of an entire topography, an entire typography of the "book yet to come" [*livre à venir*]; our goal is only to indicate in all cases the efficacy of this two-sided empty square, at once word and object.

What does it consist of, this object = *x*? Is it and must it remain the perpetual object of a riddle, the *perpetuum mobile*? This would be a way of recalling the objective consistency that the category of the problematic takes on at the heart of structures. And in the long run, it is good that the question *How do we recognize structuralism?* leads to positing something that is not recognizable or identifiable. Let us consider Lacan's psychoanalytic response:[54] the object = *x* is determined as phallus. But this phallus is neither the real organ, nor the series of associable or associated images: it is the symbolic phallus. However, it is indeed sexuality that is in question, a question of nothing else here, contrary to the pious and ever-renewed attempts in psychoanalysis to renounce or minimize sexual references. But the phallus appears not as a sexual given or as the empirical determination of one of the sexes. It appears rather as the symbolic organ that founds sexuality *in its entirety* as system or structure, and in relation to which the places occupied variously by men and women are distributed, as also the series of images and realities. In designating the object = *x* as phallus, it is thus not a question of identifying this object, of conferring to it an identity, which is repellant to its nature. Quite the contrary, for the symbolic phallus is precisely that which does not coincide with its own identity, always found there where it is not since it is not where one looks for it, always displaced in relation to itself, *from the side of the mother*. In this sense, it is certainly the letter and the debt, the handkerchief or the crown, the Snark and the "mana." Father, mother, etc., are symbolic elements held in differential relations. But the phallus is quite another thing, the object = x that determines the relative place of the elements and the variable value of relations, making a structure of the entirety of sexuality. The relations vary as a function of the displacements of the object = x, as relations between "partial drives" constitutive of sexuality.[55]

Obviously the phallus is not a final word, and is even somewhat the locus of a question, of a "demand" that characterizes the empty square of the sexual structure. Questions, like answers, vary according to the structure under consideration, but never do they depend on our preferences, or on an order of abstract causality. It is obvious that the empty square of an economic structure, such as commodity exchange, must be determined in quite another way. It consists of "something" which is reducible neither to the terms of the exchange, nor to the exchange relation itself, but that forms an eminently symbolic third term in perpetual displacement, and as a function of which the relational variations will be defined. Such is *value* as expression of a "*generalized* labor," beyond any empirically observable quality, a locus of the question that runs through or traverses the economy as structure.[56]

A more general consequence follows from this, concerning the different "orders." From a structuralist perspective, it is no doubt unsatisfactory to resurrect the problem of whether there is a structure that determines all the others in the final instance. For example, which is first, value or the phallus, the economic fetish or the sexual fetish? For several reasons, these questions are meaningless. All structures are infrastructures. The structural orders—linguistic, familial, economic, sexual, etc.—are characterized by the form of their symbolic elements, the variety of their differential relations, the species of their singularities, finally and, above all, by the nature of the object = x that presides over their functioning. However, we could only establish an order of linear causality from one structure to another by conferring on the object = x in each case the type of identity that it essentially repudiates. Between structures, causality can only be a type of structural causality. In each structural order, certainly, the object = x is not at all something unknowable, something purely undetermined; it is perfectly determinable, including within its displacements and by the mode of displacement that characterizes it. It is simply not assignable: that is, it cannot be fixed to one place, nor identified with a genre or a species. Rather, it constitutes itself the ultimate genre of the structure or its total place: it thus has no identity except in order to lack this identity, and has no place except in order to be displaced in relation to all places. As a result, for each order of structure the object = x is the empty or perforated site that permits this order to be articulated with the others, in a space that entails as many directions as orders. The orders of the structure do not communicate in a common site, but they all communicate through their empty place or respective object = x. This is why, despite several of Lévi-Strauss's hasty pages, no privilege can be claimed for ethnographic social structures, by referring the psychoanalytic sexual structures to the empirical determination of a more or less de-socialized individual. Even linguistic structures cannot pass as symbolic elements or as ultimate signifiers. Precisely to the extent that the other structures are not limited simply to applying by analogy methods borrowed from linguistics, but discover on their own account veritable languages, be they non-verbal, always entailing their signifiers, their symbolic elements and differential relations. Posing, for example, the problem of the relations between ethnography and psychoanalysis, Foucault is right to say: "They intersect at right angles; for the signifying chain by which the unique experience of the individual is consti-tuted is perpendicular to the formal system on the basis of which the significations of a culture are constituted: at any given instant, the structure proper to individual experience finds a certain number of possible choices (and of excluded possibilities) in the systems of the society; conversely, at each of their points of choice the social structures encounter a certain number of possible indi-viduals (and others who are not)."[57]

And in each structure, the object = x must be disposed to give an account 1) of the way in which it subordinates within its order the other orders of structure, that then only intervene as dimensions of actualization; 2) of the way in which it is itself subordinated to the other orders in their own order (and no longer inter-venes except in their own actualization); 3) of the way in which all the objects = x and all the orders of structure communicate with one another, each order defin-ing a dimension of the space in which it is absolutely primary; 4) of the conditions in which, at a given moment in history or in a given case, a particular dimension corresponding to a particular order of the structure is not deployed for itself and remains subordinated to the actualization of another order (the Lacanian concept of "foreclosure" would again be of decisive importance here).

VII. Final Criteria: From the Subject to Practice

In one sense, places are only filled or occupied by real beings to the extent that the structure is "actualized." But in another sense, we can say that places are already filled or occupied by symbolic elements, at the level of the structure itself. And the differential relations of these elements are the ones that determine the order of places in general. Thus there is a primary symbolic filling-in [remplissement], before any filling-in or occupation by real beings. Except that we again find the paradox of the empty square. For this is the only place that cannot and must not be filled, were it even by a symbolic element. It must retain the perfection of its emptiness in order to be displaced in relation to itself, and in order to circulate throughout the elements and the variety of relations. As symbolic, it must be for itself its own symbol, and eternally lack its other half that would be likely to come and occupy it. (This void is, however, not a non-being; or at least this non-being is not the being of the negative, but rather the positive being of the "problemat-

189

ic," the objective being of a problem and of a question.)[58] This is why Foucault can say: "It is no longer possible to think in our day other than in the void left by man's disappearance. For *this void does not create a deficiency; it does not constitute a lacuna that must be filled in*. It is nothing more and nothing less than the unfolding of a space in which it is once more possible to think."[59]

Nevertheless, if the empty square is not filled by a term, it is nevertheless accompanied by an eminently symbolic instance which follows all of its displacements, accompanied without being occupied or filled. And the two, the instance and the place, do not cease to lack each other, and to accompany each other in this manner. The *subject* is precisely the agency [*instance*] which follows the empty place: as Lacan says, it is less subject than subjected [*assujetti*]—subjected to the empty square, subjected to the phallus and to its displacements. Its agility is peerless, or should be. Thus, the subject is essentially intersubjective. To announce the death of God, or even the death of man is nothing. What counts is *how*. Nietzsche showed already that God dies in several ways; and that the gods die, but from laughter, upon hearing one god say that he is the Only One. Structuralism is not at all a form of thought that suppresses the subject, but one that breaks it up and distributes it systematically, that contests the identity of the subject, that dissipates it and makes it shift from place to place, an always nomad subject, made of individuations, but impersonal ones, or of singularities, but pre-individual ones.[60] This is the sense in which Foucault speaks of "dispersion"; and Lévi-Strauss can only define a subjective agency as depending on the Object conditions under which the systems of truth become convertible and, thus, "simultaneously receivable to several different subjects."[61]

Henceforth, two great accidents of the structure may be defined. Either the empty and mobile square is no longer accompanied by a nomad subject that accentuates its trajectory, and its emptiness becomes a veritable lack, a lacuna. Or just the opposite, it is filled, occupied by what accompanies it, and its mobility is lost in the effect of a sedentary or fixed plenitude. One could just as well say, in linguistic terms, either that the "signifier" has disappeared, that the stream [*flot*] of the signified no longer finds any signifying element that marks it, or that the "signified" has faded away, that the chain of the signifier no longer finds any signified that traverses it: the two pathological aspects of psychosis. One could say further, in theo-anthropological terms, that either God makes the desert grow and hollows out a lacuna in the earth, or that man fills it, occupies the place, and in this vain permutation makes us pass from one accident to the other: this being the reason why man and God are the two sicknesses of the earth, that is to say, of the structure.

What is important is knowing according to what factors and at what moments these accidents are determined in structures of one order or another. Let us again consider the analyses of Althusser and his collaborators: on the one hand, they show in the economic order how the adventures of the empty square

(Value as object = x) are marked by the goods, money, the fetish, capital, etc., that characterize the capitalist structure. On the other hand, they show how contradictions are thus born in the structure. Finally, they show how the real and the imaginary—that is, the real beings who come to occupy places and the ideologies which express the image that they make of it—are narrowly determined by the play of these structural adventures and the contradictions resulting from it. Not that the contradictions are at all imaginary: they are properly structural, and qualify the effects of the structure in the internal time that is proper to it. Thus it cannot be said that the contradiction is apparent, but rather that it is derived: it derives from the empty place and from its becoming in the structure. *As a general rule, the real, the imaginary and their relations are always engendered secondarily by the functioning of the structure, which starts with having its primary effects in itself.*

This is why what we were earlier calling accidents does not at all happen to the structure from the outside. On the contrary, it is a matter of an "immanent" tendency,[63] of ideal events that are part of the structure itself, and that symbolically affect its empty square or subject. We call them "accidents" in order better to emphasize not a contingent or exterior character, but this very special characteristic of the event, interior to the structure in so far as the structure can never be reduced to a simple essence.

Henceforth, a set of complex problems are posed for structuralism, concerning structural "mutations" (Foucault) or "forms of transition" from one structure to another (Althusser). It is always as a function of the empty square that the differential relations are open to new values or variations, and the singularities capable of new distributions, constitutive of another structure. The contradictions must yet be "resolved," that is, the empty place must be rid of the symbolic events that eclipse it or fill it, and be given over to the subject which must accompany it on new paths, without occupying or deserting it. Thus, there is a structuralist *hero*: neither God nor man, neither personal nor universal, it is without an identity, made of non-personal individuations and pre-individual singularities. It assures the break-up [*l'éclatement*] of a structure affected by excess or deficiency; it opposes *its own* ideal event to the ideal events that we have just described.[64] For a new structure not to pursue adventures that again are analogous to those of the old structure, not to cause fatal contradictions to be reborn, depends on the resistant and creative force of this hero, on its agility in following and safeguarding the displacements, on its power to cause relations to vary and to redistribute singularities, always casting another throw of the dice. This mutation point precisely defines a praxis, or rather the very site where praxis must take hold. For structuralism is not only inseparable from the works that it creates, but also from a practice in relation to the products that it interprets. Whether this practice is therapeutic or political, it designates a point of permanent revolution, or of permanent transfer.

191

These last criteria, from the subject to practice, are the most obscure—the criteria of the future. Across the six preceding characteristics, we have sought only to juxtapose a system of echoes between authors who are very independent from each other, exploring very diverse domains, and as diverse as the theory that they themselves propose regarding these echoes. At the different levels of the structure, the real and the imaginary, real beings and ideologies, sense and contradiction, are "effects" that must be understood at the conclusion of a "process," of a properly structural, differenciated production: strange static genesis for physical (optical, sound, etc.) "effects." Books against structuralism (or those against the "New Novel") are strictly without importance; they cannot prevent structuralism from exerting a productivity which is that of our era. No book *against* anything ever has any importance; all that counts are books *for* something, and that know how to produce it.

Three Group-Related Problems[1]

A militant political activist and a psychoanalyst just so happen to meet in the same person,[2] and instead of each minding his own business, they ceaselessly communicate, interfere with one another, and get mixed up—each mistaking himself for the other. An uncommon occurrence at least since Reich. Pierre-Félix Guattari does not let problems of the unity of the Self preoccupy him. The self is rather one more thing we ought to dissolve, under the combined assault of political and analytical forces. Guattari's formula, "we are all groupuscles," indeed heralds the search for a new subjectivity, a group subjectivity, which does not allow itself to be enclosed in a whole bent on reconstituting a self (or even worse, a superego), but which spreads itself out over several groups at once. These groups are divisible, manifold, permeable, and always optional. A good group does not take itself to be unique, immortal, and significant, unlike a defense ministry or homeland security office, unlike war veterans, but instead plugs into an outside that confronts the group with its own possibilities of non-sense, death, and dispersal "precisely as a result of its opening up to other groups." In turn, the individual is also a group. In the most natural way imaginable, Guattari embodies two aspects of an anti-Self: on the one hand, he is like a catatonic stone, a blind and hard body invaded by death as soon as he takes off his glasses; on the other hand, he lights up and seethes with multiple lives the moment he looks, acts, laughs, thinks or attacks. Thus he is named Pierre and Félix: schizophrenic powers.

In this meeting of the militant and the psychoanalyst, there are at least three different problems that emerge: 1) In what form does one introduce politics into psychoanalytic theory and practice (it being understood that, in any case, politics is already in the unconscious)?; 2) Is there a reason to introduce psychoanalysis into militant revolutionary groups, and if so, how?; 3) How does one conceive and form specific therapeutic groups whose influence would impact political groups, as well as psychiatric and psychoanalytic groups? The series of articles from 1955 to 1970 which Guattari presents here, addresses these three different problems and exhibits a particular evolution, whose two major focal points are the hopes-and-despair after the Liberation, and the hopes-and-despair following May '68—while in-between the double agent is hard at work preparing for May.

As for the first problem, Guattari early on had the intuition that the unconscious is directly related to a whole social field, both economic and political, rather than the mythical and familial grid traditionally deployed by psychoanalysis. It is indeed a question of libido as such, as the essence of desire and sexuality: but now it invests and disinvests flows of every kind as they trickle through the social field, and it effects cuts in these flows, stoppages, leaks, and retentions. To be sure, it does not operate in a manifest way, as do the objective interests of consciousness or the chains of historical causality. It deploys a latent desire coextensive with the social field, entailing ruptures in causality and the emergence of singularities, sticking points as well as leaks. The year 1936 is not only an event in historical consciousness, it is also a complex of the unconscious. Our love affairs, our sexual choices, are less the by-products of a mythical Mommy-Daddy, than the excesses of a social-reality, the interferences and effects of flows invested by the libido. What do we not make love with, including death? Guattari is thus able to reproach psychoanalysis for the way in which it systematically crushes the socio-political contents of the unconscious, though they in reality determine the objects of desire. Psychoanalysis, says Guattari, starts from a kind of absolute narcissism (*Das Ding*) and aims at an ideal social adaptation which it calls a cure; this procedure, however, always obscures a singular social constellation which in fact must be brought to light, rather than sacrificed to the invention of an abstract, symbolic unconscious. *Das Ding* [The Thing] is not some recurrent horizon that constitutes an individual person in an illusory way, but a social body serving as a basis for latent potentialities (why are these people lunatics, and those people revolutionaries?). Far more important than mommy, daddy, and grandma are all the characters haunting the fundamental questions of society, such as the class conflict of our day. More important than recalling how, one fine day, Oedipus "totally changed" Greek society, is the enormous *Spaltung* [division, rift, fissure] traversing the communist party today. How does one overlook the role the State plays in all the dead-ends where the libido is caught, and reduced to investing in the intimist images of the family? Are we to believe that the castration complex will find a satisfactory solution as long as society assigns it the unconscious role of social repression and regulation? In a word, the social relation never constitutes something beyond or something added after the fact, where individual or familial problems occur. What is remarkable is how manifest the economic and political social contents of the libido become, the more one confronts the most desocialized aspects of certain syndromes, as in psychosis. "Beyond the Self, the subject explodes in fragments throughout the universe, the madman begins speaking foreign languages, rewriting history as hallucination, and using war and class conflict as instruments of personal expression [...] the distinction between private life and the various levels of social life no longer holds." (Compare this with Freud, who derives from war only an undetermined death-drive, and a non-qualified shock or excess of excitation caused by a big boom). Restoring to the unconscious its historical perspectives, against a backdrop of disquiet and the unknown, implies a reversal of psychoanalysis and certainly a rediscovery of psychosis underneath the cheap trappings of neurosis. Psychoanalysis has indeed joined forces with the most traditional psychiatry to stifle the voices of the insane constantly talking politics, economics, order, and revolution. In a recent article, Marcel Jaeger shows how "the discourse produced by the insane does not only contains the depth of their individual psychic disorders: the discourse of madness also connects with the discourse of political, social, and religious history that speaks in each of us. [...] In certain cases, the use of political concepts provokes a state of crisis in the patient, as though these concepts brought to light the very contradictions in which the patient has become entangled. [...] No place is free, not even the asylum, from the historical inscription of the workers' movement."[3] These formulations express the same orientation that Guattari's work displays in his first articles, the same effort to reevaluate psychosis.

We see the difference here with Reich: there is no libidinal economy to impart, by other means, a subjective prolongation to political economy; there is no sexual repression to internalize economic exploitation and political subjection. Instead, desire as libido is everywhere already present, sexuality runs through the entire social field and embraces it, coinciding with the flows that pass under the objects, persons and symbols of a group, and it is on desire as libido that these same objects, persons and symbols depend for their distribution and very constitution. What we witness here, precisely, is the latent character of the sexuality of desire, which becomes manifest only with the choice of sexual objects and their symbols (if it needs to be said that the symbols are consciously sexual). Consequently, this is political economy as such, an economy of flows, which is unconsciously libidinal: there is only one economy, not two; and desire or libido is just the subjectivity of political economy. "In the end, the economic is the motor of subjectivity." Now we see the meaning of the notion of *institution*, defined as a subjectivity of flows and their interruption in the objective forms of a group. The dualities of the objective and the subjective, of infrastructure and superstructure, of production and ideology, vanish and give way to the strict complementarity of the desiring subject of the institution, and the institutional object. (Guattari's institutional analyses should be compared with those Cardan did around the same time in *Socialisme ou Barbarie*, both assimilated in the same bitter critique of the Trotskyites.)[4]

195

The second problem—is there a reason to introduce psychoanalysis into political groups, and if so how?—excludes, to be sure, any "application" of psychoanalysis to historical and social phenomena. Psychoanalysis has accumulated many such ridiculous applications, Oedipus being foremost among them. Rather, the problem is this: the situation that has made capitalism the thing to be overthrown by revolution is the same situation that made the Russian Revolution, as well as the history immediately following it, not to mention the organization of communist parties, and national unions, all into so many authorities incapable of effecting the destruction of capitalism. In this regard, the proper character of capitalism, which is presented as a contradiction between the development of productive forces and the relations of production, is essentially the reproduction process of capital. This process, however, on which the productive forces of capital in the system depend, is in fact an international phenomenon implying a worldwide division of labor; nevertheless, capitalism cannot shatter the national frameworks within which it develops its relations of production, nor can it smash the State as the instrument of the valuation of capital.[5] The internationalism of capital is thus accomplished by national and state structures that curb capital even as they make it work; these "archaic" structures have genuine functions. State monopoly capitalism, far from being an ultimate given, is the result of a compromise. In this "expropriation of the capitalists at the heart of capital," the bourgeoisie maintains its stranglehold on the State apparatus through its increasing efforts to institutionalize and integrate the working class, in such a way that class conflict is decentered with respect to the real places and deciding factors that go beyond States and point to the international capitalist economy. It is by virtue of the same principle that "a narrow sphere of production is alone inserted in the worldwide reproduction process of capital," while in third-world States, the rest remains subjected to precapitalist relations (genuine archaisms of a second kind).

Given this situation, we see the complicity of national communist parties promoting the integration of the proletariat into the State, such that "the bourgeoisie's national sense of identity results in large measure from the proletariat's own national sense of identity; so, too, does the internal division of the bourgeoisie result from the division of the proletariat." Moreover, even when the necessity of revolutionary struggle in the third world is affirmed, these struggles mostly serve as chips in a negotiation, indicating the same renunciation of an international strategy and the development of class conflict in capitalist countries. It comes down to this imperative: *the working class must defend national productive forces*, struggle against monopolies, and appropriate a State apparatus.

This situation originates in what Guattari calls "the great Leninist rupture" of 1917, which determined for better or worse the major attitudes, the principal discourse, initiatives, stereotypes, phantasms, and interpretations of the revolutionary movement. This rupture was presented as the possibility of effecting a real break in historical causality by "interpreting" the military, economic, political and social disarray as a victory of the masses. Arising to replace the necessity of a sacred union of the center with the left was the possibility of a socialist revolution. But this possibility was only accepted by turning the party, once a modest clandestine group, into an embryonic State apparatus able to direct everything, to fulfill a messianic vocation and substitute itself for the masses. Two more or less long-term consequences ensued. Inasmuch as the new State confronted capitalist States, it entered into relations of force with them, and the ideal of such relations was a kind of status quo: what had been the Leninist tactic at the creation of the NEP was converted into an ideology of peaceful coexistence and economic competition with the West. This idea of competition spelled the ruin of the revolutionary movement. And inasmuch as the new State assumed responsibility for the proletariat the world over, it could develop a socialist economy only in accordance with the realities of the global market and according to objectives similar to those of international capital. The new State all the more readily accepted the integration of local communist parties into the relations of capitalist production since it was in the name of the working class defending the national forces of production. In short, there is no reason to agree with the technocrats when they say that two kinds of regimes and States converged as they evolved; nor with Trotsky, when he supposes that bureaucracy corrupted a healthy proletarian State, with the cure consisting in a simple political revolution. The outcome was already decided or betrayed in the way in which the State-party *responded* to the city-States of capitalism, even in their relations of mutual hostility and annoyance. The clearest evidence of this is that weak institutions were created in every sector in Russia as soon as the Soviets liquidated everything early on (for example, when they imported pre-assembled automobile factories, they unwittingly imported certain types of human relations, technological functions, separations between intellectual and manual work, and modes of consumption deeply foreign to socialism).

What gives this analysis its force is the distinction Guattari proposes between *subjugated groups* and *group-subjects*. Groups are subjugated no less by the leaders they assign themselves, or accept, than by the masses. The hierarchy, the vertical or pyramidal organization, which characterizes subjugated groups is meant to ward off any possible inscription of nonsense, death or dispersal, to discourage the development of creative ruptures, and to ensure the self-preservation mechanisms rooted in the exclusion of other groups. Their centralization works through structure, totalization, unification, replacing the conditions of a genuine collective "utterance" with an assemblage of stereotypical utterances cut off both from the real and from subjectivity (this is when imaginary phenomena such as Oedipalization, superegofication, and group-castration take place). Group-subjects, on the other hand, are defined by coefficients of *transversality* that ward off totalities and hierarchies. They are agents of enunciation, environments of desire, elements of institutional creation. Through their very practice, they ceaselessly conform to the limit of their own nonsense, their own death or rupture. Still, it is less a question of two groups than two sides of the institution, since a group-subject is always in danger of allowing itself to be subjugated, in a paranoid contraction where the group wants to perpetuate itself at all cost and live forever as a subject. Conversely, "a party that was once revolutionary and now more or less subjugated to the dominant order can still occupy, in the eyes of the masses, the place which the subject of history has left empty, can still become in spite of itself the mouthpiece of a discourse not its own, even if it means betraying that discourse when the evolution of the relations of force causes a return to normalcy: the group nonetheless preserves, almost involuntarily, a potentiality of subjective rupture which a transformation of context will reveal." (To take an extreme example: the way in which the worst archaisms can become revolutionary, i.e. the Basques, the Irish Republican Army, etc.)

It is certainly true that if the problem of the group's functioning is not posed to begin with, it will be too late afterwards. Too many groupuscles that as yet inspire only phantom masses already possess a structure of subjugation, complete with leadership, a mechanism of transmission, and a core membership, aimlessly reproducing the errors and perversions they are trying to oppose. Guattari's own experience begins with Trotskyism and proceeds through Entryism, the Leftist Opposition (*La Voie communiste*), and the March 22nd Movement. Throughout this trajectory, the problem remains one of desire or unconscious subjectivity: how does a group carry its own desire, connect it to the desires of other groups and to the desires of the masses, produce the appropriate creative utterances and constitute the conditions not of unification, but of multiplication conducive to utterances in revolt? The misreading and repression of phenomena of desire inspire structures of subjugation and bureaucratization: the militant style composed of hateful love determining a limited number of exclusive dominant utterances. The constancy with which revolutionary groups have betrayed their task is well known. These groups operate through detachment, election, and residual selection: they detach a supposedly expert avant-garde; they elect a disciplined, organized, hierarchized proletariat; they select a residual sub-proletariat to be excluded or reeducated. But this tripartite division reproduces precisely the divisions which the bourgeoisie introduced into the proletariat, and on which it has based its power within the framework of capitalist relations of production. Attempting to turn these divisions against the bourgeoisie is a lost cause. The revolutionary task is the suppression of the proletariat itself, that is to say, the immediate suppression of the distinctions between avant-garde and proletariat, between proletariat and sub-proletariat—the effective struggle against all mechanisms of detachment, election, and residual selection—such that subjective and singular positions capable of transversal communication may emerge instead (cf. Guattari's text, "L'étudiant, le fou et le Katangais").

Guattari's strength consists in showing that the problem is not at all about choosing between spontaneity and centralism. Nor between guerrilla and generalized warfare. It serves no purpose to recognize in one breath the right to spontaneity during a first stage, if it means in the next breath demanding the necessity of centralization for a second stage: the theory of stages is the ruin of every revolutionary movement. From the start we have to be more centralist than the centralists. Clearly, a revolutionary machine cannot remain satisfied with local and occasional struggles: it has to be at the same time super-centralized and super-desiring. The problem, therefore, concerns the nature of unification, which must function in a transversal way, through multiplicity, and not in a vertical way, so apt to crush the multiplicity proper to desire. In the first place, this means that any unification must be *the unification of a war-machine and not a State apparatus* (a Red Army stops being a war-machine to the extent that it becomes a more or less important cog in a State apparatus). In the second place, this means that unification must occur through *analysis*, that it must play *the role of an analyzer* with respect to the desire of the group and the masses, and not the role of a synthesizer operating through rationalization, totalization, exclusion, etc. What exactly a war-machine is (as compared to a State-apparatus), and what exactly an analysis or an analyzer of desire is (as opposed to pseudo-rational and scientific synthesis), are the two major lines of thought that Guattari's book pursues, signaling in his view the theoretical task to be undertaken at the present time.

This pursuit, however, is not about "applying" psychoanalysis to group phenomena. Nor is it about a therapeutic group that would somehow "treat" the masses. It's about constituting in the group the conditions of an analysis of desire, for oneself and for others; it's about pursuing the flows that constitute myriad lines of flight in capitalist society, and bringing about ruptures, imposing interruptions at the very heart of social determinism and historical causality; it's about allowing collective agents of enunciation to emerge, capable of formulating new utterances of desire; it's about constituting not an avant-garde, but groups adjacent to social processes, whose only task is to advance a truth along paths it usually never takes—in a word, it's about constituting a revolutionary subjectivity about which there is no more reason to ask whether libidinal, economic, or political determinations should come first, since this subjectivity traverses traditionally separate orders; it's about grasping that point of *rupture* where, precisely, political economy and libidinal economy are *one and the same*. The unconscious is nothing else than the order of group subjectivity which introduces explosive machines into so-called signifying structures as well as causal chains, forcing them to open to liberate their hidden potentialities as a future reality influenced by the rupture. The March 22nd Movement is exemplary in this respect, because while it was insufficient as a war-machine, it nonetheless functioned exceedingly well as an analytic and

desiring group which not only held a discourse on the mode of truly free association, but which was able also "to constitute itself as an analyzer of a
considerable mass of students and workers," without any claims to hegemony
or avant-garde status; it was simply an environment allowing for the transfer
and the removal of inhibitions. Analysis and desire finally on the same side,
with desire taking the lead: such an actualization of analysis indeed characterizes group-subjects, whereas subjugated groups continue to exist under the
laws of a simple "application" of psychoanalysis in a closed environment (the
family as a continuation of the State by other means). The political and economic content of libido as such, the libidinal and sexual content of the
politico-economic field—this whole *turn of history*—become manifest only in
an open environment and in group-subjects, wherever a truth shows up.
Because "truth is not theory, and not organization." It's not structure, and not
the signifier; it's the war-machine and its nonsense. "When the truth shows
itself, theory and organization will just have to deal with it; it's not desire's role
to perform self-criticism, theory and organization have to do it."

The transformation of psychoanalysis into schizo-analysis implies an evaluation of the specificity of madness. This is just one of the points Guattari
insists on, joining forces with Foucault, who says that madness will not be
replaced by the positivist determination, treatment, and neutralization of mental illness, but that mental illness will be replaced by something we have not
yet understood in madness.[6] Because the real problems have to do with psychosis (not the neuroses of application). It is always a pleasure to elicit the
mockery of positivists: Guattari never tires of proclaiming the legitimacy of a
metaphysical or transcendental point of view, which consists in purging madness of mental illness, and not mental illness of madness: "Will there come a
day when we will finally study President Schreber's or Antonin Artaud's definitions of God with the same seriousness and rigor as those of Descartes or
Malebranche? For how long will we perpetuate the split between the inner
workings of pure theoretical critique and the concrete analytical activity of the
human sciences?" (It should be understood that mad definitions are more serious and more rigorous than the unhealthy-rational definitions by means of
which subjugated groups relate to God in the form of reason.) More precisely,
Guattari's institutional analysis criticizes anti-psychiatry not only for refusing
to acknowledge any pharmacological function, not only for denying the institution any revolutionary possibility, but especially for confusing mental
alienation with social alienation and thereby suppressing the specificity of
madness. "With the best intentions, both moral and political, they managed to
refuse the insane their right to be insane, the *it's-all-society's-fault* can mask a
way of suppressing deviance. The negation of the institution would then be the
denial of the singular fact of mental alienation." Not that some general theory

of madness must be posited, nor must a mystical identity of the revolutionary and lunatic be invoked. (Certainly, it is useless to attempt to forestall such a criticism, which will be made in any event.) Rather, it's not madness which must be reduced to the order of the general, but the modern world in general or the entire social field which must *also* be interpreted in terms of the singularity of the lunatic, in its very own subjective position. Militant revolutionaries cannot be concerned with delinquency, deviance, and madness—not as educators or reformers, but as those who can read the face of their proper difference only in such mirrors. Take for example this bit of dialogue with Jean Oury, at the start of this collection: "Something specific to a group of militants in the psychiatric domain is being committed to social struggle, but also being insane enough to entertain the possibility of *being with* the insane; but there are definitely people in politics who are incapable of belonging to such a group..."

Guattari's proper contribution to institutional psychotherapy resides in a certain number of notions (whose formation we can actually trace in this collection): the distinction between two kinds of groups, the opposition between group phantasms and individual phantasms, and the conception of transversality. And these notions have a precise practical orientation: introducing a militant political function into the institution, constituting a kind of "monster" which is neither psychoanalysis, nor hospital practice, even less group dynamics, and which is everywhere applicable, in the hospital, at school, in a militant group—a machine to produce and give voice to desire. This is why Guattari claimed the name of institutional analysis for his work rather than institutional psychotherapy. In the institutional movement led by Tosquelles and Jean Oury there indeed begins a third age of psychiatry: the institution as model, beyond the contract and the law. If it is true that the old asylum was governed by repressive law, insofar as the insane were judged "incapable" and therefore excluded from the contractual relations that unite so-called reasonable beings, Freud's stroke of genius was to show that bourgeois families and the frontiers of the asylum contained a large group of people ("neurotics") who could be brought under a particular contract, in order to lead them, using original means, back to the norms of traditional medicine (the psychoanalytic contract as a particular case of the liberal-medical contractual relation). The abandonment of hypnosis was an important step in this development. It seems to me that no one has yet analyzed the role and effects of this contractual model in which psychoanalysis lodged itself; one of the principal consequences of this was that psychosis remained on the horizon of psychoanalysis, as a genuine source of clinical material, and yet was excluded as beyond the contractual field. It will come as no surprise, as several texts in this collection demonstrate, that institutional psychotherapy entails in its principal propositions a critique of repressive law as well as the so-called liberal contract, for which it hoped to substitute the model of the institution. This critique was meant to be extended in several directions at once, inasmuch as the pyramidal organization of groups, their subjugation and hierarchical division of labor are based on contractual relations no less than legalist structures. In the collection's first text, dealing with doctor-nurse relationships, Oury interjects: "There is a rationalism in society that is nothing more than a rationalization of bad faith and rotten behavior. The view from the inside is the relationship one has with the insane on a day-to-day basis, *provided a certain "contract" with the traditional has been voided*. So, in a sense, we can say that knowing what it is to be in contact with the insane is at the same time being a progressive. [...] Clearly, the very terms doctor-nurse belong to the contract we said we had to void." There is in institutional psychotherapy a kind of psychiatric inspiration à la Saint-Just, in the sense that Saint-Just defines the republican regime by many institutions and few laws (few contractual relations also). Institutional psychotherapy threads a difficult passage between anti-psychiatry, which tends to fall back into desperate contractual forms (cf. a recent interview with Laing), and psychiatry today, with its tight police controls, its planned triangulation, which will very likely cause us to regret the closed asylums of old, ah the good old days, the good old style.

What comes into play here are Guattari's problems concerning the nature of cured-curing groups capable of forming group-subjects, that is to say, capable of making the institution the object of a genuine creation where madness and revolution each reflect, without combining, the face of their difference in the singular positions of a desiring subjectivity. For example, in the article entitled "Where does group psychotherapy begin?," there is the analysis of BTUs (basic therapeutic units) at La Borde. How does one ward off subjugation from already subjugated groups, with which traditional psychoanalysis is in competition? And psychoanalytic associations: on what side of the institution, in what group, do they fall? A great portion of Guattari's work prior to May '68 was dedicated to "patients taking charge of their own illness, with the support of the entire student movement." A particular dream of nonsense and *empty words*, instituted as such, against laws or the contract of saturated speech, and legitimized *schizo-flow* have ceaselessly inspired Guattari in his endeavor to break down the divisions and hierarchical or pseudo-functional compartmentalizations—educator, psychiatrist, analyst, militant... Every text in this collection is an article written for a specific occasion. And they have a twofold goal: the one is connected to their origin at a certain juncture of institutional psychotherapy, a certain moment of militant political life, a certain aspect of the Freudian school and Lacan's teaching; the other looks to their function, their possible functioning in other circumstances. This book must be taken in bits and pieces, like a montage or installation of the cogs and wheels of a machine. Sometimes the cogs are small, miniscule, but disorderly, and thus all the more indispensable. This book is a machine of desire, in other words, a war-machine, an analyser. So, I would like to single out two texts in particular that seem especially important in this collection: a theoretical text, where the very principle of a machine is distinguished from the hypothesis of structure and detached from structural ties ("Machine and Structure"), and a schizo-text where the notions of "sign-point" and "sign-blot" are freed from the obstacle of the signifier.

"What Our Prisoners Want
From Us..."[1]

Something new is happening in and around our prisons. Inmates are deciding what form they wish to give their collective action within the context of each particular prison (since Toul, for example: the Tract / Final warning at Melun, the work stoppage at Nîmes, the break out and occupation of the roof tops at Nancy).[2] But in this great variety there appears to be a series of precise demands, which are no longer addressed to the penitentiary administration, but are directly addressed to the powers that be and call directly on the French people. These demands in common essentially deal with censure: the "court" and "solitary confinement" as brutal repression without any possible defense on the prisoner's part; the exploitation of work in the prisons; conditional freedom, the police record, interdiction from visiting a place; and the call to establish monitoring commissions that are independent of the government and prison administration.

The fact itself of punishment and imprisonment has not yet been called into question; still, a front of political struggle has already moved into the prisons. The realization that prison is essentially about class, that it concerns above all the working class, and that it also has to do with the labor market (repression will be all the more harsh, especially on the young, to the extent that unemployment is a threat and their labor superfluous on the market)—these realizations are becoming more and more clear in the prisons. The essential principle articulated by the inmates at Melun is that "social reinsertion of the prisoners could be the work only of the prisoners themselves."

An active grass roots base inside the prison is not enough; there must be a grass roots base on the outside, an activist base, supporting and propagating the prisoners' demands. The GIP is not, as Mr. Pleven and the newspaper *Minute* would have the public believe, a subversive group inspiring the actions of prisoners from the exterior. Nor as the President of the Toul Inquiry Commission M. Schmelck contends, is the GIP a group of intellectual dreamers. It aims to

204

organize activist external help, which first must be led by former inmates and the families of inmates, but then must recruit more and more workers and democrats to the cause.

In this respect also, there is something unprecedented going on. In Toul, Lille, Nancy, and elsewhere, a new kind of public gathering is taking place, which has nothing to do with the "public confession," and which is not the classical town meeting either: former prisoners, who have settled in the cities where they paid their debt to society, are coming forward to say what was done to them, what they saw, physical abuse, reprisals, lack of medial care, etc. This is a *personalized critique*, the example of which was given by Dr. Rose, whose report took up the prisoners' cause.[3]

This is what took place in Nancy, in an extraordinary gathering of more than one thousand individuals, which the press passed over in silence.

This is what took place in Toul, where the prison guards, from the last row, kept shouting at the inmates; only the former inmates were able to shut them up, when without hesitation each explained why he went to prison and singled out this or that prison guard to remind him of his brutality. The phrase "I know him," with which the prison guards wanted to intimidate the inmates, became the phrase the inmates co-opted to silenced the prison guards.

The day is coming when not one prison guard will be able to beat a prisoner without being publicly denounced a day or month later by his victim or a witness, in the very city where it has taken place. Former prisoners, and current prisoners alike, have ceased to be afraid and no longer feel ashamed.

Faced with such a movement, the government has responded only with increased repression (the CRS is ever ready to intervene in the prisons) and administrative reforms (in which prisoners and former prisoners have no right to make themselves heard). They are giving power back to the prefects of police: which once again amounts to nothing more than the Minister of Justice passing the buck to the Minister of the Interior. The gulf between the Pleven reforms[4] and the more moderate demands of the prisoners expresses in all their nakedness the relationships of class, violence, and power.

Intellectuals and Power[1]

Michel Foucault: A Maoist told me: "I can see why Sartre is on our side, for what and why he is involved in politics; and you, I can even see why you do it, since you've always considered imprisonment a problem. But Deleuze, really, I don't see it." His question took me totally by surprise, because it's crystal clear to me.

Gilles Deleuze: Maybe it's because for us the relationships between theory and praxis are being lived in a new way. On the one hand, praxis used to be conceived as an application of theory, as a consequence; on the other hand, and inversely, praxis was supposed to inspire theory, it was supposed to create a new form of theory. In any case, their relationship took the form of a process of totalization, in one shape or another. Maybe we're asking the question in a new way. For us the relationships between theory and praxis are much more fragmentary and partial. In the first place, a theory is always local, related to a limited domain, though it can be applied in another domain that is more or less distant. The rule of application is never one of resemblance. In the second place, as soon as a theory takes hold in its own domain, it encounters obstacles, walls, collisions, and these impediments create a need for the theory to be relayed by another kind of discourse (it is this other discourse which eventually causes the theory to migrate from one domain to another). Praxis is a network of relays from one theoretical point to another, and theory relays one praxis to another. A theory cannot be developed without encountering a wall, and a praxis is needed to break through. Take yourself, for example, you begin by theoretically analyzing a milieu of imprisonment like the psychiatric asylum of nineteenth-century capitalist society. Then you discover how necessary it is precisely for those who are imprisoned to speak on their own behalf, for them to become a relay (or perhaps you were already a relay for them), but these people are prisoners, they're *in* prison. This was the logic behind your creating the GIP (Group for Information on Prisons):

206

to promote the conditions in which the prisoners themselves could speak.[2] It would be totally misguided to say, as the Maoist seemed to be saying, that you were making a move toward praxis by applying your theories. In your case we find neither an application, nor a reform program, nor an investigation in the traditional sense. It is something else entirely: a system of relays in an assemblage, in a multiplicity of bits and pieces both theoretical and practical. For us, the intellectual and theorist have ceased to be a subject, a consciousness, that represents or is representative. And those involved in political struggle have ceased to be represented, whether by a party or a union that would in turn claim for itself the right to be their conscience. Who speaks and who acts? It's always a multiplicity, even in the person that speaks or acts. We are all groupuscles. There is no more representation. There is only action, the action of theory, the action of praxis, in the relations of relays and networks.

Michel Foucault: It seems to me that traditionally, an intellectual's political status resulted from two things: 1) the position as an intellectual in bourgeois society, in the system of capitalist production, in the ideology which that system produces or imposes (being exploited, reduced to poverty, being rejected or "cursed," being accused of subversion or immorality, etc.), and 2) intellectual discourse itself, in as much as it revealed a particular truth, uncovering political relationships where none were before perceived. These two forms of becoming politicized were not strangers to one another, but they didn't necessarily coincide either. You had the "cursed" intellectual, and you had the "socialist" intellectual. In certain moments of violent reaction, the powers that be willingly confused these two politicizations with one another—after 1848, after the Commune, after 1940: the intellectual was rejected, persecuted at the very moment when "things" began to appear in their naked "truth," when you were not supposed to discuss the king's new clothes.

Since the latest resurgence, however, intellectuals realize that the masses can do without them and still be knowledgeable: the masses know perfectly well what's going on, it is perfectly clear to them, they even know better than the intellectuals do, and they say so convincingly enough. But a system of power exists to bar, prohibit, invalidate their discourse and their knowledge—a power located not only in the upper echelons of censorship, but which deeply and subtly permeates the whole network of society. The intellectuals are themselves part of this system of power, as is the idea that intellectuals are the agents of "consciousness" and discourse. The role of the intellectual is no longer to situate himself "slightly ahead" or "slightly to one side" so he may speak the silent truth of each and all; it is rather to struggle against those forms of power where he is both instrument and object: in the order of "knowledge," "truth," "consciousness," and "discourse."

So it is that theory does not express, translate, or apply a praxis; it is a praxis—but local and regional, as you say: non-totalizing. A struggle against power, a struggle to bring power to light and open it up wherever it is most invisible and insidious. Not a struggle for some "insight" or "realization" (for a long time now consciousness as knowledge has been acquired by the masses, and consciousness as subjectivity has been taken, occupied by the bourgeoisie)—but a struggle to undermine and take power side by side with those who are fighting, and not off to the side trying to enlighten them. A "theory" is the regional system of this struggle.

Gilles Deleuze: Yes, that's what a theory is, exactly like a tool box. It has nothing to do with the signifier... A theory has to be used, it has to work. And not just for itself. If there is no one to use it, starting with the theorist himself who, as soon as he uses it ceases to be a theorist, then a theory is worthless, or its time has not yet arrived. You don't go back to a theory, you make new ones, you have others to make. It is strange that Proust, who passes for a pure intellectual, should articulate it so clearly: use my book, he says, like a pair of glasses to view the outside, and if it isn't to your liking, find another pair, or invent your own, and your device will necessarily be a device you can fight with. A theory won't be totalized, it multiplies. It's rather in the nature of power to totalize, and you say it exactly: theory is by nature opposed to power. As soon as a theory takes hold at this or that point, it runs up against the impossibility of having the least practical consequence without there being an explosion, at some distant point if necessary. That's why the idea of reform is so stupid and hypocritical. Either the reform is undertaken by those who claim to be representatives, whose business it is to speak for others, in their name, and this is how power adjusts, distributing itself along reinforced lines of repression. Or else the reform is demanded by those who have a stake in it, and then it is no longer a reform but a revolution. A revolutionary action, by virtue of its partial character, is determined to call into question the totality of power and its hierarchy. This is nowhere clearer than in the prisons: the tiniest, meekest demand by the prisoners is enough to kill Pleven's pseudo reform bill.[3] If little children managed to make their protests heard in nursery school, or even simply their questions, it would be enough to derail the whole educational system. In reality, the system in which we live *cannot tolerate anything*: whence you see its radical fragility at every point, and at the same time its global repression. In my opinion, you were the first to teach us a fundamental lesson, both in your books and in the practical domain: the indignity of speaking for others. What I mean is, we laughed at representation, saying it was over, but we didn't follow this "theoretical" conversion through—namely, theory demanded that those involved finally have their say from a practical standpoint.

Michel Foucault: And when the prisoners began to speak, they had their own theory of prison, punishment, and justice. What really matters is *this* kind of discourse against power, the counter-discourse expressed by prisoners or those we call criminals, and not a discourse *on* criminality. The problem of imprisonment is a local and marginal problem, because no more than 100,000 people go through prison in any year. But this marginal problem shakes people up. I was surprised to see how many who were *not* in prison interested in the problem, to see so many people respond who were in no way predisposed to hearing this discourse, and surprised to see how they took it. How do you explain it? Is it not simply that, generally speaking, the penal system is that form where power shows itself as power in the most transparent way? To put someone in prison, to keep him there, deprive him of food and heat, keep him from going out, from making love, etc., is that not the most delirious form of power imaginable? The other day I was talking with a woman who had been in prison, and she said: "To think that one day in prison they punished me, a forty year old woman, by forcing me to eat stale bread." What is striking in this story is not only the puerility of the exercise of power, but the cynicism with which it is exercised as power, in a form that is archaic and infantile. They teach us how to be reduced to bread and water when we're kids. Prison is the only place where power can be exercised in all its nakedness and in its most excessive dimensions, and still justify itself as moral. "I have every right to punish because you know very well how evil it is to steal, to kill..." This is what is so fascinating about prisons: for once power does not hide itself, does not mask itself, but reveals itself as tyranny down to the most insignificant detail, cynically applied; and yet it's pure, it's entirely "justified," because it can be entirely formulated in a morality that frames its exercise: its brute tyranny thus appears as the serene domination of Good over Evil, of order over disorder.

Gilles Deleuze: Now that I think about it, the inverse is equally true. It's not only prisoners who are treated like children, but children who are treated like prisoners. Children are subjected to an infantilization which is not their own. In this sense, schools are a little like prisons, and factories are very much like them. All you have to do is look at Renault's entrance. Or anywhere: you need three vouchers to go make pee-pee during the day. You uncovered a text by Jeremy Bentham in the eighteenth-century, a proposal for prison reform: it is in the name of this noble reform that Bentham establishes a circular system, where at one and the same time the renovated prison serves as a model, and where without noticing it, one moves from the school to the factory, from the factory to the prison and vice versa. There you have the essence of reformism, of representation which has been reformed. However, when people begin to speak and act in their own name, they don't oppose one representation, even one which has been reformed, to another representation; they don't oppose another mode of representation to power's false mode of representation. For example, I recall when you said that there was no popular justice against justice, it happens at another level altogether.[4]

Michel Foucault: In my view, what comes to light beneath the hatred which the people have for the judicial system, judges, tribunals, prisons, etc., is not only the idea of some other, better justice, but first and foremost the perception of a singular point where power is exercised to the detriment of the people. The anti-judicial struggle is a struggle against power, and in my opinion it's not a struggle against injustice, against the injustice of the judicial system, nor is it for a judicial institution that would work more efficiently. Still, isn't it striking that every time there are riots, revolts and seditions, the judicial apparatus has come under fire, in the same way and at the same time as the fiscal apparatus, the army, and the other forms of power? My hypothesis, but it's just a hypothesis, is that popular tribunals, for example, those during the Revolution, have been a way for the lower middle class, in alliance with the masses, to recuperate and harness the movement unleashed by the struggle against the judicial system. To harness it, they proposed this system of tribunals, which defers to a justice that could be just, to a judge that could pronounce a just sentence. The very form of the tribunal belongs to an ideology of justice which is a bourgeois ideology.

Gilles Deleuze: If we look at today's situation, power necessarily has a global or total vision. What I mean is that every form of repression today, and they are multiple, is easily totalized, systematized from the point of view of power: the racist repression against immigrants, the repression in factories, the repression in schools and teaching, and the repression of youth in general. We mustn't look for the unity of these forms of repression only in reaction to May '68, but more so in a concerted preparation and organization concerning our immediate future. Capitalism in France is dropping its liberal, paternalistic mask of full employment; it desperately needs a "reserve" of unemployed workers. It's from this vantage point that unity can be found in the forms of repression I already mentioned: the limitation of immigration, once it's understood that we're leaving the hardest and lowest paying jobs to them; the repression in factories, because now it's all about once again giving the French a taste for hard work; the struggle against youth and the repression in schools and teaching, because police repression must be all the more active now that there is less need for young people on the job market. Every category of professional is going to be urged to exercise police functions which are more and more precise: professors, psychiatrists, educators of all stripes, etc. Here we see something you predicted a long time ago, and which we didn't think possible: the global reinforcement of the structures of imprisonment. So, faced with such a global politics of power, our response is local: counter-attacks, defensive fire, an active and sometimes preventative defense. We mustn't totalize what is totalizable only by power, and which we could totalize only by restoring the representative forms of centralism and hierarchy. On the other hand, what we must do is find a way to create lateral connections, a system of networks, a grass roots base. And that is what is so difficult. In any case, reality for us does not pass through the usual political channels in the traditional sense, i.e. competition and the distribution of power, like the so-called representative authorities of the French Communist Party or the French Trade Union. Reality is what is actually going on in a factory, a school, a barracks, a prison, a police station. Consequently, action there entails a type of information of another nature altogether than what passes for information in the papers (such as the type of information we get from Liberation Press Agents).

Michel Foucault: Doesn't this difficulty, the trouble we have finding adequate forms of struggle, derive in large measure from the fact that we still don't know what power is? After all, we had to wait till the nineteenth-century before we knew what exploitation was, and maybe we still don't really know what power is. Maybe both Marx and Freud are not enough to help us come to know this thing which is so enigmatic, at once visible and invisible, open and hidden, invested everywhere, this thing we call power. The theory of the State, the traditional analysis of State apparatuses certainly do not exhaust the field in which power functions and is exercised. This is today's great unknown: who exercises power? and where? Today, we know more or less who does the exploiting, where the profit goes, into whose hands, and where it gets reinvested, whereas power... We know very well that power is not in the hands of those who govern. But the notion of "ruling class" is neither clear nor well developed. There is a whole loosely knit group of notions that need analysis: "dominate," "manage," "govern," "state apparatus," "party," etc. Similarly, we need to learn just how far power extends, through which relays, down to the smallest instances of hierarchy, control, surveillance, prohibitions, constraints. Power is being exercised wherever we find it. No one person, properly speaking, holds it; and yet it is always exercised in one direction and not another, by this group in this case, by this other group in this other case. We don't really know who has power, but we do know who doesn't. If reading your books (starting with *Nietzsche* and in anticipation of *Capitalism and Schizophrenia*) has been so crucial for me, it's because they seem to go a long way toward setting up this problem: using old themes like meaning and sense, signifier and signified, etc., to pose the questions of power, the inequality of powers, and their struggle. Every struggle develops around a particular focal point of power (one of the innumerable focal points such as a boss, a security guard, a prison warden, a judge, a union representative, a newspaper's editor-in-chief). And if pointing out these focal points of power, denouncing them as such, talking about them in a public forum, constitutes a struggle, it's not because people were unaware of them, it's because speaking up on this topic, breaking into the network of institutional information, naming and saying who did what, is already turning the tables on power, it's a first step for other struggles against power. If making a speech is already a struggle, like those made by the medical doctors who work in prisons or by the inmates themselves, it's because such an action momentarily confiscates the prison's power to speak, which is in reality controlled exclusively by the administration and its accessories, the reformers. The discourse of struggle is not opposed to the unconscious, it's opposed to the secret. This seems a let down, but what if

211

the secret were worth much more? A whole series of equivocations concerning what is "hidden," "repressed," "unspoken," enables a cheap "psychoanalysis" of what should be the object of political struggle. The secret is perhaps more difficult to bring to light than the unconscious. The two themes which only yesterday we came across once again, that "writing is the repressed" and that "writing is by rights subversive," in my opinion betray several operations which must be severely criticized.

Gilles Deleuze: About the problem you just raised: that we see who does the exploiting, who profits, who governs, but power is still something rather diffuse— I would offer the following hypothesis: even Marxism, especially Marxism, has posed the problem in terms of interest (it is a ruling class, defined by its interests, that holds the power). Suddenly, we run smack into the question: how does it happen that those who have little stake in power follow, narrowly espouse, or grab for some piece of power? Perhaps it has to do with *investments*, as much economic as unconscious: there exist investments of desire which explain that one can if necessary desire not against one's interest, since interest always follows and appears wherever desire places it, but desire in a way that is deeper and more diffuse than one's interest. We must be willing to hear Reich's cry: No, the masses were not fooled, they wanted fascism at a particular moment! There are certain investments of desire that shape power, and diffuse it, such that power is located as much at the level of a cop as that of a prime minister: there is absolutely no difference in nature between the power wielded by a cop and that wielded by a politician. It is precisely the nature of the investments of desire that explains why parties or unions, which would or should have revolutionary investments in the name of class interest, all too often have investments which are reformist or totally reactionary at the level of desire.

Michel Foucault: As you point out, the relationships among desire, power, and interest are more complex than we ordinarily imagine, and it is not necessarily those who exercise power that have an interest in exercising it; those who have an interest in exercising it don't necessarily, and the desire of power plays a game between power and interest which is quite singular. When fascism comes into play, it happens that the masses want particular people to exercise power, but those particular people are not to be confused with the masses, since power will be exercised *on* the masses and at their expense, all the way to their death, sacrifice, and massacre, and yet the masses want it, they want this power to be exercised. The play of desire, power and interest is still relatively unknown. It took a long time to know what exploitation was. And desire, it has been and promises still to be a lengthy affair. It's possible that the struggles now under way, and the local, regional, discontinuous theories being elaborated in the course of these struggles, and which are absolutely of a piece with them, are just beginning to uncover the way in which power is exercised.

Gilles Deleuze: So I come back to the question: today's revolutionary movement has multiple focal points, and this isn't a weakness, it isn't a deficiency, since a particular totalization belongs rather to power and its reaction; Vietnam, for example, is a formidable local response. But how do you view the networks, the transversal connections between discontinuous active points from one country to another or within the same country?

Michel Foucault: This geographic discontinuity you've mentioned perhaps means that the moment we struggle against exploitation, the proletariat not only leads the struggle but defines the targets, methods, places and instruments of struggle; to make an alliance with the proletariat is to embrace its positions, its ideology; we effectively assume the motivations of its fight. We all melt together. But if we choose to struggle against power, then all those who suffer the abuses of power, all those who recognize power as intolerable, can engage in the struggle wherever they happen to be and according to their own activity or passivity. By engaging in this struggle which is their own (they are perfectly familiar with its targets, and they themselves determine the methods), these people enter the revolutionary process—as allies of the proletariat, of course, since power is exercised in the way that maintains capitalist exploitation. These people truly serve the cause of the proletariat revolution by fighting precisely at that point where they suffer oppression. Women, prisoners, conscripts, homosexuals, the sick in hospitals have, as we speak, each begun a specific struggle against the particular form of power, constraint, control being exercised over them. Such struggles belong to the revolutionary movement today, provided they are radical, without compromise or reformism, provided they do not attempt to readjust the same power through, at most, a change of leadership. And these movements are connected to the revolutionary movement of the proletariat itself insofar as the proletariat must fight every control and constraint which are the conduits of power everywhere.

In other words, the generality of the struggle most certainly does not occur in the form you mentioned before: theoretical totalization in the form of the "truth." What constitutes the generality of the struggle is the system of power itself, all the forms in which it is exercised and applied.

Gilles Deleuze: And one cannot make the slightest demand whatsoever on any point of application without being confronted by the diffuse whole, such that as soon as you do, you are necessarily led to a desire to explode it. Every partial revolutionary attack or defense in this way connects up with the struggle of the working class.

213

Remarks (on Jean-François Lyotard)[1]

Lyotard's book is at once dispersed, flying off in every direction, and yet as self-contained as an egg. The text is both full of gaps and tight, both adrift and moored. *Discours, Figure*: the figures, even the illustrations, are an integral part of the discourse; they slip into the discourse, while the discourse turns back on the operations that make figures possible. This book is built on two heterogeneous expanses that do not mirror one another, though they do assure a free circulation of writing energy (or desire?). An egg, a variable interior in the middle, on a mobile surface. A schizo-book which through its complex technique, achieves the highest degree of clarity. Like every great book, difficult to write, but not difficult to read.

The importance of this book is that it marks the first generalized critique of the *signifier*. It tackles this notion which for so long has exerted a kind of terrorism in literature, and has even contaminated art or our comprehension of art. Finally, a little fresh air in those musty spaces. The book shows how the signifier-signified relation is surpassed in two directions: 1) Towards the exterior, on the side of designation, by those figure-images, because it is not words that are signs, but they make signs with the objects they designate, whose identity they break open to discover a hidden content, another face which we will not be able to see, but which yet will make us "see" the word (I am thinking of those beautiful pages on dance as designation, and the visibility of the word, the word as visible thing, as distinct from both its legibility and its audition); but the signifier-signified relation is again surpassed in another way: 2) Towards the interior of discourse, by a *pure figural* which upsets the coded gaps of the signifier, works its way into them, and there labors under the conditions of the identity of their elements (the pages on the dream work, which violates the order of speech and crumples the text, creating new unities that are not linguistic, like so many rebuses under hieroglyphics).

Lyotard's book on every page participates in an anti-dialectic that performs a total reversal of the figure-signifier relation. It is not the figures that depend on the signifier and its effects; on the contrary, it is the signifying chain that depends on figural effects, creating variable configurations of images with non-figurative figures, causing lines to flow and breaking them according to singular points, crushing and twisting signifiers as well as signifieds. And Lyotard does not even say all this, he shows it, he makes us see it, he makes it visible and mobile: a destruction of identities that carries us off on a profound journey.

Deleuze and Guattari Fight Back...[1]

Maurice Nadeau: Gilles Deleuze and Félix Guattari would very much like to begin this round-table by taking your questions. I would just ask them to explain briefly the thesis of their book, and then tell us how they carried out their collaboration.

Félix Guattari: This collaboration is not the product of a simple meeting of two individuals. Aside from a variety of circumstances, there was a whole political context that led up to it. Initially, it was less a question of pooling our knowledge than an accumulation of our uncertainties; we were confused about the turn of events after May '68.

We both belong to that generation whose political consciousness awoke during the Liberation, in the enthusiasm and naiveté and the conspiracy myths of fascism that came with it. Also, the questions left unanswered by the aborted revolution in May '68 developed in a counter-point that we found troubling: we were worried, like many others, about the future being prepared for us by those singing the hymns of a newly made-over fascism that would make you wish for the Nazis of the old days.

Our starting point was to consider how during these crucial periods, something along the order of desire was manifested throughout the society as a whole, and then was repressed, liquidated, as much by the government and police as by the parties and so-called workers unions and, to a certain extent, the leftist organizations as well.

And certainly we would have to go way back in history! The history of betrayed revolutions, betraying the desires of the masses, is quite simply the history of the workers movement. Whose fault is that? Beria's? Stalin's? Kruschev's? This was not the program, organization, alliance we hoped for. Marx wasn't read sufficiently in the original... Obviously. But this brute fact remains: the revolution was possible, the socialist revolution was within reach. It truly exists and is not some myth that has been invalidated by the transformations of industrial societies.

Given the right conditions, the masses express a revolutionary will. Their desires clear away all obstacles and open up new horizons. But the last to realize it are the organizations and leaders who are supposed to represent them. Clearly! But then why do the masses pay them any mind? Could it be the result of an unconscious complicity, an internalization of repression that works in successive stages, from Power to the bureaucrats, from the bureaucrats to the militants, and from the militants to the masses themselves? This is what we witnessed after May '68.

Fortunately, the attempt to recuperate and brainwash the masses has spared some tens of thousands—maybe more—who are now immune to the ill effects of bureaucracies of all kinds, and who intend to retaliate against the repressive dirty tricks of power and its bosses, against their maneuvers of dialogue, participation, and integration, which rely on the complicity of traditional workers organizations.

Admittedly, the current attempts to renew forms of popular struggle are difficult to wrest from the grip of boredom and revolutionary boy-scouts who, to say the least, are not too concerned with a systematic liberation of desire! "Desire! That's all you ever talk about!" This ruffles the feathers of the serious types, the responsible militants. We are certainly not going to suggest that desire be taken seriously. We would much rather undermine the spirit of seriousness, beginning with the domain of theoretical inquiry. A theory of desire in history should be presented as something not too serious. And from this standpoint, perhaps *Anti-Oedipus* is still too serious a book, too intimidating. The work of theory should no longer be the business of specialists. The desire of a theory and its propositions should stick as closely as possible to the event and the expression of the masses. To achieve this, we must knit a new breed of intellectual, a new breed of analyst, a new breed of militant: blending the different types and running them together.

We started with the idea that desire must not be conceived as a subjective superstructure that is more or less occluded. Desire never stops investing history, even in its darkest periods. The German masses had come to desire Nazism. After Wilhelm Reich, we cannot avoid coming to grips with this fact. Under certain conditions, the desire of the masses can turn against their own interests. What are those conditions? That is the question.

To formulate an answer, we realized that we couldn't just hook a Freudian engine up to the Marxist-Leninist train. We first had to undo a stereotypical hierarchy between an opaque economic infrastructure and social-ideological superstructures conceived in such a way that they confine the questions of sex and expression to representation, as far away from production as possible. The relations of production and those of reproduction participate in the same pairing of productive forces and anti-productive structures. We wanted to move desire into

217

the infrastructure, on the side of production, while we moved the family, the ego, and the individual on the side of anti-production. This is the only way to ensure that sexuality is not completely cut off from the economy.

In our view, there exists a desiring production prior to any actualization in the familial division of the sexes and individuals or in the social division of labor, and this production invests the diverse forms of the production of pleasure as well as the structures intended to repress them. Though it obeys different regimes, the desiring energy found in the revolutionary aspect of history—with the working class, the sciences and the arts—is the same as that found in the aspect of exploitation and how it relates to State power. Both aspects presuppose the unconscious participation of the oppressed.

If it is true that the social revolution is inseparable from a revolution of desire, then this changes the question. We now must ask: what conditions will enable the revolutionary avant-garde to free itself from its unconscious complicity in repressive structures, and undermine Power's manipulations of the desire of the masses who "fight for their servitude as though it were their salvation"? If the family and the ideologues of the family have a crucial role to play here, as we believe they do, then one cannot overestimate the function of psychoanalysis in this respect, since it was the first to raise these questions—and the first to stifle them, privileging instead the modern myth of familial repression through Oedipus and castration.

To make progress in this direction, we feel it necessary to abandon an approach to the unconscious through neurosis and the family, and to adopt instead an approach more specific to the schizophrenic process of desiring-machines—and this process has little to do with institutionalized madness.

From that point on, a militant struggle becomes imperative against reductive explanations, against the adaptive techniques of suggestion based on the Oedipal triangle. This entails giving up on the compulsive grasping after a total object, symbolic of every despotism. It entails going over to the side of real multiplicities, and ceasing to oppose human beings to machine, whose relationship in fact constitutes desire. It entails promoting an other logic: a logic of real desire which establishes the primacy of history over structure. It entails promoting a whole other analysis disentangled from symbolism and interpretation, as well as a whole other militancy with the means to free itself from the fantasies of the dominant order.

Gilles Deleuze: As for the technical side of writing the book, the two of us working together was not a problem, but it did serve a precise function, as we came to realize. One thing is rather shocking about books of psychiatry or even psychoanalysis, and that is the pervasive duality between what an alleged mental patient says and what the doctor reports—between the "case" and the commentary on the case, the analysis of the case. It's logos against pathos: the mental patient is supposed to say something, and the doctor says what it means in terms of symptoms or sense. This allows what the patient says to be crushed. It's hypocritically selective.

Now we didn't think for a minute of writing a madman's book, but we did write a book in which you no longer know who is speaking: there is no basis for knowing whether it's a doctor, a patient, or some present, past, or future madman speaking.

This is precisely why we used so many writers and poets: you would have to be really clever to decide whether they speak as mental patients or doctors—mental patients and doctors of civilization. Strangely enough, if we tried to get beyond this traditional duality, it's because there were two of us writing. Neither of us was the madman, and neither the doctor: there had to be two of us if we were to uncover a process that would not be reducible to the psychiatrist and his mental patient, or to the mental patient and his psychiatrist.

This process is what we call *a flow*. But, again, flow is an everyday, unqualified notion that we needed. It can be a flow of words, a flow of ideas, a flow of shit, a flow of money. It can be a financial mechanism or a schizophrenic machine: it surpasses all duality. We imagined this book as a flow-book.

Maurice Nadeau: Indeed, in your first chapter, there is this notion of a "desiring-machine," which is obscure to the layman and needs to be defined. Especially since it answers everything, suffices for everything...

Gilles Deleuze: Yes, we've given the notion of machine its maximum extension: in relation to flows. We define the machine as any system that interrupts flows. So, sometimes we're referring to technological machines, in the ordinary sense of the word, and sometimes to social machines, and sometimes to desiring-machines. In our view, the machine is not opposed to humanity or nature (you would really have to persuade us that the forms and relations of production are not machines). Furthermore, machine is not reducible to mechanism. Mechanism serves to designate specific processes in certain technological machines, or else a specific organization of a living being. But *machinism* is totally different: again, it is any system that interrupts flows, and it goes beyond both the mechanism of technology and the organization of the living being, whether in nature, society, or human beings. A desiring-machine is a non-organic system of the body, and this is what we mean when we talk about molecular machines or micro-machines.

More specifically, in reference to psychoanalysis, we have two criticisms: 1) psychoanalysis does not understand what delirium is, because it does not see how delirium invests the social field in its widest extension; and 2) it does not understand that this is desire, because it fails to grasp that the unconscious is a factory, and not a theatre. If psychoanalysis misunderstands both delirium and desire, what is left? These two criticisms are one and the same: we're interested in the presence of desiring-machines, molecular micro-machines and the large molar social machines—how they interact and work *in* one another.

Raphaël Pividal: If you're going to define your book in terms of desire, I want to know how this book reponds to desire. Which desire? Whose desire?

Gilles Deleuze: It's not as a book that it could respond to desire, but only in relation to what surrounds it. A book is not worth much on its own. It's always a question of flow: there are many people doing similar work in other fields. And there are the younger generations, too. I doubt they will buy the current type of discourse, at once epistemological, psychoanalytical, and ideological, which is beginning to wear thin with everyone.

What we're saying is this: take advantage of Oedipus and castration while you still can, it won't last forever. Until now psychoanalysis has been spared: psychiatry was attacked, along with the psychiatric hospital. Psychoanalysis seemed untouchable and uncompromised. But we want to show that psychoanalysis is worse than the hospital, precisely because it operates in the pores of capitalist society and not in the special places of confinement. And that it's profoundly reactionary in theory and practice, not just ideologically. Psychoanalysis fulfils precise functions in this society.

Félix thinks our book is addressed to people who are now somewhere between the ages of seven and fifteen. Ideally so, because the fact is the book is still too difficult, too cultivated, and makes too many compromises. We weren't able to make it clearer and more direct. However, I'll just point out that the first chapter, which many favorable readers have said is too difficult, does not require any prior knowledge. In any case, a book responds to a desire only because there are many other people fed up with a current type of discourse. So, it is only because the book participates in a larger reshuffling, a resonance between research and desire. A book can respond to a desire only in a political way, outside the book. For example, an association of angry users of psychoanalysis wouldn't be a bad place to start.

François Châtelet: What strikes me as important here is the eruption of such a text among books of philosophy (because this book is conceived as a book of philosophy). *Anti-Oedipus* smashes everything. In an exterior way at first, by the very "form" of the text: "curse words" are used in the first sentence, as though to provoke the reader. At first you think it can't go on, and then it does. There are nothing but "coupled machines," and these "coupled machines" are particularly obscene or scatological.

Furthermore, I felt this eruption as an eruption of materialism. It's been too long since we've witnessed such a thing. Methodology, I have to admit, is starting to bug the shit out of me. The whole enterprise of research and furthering knowledge is ruined by the imperialism of methodology. I fell into the trap myself, so I know what I'm talking about. Anyway, if I call it a materialist eruption, I'm thinking primarily of Lucretius. I don't know if I'm flattering you—perhaps too much, or not enough.

Gilles Deleuze: If it's true, excellent. That would be perfect. In any case, there is no methodological problem in our book. Nor any problem of interpretation, because the unconscious doesn't mean anything. Machines don't mean anything, they merely work, produce, break down. What we're after is only how something works in the real.

Nor is there an epistemological problem: we're not worried about a return to Freud, or to Marx. If they tell us we've misunderstood Freud, we'll say: "Ooh well, we have too much else to do." It's interesting how epistemology has always been a cover for an imposition of power, an organization of power, a kind of ideological technocracy at the university level. In our view, writing or thought has no specificity whatsoever.

Roger Dadoun: Up to this point, the discussion has taken place at a "molar" level—to use a dichotomy fundamental to your interpretation—that is, the level of major conceptual schema. We have yet to break through to the "molecular" level, that is, the micro-analyses that would allow us to grasp how you "machined" your work together. This would be particularly useful for the analysis—a schizo-analysis, perhaps?—of the political parts of your text. In particular, I would like to know how fascism and May '68, the dominant "note" of the book, entered into its make-up—not in a "molar" way, that's too banal, but in a "molecular" way, in the very construction of the text.

Serge Leclaire: Since you bring it up, I get the feeling that the book is machined in such a way that any intervention "on a molecular level" will be digested by the machine of the book.

I think your intention to write "a book in which every possible duality would be suppressed," an intention you just reaffirmed, has succeeded beyond your wildest dreams. The book puts your more perceptive readers in the situation of a single and unique perspective that leaves them feeling absorbed, digested, bound, even negated by the admirable workings of your so-called machine!

So, this is a dimension that puzzles me and something I would gladly ask you about: What is the function of this machine-book, since it too seems, from the start, perfectly totalizing, absorbing, in a way that integrates, absorbs any question which we might try to raise? First, it seems to put the reader in the situation of feeling cornered, by the simple fact of speaking and asking a question.

Why don't we do the experiment right now, if you don't mind, let's see what happens.

One of the essential pieces of the desiring-machine, if I have understood you correctly, is the "partial object." For someone who has not yet managed to strip off the vestiges of psychoanalysis, this concept simply recalls a psychoanalytic concept, Klein's partial object—even if, as you claim with a touch of humor, you're "laughing at concepts."

In your use of the partial object as an essential piece of the desiring-machine, I noticed something very important: you indeed try to define it. You say: the partial object can be defined only positively. That's a surprise to me. How does the positive qualification essentially differ from the negative imputation that you criticize?

Most importantly, the least psychoanalytic experience makes it clear that the partial object can be defined only "by difference" and "in relation to the signifier."

In this case, if I may say so, your "contraption" can only miss its object (Look! The banished lack pops up again!): even though your contraption is written, as a book is, it claims to be a text without a signifier, a text to speak the truth about the truth, sticking close to some alleged real, to put it simply. As though that were possible, without any distance or any mediation. A text from which all duality (in theory) has been expunged. OK. A contraption of this sort can have its use; only time will tell. As for the good news it claims to bring society, and much better than psychoanalysis can, I repeat, your contraption can only miss its object.

In my opinion, you yourselves have disarmed your desiring-machine, which should work only by breaking down, through its failures and backfires: whereas thanks to this "positive" object and the absence of any duality, as well as any lack, it is going to work like...a Swiss clock!

Félix Guattari: I don't think the object should be situated positively or negatively: you have to think of it as participating in non-totalizable multiplicities. The object is only mistakenly inscribed as a complete body such as the body proper, or even the fragmented body. When Jacques Lacan opens up the series of partial objects to the voice and the gaze, beyond the breast and the buttocks, he signals his refusal to close them off and reduce them to the body. The voice and the gaze escape the body, for example, as they and audiovisual machines become increasingly contiguous.

I'll leave aside for now the question of how Lacan's phallic function, in so far as it over-codes each partial object, does not give them back a particular identity, and how, distributing a lack to each, does not call on another form of totalization, this time in the symbolic order. Whatever the case may be, it seems to me that Lacan always strove to disentangle the object of desire from all totalizing referents that might threaten it: beginning with the mirror-stage, the libido escapes the "substantialist hypothesis" and symbolic identification supplants an exclusive reference to the organism; tied down to the function of speech and to the field of language, the drive shatters the framework of those topics closed in on themselves, whereas the theory of the object "a" perhaps sows the destruction of the signifier's totalitarianism.

As object "a," the partial object is de-totalized and deterritorialized; it has permanently distanced itself from any individuated corporeity; and it is now in a position to tip in the direction of real singularities and open up to the molecular machinisms of every kind that shape history.

Gilles Deleuze: Yes, isn't it strange? Leclaire saying our machine works too well, that it is capable of digesting anything and everything? This is precisely our criticism of psychoanalysis, so it's strange that a psychoanalyst would accuse us of that very thing. I mention it only because we have a particular relationship to Leclaire: he wrote a text on "La réalité du désir"[2] which, prior to our efforts, goes a long way toward a machinic unconscious, uncovering certain ultimate elements of the unconscious that are no longer figurative or structural.

But it seems we're not in perfect agreement here, since Leclaire says we have no idea what the partial object is. He says it's not important to define it positively or negatively because, no matter what, it is always something else; it is "different." But we're not all that interested in the category of object, partial or otherwise. It is by no means clear that desire has anything to do with objects. We're talking about machines, flows, levies, detachments, residues. We're doing a critique of the partial object. And certainly Leclaire is right to say it doesn't matter whether the partial object is defined positively or negatively. But he is right only in theory. Because if we examine how the partial object works, if we ask ourselves what psychoanalysis actually does with it, how psychoanalysis makes it work, then knowing whether it fulfils a positive or negative function is no longer a matter of indifference.

Yes or no: Does psychoanalysis use the partial object to ground its ideas of lack, absence, or the signifier of absence, and to legitimate its operations of castration? Even when it invokes notions of difference or the different, psychoanalysis uses the partial object in a negative way to weld desire to a fundamental lack. This is our critique: psychoanalysis has this pious conception of itself; through lack and castration, it makes itself out to be a kind of negative theology which entails calling on infinite resignation (the Law, the impossible, etc.). This is what we oppose. And in its place we propose a positive conception of desire: a desire that produces, not a desire that is lacking. Psychoanalysts are too self-righteous.

Serge Leclaire: I won't reject your critique any more than I acknowledge its pertinence. I just want to point out that it seems to be based on the hypothesis of a real which is somewhat…totalitarian: no signifier, no flaw, no fissure, no castration. In the end, one wonders what makes the "true difference" you invoke between pages 61 and 99. According to you, it must be situated…let's see, not between…

Gilles Deleuze: …the imaginary and the symbolic…

Serge Leclaire: …but between the real on the one hand, which you present as the ground, the underlying element, and on the other hand, something like superstructures such as the imaginary and the symbolic. In my view, however, the question of "true difference" is in fact a question raised by the problem of the object. Just a moment ago, Félix, you brought it up, in reference to Lacan's teachings: you situated the object "a" in relation to the "ego," the person, etc.

Félix Guattari: … the person and the family…

Serge Leclaire: Yes, but the concept of the object "a" in Lacan belongs in a fourfold structure that includes the signifier, which is dual (S1 and S2), and the subject (crossed-out S). True difference, if we are going to use this term, must be situated between the signifier on the one hand, and the object "a" on the other.

I will concede that for pious or impious reasons, whatever, at no point is it advisable to use the term signifier. In any case, I don't see how in this instance you can reject any and all duality and privilege the object "a" as somehow self-sufficient, like a cheap substitute for an impious God. In my view, there is no thesis, no project, no action or "contraption" that you can defend without introducing a lack somewhere and everything that it entails.

Félix Guattari: I'm not at all sure that the object "a" in Lacan is anything other than a vanishing point, a leak, an escape from the despotic character of signifying chains.

Serge Leclaire: What interests me most and what I am trying to articulate in a way obviously different from yours, is how desire unfolds in the social machine. I don't think we can do without a precise clarification of the object's function. We would have to specify its relations to the other elements at work in the social machine, "signifying" elements, properly speaking (or if you prefer, symbolic and imaginary elements). These relations are not uni-directional. In other words, the "signifying" elements also have an effect on the object.

If we want to understand what is happening with desire in the social machine, we cannot avoid going through the narrow pass which the object represents at present. It's not enough to say everything is desire, you have to show how it happens. One last question: what's the use of your *contraption*?

What relation can there be between the fascination of a flawless machine and the genuine inspiration of a revolutionary project? This is the question I'm asking, on the level of action.

Roger Dadoun: In any case, your machine or "contraption" works. It works really well in literature: for example, it helps capture the flow or "schizo" circulation of Artaud's *Heliogabalus*; and it delves deeper into the bipolar schizoid / paranoid movement of an author like Romain Rolland; it works for a psychoanalysis of dreams, too—you know, Freud's dream, "Irma's injection," which is theatrical in almost a technical sense, or cinematic, with all the staging, close-ups, etc. It remains to be seen how well it operates in terms of children…

Henri Torrubia: I work in a psychiatric ward, and I would like to underline one of the central points of your thesis on schizo-analysis. In my view, the arguments you muster to affirm the priority of social investment and the productive and revolutionary essence of desire are truly eye-opening. They raise genuine theoretical, practical, and ideological problems, so you have to be prepared for a defensive reaction.

In any event, employing an analytic psychology in a psychiatric establishment demands that "each person" be able to question the institutional network; otherwise, it's a waste of time, and even in the best circumstances, it doesn't go anywhere. In the current climate, one could never hope to get anywhere. That being the case, whenever an essential conflict emerges somewhere, when something goes awry—which is precisely an indication that something at the level of desiring production is able to manifest itself and challenge the social field and its institutions—then we see a panic reaction set in, and resistance is organized. This resistance takes different forms: meetings are called to synthesize developments, to coordinate efforts, to sum things up, etc. And in a much more subtle way, the classical psychoanalytic interpretation has its usual effect—crushing desire, as you say.

Raphaël Pividal: I'd like to say something to Serge Leclaire: you've spoken at length, but you failed to address what Guattari is saying. Because the book fundamentally examines your profession, the practice of analysis, you understand the problem in a partial way. You acknowledge the problem only by drowning it in the jargon of your theories, in which you accord greater importance to fetishism, that is, the partial object. You hide behind this jargon to quibble over details. Everything in *Anti-Oedipus* that concerns the birth of the State, the role of the State, schizophrenia, etc., you pass over in silence. Your day-to-day practice—this, too, you pass over in silence. And the real problem of psychoanalysis—the patient—you pass over in silence. Of course, *you* are not on trial here. However, these are the issues you must address: the relationship of psychoanalysis to the State, to capitalism, to history, and to schizophrenia.

Serge Leclaire: I agree with the aim you propose. I only insisted on this one precise point, the object, to emphasize by a concrete example how their contraption's type of functioning is produced.

Having said that, I don't entirely reject the criticism Deleuze and Guattari level against the concealment, the crushing of the psychoanalytic discovery: indeed nothing, or almost nothing, has been said about the relation of psychoanalytic practice or schizophrenia to the political or social field. But it's not enough to announce your intention to do so. It must be done in a felicitous manner. Our two authors had a go at it, and it's their attempt that we're discussing here.

Let me remind you of what I said. In my view, the correct approach to the problem passes through an extremely precise corridor: the place of the object, and the function of the drive in a social formation.

And let me just say this about the argument—"it works"—advanced to defend the felicity of this machine, the book under discussion. Of course it works! I was going to say that to a certain extent, it works for me too. It's no secret that almost any theoretically invested practice has some chance of working, at least to begin with. That is not in itself a criterion of success.

Roger Dadoun: Certainly a problem which your book raises is how it is going to work politically, since you conceptualize the political domain as a primary "machination." It is just a question of examining the thoroughness and detail with which you analyzed the "*socius*," especially its ethnographic and anthropological aspects.

Pierre Clastres: A philosopher and a psychoanalyst, Deleuze and Guattari, have together produced a reflection on capitalism. To think about capitalism, they go through schizophrenia, in which they see the effect and the limit of our society. And to think about schizophrenia, they go through Oedipal psychoanalysis. But like Attila the Hun, there is not much left in their wake. Between these two, that is, between the description of familialism (the Oedipal triangle) and the schizo-analysis project, you find the largest chapter in *Anti-Oedipus*: "Savages, Barbarians, and Civilizations," which is essentially about those societies which ethnologists have traditionally studied. What is ethnology doing there?

It ensures the coherence of their enterprise by shoring up their argument with non-Western examples (taking into account primitive societies and barbarian empires). If the authors had been content to say: capitalism works in this particular way, but other societies work differently—we would never have left the most banal form of comparison. But this is not the case. They show "how the unconscious [*ça*] works differently." *Anti-Oedipus* is also a general theory of society and societies. In other words, Deleuze and Guattari have written about Savages and Barbarians what ethnologists up to now have not.

It is certainly true (we didn't write it, but we knew it) that the world of Savages is a place where flows are encoded: nothing escapes the control of primitive societies, and if something like a runaway train occurs—it happens—these societies always find a way to stop it. It is also true that imperial formations impose an over-encoding on the savage elements integrated into the empire, though without necessarily destroying the encoding of the flows that persist at the local level for each element. The example of the Incan Empire perfectly illustrates Deleuze and Guattari's point of view. They say some interesting things about the system of cruelty as writing on the Savage body, about writing as a mode of the system of terror among the Barbarians. I think ethnologists will feel perfectly at home in *Anti-Oedipus*. That doesn't mean everything will be accepted right away. I can see there will be some reticence, to say the least, about their preference for a theory that posits the priority of a genealogy of debt over the accepted structuralist theory of exchange. We might also ask whether the idea of Earth doesn't overwhelm the idea of territory. In any case, Deleuze and Guattari are not laughing at ethnologists: they're asking us real questions, questions to make us think.

Is this some return to an evolutionist interpretation of history? A return to Marx, beyond Morgan? Not at all. Marxism could get its bearings among the Barbarians (the Asiatic mode of production), but it never quite knew what to do with Savages. Why? Because if the Marxist perspective indeed explains the movement from barbarism (oriental despotism or feudalism) to civilization (capitalism), it is powerless to explain the movement from savagery to barbarism. There is nothing in territorial machines (primitive societies) that would indicate or prefigure what comes next: no caste-system, no class, no exploitation, not even labor (if labor is essentially alienation). So where does History come from? And class-struggle? Deterritorialization, etc.?

Deleuze and Guattari have an answer to this question, because they do know what to do with Savages. And their answer, in my view, is the strongest and most rigorous discovery in *Anti-Oedipus*: the "*Urstaat*," the cold monster, the nightmare, the State, which is the same everywhere and which "has always existed." Yes, the State exists in the most primitive societies, even in the smallest band of nomadic hunters. It exists, but it is ceaselessly warded off. It is ceaselessly prevented from becoming a reality. A primitive society directs all its efforts toward preventing its chief from becoming a chief (and that can go as far as murder). If history is the history of class struggle (I mean, in societies that have classes), then the history of classless societies is the history of their struggle against the latent State. Their history is the effort to encode the flows of power.

Of course, *Anti-Oedipus* doesn't tell us why the primitive machine, here and there, failed to encode the flows of power, this death which keeps rising from within. Indeed there is no reason why the tribe should permit its chief to act the part at all (there are plenty of examples to support this). So, where does the "*Urstaat*" come from? How does it emerge fully formed and all at once? It must come from the outside, and we can hope that the follow-up to *Anti-Oedipus* will have more to say about it.

Encoding, over-coding, decoding, flows: these categories establish the theory of society, whereas the idea of the "*Urstaat*," warded off or triumphant, establishes the theory of history. What we have here is a radically new thought, a revolutionary reflection.

Pierre Rose: For me, what proves the practical importance of Deleuze and Guattari's book is that it repudiates the virtues of commentary. This book wages war. It's about the situation of the working classes and Power. Deleuze and Guattari use an oblique approach through a critique of the analytic institution, but the question cannot be reduced to that.

"The unconscious is politics," said Lacan in '67. This was analysis's bid for universality. It's when analysis takes on politics, that it most blatantly legitimates oppression. This is a sleight-of-hand which transforms the subversion of the alledgedly knowing Subject into submission before a new transcendental trinity: Law, Signifier, and Castration: "Death is the life of the Spirit, what's the point of revolting?" The question of Power was erased by the conservative irony of Hegelianism on the right, which undermines the question of the unconscious, from Kojève to Lacan.

At least this legacy had high standards. More sordid is the tradition of the theory of ideologies, which haunted Marxist theory since The Second International, that is, since the thought of Jules Guesde crushed the thought of Fourier. This, too, is over.

What the Marxists never managed to overcome is the theory of reflection, or what had been made of it. Still, the Leninist metaphor of the "little screw" in "the big machine" is illuminating: the reversal of Power in people's minds is a transformation that is produced in every gear and wheel of the social machine.

The Maoist "ideological revolution"—thanks to how it breaks with the mechanical opposition between political-economy and ideology—sweeping away the reduction of desire to "politics" (Parliament and party struggle), as well as the reduction of politics to discourse (speeches by the leader), in order to restore the reality of multiple wars on multiple fronts, is the only method that even comes close to the critique of the State in *Anti-Oedipus*. There is no way that a critical project set in motion by *Anti-Oedipus* can become a university industry, just another lucrative activity for the whirling dervishes of *Being and Time*. The effect of *Anti-Oedipus* has been wrested from the instruments of Power and delivered back to the real: the book can only reinforce the assaults against the police, justice, the army, and State power, in the factory and beyond.

Gilles Deleuze: I think what Pividal said just a moment ago, and what Pierre just said, is right on target. For us, the essential thing is the relation of desiring-machines and social machines, their different regimes, and their immanence with respect to one another. In other words, how is unconscious desire invested in a social, economic and political field? How does sexuality, or what Leclaire might call choice of sexual objects, merely express these investments, whereas in reality these investments are investments of flow? How do our love affairs derive from universal history and not mommy and daddy? A whole social field is invested through a man or a woman that we love, and this investment happens in a variety of ways. So, we try to show how the flows invest different social fields, what they are flowing on, and by what means they are invested: encoding, over-coding, decoding.

Can one say that psychoanalysis has touched on any of this in the slightest? For example, its ridiculous explanations of fascism: it would have everything derive from images of the father and mother, or from familial and pious signifiers like the Name-of-the-Father. Serge Leclaire says that it is no proof that our system works, because anything and everything works. True enough. That's what we're saying: Oedipus and castration work like a charm. But we want to know what are their effects: they work but at what price? It is certain that psychoanalysis pacifies and mollifies, that it teaches us resignation we can live with. But we're saying it has usurped its reputation for promoting, or even participating in, any effective liberation. It has smashed the phenomena of desire onto a familial stage, and crunched the whole economic and political dimension of libido into a conformist code. As soon as the "mental patient" starts talking politics, goes into a political delirium, just look at what psychoanalysis does with it. It's what Freud did to Schreber.

Pierre Clastre said all there was to say about ethnology, at least much to our advantage. What we're trying to do is put libido in relation with an "outside." The flow of women among the primitives is in relation with flows of herd animals, flows of arrows. One day a group becomes nomadic. One day warriors show up in the village square: look at Kafka's "Great Wall of China." What are the flows of a society? Which flows are capable of subverting that society? And where is desire's place in all this? Something always happens to the libido, and it happens from far off on the horizon, not from within. Shouldn't ethnology, as well as psychoanalysis, be in relation with an outside?

Maurice Nadeau: We should perhaps stop here... if we want to print this interview in *La Quinzaine* (we've probably filled more pages than we have in a single issue!). Let me thank Gilles Deleuze and Félix Guattari for the insights they've given us into a book that seems likely to revolutionize many disciplines, and which seems all the more important when we consider the particular way in which its authors approach questions that concern us all. Let me also thank François Châtelet for having organized and presided over this debate and, of course, all the specialists who agreed to participate today.

Hélène Cixous, or Writing in Strobe[1]

For several years now Hélène Cixous has pursued a subterranean body of work which remains relatively unknown despite the Medici prize awarded her for *Inside* in 1969.[2] She wrote a beautiful book on *The Exile of James Joyce*,[3] in which fiction, theory and criticism are tightly knit. On first impression, her work indeed stems from a Joycean tradition: a narrative in process, which includes itself or takes itself as an object, with a plural "author" and a "neuter" subject, neuter plural, and the simultaneity of every kind of scene: historical and political, mythical and cultural, psychoanalytic and linguistic. But maybe this first impression, being only apparent, leads to a misunderstanding, like the idea that Cixous is an exceedingly difficult author or that her work follows the well known trends of contemporary literature. The real originality of an author is revealed only once we manage to position ourselves within the point of view she herself has invented and from which the work becomes easy to read, leading the reader by the hand. This is the mystery: every truly new work is simple, easy, and joyful. Look at Kafka, look at Beckett.

We see the Cixous mystery in her last book *Neutre*: an author acknowledged as difficult generally demands to be read slowly: in this case, however, the work asks us to read it "fast," and we are bound to read it again, faster and faster. The difficulties which a slow reader would experience dissolve as the reading speed increases. In my view, Cixous has invented a new and original kind of writing, which gives her a particular place in modern literature: writing in strobe,[4] where the story comes alive, different themes connect up, and words form various figures according to the precipitous speeds of reading and association.

Paul Morand's great significance, so poorly understood today, was to bring speed into literature around 1925, bringing it into style itself, in relation to jazz, the automobile, and the airplane. Cixous is inventing other speeds, sometimes crazy speeds, in relation to the contemporary. *Neutre* never tires of saying it: mix colors in such a way that through movement they produce unknown shades and hues. Writing per second, per tenth of a second: "The rule is simple: move from one tree to another either by exchanging the active bodies, or by exchanging the supplementary terms, or by exchanging the names of the terms that function in pairs. This all happens so fast that it is difficult, from the exterior, to see which of the three operations is in process, and whether there is a transfer from one tree to the other via body or name. The movement is such that the trees by a strobe effect produce a kind of pole that is smooth or barely striated by dark vertical cross-hatching, the specters of generations: Paper... Each plays the other: For example, the statement 'None is Without its Other: Samson haunts it.'"

So what is the effect that Cixous creates? The material of *Neutre* is composed of associated elements: fictive elements made of desires; phonological elements made of letters; linguistic elements made of figures; elements of criticism made of citations; active elements made of scenes, etc. These elements comprise an immobile group, complex and difficult to decipher, as long as the speed = 0. At intermediate speeds, the elements form chains that splice into one another, and then splice into this or that group, which has determinations, thus making up distinct stories or distinct versions of a story. And at higher and higher speeds, the elements reach a perpetual slippage, an extreme rotation which prevents them from splicing into any group whatsoever, driving them ever faster through each and every story. In a word, the reading functions according to the reader's speeds of association. For example, the extraordinary scene of the son's death, which varies according to three degrees at least. Or else those hilarious pages where one sees the letter F contaminate all neighboring words and quickly overtake them. This is pleasure which comes from a book-as-drug, a disquieting strangeness, in accordance with a Freudian notion that Cixous loves: in every sense, a reading of *Neutre* must be fast and taut, as in a modern mechanism of decisive precision.

Capitalism and Schizophrenia[1]

Vittorio Marchetti: Your book *Anti-Oedipus* is subtitled *Capitalism and Schizophrenia*. Why is that? What were the fundamental ideas you started from?

Gilles Deleuze: Perhaps the most fundamental idea is that the unconscious "produces." What this means is that we must stop treating the unconscious, as everyone has done up to now, like some kind of theatre where a privileged drama is represented, the drama of Oedipus. We believe the unconscious is not a theatre, but a factory. Artaud said something really beautiful in this regard. He said the body, and especially the ailing body, is like an overheated factory. So, no more theatre. Saying the unconscious "produces" means that it's a kind of mechanism that produces other mechanisms. In other words, we believe the unconscious has nothing in common with theatrical representation, but with something called a "desiring-machine." Let's be clear about the word "mechanism." The biological theory of mechanism was never able to understand desire and remains totally in the dark in this area because desire cannot be integrated into mechanical models. When we talk about desiring-machines, or the unconscious as a mechanism of desire, we mean something completely different. Desiring consists in interruptions, letting certain flows through, making withdrawals from those flows, cutting the chains that become attached to the flows. This system of the unconscious, or desire that flows, interrupts, begins flowing again—it's totally literal; and contrary to what traditional psychoanalysis tells us, it is perfectly meaningless. Without any sense, there is nothing to interpret. Interpretation is meaningless here. The problem is knowing how the unconscious works. It is knowing how "desiring-machines" work, and knowing how to use those machines.

Guattari and I began with the assumption that desire could be understood only as a category of "production." So we had to reintroduce production into desire itself. Desire does not depend on lack, it's not a lack of something, and it doesn't refer to any Law. Desire produces. So it's the opposite of a theatre. An idea like Oedipus, the theatrical representation of Oedipus, mutilates the unconscious and gives no expression to desire. Oedipus is the effect of social repression on desiring production. Even with a child, desire is not Oedipal, it functions like a mechanism, produces little machines, establishing connections among things. What this means in different terms, perhaps, is that desire is revolutionary. This doesn't mean that it wants revolution. It's even better. Desire is revolutionary by nature because it builds desiring-machines which, when they are inserted into the social field, are capable of derailing something, displacing the social fabric. Traditional psychoanalysis, however, has turned everything upside down in its little theatre. It's exactly as if something that really belongs to humanity, to a factory, to production, were translated by means of a representation at the Comédie Française. So there you have our point of departure: the unconscious as producing these little machines of desire, which we call desiring-machines.

Vittorio Marchetti: So what about *Capitalism and Schizophrenia*?

Félix Guattari: We wanted to emphasize the extremes. Everything in human existence is brought back to the most abstract categories. Capital and, on the other extreme, or rather, the other pole of nonsense, madness—and within madness, schizophrenia. In our view, it was these two poles' common tangent of nonsense that seemed to have a relation. And not just a contingent relation making it possible to say that modern society drives people crazy. Much more than that: if we want to explain alienation, or the repression which the individual suffers in the capitalist system, if we want to understand the real meaning of the politics of the appropriation of surplus value, we must bring into play those same concepts to which one turns to analyze schizophrenia. We privileged these extreme poles, but it goes without saying that all the intermediate terms must also be examined: everything from the way in which neurosis is confronted to the study of childhood or primitive societies. All the themes which the human sciences deal with are fair game. But rather than establish some coexistence of all the human sciences, one in relation to the other, we decided to relate capitalism and schizophrenia in an attempt to encompass these fields as a whole; that way we avoided limiting ourselves to the various pathways that allow you to pass between them.

Vittorio Marchetti: Did your research come out of concrete experience? Do you see any practical development? If so, in which fields?

Félix Guattari: To answer the first part of your question, the research comes out of psychiatric practice, psychoanalysis, and in particular, the study of psychosis.

We feel that the semiotic chains, the descriptions of Freudian theory, and psychiatry are relatively inadequate to explain what is really going on in mental illness. We noticed this as soon as a new kind of listening to mental illness became possible.

Freud developed his concepts, to begin with at least, within the framework of a particular kind of access he had to neuroses, and hysteria in particular. He himself complained toward the end of his life about not having had access to another field, about not having had any other way to approach psychosis. He was able to approach psychotic patients only accidentally and from the outside. It should be added, too, that within the framework of repressive hospitalization, you don't have access to schizophrenia. You have access to mental patients locked in a system that prevents them from expressing the very essence of madness. They express only a reaction to the repression to which they are subjected, which they are forced to endure. As a result, psychoanalysis is practically impossible with cases of psychosis. And things will continue this way as long as psychotic patients are trapped in the repressive hospital system. However, rather than transpose the descriptive chains of neurosis onto psychosis, we tried to do the opposite. In other words, we tried to reexamine the concepts used to describe neurosis in the light of the indications we received from contact with psychosis.

Gilles Deleuze: We began with the feeling, and I do mean a feeling, and the knowledge, that something was not right with psychoanalysis. It has become interminable, spinning its wheels and going nowhere. Just look at the psychoanalytic cure. Well, the cure has become an endless process in which both the patient and the doctor chase each other round and round, and this circle, whatever modifications are applied, remains Oedipal. It's like "OK, talk!" But it's always about the same thing: mommy and daddy. The reference turns on an Oedipal axis. They can insist all they want that it's not about a real mother and father, that it's about some higher structure, whatever you like, some symbolic order, and that it shouldn't be interpreted as imaginary, but the discourse remains the same: the patient is there to talk about mommy and daddy, and the analyst listens in terms of mommy and daddy. There are problems that troubled Freud toward the end of his life: something is not right with psychoanalysis, something is stuck. Freud thought that it was becoming endless, the cure looked interminable, it was going nowhere. And Lacan was the fist to indicate how far things had to be revamped. He believed the problem could be resolved in a profound return to Freud. We on the other hand began with the feeling that psychoanalysis was going round and round in a circle, a familial circle, so to speak, represented by Oedipus. And today a rather worrisome situation has developed. Although psychoanalysis has changed its methods, it has nonetheless come into line with the most classical psychiatry. As Michel Foucault has so admirably shown, it was in the nineteenth-century that psychiatry fundamentally linked madness to the family. Psychoanalysis has reinterpreted this connection, but what is so striking is that the connection has stayed in place. And even anti-psychiatry, which points in new and revolutionary directions, preserves this family-madness reference. Everyone talks about familial psychotherapy. So, everyone continues to locate the fundamental reference of mental derangement in familial determinations of the mommy-daddy type. And even if these determinations are interpreted in a symbolic way—the father symbolic function, the mother symbolic function—it doesn't change a thing.

Now I suppose everyone is familiar with the amazing text by that lunatic, as they call him, President Schreber, a paranoid or a schizophrenic, it doesn't matter. His memoirs are a kind of racial, racist, historical delirium. His delirium encompasses whole continents, cultures, and races. What takes you by surprise is the political, historical, and cultural content of his delirium. When you read Freud's commentary, this whole aspect of the delirium has disappeared: it has been crushed by the reference to a father that Schreber never mentions. Psychoanalysts will say that it is precisely because he never mentions it that it's so important. Well, we say that we've never seen a schizophrenic delirium that is not first and foremost racial, racist, and political, that is not running off in every direction of history, that does not invest cultures, that does not talk about continents, kingdoms, etc. We say that the problem of delirium is not related to the family, that it concerns mommy and daddy only secondarily, if it concerns them at all. The real problem of delirium is the extraordinary transitions between two poles: the one is a reactionary pole, so to speak, a fascist pole of the type: "I am a superior race," which shows up in every paranoid delirium; and the other is a revolutionary pole: like Rimbaud, when he says: "I am an inferior race, always and forever."[2] Every delirium invests History before investing some ridiculous mommy-daddy. And so, even where therapy or a cure is concerned—provided this is indeed a mental illness—if the historical references of the delirium are ignored, if you just go round and round between a symbolic father and an imaginary father, you never escape familialism and you remain locked within the framework of the most traditional psychiatry.

Vittorio Marchetti: Do you think linguistic studies can contribute something to the interpretation of schizophrenic language?

Félix Guattari: Linguistics is a rapidly expanding science still very much in search of itself. You sometimes see an abusive use of concepts, too hastily employed, given that they're still being formulated. There is one notion in particular we felt it necessary to rethink: the signifier. We believe the notion poses several problems in different linguistics. Perhaps the signifier is less problematic for psychoanalysis, but as far as we're concerned, we think it needs further development. Faced with the problems of contemporary society, we have to be in a position to question the traditional culture which has been divided up, so to speak, among the human sciences, science, scientism (a fashionable word for a while now), and political responsibility. Especially after May '68, a revision of this separation seems important and necessary. From this perspective, until recently, the various disciplines have enjoyed a kind of autonomy. The psychoanalysts have their own cooking utensils, and the politicians have their own, etc. The necessity to reexamine this division is not born from some concern for eclecticism and does not necessarily lead to some sort of confusion. The same way that it is not due to confusion that a schizophrenic jumps from one register to the next. It is the reality he finds himself confronted with that drives him to it. The schizophrenic, without any epistemological guarantee, so to speak, sticks closely to reality and this reality causes him to move from one level to the next, from a questioning of semantics and syntax to the revision of the themes of history, etc. Well, from this perspective, people in the human sciences and in politics should, in a sense, go a little schizo. And not to embrace that illusory image which the schizophrenic gives us when he is trapped in repression, according to which he is supposedly "autistic," withdrawn into himself, etc. On the contrary, to have the same ability to embrace all the disciplines together. In the aftermath of May '68, the question is precisely this: either we attempt to unify our comprehension of phenomena such as, I don't know, bureaucratization in political organizations, or bureaucratization in State capitalism, with our comprehension of distant and disparate phenomena such as, for example, obsession, or the descriptions given by repetitive autism—or else, if we stick to the idea that things are separate, that each of us is a specialist and should mind his own business while making advances in his field, explosions that totally escape our powers of description and comprehension, from a political as well as anthropological point of view, will nonetheless show up in the world. In this sense, the point of calling into question the division of the various disciplines, as well as the self-satisfaction of psychoanalysts, linguists, ethnologists, and teachers of pedagogy, is not the dissolution of these sciences. The point is to refit these sciences so they better measure up to their object of inquiry. A whole line of research conducted prior to May '68 by some small, privileged groups suddenly found itself at the center of debate, and that Spring, institutional revolution was the order of the day. Psychoanalysts are increasingly "interpolated" in public discourse; they have been forced to broaden their discipline. The same goes for psychiatrists. This is a totally new phenomenon. What does it mean? Is it just a fad? Or as some in the political sphere contend, is it a way of diverting militant revolutionaries from their objectives? But is it not rather a call, however confused, for a profound revision of conceptualization as it is practiced today?

Vittorio Marchetti: Could psychiatry play this role and become, so to speak, the new human science, the human science par excellence?

Félix Guattari: Rather than psychiatry, why not the schizophrenics, the crazies themselves? It seems to me that those who work in the field of psychiatry, at least right now, are hardly on the cutting edge!

Gilles Deleuze: And there's no reason anyway why psychiatry rather than any other discipline should become the human science par excellence. The whole idea of some "human science par excellence" is misguided. Why couldn't bibliophilia be the human science par excellence? Or how about textual criticism? The fact is too many sciences would like to play such a role. The problem is not determining which science will be the human science par excellence; the problem is determining how a certain number of "machines" endowed with revolutionary potential are going to fit together. For example, the literary machine, the psychoanalytic machine, and political machines: either they will find a unifying point, as they have done so up to now, in a particular system of adaptation to capitalist regimes, or else they will find a shattering unity in a revolutionary utilization. We mustn't pose the problem in terms of priority, we have to pose it in terms of use or utilization. So, the question is: to what use are they put? In our view, psychiatry has up to now concealed a particular use of familialism, of the familial perspective, and this utilization seems reactionary, even necessarily so, no matter how revolutionary those people are now working in the field of psychiatry.

Vittorio Marchetti: Lévi-Strauss says that philosophical or scientific thought operates by proposing and opposing concepts, whereas mythic thought operates through images taken from the sensible world. Arieti, in his book *Interpretation of Schizophrenia*, affirms that those suffering from mental illness have recourse to an intelligible logic, to a "coherent logical system" even if it has nothing to do with the logic founded on concepts. Arieti talks about "paleo-logic" and claims that this "coherent logical system" resembles mythical thought, the thought of so-called primitive societies, that it operates in the same way, by "associating sensible qualities." How do you explain this phenomenon? Is schizophrenia a defensive strategy pressed into the refusal of our logical system? And if so, doesn't the analysis of schizophrenic language offer an invaluable instrument for the human sciences in the study of our society?

Gilles Deleuze: I understand your question, it's pretty technical. I'd like to hear what Guattari thinks.

Félix Guattari: I don't really like the word 'paleo-logic' because it still implies a "prelogical mentality" and other definitions of the kind that opened the way for a literal segregation, not to mention its associations with the childishness of mental patients.

Gilles Deleuze: And 'logic' is a concept that doesn't interest us in the least. It's too vague a term. Everything is logical, or nothing is. As for the question, its technical aspect, I would question whether what schizophrenics, primitives, or children are really about is a logic of sensible qualities.

In our own research, what we're doing now, this question doesn't come up. What strikes me is how easily everyone forgets that a formulation such as 'the logic of sensible qualities' is already too theoretical. What we neglect is "pure lived experience." Whether we're talking about the lived experience of the child, the lived experience of the primitive, or the lived experience of the schizophrenic, 'lived experience' doesn't mean sensible qualities. Lived experience is "intensive": *I feel…* 'I feel' means that something is happening in me, I am experiencing an intensity, and intensity is not the same thing as sensible qualities; in fact, it's totally different. This happens all the time with schizophrenics. A schizophrenic says: "I feel I'm becoming a woman" or "I feel I'm becoming God." Sensible qualities have nothing to do with it. It seems that Arieti stays at the level of a logic of sensible qualities, but that doesn't correspond at all to what schizophrenics say. When a schizophrenic says: "I feel I'm becoming a woman," "I feel I'm becoming God," "I feel I'm becoming Joan of Arc," what does it mean in reality? Schizophrenia is a shocking and very very acute experience, an involuntary experience, of intensity and the passings of intensities. When a schizophrenic says: "I feel I'm becoming a woman," "I feel I'm becoming God," it's like the body is crossing a threshold of intensity. Biologists talk about the egg and the schizophrenic body as a kind of egg; the catatonic body is nothing more than an egg. Well, when a schizophrenic says: "I'm becoming God," "I'm becoming a woman," it's like crossing what biologists call a gradient, traversing a threshold of intensity. A schizophrenic is still crossing it, going above it, beyond it, etc. This whole phenomenon is what traditional analysis fails to take into account. That's why the pharmacological research being done on schizophrenia could be so rich, although it is poorly utilized at present. Pharmacological studies and drug research pose the problem in terms of variations in intensity of the metabolism. The "I feel…" must be considered in the light of passing sensations, degrees of intensity. So, the difference between our conception and Arieti's, with all due respect to Arieti's work, resides in the fact that we interpret schizophrenia in terms of intensive experience.

Vittorio Marchetti: But what do you mean by the "intelligibility" of schizophrenic discourse?

Félix Guattari: What we want to know is whether coherence derives from, say, an order of rational expression, or some semantic order, or whether it derives from an order which one might call machinic. After all, we do the best we can with representation, everyone does the best he can with it: both the research scientist, trying to reconstitute something in the order of expression, and the schizophrenic. But the schizophrenic doesn't have the possibility of making intelligible what he is trying to reconstitute, with the means ready to hand, those he has at his disposal. In this sense, we're saying that the descriptions made within the framework of psychoanalysis, and which we call Oedipal, to simplify things, constitute a repressive representation. Even the most important authors, those who have gone the farthest in the exploration of psychosis and childhood, or those who spotted the problem of the passages of intensive quantities—even *they* end up describing everything in Oedipal terms all over again. A famous researcher, and I mean someone really important, still spoke of micro-Oedipalism in a case of psychosis, despite the fact that he had noticed—at the level of its functioning, in other words, the level of partial impulses—a landscape reminiscent of Hieronymous Bosch, composed of an infinity of fragments, bits and pieces, where the idea of the father, the mother, and the holy trinity was not to be found. What this suggests, on one level at least, is that such a representation is taken literally from a single dominant ideology.

Vittorio Marchetti: There exist typical alterations in schizophrenic language. Are there identical alterations in language specific to certain social categories such as the military or politics?

Félix Guattari: Definitely. We can even speak of a "para-phrenic" military language, the language of militant political activists today. But we would have to generalize. The categories used by psychiatrists, psychoanalysts, and research scientists rely on a language of representational closure. To such an extent, that whatever escapes the production of desiring-machines is always redirected back to restrictive, exclusive syntheses, with a continual return to dualist categories, and a perpetual separation of levels. An epistemological reform would be insufficient to redress such a situation, because the whole balance of power is at stake, even at the level of class conflict. That means it is pointless to remind certain psychoanalysts, or research scientists, to pay attention. In so far as what is at stake is not a separate order, as it would be in the case of a pulsional order, for instance, but rather the very totality of social mechanisms and their functioning, as much in the order of desire as in the order of revolutionary struggle or science and industry—in so far as all this is at stake, the system in its totality would have to secrete its models, its casts, and its stereotyped expressions all over again. We ought to ask ourselves whether the expression of politicians, scientists, and the military is not in fact precisely a kind of anti-production, a kind of repression working at the level of expression, whose goal is to stop the work of questioning, which never stops in fact, but overflows and then is simply lost in the real movement of things.

Vittorio Marchetti: Nietzsche, Artaud, Van Gogh, Roussel, Campana: what does mental illness mean in their case?

Gilles Deleuze: It means many things. Jaspers and, more recently, Laing have displayed penetrating insight on this topic, even if they are still pretty much misunderstood. Essentially, they say that what is called *madness* is composed, roughly speaking, of two things: there is a breach, a tearing open, like a sudden light, a wall that is punched through, and then there is this other, very different dimension which could be called collapse. I remember a letter by Van Gogh: "We have to undermine the wall," he says. Except knocking down the wall is really difficult, and if you do it in a way that is too brutal, you knock yourself out, you fall down, you collapse. And Van Gogh added: "Just file away at it, slowly, patiently." So there is this breach, and a possible collapse. Jaspers, when he talks about the schizophrenic process, emphasizes the coexistence of two elements: a kind of intrusion, the arrival of something for which there is no possible expression, something wonderful, so wonderful in fact that it is difficult to articulate; but it is so repressed in our society—and here you have the second element— that it runs the risk of coinciding with collapse. Here you see the autistic schizophrenic, who no longer moves, and who can remain motionless for years. In the case of Nietzsche, Van Gogh, Artaud, Roussel, Campana, etc., the two elements certainly coexist. A fantastic breach, a hole in the wall. Van Gogh, Nerval—and so many others—have knocked down the wall of the signifier, the wall of mommy-daddy, they went beyond it and speak to us in a voice which is our future. But the second element is nonetheless present in this process, and it is the danger of collapse. No one has the right to deride, to treat with flippancy, the fact that the tearing open, the breach slips into or coincides with a kind of collapse. This danger must be considered fundamental. The two elements are connected. It is meaningless to say that Artaud was not schizophrenic—worse, it's shameful and stupid. Artaud was clearly schizophrenic. He achieved a "wonderful breakthrough," he knocked down the wall, but at what price? The price of a collapse that must be qualified as schizophrenic. The breakthrough and the breakdown are two different moments. It would be irresponsible to turn a blind eye to the danger of collapse in such endeavors. But they're worth it.

Vittorio Marchetti: I heard about these interns in a psychiatric hospital who, against the wishes of the director of the clinic, had the habit of playing cards in the room of a patient who had been in a profound catatonic state for years: a vegetable. Not a word, not a gesture, not the least movement. One day, while the interns are playing cards, the patient, whose head had been turned toward the window by the nurse, suddenly says: "It's the director!" His perpetual silence ensues and he dies a few years later without ever saying another word. That is his message to the world: "It's the director!"

Gilles Deleuze: A beautiful story. In the light of schizoanalysis, and that's what we're after, we should not ask so much what the phrase "It's the director!" means, as what happened such that the autistic patient, withdrawn into his body, was able to constitute, with the arrival of the director, a little machine that served his purposes, even for a short time.

Félix Guattari: It seems to me far from obvious that the patient in the story actually saw the director. From the standpoint of the story, it would even be better if the patient didn't see him. The simple fact that there was a modification, a change of habits due to the presence of the young interns, the transgression of the director's law on account of the card game, could have provoked the patient to foreground the hierarchical figure of the director, to articulate simply an analytic interpretation of the situation. This represents a beautiful illustration of the transfer, the translation of the analytic function. It's not a psychoanalyst, or whoever you like, a psycho-sociologist, who is interpreting the structure of the situation. It is literally a crying out, a kind of slip of the tongue, that interprets the sense of the alienation which not the schizophrenic, but the people for whom it is such a big deal simply to play cards in the presence of patients find themselves in.

Vittorio Marchetti: Yes, but the patient is still present to himself when he cries out, even if he hasn't seen the director...

Félix Guattari: Present to himself! I'm not at all sure about that. He could have seen a cat or something. In the practice of institutional psychotherapy, it is well known that the most zoned-out schizophrenic can suddenly dredge up the most incredible stories about your private life, things you would never have believed anyone knew, and then will proceed to articulate, in the crudest manner possible, truths you thought were secret. It's no mystery. The schizophrenic has instant access to such insight, because he is directly flayed, so to speak, on the hooks that constitute the group in its subjective unity. He finds himself in a "clairvoyant" situation with respect to those individuals who, crystallized in their logic, in their syntax, in their own interests, are absolutely blind.

Your Special "Desiring-Machines": What Are They?

The readers of *Les Temps Modernes* will find a strange report here. Pierre Béni-chou has revealed some of the results from his inquiry on masochists (the "real" masochists, those who have others inflict severe and often bloody treatment on themselves). For this inquiry, however, he does not address the masochists themselves; he does not have them talk. They would gladly talk. Were they to talk, however, they would enter a preformed, prefabricated circuit: the circuit of their myths and fantasies, including the circuit of that psychoanalysis whose ideas everyone today is more or less familiar with, a circuit in which each of us knows more or less in advance what is expected of us, answering "Oedipus" or "mommy-daddy" as soon as we are asked—that world of interiority which we find so tiresome.

Pierre Bénichou substitutes an entirely different trinity for the psychoana-lytic father-mother-ego: cop-prostitute-client. We must not too hastily conclude that they are the same. And rather than the subject speaking, and the psychoanalyst writing for eventual publication in a scientific journal, the sub-ject does not speak, does not have the right to speak; he only writes, he writes his wishes and demands, he passes a note in which he criticizes the last session, or plans for the next one. But on the other hand, the prostitute, the cop speak. Pierre Bénichou's inquiry provides what is so lacking in psychoanalysis today: a new relation with the Outside.

This is all we are asking of the psychoanalytic relation: an inversion, a car-icature, an extreme tightening. Masochism is that perversion par excellence which takes the form of a contract, even if it is within the terms of the contract for it to be exceeded each time, to be subverted by the caprice or superior authority of the all powerful "Mistress." (P.B. instances the monthly payment that entitles the client to a certain number of sessions.) And so, just as in psy-choanalysis, the contract here takes on a dimension that has its equivalent nowhere else: it is not possible to distinguish between the contracting parties and the object which the contract specifies. As Pierre Bénichou remarks: "sexual deviation, *properly speaking*, is the only domain in which a direct relation obtains. The prostitute does more than provide an object; she *is* the object. A living material that listens, records, answers, questions, decides; a drug that itself prescribes its own dose; a roulette wheel that chooses its own number and color—always the other number and color, of course. She has seen everything, heard everything... And understood nothing? What does it matter, she talks, she knows what she's talking about, she has 'experience.'" Does the perverse relation deface the psychoanalytic relation, or does the psychoanalytic relation deface the perverse relation?

For a long time psychiatry was a normalizing discipline, speaking in the name of reason, authority, and law, in a double relation with the asylums and the courts. Then a new interpreting discipline came along: psychoanalysis. Madness, perversion, neurosis—psychoanalysts wanted to know "what did it mean," from the inside. Today we are calling for the rights of a new functionalism: no longer what it means, but how it works, how it functions. As if desire had nothing to say, but rather was the assemblage of tiny machines, *desiring-machines*, always in a particular relation with the big social machines and the technological machines. Your particular desiring-machines: what are they? In a difficult and beautiful text, Marx called for the necessity to think human sexuality not only as a relation between the human sexes, masculine and feminine, but as a relation "between human sex and non-human sex." He was clearly not thinking of animals, but of what is non-human in human sexuality: the machines of desire. Perhaps psychoanalysis had gotten no further than an anthropomorphic idea of sexuality, even in its conception of fantasy and dreams. An exemplary investigation like Pierre Bénichou's, in giving us real masochistic machines (real paranoid machines, real schizophrenic machines, etc.), maps out the road to such a functionalism as we are calling for: the analysis of "non-human sex" in human kind.

H.M.'s Letters[1]

Our prisons are filled primarily with loners of every kind, the unemployed, and young "small-time crooks" with or without work. As many officials admit in private, these young people have no business being in prison; the Arpaillanges report,[2] still secret, confirms as much. A counter-expert will dare say to H.M.: "Prison is *not* a solution to your problem." We would like to ask this counter-expert: for whom and for which problem *is* prison a "solution"? A precise system comprised of police officers, criminal records, and parole officers lowers the chances of escaping a first conviction; these young people are destined to return to prison almost as soon as they leave. One conviction after another gets them labeled "hardened criminals."

Young people today walk a fine line indeed between a persistent temptation to commit suicide and the birth of a certain form of political consciousness peculiar to prison. It's not about making vague recriminations against society, or fate, or making new resolutions; it's about analyzing their lived experience: the personified mechanisms that ceaselessly push them into reform school, the hospital, the army, confinement.

The need to write to family and friends is born of isolation, and their political reflection is nourished by a new genre of writing in which the traditional distinctions between public and private, the sexual and the social, collective demands and personal lifestyle are blurred. In many of H.M.'s letters, the writing progressively changes, under Mandrax, "Mandrax the Magnificent," and bears witness to complementary or opposed personalities restlessly stirring in the prisoner, all of them participating in the same "effort to reflect." The suicidal personality won out; there could have been another outcome, if penitentiary medicine were not just a simple extension of policing. H.M.'s correspondence is exemplary because its heartfelt reflections express what exactly a prisoner is thinking.

These letters keep turning over all kinds of obsessions: write me, if you only knew what a word from you means…, include a stamp, it's no use giving our money to P. and T., I write like a pig with my hand broken, they broke my cast and won't replace it, "it's perhaps good people who have done me the most harm," Mandrax, I'm losing it…FREEDOM, send me books, *The Anti-Psychiatrist*, and Sartre's *Saint Genet, Actor & Martyr*…. These letters talk about all sorts of desires to flee, and to live. Not some impossible escape. But fleeing the traps of the police who led him back to prison. To flee to India, where he wanted to go before his last arrest. A spiritual flight, like Krishna. Or even in prison, fleeing right there, fleeing himself, as he undoes certain personalities that inhabit him, fleeing like a schizophrenic, in an anti-psychiatric way. Fleeing like Genet, when he's "staying cool" about the feelings of persecution he senses rising within himself, and which he knows are provoked by persecutions that are all too real. Community-flights, where the "community" is defined in opposition to "little hippy societies that do nothing but imitate our fascist society." Or active flights, in the political sense, like Jackson,[3] where one flees while looking for a weapon, while attacking: "I don't have a lawyer and I don't know if I'll ask for one. I don't want a lawyer who whines and pleads for clemency. I want a lawyer who's gonna scream and raise hell…." "I feel like I'm suffocating, I won't ask the tribunal to show any mercy, I'll scream injustice, I'll proclaim the police are corrupt…, I have to go now because I'm half-crazy, and they'll use these letters to lock me away for good…" And if nothing else is possible, to flee by committing suicide: "I'll wait for the verdict unless life becomes too difficult to bear and I decide not to wait any longer. It's something I contemplate everyday, but it's just as difficult to live as to die. Well, I'm going to bed and will continue my book by Laing, because I'm really down today" (written the day before his suicide). There is every chance that the warden and the guards considered it blackmail, bad reading material, or simply play acting.

H.M. was homosexual. There are some who believe that a homosexual has it easier in prison, since everybody becomes homosexual in prison. The opposite is true: prison is the last place where one can be "naturally" homosexual, because one is caught in a system of harassment and prostitution, in which *the administration voluntarily plays a part in order to divide the prison population against itself*. H.M., however, was appreciated and loved by the prisoners without having to hide his homosexuality. And it is precisely due to a report by a guard, following an incident, that H.M. was sent to solitary confinement—for being "caught in the act." We have to ask ourselves what right the prison has to judge and punish homosexuality.

H.M. thinks they never give him a moment's peace, indeed, that punishment on punishment is relentlessly delivered. But prison has an even more secret prison, solitary confinement, which the Pleven "reform" is careful to overlook.[4] During a previous conviction for attempted larceny, when H.M. had served his time, they added forty-five more days of confinement (for non-payment of his court fees), and then when he was leaving the premises, he was retaken into custody on a complaint filed by a guard who, having beaten him, swears he was attacked by the prisoner. Or how about this: having taken some drugs for a psychotherapeutic treatment, and being at the hospital for some other reason (viral hepatitis), H.M. was pursued by someone who telephones, asking him to cop a few bricks of opium, and keeps calling, insisting, till he finally denounces H.M. to the police. This is how they turn a drug user, former or current, into a "dangerous dealer" for police statistics and the editorials of reactionary newspapers like *Aurore*. He was immediately arrested, given a new preventive detention; a new provocation, being "caught in the act" of homosexuality lands him in solitary, where he kills himself. What is at stake here is not only a social system in general with its exclusions and condemnations, but the deliberate and personified provocations by means of which this system functions and ensures its order, by means of which the system creates its excluded and condemned, in conformity with a politics shared by Power, the police, and the administration. A specific number of people are directly and personally responsible for the death of H.M.

Hot and Cool[1]

The painter's model is commodity. All sorts of commodities: apparel, toiletries, bridal accessories, erotica, food. And the painter is always present in his paintings, a black silhouette who seems to watch: painter and love, painter and death, painter and food, painter and car… But from one model to the other, they are all measured by the unique model of Commodity moving with the painter. Each painting is built on a dominant color, and the paintings form a series. It is as if the series began with the painting *Rouge de cadmium* and finished with *Vert Véromèse*, representing the same painting, but this time exhibited in the dealer's shop: the painter and his painting have themselves become commodities. Still, we could imagine other beginnings and other endings. In any case, from one painting to the other, not only is the painter strolling through the shops, but the values of exchange are in circulation; it is a journey of colors, and a journey in each painting, a circulation of intonations.

Nothing is neutral or passive. And yet the painter doesn't mean anything by his work: neither approbation nor anger. Nor do the colors mean anything: green is not hope; yellow is not sadness; red is not happiness or joy. Only hot or cool, hot *and* cool. Art as machinery: Fromanger paints, that is to say, he knows how to operate his paintings. The painting-machine of an artist-engineer. The artist-engineer of a civilization: how does he operate his paintings?

Newspaper photograph in hand, the painter has plotted the positions: street, store, people. It's not about grasping the atmosphere, but rather an ever-suspended immanence, the uniform possibility that something like a new Kennedy assassination could come out of nowhere, in a system of indifference where the values of exchange circulate. The photograph captures a number of colorless cliches, and the painter chooses the one he likes. But he will have chosen the photo based on a different choice: the single dominant color that flows from the paint-tube (the two choices compliment each other). The painter projects the image onto the canvas and paints the projected image, just like the technique of creating tapestries. The painter paints in the darkness for hours. This nocturnal activity reveals an eternal truth about painting: a painter has never painted on a blank canvas, reproducing an object that functions as a model. Rather, he has always painted an image, a simulacrum, a shadow of the object, producing a canvas whose very functioning reverses the relationship between model and copy. Consequently, there is no longer model or copy. The copy, and the copy of the copy, is pushed to the point where it reverses itself, and produces the model: Pop Art or painting for a "higher reality."

Having chosen a color, the painter applies it straight from the tude, mixing it only with zinc white. This color, in relation to the photo, could be hot like *Rouge Chine vermillionné* or *Violet de Bayeux*, or cool like *Vert Aubusson* or *Violet d'Egypte*. He starts with the lightest areas (where there is the most white) and constructs his painting on a gradient that doesn't allow for back-tracking, drips, or blends. An irreversible ascending series of flat tints rises toward the pure color squeezed from the tube, or rejoins this pure color, as though the painting in the end were going to crawl back into the tube.

Still, this doesn't fully explain how the painting operates, because a color is only potentially hot or cool, and this potential will be actualized only in relation to the other colors. For example, a second color affects a particular part of the photo: a pedestrian. Not only is this color lighter or darker than the dominant color, but being hot or cool in its own right, it can heat it up or cool it down. A circuit of exchange and communication is set up in the painting, and from one painting to another. Look at *Violet de Bayeux* with its hot ascending gradient: a child in the background is painted a cool green, and so, by contrast, begins heating up the potentially hot violet. But this isn't enough to animate the violet. In the foreground, a man painted a hot yellow will kindle or re-kindle the violet and, with the green acting as intermediary, will actualize the violet's potential over and above the green. But now the cool green is out of the loop, isolated, as though exhausting its function all at once. It must itself be sustained, inserted back into the painting, reanimated or reactivated within the painting as a whole. It does this through a third character-color: the cool blue behind the yellow. Sometimes these secondary and circulatory colors are grouped around one single color, which they divide up into bands or arcs. And sometimes the photo resists being transformed into a living painting. It leaves a residue, as in *Violet de Bayeux*, where one of the character-colors in the foregrounded group remains undetermined. This color will be treated like black, with a dual potential that can be actualized in *both* directions; or it can "drift" toward cool blue as easily as move toward hot red. The residue is re-injected into the painting, such that the painting operates using the refuse of the photo, just as the photo operates using the colors that make up the painting.

We have to consider another element which is present in all the paintings from the start, an element that jumps from one painting to another: the black painter in the foreground. The painter who paints in the blackness is himself black: his silhouette is massive; the curves of his body are salient; his chin is hard and heavy, and his hair is braided like a rope. He observes the commodities. He waits. But the black doesn't exist; the black painter doesn't exist. The black doesn't even have a potential in the same way a hot or cool color does. Its potential is below the surface: black is both hot and cool: cool when pulled toward blue, and hot when pulled toward red. Though present with such force, this black has no existence. Instead, it serves a primordial function in the painting. Whether hot or cool, it will be the antithesis of the dominant color, or the same as this color: for example, to reheat what was cool. Take the painting *Vert Aubusson*: the black painter watches and loves the seated model, a dead cool green woman. She is beautiful in death. But to make her death hot, some yellow must be extracted from the green, and to do this, blue must be drawn out as the compliment of yellow. So, the black painter must be cooled off again in order to reheat the green death. (See, too, in *Rouge de cadmium clair*, how the young married models are very discreetly given death's-heads, or in *Violet de Mars*, the dead bathing beauties are elegant vampires caught in a variable relation with the black silhouette). In a word, the black painter has two functions in the painting, according to two different circuits: 1) he is a paranoid, immobile, heavy silhouette just as fixated on commodity as commodity is fixated on him; but 2) he is also a mobile schizoid shadow perpetually displaced with respect to himself, traversing the whole gradient of hot and cool, reheating the cool and cooling down the hot: a never-ending trip while standing still.

The painting and its series don't mean anything, they function. And they function using at least four elements (though there are many others): 1) the irreversible ascending gradient of the dominant color which traces in the painting a whole system of *connections* marked with white points; 2) the network of secondary colors, which forms *disjunctions* of the hot and the cool, a reversible exchange of transformations, reactions, inversions, inferences, heatings and coolings; 3) the black painter as major *conjunction* which contains in itself the disjunctive, and which distributes the connections; and 4), when necessary, the *residue* of the photo that re-injects into the painting everything that was about to escape. A life force circulates here, a strange and vital force.

There are two coexisting circuits, each entangled in the other. There is the circuit of the photo, or the photos, which serves as the support of the commodities; there is the circulation of exchange value, and whose importance lies in mobilizing what remains indifferent. This indifference occurs at three levels of the painting: 1) the indifference of the commodity in the background, which is equivalent to love, death or nourishment, to the naked or the clothed, to a still life, or to a machine; 2) the indifference of the pedestrians, some stationary, others slipping away, such as the blue man or the green woman in *Violet de Mars*, or the man who is eating as he passes by the newlyweds; 3) the indifference of the black painter in the foreground, his indifferent equivalence to every commodity and passer-by. But perhaps these respective circuits of indifference, each one mirroring the other, exchanging with the other, introduce something like a declaration: the feeling that something is not right, that something keeps disrupting the apparent equilibrium of circuits, that each thing is keeping to itself in the compartmentalized depth of the painting: the commodity keeps to commodities, the humans to the human, and the painter to himself. This is the circuit of death, where everyone is heading towards the grave, or is already there. It is at this rupture point, everywhere present, that the other circuit connects up, rejoining the painting, reorganizing it, turning the discrete planes into the rings of a spiral that causes the background to come forward, and the various elements to react with each other in a system of simultaneous inductions. But now it is a vital circuit, with its black sun, its ascending color and its radiant hots and cools. And still the circuit of life is nourished by the circuit of death and carries it along, ultimately to triumph over it.

It is hard to ask a painter, 'Why do you paint?' The question makes no sense. But what about: How do you paint? How does the painting function? And suddenly: What do you get out of painting? Imagine that Fromanger answers: "I paint in the dark, and what I'm after is *hot* and *cool*, and I want to get it from the colors, through the colors." A cook, too, can be after *hot* and *cool*, or a junky. Maybe the paintings are Fromanger's food, or his drugs. Hot and cool: that's what can be extracted from color as much as from anything else (like writing, dance, music, or the media). Conversely, there are other things to be extracted from color as well, and this extraction is never easy, no matter what it is. What this means is that the operation of extracting, or extricating something doesn't happen all by itself. As McLuhan has shown,[2] when the medium is hot, nothing circulates or communicates except through the cool, which controls every active interaction, including painter with model, spectator with painter, and model with copy. What counts is the perpetual reversals of hot and cool, according to which the hot can cool down the cool and the cool reheat the hot: it's like heating an oven with snow balls.

What is revolutionary about this painting? Perhaps it's the radical *absence* of bitterness, tragic grief, and anguish—all that annoying crap in the pseudo-great painters who are supposedly the witnesses of their times. All those fascist and sadistic fantasies that make a painter seem like an incisive critic of the modern world, when in fact he is only reveling in his own resentment and complacency, not to mention the complacency of his patrons. Though such a painting may be abstract, it is none the less dirty, disgusting, and sad. Like the game-keeper says to the painter: "All these tubes and vibrations of corrugated iron are really stupid, and too sentimental; they exhibit way too much self-pity and vain insecurity." Fromanger does the opposite: he exhibits something vital and powerful. Perhaps this explains why he is not liked by connoisseurs, and why his work doesn't sell. His paintings are full of shop windows, and his silhouette is everywhere: and yet he offers no mirror to reflect our gaze. He paints against the fantasy which mutilates life, which turns life toward death, and the past, even when it's done in a modern style: to this Fromanger opposes a life-giving process that has been wrested from the grip of death, and from the past. Fromanger understands the poisonous nature of his model, the ruse of commodity, the pedestrian's inevitable stupidity, and the hatred that follows a painter as soon as he becomes political, and the hatred he himself can feel. However, out of this poisonous nature, this ruse, this ugliness and hatred, Fromanger refuses to create a narcissistic mirror for some hypocritical, generalized reconciliation, exciting pity for himself and for the world. Out of everything ugly, repugnant, hateful and detestable, he knows how to extract the hots and the cools that create a life for tomorrow. We have to imagine the cool revolution as necessarily reheating today's over-heated world. Is this hyper-realism? Why not, if it wrests a "more-real" from a melancholy and oppressive reality to create joy, to cause an explosion, to start a revolution. Fromanger loves the dead green woman-commodity, and gives her life by making his blackness more blue. Maybe he even loves the fat violet woman awaiting, and mourning, who knows what client. He loves everything he paints. This presupposes no abstraction, and no agreement either, but demands much extracting and extractive force. It's strange to what extent the acts of a revolutionary are governed by what he loves in the very world he wants to destroy. The only revolutionary is a joyful revolutionary, and the only painting that is esthetically and politically revolutionary is joyful. Fromanger lives and accomplishes what Lawrence says: "In my opinion, either there is joy in a painting, or it's not a painting. The most somber paintings of Piero della Francesca, Sodoma and Goya, breath out this indescribable joy found in real painting. Modern critics talk a lot about the ugliness of paintings, but I have never seen a real painting that I thought was ugly. The subject can be ugly, it can have a terrifying quality, a desperate, almost repugnant quality, as in El Greco's paintings. But all of this is strangely swept away by the joy of the painting. No artist, even the most desperate, has ever painted something without experiencing the strange joy which the creation of the image begets"[3]—that is to say, the transformation which the image undergoes in the painting, and the change that the painting produces in the image.

Nomadic Thought[1]

If we want to know what Nietzsche is or is becoming today, we know very well whom we should ask—the young people now reading Nietzsche, those who are just discovering Nietzsche. Those of us here today are, for the most part, already too old. What is a young person discovering in Nietzsche that was clearly not discovered by earlier generations? How is it that young musicians today feel some connection with Nietzsche in their music, although they do not at all make music that is Nietzschean in any sense that Nietzsche would understand? How is it that young painters, young film makers feel some connection with Nietzsche? What is going on? What we want to know is how *they* have received Nietzsche. On the outside, the only thing we can really explain is how Nietzsche reserved for himself and for his readers, both contemporary and future generations, a particular right to misinterpret. Not just any right, to be sure, because it has its own secret rules—but a particular right to misinterpret, which I will explain in a minute, and which makes commenting on Nietzsche very unlike commenting on Descartes or Hegel. I ask myself: who is the young Nietzschean today? Is it whoever is working on Nietzsche? Perhaps. Or is it whoever, voluntarily or involuntarily—it doesn't matter which, utters things which are singularly Nietzschean in the course of an action, passion, or experience? This is also the case. A beautiful recent text, one of the most profoundly Nietzschean to my knowledge, is Richard Deshayes's *Vivre, c'est pas survivre*, which he wrote just before being wounded by a grenade during a demonstration.[2] Perhaps the two cases are not mutually exclusive. Perhaps one can write on Nietzsche, and then in the course of experience produce Nietzschean utterances.

What is Nietzsche today? In that question, we can feel the dangers lying in wait for us. A demagogic danger ("young people are on our side..."). A paternalistic danger (advice to a young reader of Nietzsche...). And above all, the danger of an appalling synthesis. The trinity of Nietzsche, Freud, and Marx is thought

252

to be the dawn of our modern culture. Never mind that by doing so you defuse the explosiveness of each from the start. Perhaps Marx and Freud are the dawn of our culture, but Nietzsche is something else entirely, the dawn of a counter-culture. It seems clear that our society does not function according to codes. Our society has other foundations by virtue of which it functions. However, if one examines not the letter of Marx or Freud, but the becoming of Marxism and the becoming of Freudianism, we see, paradoxically, Marxists and Freudians engaged in an attempt to recode Marx and Freud: in the case of Marxism, you have a recoding by the State ("the State has made you ill, the State will cure you"—this cannot be the same State); and in the case of Freudianism, you have a recoding by the family (you fall ill *from* the family and recover *through* the family—this is not the same family). What at the horizon of our culture in fact constitutes Marxism and psychoanalysis as those two fundamental bureaucracies, the one public, the other private, is their effort to recode as best they can precisely that which on the horizon ceaselessly tends to come uncoded. This is not at all what Nietzsche is about. His problem is elsewhere. For Nietzsche, it is about getting something through in every past, present, and future code, something which does not and will not let itself be recoded. Getting it through on a new body, inventing a body on which it can pass and flow: a body that would be ours, the body of Earth, the body of writing...

We are familiar with the great instruments of encoding; societies are not that different in this respect; there are only so many means of encoding at their disposal. The three principle means are: the law, the contract, and the institution. For example, the relationship to books which people have or have had exhibits all three. There are books of law: here the relation of the reader to the book passes through the law. In particular, moreover, they are called codes, canons, or sacred books. And the other sort of book you have passes through the contract, the bourgeois contractual relation. This other book is the basis of secular literature and book-selling: I purchase, and you give me something to read—a contractual relation in which everyone is caught: author, publisher, reader. And there is the third sort of book, the political book, preferably revolutionary, which is presented as a book of institutions, either present or to come. You find every possible combination of the three: contractual or institutional books considered sacred, etc. This is because every type of code is so present, and so underlies every other code, that we find each in the other. Take an entirely different example: madness. The attempt to encode madness has been carried out in three forms. First, the forms of law, i.e. the hospital, the asylum—this is the repressive code, locking someone away, but the old style of locking someone away, which is destined to become a last hope, when people will say: "those were the good old days when they used to lock us away, because much worse is in store for us." And then you have this brilliant move which was psychoanalysis: it was understood that there were people who escaped the bourgeois contractual relation as it was manifested in medicine, and those people were the disturbed, because they couldn't be contractual parties, they were juridically "incapable." Freud's stroke of genius was to get at least some of the disturbed, in the largest sense of the word, the neurotics, to pass through the contractual relation, proving that a contract with such people could be done (thus he abandons hypnosis). This is finally the novelty of psychoanalysis: Freud was the first to introduce into psychiatry the bourgeois contractual relation which up to that point had been excluded from psychiatry. And then there are the still more recent attempts to encode madness, whose political implications, and at times revolutionary ambitions, are clear; such attempts are called institutional. In this case, we find the triple means of encoding: either it will be the law, or if it is not the law, it will be the contractual relation; if not the contractual relation, it will be the institution. And it is thanks to these encodings that our bureaucracies flourish.

Faced with the way in which our societies come uncoded, codes leaking away on every side, Nietzsche does not try to perform a recoding. He says: this hasn't yet gone far enough, you're nothing but children ("the equalization of European individuals is the great irreversible process: we should accelerate it still more.") In terms of what he writes and thinks, Nietzsche's enterprise is an attempt at uncoding, not in the sense of a relative uncoding which would be the decoding of codes past, present, or future, but an absolute encoding—to get something through which is not encodable, to mix up all the codes. It is not so easy to mix up all the codes, even at the level of the simplest writing, and language. The similarity I see here is with Kafka, what Kafka does with German, in accordance with the linguistic situation of the Jews in Prague: he builds a war-machine in German against German; through sheer indetermination and sobriety, he gets something through in the German code which had never been heard before. Nietzsche, for his part, wants to be or sees himself as Polish with respect to German. He seizes on German to build a war-machine which will get something through that will be uncodable in German. That's what style as politics means. More generally, how do we characterize such thought, which claims to get its flows through, underneath the laws by challenging them, and underneath contractual relations by contradicting them, and underneath institutions by parodying them? Let me come back quickly to the example of psychoanalysis. In what respect does a psychoanalyst as original as Melanie Klein still remain within the psychoanalytic system? She explains it herself quite well: the partial objects that she tells us about, with their explosions, their flows, etc., are only fantasy. The patients bring lived experiences, intensely lived experiences, to Melanie Klein and she translates them into fantasy. There you have a contract, specifically a contract: give me your lived experiences, and I will give you fantasies. And the contract implies an exchange, an exchange of money and words. In this respect, a psychoanalyst like Winnicott truly occupies the limit of psychoanalysis, because he feels that this procedure is no longer appropriate after a certain point. There comes a point where it is no longer about translating, or interpreting, translating into fantasies, interpreting into signifiers and signifieds—no, not in the least. There comes a point where you will have to share, have to put yourself in the patient's shoes, go all the way, and share his experience. Is it about a kind of sympathy, or empathy, or identification? But surely it's more complicated than that. What we feel is rather the necessity of a relation that would be neither legal, nor contractual, nor institutional. That's how it is with Nietzsche. We read an aphorism or a poem from *Thus Spoke Zarathustra*. But materially and formally, texts like that cannot be understood by the establishment or the application of a law, or by the offer of a contractual relation, or by the foundation of an institution. Perhaps the only conceivable equivalent is something like "being in the same boat." Something of Pascal turned against Pascal. We're in the same boat: a sort of lifeboat, bombs falling on every side, the lifeboat drifts toward subterranean rivers of ice, or toward rivers of fire, the Orenoco, the Amazon, everyone is pulling an oar, and we're not even supposed to like one another, we fight, we eat each other. Everyone pulling an oar is sharing, sharing something, beyond any law, any contract, any institution. Drifting, a drifting movement or "deterritorialization": I say all this in a vague, confused way, since this is an hypothesis or a vague impression on the originality of Nietzsche's texts. A new kind of book.

So what are the characteristics of a Nietzschean aphorism that give this impression? There is one in particular that Maurice Blanchot has brought to light in *The Infinite Conversation*.[3] It is the relation with the outside. Indeed, when we open at random one of Nietzsche's texts, it is one of the first times we no longer pass through an interior, whether it is the interior of the soul or consciousness, the interior of essence or the concept, in other words, that which has always constituted the principle of philosophy. What constitutes the style of philosophy is that the relation to the exterior is always mediated and dissolved by an interior, in an interior. On the contrary, Nietzsche grounds thought, and writing, in an immediate relation with the outside. What is this: a beautiful painting or a beautiful drawing? There is a frame. An aphorism has a frame, too. But whatever is in the frame, at what point does it become beautiful? At the moment one knows and feels that the movement, that the line which is framed comes from elsewhere, that it does not begin within the limits of the frame. It began above, or next to the frame, and the line traverses the frame. As in Godard's film, you paint the painting *with* the wall. Far from being the limitation of the pictorial surface, the frame is almost the opposite, putting it into immediate relation with the outside. However, hooking up thought to the outside is, strictly speaking, something philosophers have never done, even when they were talking about politics, even when they were talking about taking a walk or fresh air. It is not enough to talk about fresh air, to talk about the exterior if you want to hook thought up directly and immediately to the outside.

"...They show up like destiny, without cause or reason, without consideration or pretext, there they are with the speed of lightning, too terrible, too
sudden, too conquering, too *other* even to be an object of hatred..." This is Nietzsche's famous text on the founders of States, "those artists with eyes of bronze"
(*The Genealogy of Morals*, II, 17). Or is it Kafka, writing *The Great Wall of China*?
"It's impossible to understand how they made it all the way to the capital, which
is nonetheless quite far from the frontier. But there they are, and every morning
seems to increase their number. [...] Impossible to converse with them. They
don't know our language. [...] Even their horses are meat-eaters!"[4] Well then,
what I am saying is that texts like these are traversed by a movement which comes
from the outside, which does not begin in the page of the book, nor in the preceding pages, which does not fit in the frame of the book, and which is totally
different from the imaginary movement of representations or the abstract movement of concepts as they are wont to take place through words and in the reader's
head. Something leaps from the book, making contact with a pure outside. It is
this, I believe, which for Nietzsche's work is the right to misinterpret. An aphorism is a play of forces, a state of forces which are always exterior to one another.
An aphorism doesn't mean anything, it signifies nothing, and no more has a signifier than a signified. Those would be ways of restoring a text's interiority. An
aphorism is a state of forces, the last of which, meaning at once the most recent,
the most actual, and the provisional-ultimate, is *the most external*. Nietzsche
posits it quite clearly: if you want to know what I mean, find the force that gives
what I say meaning, and a new meaning if need be. Hook the text up to this
force. In this way, there are no problems of interpretation for Nietzsche, there are
only problems of machining: to machine Nietzsche's text, to find out which actual external force will get something through, like a current of energy. In this
respect, we come across the problem raised by some of Nietzsche's texts which
have a fascist or anti-Semitic resonance... And since we are discussing Nietzsche
today, we must acknowledge that he has inspired and inspires still many a young
fascist. There was a time when it was important to show how Nietzsche was used,
twisted, and completely distorted by the fascists. This was done in the revue
Acéphale, with Jean Wahl, Bataille, and Klossowski. Today, however, this is perhaps no longer the problem. It is not at the level of the text that we must fight.
Not because we are incapable of fighting at that level, but because such a fight is
no longer useful. Rather, we must find, assign, join those external forces which
give to any particular Nietzschean phrase its liberating meaning, its sense of exteriority. It is at the level of method that the question of Nietzsche's revolutionary
character is raised: it is the Nietzschean method that makes Nietzsche's text not
something about which we have to ask: "is this fascist, bourgeois, or revolutionary in itself?"—but a field of exteriority where fascist, bourgeois, and
revolutionary forces confront one another. And if we pose the problem in this
way, the answer that necessarily conforms with the method is: find the revolu-

tionary force (who is superman?) always calling on new forces which come from the exterior, and which traverse and intersect with the Nietzschean text in the frame of the aphorism. *There* is your legitimate misinterpretation: to treat the aphorism like a phenomenon awaiting new forces that will "subjugate" it or make it work or explode.

The aphorism is not only relation with the outside. Its second characteristic is relation with the intensive. And they're the same thing. Klossowski and Lyotard have said all there is to say on the matter. What I said about *lived experiences* a moment ago, how they mustn't be translated into representations or fantasies, how they mustn't be made to pass through the codes of law, contract, or institution, they mustn't be cashed in—it's quite the opposite: they must be treated as flows which carry us always farther out, ever further toward the exterior; this is precisely intensity, or intensities. The lived experience is not subjective, or not necessarily. It is not of the individual. It is flow and the interruption of flow, since each intensity is necessarily in relation to another intensity, in such a way that something gets through. This is what is underneath the codes, what escapes them, and what the codes want to translate, convert, cash in. But what Nietzsche is trying to tell us by this writing of intensities is: don't exchange the intensity for representations. The intensity sends you back neither to signifieds which would be like the representations of things, nor to signifiers which would be like the representations of words. So in what does intensity consist, as both agent and object of uncoding? This is where Nietzsche is at his most mysterious. The intensity has to do with proper names, and these are neither representations of things (or persons), nor representations of words. Whether they are collective or individual names, the pre-Socratics, the Romans, the Jews, Christ, the Anti-Christ, Julius Caesar, Borgia, Zarathoustra, all the proper names which come and go in Nietzsche's texts are neither signifiers or signifieds, but designate intensities on a body which can be the body of the Earth, the body of the book, as well as Nietzsche's own suffering body: *I am every name in history...* There is a kind of nomadism, a perpetual migration of the intensities designated by proper names, and these interpenetrate one another as they are lived on a full body. The intensity can be lived only in relation to its mobile inscription on a body, and to the moving exteriority of a proper name, and this is what it means for a proper name to be always a mask, the mask of an operator.

The relation of the aphorism to humor and irony is the third point. Whoever reads Nietzsche without laughing, and laughing heartily and often and sometimes hysterically, is almost not reading Nietzsche at all. This is true not only for Nietzsche, but for all the authors who comprise the same horizon of our counter-culture. What shows us our own decadence and degeneracy is the way we feel the need to read in them anguish, solitude, guilt, the drama of communication, the whole tragedy of interiority. Even Max Brod tells us how the audience would laugh hysterically when Kafka used to read *The Trial*. And

Beckett, I mean, it is difficult not to laugh when you read him, moving from one joyful moment to the next. Laughter, not the signifier. What springs from great books is schizo-laughter or revolutionary joy, not the anguish of our pathetic narcissism, not the terror of our guilt. Call it the "comedy of the superhuman," or the "clowning of God." There is always an indescribable joy that springs from great books, even when they speak of ugly, desperate, or terrifying things. The transmutation already takes effect with every great book, and every great book constitutes the health of tomorrow. You cannot help but laugh when you mix up the codes. If you put thought in relation to the outside, Dionysian moments of laughter will erupt, and this is thinking in the clear air. It often happens that Nietzsche comes face to face with something sickening, ignoble, disgusting. Well, Nietzsche thinks it's funny, and he would add fuel to the fire if he could. He says: keep going, it's still not disgusting enough. Or he says: excellent, how disgusting, what a marvel, what a masterpiece, a poisonous flower, finally the "human species is getting interesting." For example, this is how Nietzsche looks at and deals with what he calls unhappy consciousness. Thus, there are the Hegelian commentators, those commentators of interiority, who really have no sense of humor. They say: you see, Nietzsche takes the unhappy consciousness seriously; he makes it one of the moments in the becoming-spirit of spirituality. They pass over quickly what Nietzsche makes of spirituality because they sense the danger. So we see that while Nietzsche entitles legitimate misinterpretations, there are also misinterpretations which are totally illegitimate, those which are explained by the spirit of seriousness, by the spirit of gravity, by the monkey of Zarathoustra, in other words, by the cult of interiority. Laughter in Nietzsche always harks back to the external movement of humors and ironies, and this is the movement of intensities, as Klossowski and Lyotard have made clear: the way in which there is a play of high and low intensities, the one in the other, such that a low intensity can undermine the highest intensity and even be as high as the highest, and vice versa. This play of levels of intensity controls the peaks of irony and the valleys of humor in Nietzsche, and it is developed as the consistency or the quality of what is lived in relation to the exterior. An aphorism is the pure matter of laughter and joy. If you cannot find something to make you laugh in an aphorism, a distribution of irony and humor, a partition of intensities, then you have found nothing.

There is one last point. Let's come back to that great text, *The Genealogy of Morals*, on the State and the founders of empires: "They show up like destiny, without cause or reason...." In this we recognize the men of that social production known as Asiatic. On the foundation of primitive rural communities, the despot sets up his imperial machine which over-codes everything, with a bureaucracy, an administration that organizes major enterprises and appropriates the surplus work for itself ("wherever they appear, in no time at all you find something new, a sovereign machinery that has come alive, in which every part, every function is defined and determined with respect to the whole...”). But we can ask ourselves whether this text does not bring together two forces that are in other ways distinct—which Kafka, for his part, kept separate and even opposed in *The Great Wall of China*. Because when we seek to learn how primitive segmentary communities gave way to other formations of sovereignty, a question which Nietzsche raises in the second essay of his *Genealogy*, we see two phenomena produced which are strictly correlative, but quite different. It is true that rural communities at their center are caught and transfixed in the despot's bureaucratic machine, with its scribes, its priests, its bureaucrats; but on the periphery, the communities embark on another kind of adventure, display another kind of unity, a nomadic unity, and engage in a nomadic war-machine, and they tend to come uncoded rather than being coded over. Entire groups take off on a nomadic adventure: archeologist have taught us to consider nomadism not as an originary state, but as an adventure that erupts in sedentary groups; it is the call of the outside, it is movement. The nomad and his war-machine stand opposite the despot and his administrative machine, and the extrinsic nomadic unity opposite the intrinsic despotic unity. And yet they are so interrelated or interdependent that the despot will set himself the problem of integrating, internalizing the nomadic war-machine, while the nomad attempts to invent an administration for his conquered empire. Their ceaseless opposition is such that they are inextricable from one another.

Imperial unity gave birth to philosophical discourse, through many an avatar, the same avatars which lead us from imperial formations to the Greek city-state. Even in the Greek city-state, philosophical discourse maintains an essential relation to the despot or the shadow of a despot, to imperialism, to the administration of things and persons (you will find ample evidence in the books by Strauss and Kojève on tyranny).[5] Philosophical discourse has always maintained an essential relation to the law, the institution, and the contract, all of which are the Sovereign's problem, traversing the ages of sedentary history from despotic formations to democracies. The "signifier" is in fact the latest philosophical avatar of the despot. And if Nietzsche does not belong in philosophy, perhaps it is because he is the first to conceive of another kind of discourse, a counter-philosophy, in other words, a discourse that is first and foremost nomadic, whose utterances would be produced not by a rational administrative machine—philosophers would be the bureaucrats of pure reason—but by a mobile war-machine. Perhaps this is what Nietzsche means when he says that a new politics begins with him (Klossowki calls it the conspiracy against his own class). We know all too well that nomads are unhappy in our regimes: we use any means necessary to pin them down, so they lead a troubled life. And Nietzsche lived like a nomad, reduced to this shadow, wandering from one furnished room to another. But also, the nomad is not necessarily someone who moves around: some journeys take place in the same place, they're journeys in intensity, and even historically speaking, nomads don't move around like migrants. On the contrary, nomads are motionless, and the nomadic adventure begins when they seek to stay in the same place by escaping the codes. As we know, the revolutionary problem today is to find some unity in our various struggles without falling back on the despotic and bureaucratic organization of the party or State apparatus: we want a war-machine that would not recreate a State apparatus, a nomadic unity in relation with the Outside, that would not recreate the despotic internal unity. This is perhaps Nietzsche at his most profound, a measure of his break with philosophy, as it appears in the aphorism: to have made a war-machine of thought, to have made thought a nomadic power. And even if the journey goes nowhere, even if it takes place in the same place, imperceptible, unlooked for, underground, we must ask: who are today's nomads, who are today's Nietzscheans?

Discussion

André Flécheux: What I would like to know is how [Deleuze] thinks he can pass over deconstruction, I mean, how he thinks a monadic reading of each aphorism from an empirical stance and as though from the outside could suffice—which from a Heideggerian point of view seems extremely suspect. I wonder whether the problem of the "already there," constituted by language, the reigning order, what you call the despot, allows us to understand Nietzsche's writing as a kind of erratic reading, which would itself derive from an erratic writing, with Nietzsche applying to himself what he calls auto-critique, the current editions of his work revealing him to be an exceptional stylist, and consequently, each aphorism is not a closed system, but is implicated in a total structure of relays. Perhaps your thinking on the status of an undeconstructed outside is connected to the status of the energetic in Lyotard.

My second question is related to the first: in an era that has seen the state organization, or the capitalist organization, whatever you call it, issue a challenge which is what Heidegger calls rationalization by technology, do you honestly believe nomadism, as you describe it, to be a serious response?

Gilles Deleuze: If I understand you correctly, you're saying that there is reason to suspect my loyalties to the Heideggerian point of view. I'm glad there is. As for the method of textual deconstruction, I know what it is, and I admire it, but it has nothing to do with my own method. I don't really do textual commentary. For me, a text is nothing but a cog in a larger extra-textual practice. It's not about using deconstruction, or any other textual practice, to do textual commentary; it's about seeing what one can do with an extra-textual practice that extends the text. You ask me whether I believe in nomads as an answer. Yes, I do. Genghis Kahn is nothing to sneeze at. Will he come back from the dead? I don't know, but if he does it will be in some other form. Just as the despot internalizes the nomadic war-machine, capitalist society never stops internalizing a revolutionary war-machine. It's not on the periphery that the new nomads are being born (because there is no more periphery); I want to find out what sort of nomads, even motionless and stationary if need be, our society is capable of producing.

André Flécheux: Yes, but you omitted in your presentation what you referred to as interiority...

Gilles Deleuze: You're punning on the word "interiority"...

André Flécheux: The inner journey?

Gilles Deleuze: I said "motionless journey." It's not an inner journey, it's a journey on a body, and collective bodies if necessary.

Mieke Taat: Gilles Deleuze, if I have understood you correctly, you oppose laughter, humor, and irony to unhappy consciousness. Would you agree that the laughter of Kafka, Beckett, and Nietzsche does not exclude the weeping of these writers, provided that their tears do not spring from some inner or internalized source, but are simply the production of flows on the surface of a body...?

Gilles Deleuze: I think you're right.

Mieke Taat: One more question. When you oppose irony and humor to unhappy consciousness, you no longer make a distinction between humor and irony, as you did in *The Logic of Sense*, where one was surface and the other depth. Are you not afraid that irony is dangerously close to unhappy consciousness?

Gilles Deleuze: I've undergone a change. The surface-depth opposition no longer concerns me. What interests me now is the relationships between a full body, a body without organs, and flows that migrate.

Mieke Taat: But then resentment would not be excluded, would it?

Gilles Deleuze: Yes, it would!

On Capitalism and Desire[1]

Actuel: In your description of capitalism, you say: "There isn't the slightest operation, the slightest industrial or financial mechanism that fails to manifest the dementia of the capitalist system and the pathological character of its rationality (not a false rationality at all, but a true rationality of this pathology, this madness, because the machine works, there can be no doubt). There is no danger of it going insane, because through and through it is already insane, from the get-go, and that's where its rationality comes from." Does this mean that after this "abnormal" society, or outside it, there can be a "normal" society?

Gilles Deleuze: We don't use the words "normal" and "abnormal." Every society is at once rational and irrational. They are necessarily rational in their mechanisms, their gears and wheels, their systems of connection, and even by virtue of the place they assign to the irrational. All this presupposes, however, codes or axioms which do not result by chance, but which do not have an intrinsic rationality either. It's just like theology: everything about it is quite rational if you accept sin, the immaculate conception, and the incarnation. Reason is always a region carved out of the irrational—not sheltered from the irrational at all, but traversed by it and only defined by a particular kind of relationship among irrational factors. Underneath all reason lies delirium, and drift. Everything about capitalism is rational, except capital or capitalism. A stock-market is a perfectly rational mechanism, you can understand it, learn how it works; capitalists know how to use it; and yet what a delirium, it's nuts. This is what we mean when we say that the rational is always the rationality of an irrational. Something that has not been discussed in Marx's *Capital* is the extent to which he is fascinated by capitalist mechanisms, precisely because, at one and the same time, it is demented *and* it works. So then what is rational in a society? Once interests have been defined within the confines of a society, the rational is the way in which people

262

pursue those interests and attempt to realize them. But underneath that, you find desires, investments of desire that are not to be confused with investments of interest, and on which interests depend for their determination and very distribution: an enormous flow, all kinds of libidinal-unconscious flows that constitute the delirium of this society. In reality, history is the history of desire. Today's capitalist or technocrat does not desire in the same way a slave trader or a bureaucrat from the old Chinese empire would have. When people in a society desire repression, for others *and for themselves*; when there are people who like to harass others, and who have the opportunity to do so, the "right" to do so, this exhibits the problem of a deep connection between libidinal desire and the social field. There exists a "disinterested" love for the oppressive machine: Nietzsche has some beautiful things to say about this permanent triumph of slaves, about the way the embittered, the depressed, or the weak manage to impose their way of life on us.

Actuel: What, precisely, is proper to capitalism in what you've just described?

Gilles Deleuze: Perhaps it's that, in capitalism, desire and interest, or desire and reason, are distributed in a totally new way, a particularly "abnormal" way. Capital, or money, has reached such a stage of delirium that there would be only one equivalent in psychiatry: what they call the terminal state. It's too complicated to describe here, but let me just say this: in other societies, you have exploitation, you have scandals and secrets, but it's all part of the "code." There are even explicitly secret codes. In capitalism, it's completely different: nothing is secret, at least in principle and according to the code (that's why capitalism is "democratic" and "publicizes" itself, even in the juridical sense of the term). And yet nothing is *admissible*. Legality itself is inadmissible. In contrast to other societies, the regime of capitalism is both public and inadmissible. This very special delirium is proper to the regime of money. Just look at what they call scandals today: the newspapers talk about them incessantly, everyone pretends either to defend themselves or to go on the attack; but the search for anything illegal comes up empty-handed, given the nature of the regime of capital. Everything is legal: the prime minister's tax returns, real-estate deals, lobbyists, and generally the economic and financial mechanisms of capital—everything except the little screw-ups; still more to the point, everything is public but *nothing is admissible*. If the left were "reasonable," it would be satisfied with vulgarizing economic and financial mechanisms. There's no need to make the private public, just admit what is already public. Then a dementia without precedent would be found in all the hospitals. Instead, they keep talking about "ideology." Ideology has no importance here: what matters is not ideology, and not even the "economic / ideological" distinction or opposition; what matters is the *organization of power*. Because the organization of power, i.e. the way in which desire is already in the economic, the way libido invests the economic, haunts the economic and fosters the political forms of repression.

Actuel: Ideology is smoke and mirrors?

Gilles Deleuze: That's not what I mean. Saying that "ideology is smoke and mirrors" is still the traditional thesis. On one side you put the serious stuff, the economy, the infrastructure, and then on the other side you put the superstructure, to which ideology belongs. And thus you restrict the phenomena of desire to ideology. It's a perfect way to ignore how desire works on the infrastructure, invests it, belongs to it, and how desire thereby organizes power: it organizes the system of repression. We're not saying that ideology is smoke and mirrors (or any other concept that serves to designate an illusion). We're saying: there is no ideology, the concept itself is an illusion. That's why it suits the Communist Party and orthodox Marxism so well. Marxism has given such emphasis to the theme of ideologies precisely to cover up what was going on in the USSR: a new organization of repressive power. There is no ideology, there are only organizations of power, once you accept that the organization of power is the unity of desire and the economic infrastructure. Let's take two examples. Education: the Leftists of May '68 wasted a lot of time insisting that professors publicly criticize themselves as agents of bourgeois ideology. It's stupid, and it fuels the masochistic impulses of academics. They abandoned the struggle against the competitive examination and opted instead for polemic, or the great public anti-ideological confession. During which time, the most hard-line profs were able to reorganize their power without too much difficulty. The problem of education is not ideological in nature, it's a problem of the organization of power: the specificity of educational power makes it appear ideological, but that's a red-herring. Power in grammar school, now that means something, every child is subjected to it. The second example: Christianity. The Church is all too happy to be treated as an ideology. They want to discuss it—it encourages ecumenism. But Christianity has never been an ideology. It is a very original, specific organization of power which has taken diverse forms from the Roman Empire through the Middle Ages, and which was able to invent the idea of an international power. It's far more important than ideology.

Félix Guattari: The same goes for traditional political structures. It's always the same old trick: a big ideological debate in the general assembly, and the questions of organization are reserved for special committees. These look secondary, having been determined by political options. Whereas, in fact, the real problems are precisely the problems of organization, never made explicit or rationalized, but recast after the fact in ideological terms. The real divisions emerge in organization: a particular way of treating desire and power, investments, group-Oedipuses, group-super-egos, phenomena of perversion... Only then are the political oppositions built up: an individual chooses one position over another, because in the scheme of the organization of power, he has already chosen and hates his opponent.

Actuel: Your overall analysis of the Soviet Union or capitalism is convincing, but what about the particulars? If every ideological opposition by definition masks conflicts of desire, how would you analyze, for example, the divergence of three Trotskyite splinter-groups? What conflicts of desire, if any, do you see there? In spite of their political quarrels, each group seems to fulfil the same function for its members: it offers them the security of a hierarchy, a social milieu on a reduced scale, and a definitive explanation of the world... I don't see the difference.

Félix Guattari: Provided we recognize that any resemblance to an existing group is purely fortuitous, we can imagine that one of the groups initially defines itself by its fidelity to the rigid positions of the communist left during the creation of the Third International. Now you adopt a whole axiomatics, down to the phonological level—the pronunciation of certain words, the gesture that accompanies it, not to mention the structures of organization, the conception of the relationships to be maintained with allies on the left, with centrists and adversaries... This universe can correspond to a particular figure of Oedipalization, very much like the intangible and reassuring universe of the obsessive who loses his bearings as soon as you displace a familiar object. This identification with recurrent images and figures is meant to achieve a certain kind of efficacy that characterized Stalinism—except for its ideology, precisely. In other respects, they keep the overall framework of the method, but they're receptive to change: "Comrades, we must recognize that if the enemy remains the same, the conditions have changed." So the splinter group is more open. It's a compromise: the initial image has been crossed out while being maintained, and other notions have been added. Meetings and training sessions multiply, but so do external interventions. As Zazie says, the desiring will has a way of harassing students and militants.

As for the basic problems, all these groups say more or less the same thing. Where they radically differ is *style*: a particular definition of the leader or propaganda, a particular conception of discipline, or the fidelity, modesty, and asceticism of a militant. How do you propose to account for these differences if you don't go rummaging around in the social machine's economy of desire? From the anarchists to the Maoists, the diversity is incredibly wide, analytically as well as politically. And don't forget, beyond the shrinking fringe of splinter groups, that mass of people who don't know what to choose: the leftist movement, the attraction of unions, straightforward revolt, indifference... We must try to explain the role these splinter groups play in crushing desire, like machines grinding and tamping it down. It's a dilemma: to be broken by the social system, or to fall into your preordained place in these little churches. In this respect, May '68 was an astonishing revelation. Desiring power accelerated to a point where it exploded all the splinter groups. They regrouped later on when they participated in the business of restoring order with other repressive forces: the CGT [Communist Workers' Union], the PC [Communist Party], the CRS [the riot police], or Edgar Faure. I'm not saying that to be provocative. It goes without saying that the militants were courageous to fight against the police. But if we leave the sphere of struggle, the sphere of interests, to consider instead the function of desire, you must admit that the recruiters of certain splinter groups approached the youth in a spirit of repression: they wanted to contain the desire which had been liberated to re-channel it.

Actuel: Sure, but what is a liberated desire? I see how it could work on an individual or group level: artistic creation, smashing windows, burning things, or even simply having an orgy, or letting everything go to hell through sheer laziness. But then what? What would be a collectively liberated desire on the scale of a social group? Can you give any precise examples? And what does that mean for the "totality of society," if you don't reject that term as Foucault does.

Félix Guattari: We chose as our reference a state of desire at its most critical and acute: the desire of the schizophrenic. And the schizophrenic who is able to produce something, beyond or beneath the schizophrenic who has been locked up, beaten down with drugs and social repression. In our opinion, some schizophrenics directly express a free deciphering of desire. But how does one conceive of a collective form of desiring economy? Well, not locally. I have a hard time imagining a small group which has been liberated staying together as it is traversed by the flows of a repressive society, as though one liberated individual after another could just be added on. But if desire constitutes the very texture of society in its totality, including its mechanisms of reproduction, a movement of liberation can "crystallize" in that society. In May '68, from the first sparks to the local clashes, the upheaval was brutally transmitted to the whole society—including groups that had nothing at all to do with the revolutionary movement: doctors, lawyers, merchants. Vested interest prevailed in the end, but only after a month of burnings. We're headed for explosions of this type, yet more profound.

Actuel: Might there have already occurred in history a vigorous, lasting liberation of desire, beyond brief periods of celebration, war, and carnage, or revolutions for a day? Or do you believe in an end to history: after millennia of alienation, social evolution will one day turn around in a final revolution to liberate desire forever?

Félix Guattari: Neither. Not in a definitive end to history, and not in provisional excess. Every civilization and every epoch have had their ends to history. It's not necessarily insightful or liberating. The moments of excess, the celebrations are hardly more reassuring. There are militant revolutionaries who feel a sense of responsibility and say: excess, celebration, yes—"at the first stage of revolution." But there is always a second stage: organization, operation, all the serious stuff...

Nor is desire liberated in simple moments of celebration. Just look at the discussion between Victor and Foucault, in the issue of *Les Temps Modernes* devoted to the Maoists.[2] Victor consents to excess, but only at "the first stage." As for the rest, the serious stuff, Victor calls for a new State apparatus, new norms, popular justice by tribunal, invoking an authority exterior to the masses, a third party capable of resolving the contradictions of the masses. We come up against the same old schema again and again: they detach a pseudo avant-garde able to bring about syntheses, to form a party as an embryonic State apparatus; they levy recruits from a well-educated, well-behaved working class; and the rest, *lumpen proletariat*, is a residue not to be trusted (always the old condemnation of desire). These very distinctions only trap desire to serve a bureaucratic caste-system. Foucault responds by denouncing the third party, saying that if such a thing as popular justice does exist, it certainly won't come from a tribunal. He clearly demonstrates how the "avant-garde / proletariat / non-proletarian plebs" distinction is originally a distinction which the bourgeoisie introduces into the masses, to crush the phenomena of desire and marginalize it. The whole question turns on a State apparatus. Why would you look to a party or State apparatus to liberate desires? It's bizarre. Wanting improved justice is like wanting good judges, good cops, good bosses, a cleaner France, etc. And then we are told: how do you propose to unify isolated struggles without a State apparatus? The revolution clearly needs a war-machine, but that's not a State apparatus. It also needs an analytic force, an analyzer of the desires of the masses, absolutely—but not an external mechanism of synthesis. What is liberated desire? A desire that escapes the impasse of individual private fantasy: it's not about adapting desire, socializing and disciplining it, but hooking it up in such a way that its process is uninterrupted in the social body, so its expression can be collective. The most important thing is not authoritarian unification, but a kind of infinite swarming: desires in the neighborhood, the schools, factories, prisons, nursery schools, etc. It's not about a make-over, or totalization, but hooking up on the same plane at its tipping point. As long as we stick to the alternative between the impotent spontaneity of anarchy and the hierarchical and bureaucratic encoding of a party-organization, there can be no liberation of desire.

Actuel: Do you think that capitalism in its beginnings was able to subsume social desires?

Gilles Deleuze: Of course. Capitalism has always been, and still is a remarkable desiring-machine. Flows of money, flows of the means of production, flows of man-power, flows of new markets: it's all desire in flux. You just have to examine the many contingencies that gave birth to capitalism to realize how inseparable from the phenomena of desire are its infrastructure and economy, and the extent to which it is a criss-crossing of desires. And don't forget fascism.

It too "subsumes social desires," including the desires of repression and death. Hitler and the fascist machine gave people hard-ons. But if your question wants to ask: was capitalism in its beginnings revolutionary, did the industrial revolution ever coincide with a social revolution? The answer is no. At least I don't think so. From its birth capitalism has been connected with a savage repression. It very quickly acquired its organization and State apparatus. Did capitalism entail the dissolution of previous codes and powers? Absolutely. But it had already set up the gears of its power, including its State power, in the fissures of previous regimes. It's always like that: there is very little progress. Even before a social formation gets going, its instruments of exploitation and repression are already there, aimlessly spinning their wheels, but ready to swing into high gear. The first capitalist are waiting there like birds of prey, waiting to swoop on the worker who has fallen through the cracks of the previous system. This is what is meant by primitive accumulation.

Actuel: In my view, the rising bourgeoisie was imagining and preparing its revolution throughout the Enlightenment. The bourgeoisie in its own eyes was a revolutionary class "to the bitter end," since it came to power by bringing down the Ancient Regime. Whatever the movements that existed among the peasantry and the working class, the bourgeois revolution is a revolution carried out by the bourgeoisie—the two terms are synonymous. So, it is anachronistic to judge the bourgeoisie by the socialist utopias of the nineteenth- and twentieth-centuries; it leads to the introduction of a category that never existed.

Gilles Deleuze: Here again, what you're saying fits the schema of a particular kind of Marxism: it supposes that the bourgeoisie is revolutionary at some point in history, and even that it was or is necessary to go through a capitalist stage, through a bourgeois revolutionary stage. That's a Stalinist point of view, but it's hard to take seriously. When a social formation exhausts itself and begins to leak on every side, all sorts of things come uncoded, all sorts of unpoliced flows begin circulating: for example, the migrations of peasants in feudal Europe are phenomena of "deterritorialization." The bourgeoisie imposes a new code, both economic and political, so you might think it was revolutionary. Not in the least. Daniél Guérin has said some profound things about the Revolution of 1789.[3] The bourgeoisie never mistook its real enemy. Its real enemy was not the previous system, but that which had escaped the control of the previous system, and the bourgeoisie was resolved to control it in its turn. The bourgeoisie owed its power to the dissolution of the old system; but it could exercise this new power only by considering the other revolutionaries as enemies. The bourgeoisie was never revolutionary. It had the revolution carried out for it. It manipulated, channeled, repressed an enormous surge of popular desire. The people marched to their death at Valmy.

Actuel: They certainly marched to their death at Verdun.

Félix Guattari: Exactly. This is precisely what interests us. Where do these eruptions, these uprisings, these enthusiasms come from? They can't be explained by a social rationality, and the moment they're born, they're rerouted, captured by power. A revolutionary situation cannot be explained simply by the analysis of interests present at the time. In 1903, the Russian Social-Democratic party is discussing its alliances, the organization of the proletariat, and the role of the avant-garde. All of the sudden, while the Social-Democrats are "preparing" for revolution, they're rocked by the events of 1905 and have to jump aboard a moving train. A crystallization of desire on a wide social scale had occured, whose basis lay in still incomprehensible situations. The same is true of 1917. In this case, the politicians again jumped aboard, and they gained control of it. Yet no revolutionary tendency was willing or able to assume the need for a Soviet organization that would have allowed the masses to take real charge of their interests and desires. Machines called political organizations were put in circulation, and they functioned according to the model Dimitrov had developed at the Seventh International Congress—alternating between popular fronts and sectarian retractions—and they always lead to the same repressive results. We saw it again in 1936, 1945, and 1968. By their axiomatics, these mass machines refuse to liberate revolutionary energy. Red flag in hand, this politics in its underhanded way reminds one of the politics of the President or the clergy. And in our view, this corresponds to a certain position vis-à-vis desire, a profound way of envisioning the ego, the individual, and the family. This raises a simple dilemma: either we find some new type of structure to facilitate the fusion of collective desire and revolutionary organization; or we continue on the present course, heading from one repression to the next, toward a fascism that will make Hitler and Mussolini look like a joke.

Actuel: So then what is the nature of this profound, fundamental desire that we see constitutes humanity and human beings as social animals, but which is constantly betrayed? Why is it always ready to be invested in those machines of the dominant machine, like opposed political parties which are nonetheless the same? Could this mean that desire is condemned to a pure explosion without consequence, or to perpetual betrayal? One last question: can there ever be such a thing as a collective and lasting expression of liberated desire at some point in history? If so, how?

Gilles Deleuze: If we knew the answer to that, we wouldn't be discussing it, we would just go out and do it. Still, like Félix said, revolutionary organization must be the organization of a war-machine and not of a State apparatus, the organization of an analyzer and not of an external synthesis. In every social system, you will always find lines of escape, as well as sticking points to cut off these escapes, or else (which is not the same thing) embryonic apparatuses to recuperate them, to reroute and stop them, in a new system waiting to strike. I would like to see the crusades analyzed from this perspective. But in every respect, capitalism has a very particular character: its lines of escape are not just difficulties that arise, they are the very conditions of its operation. Capitalism is founded on a generalized decoding of every flow: flows of wealth, flows of labor, flows of language, flows of art, etc. It did not create any code, it created a kind of accounting, an axiomatics of decoded flows, as the basis of its economy. It ligatures the points of escape and moves ahead. It is always expanding its own borders, and always finds itself in a situation where it must close off new escape routes at its borders, pushing them back once more. It has resolved none of its fundamental problems. It can't even foresee the monetary increase in a country over a year. It is endlessly crossing its own limits which keep reappearing farther out. It puts itself in alarming situations with respect to its own production, its social life, its demographics, its periphery in the Third World, its interior regions, etc. The system is leaking all over the place. They spring from the constantly displaced limits of the system. And certainly, the revolutionary escape (the active escape, which Jackson invokes when he says: "I've never stopped fleeing, but as I flee, I'm looking for a weapon")[4] is not the same thing as other kinds of escape, the schizo-escape, the drug-escape. This is precisely the problem facing marginal groups: to make all the lines of escape connect up on a revolutionary plane. In capitalism, then, these lines of escape take on a new character, and a new kind of revolutionary potential. So, you see, there is hope.

Actuel: You mentioned the crusades just now. Do you see the crusades as one of the first manifestations of collective schizophrenia in the West?

Félix Guattari: The crusades were indeed an extraordinary schizophrenic movement. Suddenly, thousands and thousands of people, during a period that was already divided and troubled, were totally fed up with their life; spontaneous preaching rose up everywhere, and whole villages of men set out. It is only afterwards that a frightened papacy tried to give this movement direction by leading it off to the Holy Land. This strategy had two advantages: it gets rid of the wandering gangs, and it shores up the Christian outposts threatened by the Turks in the Near-East. It didn't always work: the Venetian Crusade wound up in Constantinople, and the Children's Crusade veered off to the South of France and quickly lost any sympathy people had for it. Entire villages were captured and burned by these "crusading" children, whom the regular armies finally had to round up, either killing them or selling them into slavery…

Actuel: Do you see any parallel here with contemporary movements, such as the road, or hippy colonies, fleeing the factory and the office? Is there a pope to co-opt them? The Jesus-revolution?

Félix Guattari: A recuperation by Christianity is not out of the question. It's already a reality, to a certain extent, in the United States though much less so here in France or Europe. But you can see a latent recuperation beneath the naturist movement, the idea that we could withdraw from production and reconstitute a small society out of the way, as though we weren't all branded and corralled by the capitalist system.

Actuel: What role can still be attributed to the Church in a country like ours? The Church was at the center of power in Western society well into the eighteenth-century; it bound and structured the social machine before the nation-State emerged. The technocracy has deprived it today of its old function, so the Church, too, appears adrift, a rudderless ship divided against itself. One can ask whether the Church, pressured by currents of progressive Catholicism, is not becoming less confessional than certain political organizations.

Félix Guattari: What about ecumenism? Is that not the Church's way of landing on its feet? The Church has never been stronger. I don't see any reason to oppose the Church to technocracy; the Church has its own technocracy. Historically speaking, Christianity and positivism have always gotten along quite well together. There is a Christian motor behind the development of the positive sciences. And you can't really claim that the psychiatrist replaced the priest, nor that the cop replaced him. Everyone is needed in repression! What has become outdated in the Church is its ideology, not its organization of power.

Actuel: Let's address this other aspect of your book: the critique of psychiatry. Can one say that France is already under surveillance by psychiatry at the local level? And just how far does this influence extend?

Félix Guattari: Psychiatric hospitals are essentially structured like a state bureaucracy, and psychiatrists are bureaucrats. For a long time the State had been satisfied with a politics of coercion and did nothing for almost a century. It was only after the Liberation that any signs of anxiety appeared: the first psychiatric revolution, the opening of the hospitals, free treatment, institutional psychotherapy, etc. This led to the great utopian politics of "localized" care: limiting the number of internments, and sending teams of psychiatrists out into the population like missionaries into the bush. But not enough people believed in the reform, and without the will to carry it out, it got bogged down. Now you have a few model services for official visits, and a few hospitals here and there in the more underdeveloped regions. Still, we're headed for a major crisis, on the scale of the university crisis, a disaster at every level: equipment, personnel training, therapy, etc.

The institutional surveillance of children has been, on the whole, undertaken with greater success. In this case, the initiative escaped State structure and financing, falling instead under diverse associations, such as childhood protection agencies or parental associations… Because they were subsidized by social security, the establishments proliferated. The child is immediately taken in charge by a network of psychiatrists, tagged at an early age, and followed for life. One can expect solutions of this type for adult psychiatry. Faced with the current impasse, the State will try to denationalize institutions and replace them with institutions governed by the law of 1901 and most certainly manipulated by political powers and reactionary family groups. We're indeed headed toward the psychiatric surveillance of France, if the present crisis doesn't liberate its revolutionary potentials. The most conservative ideology is spreading everywhere, an insipid transposition of the most Oedipal concepts. In the children's wards, they call the director "uncle," and the nurse "mother." I have even heard things like: game groups follow a maternal principle, and workshops a paternal principle. The psychiatry of surveillance looks progressive because it opens up the hospital. But if that implies a surveillance of the neighborhood, we will quickly come to regret the closed asylums of yesterday. It's like psychoanalysis: it functions beyond the confines of walls, but it's much worse as a repressive force, it's much more dangerous.

Gilles Deleuze: Here is a case. A woman comes in for a consultation, explaining that she's taking tranquilizers. She asks for a glass of water. Then she says: "You see, I'm a cultured woman, I've done graduate work, I love to read, and all of a sudden I can't stop crying. I can't stand the subway… And then I start crying as soon as I read anything… I watch TV, I see those images from Vietnam: I can't stand it." The doctor doesn't say too much. The woman continues: "I've been working a little for the Resistance: I act as a mail-box." The doctor asks her to explain. "Of course, I'm sorry, you don't understand, do you? I go into a café and ask: is there anything for René? Then they give me a letter to send." When the doctor hears 'René,' he wakes up: "Why did you say 'René'?" This is the first time he has asked a question. Up to this point, she has been talking about the subway, Hiroshima, Vietnam, and the effect it has on her, on her body, how it makes her feel like crying. But the doctor only says: "Well, well, 'René.' What does 'René' mean to you?" The name 'René' implies someone who is reborn [*re-né*]. A renaissance. Resistance?—forget about it, he passes that over in silence. But renaissance, that fits the universal schema, the archetype: "You want to be reborn," he says. The doctor has found his bearings: at last he's on track. And he forces her to talk about her mother and her father. This is an essential aspect of our book, and it's totally concrete. Psychiatrists and psychoanalysts have never paid attention to delirium. All you have to do is listen to someone in a state of delirium: the Russians worry him, and the Chinese; I've got no saliva left, I was sodomized in the subway, there are microbes and spermatozoa everywhere; it's Franco's fault, the Jews' fault, the Maoists' fault. Their delirium covers the whole social field. Why couldn't this be about the sexuality of a subject, the relation it has to the idea of Chinese, Whites, Blacks? Or to whole civilizations, the crusades, the subway? Psychiatrists and psychoanalysts have never heard a word of it, and they're on the defensive because they're position is indefensible. They crush the contents of the unconscious with pre-fabricated statements like: "You keep saying Chinese, but what about your father? —He's not Chinese. —So your lover is Chinese?" It's like the repressive work by the judge in the Angela Davis case, who assured us: "Her behavior is explicable only by the fact that she was in love." But what if, on the contrary, Angela Davis's libido was a revolutionary, social libido? What if she was in love because she was a revolutionary?

This is what we want to tell psychiatrists and psychoanalysts: you have no idea what delirium is; you've got it all wrong. The sense of our book is this: we've reached a stage where many people feel that the psychoanalytic machine no longer works, and a whole generation is beginning to have had it with all-purpose schemas: Oedipus and castration, the imaginary and the symbolic —they systematically efface the social, political, and cultural content from every psychic disturbance.

Actuel: Your association of capitalism with schizophrenia is the very foundation of your book. Are there cases of schizophrenia in other societies?

Félix Guattari: Schizophrenia is indissociable from the capitalist system, which is originally conceived as an escape, a leak: an exclusive illness. In other societies, escape and marginality exhibit other aspects. The asocial individual of so-called primitive societies is not locked up; prisons and asylums are recent notions. They're chased away or exiled on the margin of the village and die there, unless they can be integrated into a neighboring village. Each system, moreover, has its own particular illness: the hysteria of so-called primitive societies, the paranoid-depressives of great Empires... The capitalist economy functions through decoding and deterritorialization: it has its extreme illnesses, that is, its schizophrenics who come uncoded and become deterritorialized to the extreme, but it also has its extreme consequences, its revolutionaries.

Five Propositions on Psychoanalysis[1]

I would like to present five propositions on psychoanalysis. The first is this: psychoanalysis today presents a political danger all of its own that is different from the implicit dangers of the old psychiatric hospital. The latter constitutes a place of localized captivity; psychoanalysis, on the other hand, works in the open air. The psychoanalyst has in a sense the same position that Marx accorded to the merchant in feudal society: working in the open pores of society, not only in private offices, but also in schools, institutions, departmentalism, etc. This function puts us in a unique position with respect to the psychoanalytic project. We recognize that psychoanalysis tells us a great deal about the unconscious; but, in a certain way, it does so only to reduce the unconscious, to destroy it, to repulse it, to imagine it as a sort of parasite on consciousness. For psychoanalysis, it is fair to say there are always too many desires. The Freudian conception of the child as polymorphous pervert shows that there are always too many desires. In our view, however, there are never enough desires. We do not, by one method or another, wish to reduce the unconscious: we prefer to produce it: there is no unconscious that is already there; the unconscious must be produced politically, socially, and historically. The question is: in what place, in what circumstances, in the shadow of what events, can the unconscious be produced. Producing the unconscious means very precisely the production of desire in a historical social milieu or the appearance of statements and expressions of a new kind.

My second proposition is that psychoanalysis is a complete machine, designed in advance to prevent people from talking, therefore from producing statements that suit them and the groups with which they have certain affinities. As soon as one begins analysis, one has the impression of talking. But one talks in vain; the entire psychoanalytical machine exists to suppress the conditions of a real expression. Whatever one says is taken into a sort of tourniquet, an interpretive machine; the patient will never be able to get to what he really has to say.

Desire or delirium (which are in a deep sense the same thing), desire-delirium is by its nature a libidinal investment of an entire historical milieu, of an entire social environment. What makes one delirious are classes, peoples, races, masses, mobs. Psychoanalysis, possessed of a pre-existing code, superintends a sort of destruction. This code consists of Oedipus, castration, the family romance; the most secret content of delirium, i.e. this divergence from the social and histori- cal milieu, will be destroyed so that no delirious statement, corresponding to an overflow in the unconscious, will be able to get through the analytical machine. We say that the schizophrenic has to deal not with his family, nor with his par- ents, but with peoples, populations, and tribes. We say that the unconscious is not a matter of generations or family genealogy, but rather of world population, and that the psychoanalytical machine destroys all this. I will cite just two exam- ples: the celebrated example of President Schreber whose delirium is entirely about races, history, and wars. Freud doesn't realize this and reduces the patient's delirium exclusively to his relationship with his father. Another example is the Wolfman: when the Wolfman dreams of six or seven wolves, which is by defini- tion a pack, i.e. a certain kind of group, Freud immediately reduces this multiplicity by bringing everything back to a single wolf who is necessarily the father. The entire collective libidinal expression manifested in the delirium of the Wolfman will be unable to make, let alone conceive of the statements that are for him the most meaningful.

My third proposition is that psychoanalysis works in this way because of its automatic interpretation machine. This interpretation machine can be described in the following way: whatever you say, you mean something different. We can't say enough about the damage these machines cause. When someone explains to me that what I say means something other than what I say, a split in the ego as subject is produced. This split is well known: what I say refers to me as the sub- ject of an utterance or statement, what I mean refers to me as an expressing subject. This split is conjured by psychoanalysis as the basis for castration and prevents all production of statements. For example, in certain schools for prob- lem children, dealing with character or even psychopathology, the child, in his work or play activities, is placed in a relationship with his educator, and in this context the child is understood as the subject of an utterance or statement; in his psychotherapy, he is put into a relationship with the analyst or the therapist, and there he is understood as an expressing subject. Whatever he does in the group in terms of his work and his play will be compared to a superior authority, that of the psychotherapist who alone will have the job of interpreting, such that the child himself is split; he cannot win acceptance for any statement about what really matters to him in his relationship or in his group. He will feel like he's talk- ing, but he will not be able to say a single word about what's most essential to him. Indeed, what produces statements in each one of us is not ego as subject, it's something entirely different: multiplicities, masses and mobs, peoples and tribes, collective arrangements; they cross through us, they are within us, and they seem unfamiliar because they are part of our unconscious. The challenge for a real psychoanalysis, an anti-psychoanalytical analysis, is to discover these collective arrangements of expression, these collective networks, these peoples who are in us and who make us speak, and who are the source of our statements. This is the sense in which we set a whole field of experimentation, of personal or group experimentation, against the interpretive activities of psychoanalysis.

My fourth proposition, to be quick, is that psychoanalysis implies a fairly peculiar power structure. The recent book by Castel, *Le Psychanalysme*, demonstrates this point very well. The power structure occurs in the contract, a formidable liberal bourgeois institution. It leads to "transference" and culminates in the analyst's silence. And the analyst's silence is the greatest and the worst of interpretations. Psychoanalysis uses a small number of collective statements, which are those of capitalism itself regarding castration, loss, and family, and it tries to get this small number of collective statements specific to capitalism to enter into the individual statements of the patients themselves. We claim that one should do just the opposite, that is, start with the real individual statements, give people conditions, including the material conditions, for the production of their individual statements, in order to discover the real collective arrangements that produce them.

My last proposition is that, for our part, we prefer not to participate in any effort consistent with a Freudo-Marxist perspective. And this for two reasons. The first is that, in the end, a Freudo-Marxist effort proceeds in general from a return to origins, or more specifically to the sacred texts: the sacred texts of Freud, the sacred texts of Marx. Our point of departure must be completely different: we refer not to sacred texts that must be, to a greater or lesser extent, interpreted, but to the situation as is, the situation of the bureaucratic apparatus in psychoanalysis, which is an effort to subvert these apparatuses. Marxism and Psychoanalysis, in two different ways, speak in the name of a kind of memory, of a culture of memory, and also speak in two different ways in the name of the requirements of a development. We believe on the contrary that one must speak in the name of a positive force of forgetting, in the name of what is for each individual his own underdevelopment, what David Cooper aptly calls our inner third world. Secondly, what separates us from any Freudo-Marxist effort is that such projects seek primarily to reconcile two economies: political economy and libidinal or desiring economy. In Reich, too, we find the observance of this duality of this effort at reconciliation.

Our point of view is on the contrary that there is but one economy and that the problem of a real anti-psychoanalytical analysis is to show how unconscious desire invests the forms of this economy. It is economy itself that is political economy and desiring economy.

Discussion

A participant asks a question about memory in Freudo-Marxism and the positive force of forgetting.

In spite of my incitation not to go back to the texts, I think of two remarkable texts by Nietzsche that make a distinction between forgetting as a force of inertia and forgetting as an active force. Forgetting as an active force is the power to finish with something to one's satisfaction. In this case, it is opposed to a meditation on the past that binds us, on that which binds us to the past, even to develop it, even to take it further. If one therefore distinguishes two forms of forgetting, of which one is a sort of reactive inertia and the other a force of positive forgetting, it is obvious that the revolutionary forgetting, the forgetting that I was thinking of is the second forgetting: only it consititutes a real activity or one that can be part of real political activities. In much the same way, a revolutionary breaks free by forgetting and remains unmoved by the reproach his critics constantly make: "It has existed, therefore it will always exist."

Revolutionary forgetting can be tied to another common theme, that of an active escape that is itself opposed to a passive escape of an entirely different kind. When, for example, Jackson, in his prison, says, "yes, I can very well escape, but during my escape, I'm looking for a weapon," this is active revolutionary escape as opposed to other escapes that are capitalist or personal, etc.

A participant asks for a clarification of the notion of forgetting with respect to the relationship between Freudianism and Marxism.

In Marxism, a certain culture of memory appeared right at the beginning; even revolutionary activity was supposed to proceed to this capitalization of the memory of social formations. It is, if one prefers, Marx's Hegelian aspect, included in *Das Kapital*. In psychoanalysis, the culture of memory is even more apparent. Moreover, Marxism, like psychoanalysis, is shot through with a certain ideology of development: psychic development from a psychoanalytic point of view of psychoanalysis, social development or even the development of production from a Marxist point of view. Before, for example, in certain forms of the worker's struggle in the 19th century that Marxism crushed right from the start (I'm not thinking only of the Utopians), the call to struggle was, on the contrary, made on the basis of the need to forget, of an active force of forgetting: no culture of remembering, no culture of the past, but a call to forgetting as the condition of experimentation. Today, in certain American groups, no one considers a return to Freud or Marx; here again is a sort of culture of forgetting as the condition of any new experimentation. The use of forgetting as an active force, in order to go back to zero, in order to get away from the academic heavy-handedness that has left so dark a stamp on Freudo-Marxism, is something very important in practical terms. Whereas bourgeois culture has always spoken from within its development and in the name of the development that it asks us to pursue and perpetuate, today's counter-culture reclaims the idea that, if we have something to say, it's not according to our development, whatever that may be, but according to our underdevelopment. Revolution has nothing to do with an attempt to inscribe oneself in a movement of development and in the capitalization of memory, but in the preservation of the force of forgetting and the force of underdevelopment as properly revolutionary forces.

A participant (G. Jervis) points out a difference of content between the Five Propositions *and* Anti-Œdipus, *for example, the disappearance of the notion of "schizo-analysis" in favor of that of an "anti-psychoanalytical analysis" and he notes a distinct evolution: there is no longer an effort to critique Œdipus, but rather psychoanalysis. What is the reason for this evolution?*

What Jervis says is perfectly true. Neither Guattari nor myself are very attached to the pursuit or even the coherence of what we write. We would hope for the contrary, we would hope that the follow-up to *Anti-Œdipus* breaks with what preceded it, with the first volume, and then, if there are things that don't work in the first volume, it doesn't matter. I mean that we are not among those authors who think of what they write as a whole that must be coherent; if we change, fine, so there's no point in talking to us about the past. But Jervis says two things that are important: at present we do not attack Œdipus so much as the institution, the psychoanalytical machine in its entirety. It goes without saying that the psychoanalytical machine comprises dimensions beyond Œdipus, and consequently we have reasons to believe that this is no longer the essential problem. Jervis adds that the reason is the direction of our present work is more political, and that this morning we have also renounced the use of the term 'schizo-analysis.' I would like to make several remarks on this point, in the most modest fashion possible. When a term is introduced and has the least bit success, as has been the case for "desiring-machine" or "schizo-analysis," either one circulates it, which is already rather pernicious, a sort of co-optation, or one renounces it and seeks other terms to upset the order. There are words that Félix and I now feel it urgent not to use: 'schizo-analysis,' 'desiring-machine'—it's awful, if we use them, we're caught in the trap. We don't know very well what they mean, we no longer believe in the words; when we use a word, we want to say, if this word doesn't agree with you, find another, there's always a way. Words are totally interchangeable. As for the content of what we do, it's true that the first volume of *Anti-Œdipus* was devoted to establishing certain kinds of dualities. There was, for example, a duality between paranoia and schizophrenia, and we felt we had discovered a duality of systems: a paranoiac system and a schizophrenic system. Or the duality we tried to establish between the molar and the molecular. We had to go that route. I'm not saying that we've gone beyond all that, but it no longer interests us. At present, what we would like to try to show is how one is grounded in the other, that the one is tied to the other. In other words, how the little outbreaks of schizophrenia ultimately organize themselves at the heart of vast paranoiac orders. There are sometimes surprising examples in politics. I'll take the very recent example of what's happening in America: there is the Vietnam War, which is immense, and represents the setting in motion of a gigantic paranoiac machine, the famous military industrial complex, an entire system of signs, political programs, and economic programs. Everyone says, "bravo," except a small number, every country says, "very well," and no one is outraged. No one is outraged, except for a small number of individuals denounced as leftists. Then, all of sudden there's a minor incident, no big deal, a matter of spying, theft, of police and psychiatry, between one American political party and another. Suddenly, there is an outbreak, an escape, a leak. And all the good people who accept the war in Vietnam, who accept this large paranoiac machine, are beginning to say "The president of the United States is no longer following the rules of the game." A little schizophrenic outbreak has grafted itself onto the large psychoanalytical system, the newspapers are losing their minds or seem to be losing them. Why not the stock quotes from the market? What really matters to us are the escape routes in the systems, the conditions under which these paths form or incite revolutionary actions, or remain anecdotal. Revolutionary probabilities do not consist in the contradictions of the capitalist system, but rather in efforts at escape—always unexpected, always renewed—that undermine it. We have been criticized for using the word schizo-analysis, for confusing the schizophrenic and the revolutionary. And yet we were extremely careful to distinguish them.

A system like capitalism escapes in every direction; it escapes, and then capitalism fills in the gaps, it ties knots, it establishes links to prevent the escapes from being too numerous. A scandal here, an escape of capital there, etc. And there are also escapes of another sort: there are communities, those on the margin, the delinquents, the addicts, the escapes of drug addicts, escapes of all kinds, there are schizophrenic escapes, there are people who escape in a very different way. Our problem (we are not completely stupid, we are not saying that this would be sufficient for a revolution) is as follows: given a system that escapes in every direction and that, at the same time, continually prevents, represses, or blocks escape-routes by every available means, what can we do so that these escapes may no longer be individual attempts or small communities, but may instead truly constitute a revolutionary machine? And for what reason, until now, have revolutions gone so badly? There is no revolution without a central, centralizing war-machine. You can't brawl, and you don't fight with your fists: there must be a war-machine that organizes and unites. But until now, there hasn't existed in the revolutionary field a machine that didn't reproduce something else: a state apparatus, the very institution of repression. Hence the problem of revolution: how can a war-machine account for all the escapes that happen in the present system without crushing them, dismantling them, and without reproducing a state apparatus? So when Jervis says that our discussion is getting more and more political, I think he's right, because as much as we insisted, in the first part of our work, on large dualities, today we're looking for the new mode of unification in which, for example, the schizophrenic discourse, the intoxicated discourse, the perverted discourse, the homosexual discourse, all the marginal discourses can subsist, so that all these escapes and discourses can graft themselves onto a war-machine that won't reproduce a State or Party Apparatus. For that very reason we no longer want to talk about schizoanalysis, because that would amount to protecting a particular type of escape, schizophrenic escape. What interests us is a sort of link that leads us back to the direct political problem, and the direct political problem for us is more or less this: until now, revolutionary parties have constituted themselves as syntheses of interests rather than functioning as analyzers of mass and individual desires. Or else, what amounts to the same: revolutionary parties have constituted themselves as embryonic State apparatuses, instead of forming war-machines irreducible to such apparatuses.

Faces and Surfaces

Stefan Czerkinsky: Me, a painter? I'm no painter. And we're not going to do a preface either. We'll do some surfaces, not a presentation. Slip-slide. You do the drawings. I'll do the bits of writing. No trading places, no exchanging anything, it's no exchange, not at all...

Gilles Deleuze: Oh awright. I've got the drawings... here.[2] The worse they are, the better they work. Look, they're surface-monsters. Like brownish-violet, and every surface color. How does violet work?

Stefan Czerkinsky: How does therrory work? How does a surface-monster work?

Gilles Deleuze: Therrory is violet. Therrory is painting-desire-writing using many other things, too, on the borders, in the corners, at the centers, and elsewhere. It's that oscillating movement: the Flow Flux Klan, a.k.a. "the great thought-racket" and its organ-members "the concept squatters." This is its program:

First, the support-free construction of therrotherapy in conjunction with the active destruction of the illnesses of our day: psychopomp, hypochondiaches, schizophaguses, gonorphrenia, neurotosis, neurotyphus, mortems, sexosis, phantasmologists, scatatonics, etc. And the worst of all: glorifying depression.

Second, the production of campaigns and slogans like:

"More of the unconscious, produce more, still more, and more after that."

"Nothing to interpret."

"It's all good, but really."

"Make every French citizen carry a visa and a work permit, accompanied by regular police shakedowns."

"Of two movements, the more deterritorialized prevails over the less deterritorialized."

"Of fifty movements, the most deterritorialized wins."

What we call the most deterritorialized movement is the delirious vector. It's violet. The unconscious is violet, or it will be.

Stefan Czerkinsky: What precautions should be taken when producing a concept?

Gilles Deleuze: You put your blinker on, and check in your rearview mirror to make sure another concept isn't coming up behind you; once you've taken these precautions, you produce the concept.[3] What are the precautions to be taken when moving from one theoretical field to another?

Stefan Czerkinsky: Nothing is simpler. You arm yourself with a concept carrying case in leatherette. You take a canvas that you yourself will boldly prime, in other words, a canvas without primer. You sandwich it between the two pieces of a wooden frame, which has been sawed in such a way that it attaches to both sides of the canvas. So the frame is a raised border on either side, forming two basins. First you paint on one side, according to the directions (vectors) you've chosen, for example, beginning from the corners, like the cardinal points: e.g., you paint North-East, North-South, South-East, North-West, etc. Paint with red or blue, or with red and blue, either mixed off the canvas, or mixed on the canvas, especially if you want to produce different shades of brown or violet. Next you go around the back to see what happened on the other side, since the color has diffused through the unprimed (non-occluded) canvas. You may or may not choose to keep an eye on the diffusion with a mirror placed behind the canvas. Now you paint the other side, using a different brush, with strokes in other directions and corners. You can also rotate the canvas, or change its situation: suspend it, put it on the wall, on the floor, etc.

Incessant diffusion from one side to the other. Each side modifies the other: red, blue, blue-red / red-blue, etc., giving rise to different shades of violet (and negative brown). Each side penetrates the other: violet is PENETRAY country, where you become the color-diffuser, the side-switcher, the time-passer: the painter or the painting, the nomad.

This is how you get deterritorialized movements of color, and many other things beside, and thus you produce intensities. You have traveled around something that has no thickness.

I forgot to mention: get a canvas that is much larger than the frame, so you have a border, a margin that is at least two feet wide. This margin has several roles to play:

First, a zone of overproduction; second, an instance of anti-production; third, the body-canvas distance; fourth, reciprocal smudges and blots: who is painting and who is being painted? (The margin will become smudged and blotted in diverse ways, according to the kind of work being done, the colors employed, the positions of the canvas, and the vectors you've chosen. Your body will become smudged and blotted, too. In a way, it is also a margin.); fifth, tramplings and walks; it's a threshold for the painter, the canvas, and the visitor alike.

It sometimes happens that an infinitesimal part of the canvas will remain unpainted, forgotten; and sometimes you forget to forget. There's a hole. Think of the Vetuda of the Italian Renaissance, that's not it. Think of the Navajo women who never completely finish a tapestry: they leave a hole, they say, because they sink all their heart into the work, and they don't want their heart to be entangled in perfection. That's still not it. Or we say that the hole circulating on the canvas is a reality that opens on another reality, but that's just metaphysics and possible-worlds.

Gilles Deleuze: What it is is an interior border that echoes the exterior borders. Together they make up the difference of intensity between which everything happens and communicates: neglecting the margin and forgetting the hole; and thus they echo one another. Forgetting to paint, neglecting to paint, the canvas between inside-outside, a canvas-drum, heard as a sign of painting, an a-signifying sign. The hole-border is physical reality. It is Reality. Oh, what beautiful things physicists are saying these days, concerning border-phenomena and hole-noumena. We would have to be scholars to understand it. Long live Pauli, long live Fermi. But we can't understand it. So what, that's even better, we'll do the same. The hole-particles and the border-particles are in motion.[4]

Stefan Czerkinsky: We're not finished. After you paint the canvases, you create a simple currency: from objects, verbs, gestures, materials, etc. Then you arbitrarily establish arbitrarily equivalent relationships between the canvases and the stuff you will use as money.

For example, I'll make a few objects or utensils: wood in cotton, like a baby doll; add metal ligatures to make cloth hands; add blue metallic plastic, beveled and split; stuff hair in the splits, cement it with clay: some of them are pretty big, and others really small. I put them all in a suitcase, a metal lunchbox, and take them to some kids playing in a public garden. They always get a kick out of them. The series and different sizes make them laugh. So then I arrange all the little family-money-objects in relation to the violet canvases. They are fetishes or key-holders for the canvas-holders, the canvas-tents, the canvas-icons. Now it makes a large circuit. You have the restricted circuit: frame-canvas-border-hole; and you have the larger circuit: its equivalence with another system of signs, i.e. the little object-utensils. Ideally, you would pay for the canvases with the little objects, and make the little objects *with* the canvases. You would have to steal one or the other or both at once. The question can be asked: Were my utensils and my canvases nothing but money all along? That's what's terrible: the virtuality of money.

Preface to Hocquenghem's
L'Après-Mai des faunes[1]

The Preface. No one escapes it. Not the author, not the publisher, not the preface writer, who is the real victim. There is no need for a preface. This 'gay' book could also have been called: How the existence of homosexuality came to be doubted; or, no one can say "I am homosexual." Signed, Hocquenghem. How did he arrive at this? Was it a personal evolution, traceable in the succession and the many tones of the texts collected here? Was it a collective evolution in connection with a group-undertaking, a becoming of FHAR? It goes without saying that it is not due to a change such as becoming heterosexual, that Hocquenghem has come to doubt the validity of certain notions and declarations. It is only by remaining homosexual *forever*, remaining and being homosexual more and more, being a better and better homosexual, that one can say "well, no one is really homosexual." Which is a thousand times better than the hackneyed, insipid idea that everyone is homosexual or will be: we're all unconscious latent queers. Hocquenghem does not use the term *evolution*, nor even *revolution*, but *volutions*. Imagine an extremely mobile spiral: Hocquenghem is there on several levels simultaneously, on several turns at once: sometimes with a motorcycle, sometimes high out of his mind, sometimes sodomized or sodomizing, and sometimes in drag. On one level, he can say: yes, I'm a homosexual; on another level: no, that's not it; and on another level, it is something else altogether. This current book does not repeat his former work, *Homosexual Desire*;[2] it has a completely different organization and mobilization. It's a total transformation.

First volution: in opposition to psychoanalysis, against psychoanalytic reductions and interpretations. In principle, Hocquenghem is not opposed to homosexuality as a relationship with father, mother, and Oedipus; he even writes a letter to mother. But it doesn't work. Psychoanalysis has never been able to tolerate desire. It has to reduce desire, make it say something else. Some of the more ridiculous pages Freud ever wrote are those on "fellatio": such a bizarre and "shocking" desire can have no worth of its own; it must be traceable to a cow udder, and from there to the mother's breast. Freud thinks we would get more pleasure sucking on a cow udder. Interpret, regress, push toward regression. It just makes Hocquenghem laugh. Who knows, maybe there is such a thing as Oedipal homosexuality, a mommy-homosexuality, guilt, paranoia, whatever. But precisely, the whole interpretation sinks like a lead balloon, weighed down by what it hides, and by what the family counselor and psychoanalyst would keep out of sight: it falls off the spiral, it fails the test of lightness and mobility. Hocquenghem instead posits the specificity and the irreducibility of a homosexual desire, a flow without origin or goal, a matter of experimentation and not interpretation. It is not the past but the present that determines whether one is homosexual, once we admit that childhood was already a presence that did not refer to a past. Because desire never represents anything, and it doesn't refer back to something waiting in the wings of the familial or personal theatre. Desire makes connections, it assembles, it machines. E.g. Hocquenghem's beautiful text on the motorcycle: the motorcycle is another sex. Perhaps the homosexual does not stay with the *same* sex, but discovers innumerable sexes. But first Hocqenghem attempts to define this irreducible, specific homosexual desire—not through a regressive interiority, but through an Outside, a relationship with the Outside, whose characteristics are present: the particular movement of cruising, the mode of encounter, the "anular" structure, the mobility and exchangeability of roles, and a particular betrayal (plotting against one's own class, as Klossowski says?: "They told us we were men, they treat us like women; yes, toward our enemies, we are treacherous, underhanded, and show bad faith: yes, we can quit on you in any social situation, at any moment, we are unreliable and proud of it!")

Second volution: Homosexuality does not produce desire without at the same time formulating utterances. Because producing desire and formulating new utterances are the same thing. Of course, Hocquenghem does not sound like Gide, or Proust, even less like Peyrefitte: but style is politics—so are generational differences, and the different ways of saying "I" (cf. the world of difference between Burroughs the father and Burroughs the son, when they say "I" and talk about drugs). A new style, a new politics. This is the importance of Tony Duvert today: a new tone. Homosexuality today produces its utterances from within a new style, and these utterances do not and must not revolve around homosexuality itself. Were it simply a question of saying "every man is a queer," it would be totally devoid of interest. Such a lame proposition amuses only fools. But the marginal position of homosexuality makes it possible, and necessary, for it to have something to say about *what is not* homosexuality: "the entire gamut of human sexual problems first appeared when the homosexual movements began." For Hocquenghem, the utterances of homosexuality are of two sorts. First, about sexuality in general: far from being phallocentric, the homosexual denounces the same phenomenon in the submission of women and in the repression of homo-sexuality. This phenomenon is constitutive of phallocentrism, which operates indirectly as the heterosexual model of our society. Phallocentrism forces the sexuality of boys on girls, to whom it assigns the role of playing seductress and seduced. From that point on, whether there exists a mysterious complicity among girls who prefer girls, or boys who prefer boys, or boys who prefer motorcycles to girls, or girls who, etc., the important thing is *not* to introduce any pseudo-signifier or symbolic relation into these plots and complicities ("a movement like FHAR appears to have intimate ties with ecological movements... *even if this is inexpressible in the logic of politics*"). The second sort of utterance is complimentary to the first; it deals with the social field in general and the presence of sexuality in the social field as a whole: homosexuality enacts a micro-politics of desire by escaping the heterosexual model, by escaping both the localization of this model in a type of relationship and its diffusion in every sector of society. Homosexuality is thus able to reveal or detect the whole array of power relations to which society submits sexuality (including the case of the more or less latent homosexuality that is diffused throughout virile military or fascist groups). Precisely, homosexuality is liberational not by disrupting all power relations, but when as a marginal phenomenon, it has no *social utility*: "society fails from the outset to inscribe its power relations in homosexuality, such that the roles man-woman, active-passive, master-slave, are unstable and reversible at every moment in homosexuality."

Third volution: we thought Hocquenghem was setting up on the margin, digging himself in. But what is this margin? And the specificity of homosexual desire, the counter-utterances of homosexuality? What are they? Another Hocquenghem, on a different level of the spiral, denounces homosexuality as a word. Homosexuality as *nominalism*. And in fact there is no power in words, only words in the service of power: language is not information or communication, but prescription, order, and command. You will be on the margin. It's the center that makes the margin. "The abstract division of desire allows for the regimentation of those who escape it, bringing within the law that which escapes the Law. The category in question, and the word itself, are relatively recent inventions. It is the growing imperialism of a society wanting to assign a social status to everything unclassifiable that created this particularization of inequality... Dividing the better to conquer, the pseudo-scientific thought of psychiatry has transformed barbarous intolerance into intolerance that is civilized." But here is where something strange happens: the less homosexuality is a state of affairs, and the more homosexuality is a mere word, the more it must be taken literally and its position be taken as specific, its utterances as irreducible, acting as if... Out of defiance. Almost from a sense of duty. A necessary dialectic moment. Passage and progress. We will act like queens because you want it. We will exceed your traps. We will take you at your word: "It is by making shame all the more shameful that we progress. We claim femininity for ourselves, that femininity which women reject, *even as we declare these roles to be meaningless...* We cannot escape the concrete form of this struggle, which is homosexuality." Still another mask, still another betrayal. A Hegelian Hocquenghem is revealed: the necessary moment that must be passed through; a Marxist Hocquenghem, too: the queer as a proletariat of Eros ("it is precisely because he lives by accepting the most particular situation that what he thinks has universal value"). The reader is shocked. Is this a Hommage to dialectics, to the Ecole Normale Supérieure? Is this Homo-Hegelian-Marxism? But Hocqenghem is already elsewhere, on another place in the spiral, saying what was in his head or his heart, and what cannot be separated from a kind of evolution. Who among us has already killed Marx or Hegel within himself, and the infamous dialectic?

Fourth volution, and the last dance for the time being, the last betrayal: we must follow the succession of Hocquenghem's texts, his position with respect to FHAR and, within FHAR as a specific group, the relation to MLF—the idea that the dispersal of groups is never tragic. Far from closing itself in on "the same," homosexuality is going to open itself up to all sorts of possible new relations, micrological or micropsychic, essentially reversible, transversal relations, with as many sexes as there are assemblages, not even excluding new relations between men and women: the mobility of particular S&M relations, the potency of cross-dressing, Fourier's thirty-six thousand forms of love, or the *n*-sexes (neither one nor two sexes). It is no longer about being a man or woman, but inventing sexes, such that a homosexual man can find in a woman those pleasures which a man would give him and vice versa (to this exclusive homosexuality of the Same, Proust already opposed a more multiple and 'localized' homosexuality which includes all kinds of transsexual communications, such as flowers and bicycles). In a beautiful passage on cross-dressing, Hocquenghem talks about a transmutation from one order to another as though it were an intensive continuum of substances: "There is no intermediary between man and woman, or the universal mediator is one part of a world transferred into another as one moves from one universe to another, parallel to the first, or perpendicular, or diagonal; or rather it's a million displaced gestures, transferred characteristics, events..." Far from closing itself in on the identity of a sex, this homosexuality opens itself up to a loss of identity, to the "system actualizing non-exclusive connections of polyvocal desire." We see how the tone has changed at this precise point on the spiral: the homosexual is no longer demanding to be recognized, no longer takes himself to be a subject deprived of his rights (let us live in peace, after all, everyone's a little gay... homosexuality-demand, homosexuality-recognition, homosexuality of the same, Oedipal form, Arcadie style).[3] The new homosexual is about being in such a way that he can finally say: nobody is homosexual, it doesn't exist. You treat us like homosexuals, OK, but we're already elsewhere. There is no more homosexual subject, but homosexual productions of desire, and homosexual assemblages that produce utterances, proliferating everywhere, e.g. S&M and cross-dressing, in sexual relations as well as in political struggles. There is no more angry, divided Gide-subject, nor even a Proust-subject feeling guilty, even less a pathetic Peyrefitte-Self. We understand better how Hoc-quenghem can be everywhere on the spiral and say all at once: homosexual desire is specific, there are homosexual utterances, but homosexuality is nothing, it's just a word, and yet let's take it literally, let's pass necessarily through it, to make it yield all the otherness it contains—and this otherness is not the unconscious of psychoanalysis, but the progression of a future sexual becoming.

A Planter's Art[1]

The film's long opening shot to the music of Couperin. We see the camera move, stop in this particular decor, that particular spot, before this example of architecture.

We see the director laugh, speak, point to something; the film crew works on a particular arrangement of elements. We fear this is just one more example of that way of introducing, into the film, the film in the making. Luckily, it isn't. The opening is not long at all. The camera's mobility in this film appears to be something new. It is a way of planting. Not burying the camera on its feet, but rapidly planting it, just below the surface of the soil or terrain, and then carrying it elsewhere to plant it over again. An art of rice: the camera is stabbed in the soil, then stabbed again, farther away, in a leap. No taking root, just stabs. In the film itself, the camera, the crew and the director will pop up suddenly right next to the couple making love: this is not a "literary" effect, nor a reflection of the film-making process in the film; rather, the camera is seen because it was planted here, stabbed there, to be immediately picked up and planted elsewhere.

The film, everything which the film shows, follows this procedure without the least artifice. The film and its opening are the same mobile story in two modes. A son kills himself, and the father, as though unhinged, will pass through a series of metamorphoses: a sadistic small-time crook, a disturbing wise man, a nomadic walker, a young man in love. The actor who plays the father, Patrice Dally, displays a deep sobriety, an almost humble manner, which intensifies the violence of the metamorphoses. The pretext is a sort of inquiry into the son's death. The reality is the broken chain of metamorphoses, which operates not by transformation, but by leaps and bounds. One beautiful scene is with Roger Planchon, the wise man, jumping around a young woman, trying to persuade her of something in the Saint-Sulpice's square. With astonishing

289

movements, Planchon repeatedly plants himself before her. Another is with Pierre Julien, the nervous sadist, who pulls the player in every direction, height, depth, length, carving up space as with a knife.

It's like a story planted in Paris, not at all heavy and static, but with light stabs that correspond to each camera position. The story comes from elsewhere: it comes from South America, from the Santiago-Borges-Bioy Ceasres ensemble, bringing with it that power of metamorphosis which one finds in the novels of Asturias, and it emanates from other landscapes: the Savannah, the pampas, a fruit company, a field of corn or rice. The precise point at which the story is inserted or stuck in Paris is a small bookstore, "The Two Americas," the father's business. But there is no application in the story, no symbolism, no literary game, as though an Indian story were being told in Paris. Instead, the story is precisely shared by the two worlds, a city fragment and a pampas fragment, each of which is quite mobile; the one is stuck in the other and carries it away. What appears continuous in the one would be discontinuous in the other, and vice versa. I am thinking of the admirable way in which Santiago filmed the interior of the Meudon Observatory: a metallic and deserted city has been planted in a forest. The tam-tams leap from Couperin's music, the parrots screech in the Odéon hotel, and the Parisian bookseller is truly an Indian.

Cinema has always been closer to architecture than to theatre. A particular relation of architecture and of the camera holds everything together here. The metamorphoses have nothing to do with fantasy: the camera leaps from one point to another, around an architectural whole, just as Planchon leaps around the huge stone fountain. The bookstore's characters leap from one to the other around Valery, the heroine who knows how to strike architectural poses. Standing or bending, leaning or upright, she watches the metamorphoses from Meudon; she is at once the victim and the instigator of the game; she is the center for the bookseller's leaps. Actrice Noëlle Châtelet: what talent and beauty, what strange "gravity" in the detailed love scene. What about the way in which she, too, though differently than the bookseller, maintains her relationship with the other world? What she says in architecture, in her look, and in her position, he says in movements, in music, and in the camera. It is strange that the critics didn't care for this film, even if it were only an experiment in cinema endowed with a new mobility. Santiago's previous film, *Invasion*, was already moving in this direction. (The tiebreaker: why is the bookseller named Spinoza? Maybe because the two Americas, the two worlds, the city and the pampas, are like two attributes of an absolutely shared substance. And this has nothing to do with philosophy, it is the substance of the film itself.)

Notes

Introduction

1. In 1989, Deleuze reviewed and organized his work as a whole, including his books, according to a series of general themes: "I. From Hume to Bergson / II. Classical Studies / III. Nietzschean Studies / IV. Critical and Clinical / V. Esthetics / VI. Cinema Studies / VII. Contemporary Studies / VIII. The Logic of Sense / IX. Anti-Oedipus / X. Difference and Repetition / XI. A Thousand Plateaus"

Desert Islands

1. Jean Giraudoux, *Suzanne et le Pacifique* (Paris: Grasset, 1922); reedited in *Oeuvres romanesques complètes*, vol 1 (Paris: Gallimard Pléiade, 1990).

Jean Hyppolite's *Logic and Existence*

1. cf. *Revue philosophique de la France et de l'étranger*, vol. CXLIV, no. 7–9, juillet-septembre 1954, pp. 457–460. Hyppolite's *Logique et Existence* was published by PUF in 1953. Jean Hyppolite (1907–1968), philosopher and Hegel specialist, was Deleuze's teacher for the "khagne" program at Louis-le-Grand high school. After becoming a professor at the Sorbonne, Hyppolite later supervised, with George Canguilhem, the *Diplôme d'Etudes Supérieures* which Deleuze received for his work on Hume. Deleuze's dissertation would be published by PUF as *Empirisme et subjectivité* in 1953, in the collection "Epiméthé" headed by Hyppolite. On several occasions, when interviewed, Deleuze refers to his admiration as a student for Hyppolite, to whom *Empirisme et subjectivité* is dedeicated. Beyond paying homage, this is the first Deleuzian text that explicitly formulates the hypothesis of an "ontology of pure difference" which will constitute, as we know, one of the key theses in *Différence et répétition*. [Editor's note]

2. Jean Hyppolite, *Genesis and Structure of Hegel's Phenomonology of Spirit* (Evanston: Northwestern University Press, 1974).

3. Jean Hyppolite, *Logic and Existence* (Albany: SUNY Press, 1997).

Bergson, 1859–1941

1. Maurice Merleau-Ponty, ed. *Les Philosophes célèbres*. Editions d'Art Lucien Mazenod, 1956. Pp. 292–299. The following year Deleuze edited, for the Presses Universitaires de France, a collection of selected texts by Bergson, under the title *Mémoire et vie*; some of the reference notes specify this edition. The pagination refers to the current edition of Bergson's individual works published by the PUF in the Quadrige collection.

2. *La Pensée et le mouvant* II.

3. *Matière et mémoire* I, p. 74.

4. *L'Evolution créatrice* III.

5. *PM* II.

6. *PM* VI.

7. *MM*, III.

8. *EC* III.

9. *PM* VI.

10. *PM* VIII.

11. *EC* IV.

12. *EC* II.

13. *MM* III.

14. *PM* VI, p. 196–197.

15. *PM* IX, p. 259–260.

16. *PM* II.

17. *PM* V, *MM* IV.

18. *Essai sur les Données immédiates de la conscience* I.

19. *EC* II.

20. *MM* I.

21. *EC* III.

22. *MM* IV, *PM* VI.

23. *Les Deux sources de la morale et de la religion* III ; *L'Energie spirituelle* I.

24. *EC* II, p. 100.

25. *DI* II.

26. *MM* IV, p. 219.

27. *PM*, VI, p. 201.

28. *MM* I.

29. *MM* III.

30. *ES* V.

31. *MM* III.

32. *MM* IV, p. 269.

33. *MM* II, p. 115 and III, p. 188.

34. *MM* III.

35. *PM* VI, p. 206–207.

36. *PM* VI, p. 208.

37. *EC* IV.

38. *PM* III.

39. *PM* VI.

Bergson's Conception of Difference

1. From *Les Etudes bergsoniennes*, vol. IV, 1956, p. 77–112. All the references are Deleuze's abbreviated citations for Bergson's works in French. In their order of appearance, they are: *M. M. = Matière et Mémoire (1896); P. M. = La Pensée et le Mouvant (1941); E. S. = L'Energie spririruelle (1919); M. R. = Les Deux sources de la morale et de la religion (1932); E. C. = L'Evolution créatrice (1907); D. I. = Essai sur les données immédiates de la conscience (1889); D. S. = Durée et simultanéité (1922).* The page numbers correspond to the editions Deleuze used and are noted in the text. The pagination refers to the current editions of Bergson's work from PUF in the Quadrige collection.

2. *MM*, p. 19, p. 62–63.

3. *PM*, p. 52–53.

4. *PM*, p. 197.

5. *PM*, p. 207.

6. *PM*, 23.

7. *ES*, p. 4.

8. *ES*, first chapter.

9. *MR*, p. 263.

10. *MR*, p. 292.

11. *EC*, p. 217.

12. *PM*, p. 61.

13. *EC*, p. 107.

14. *EC*, p. 107.

15. *EC*, p. 184, 264–265.

16. *MR*, p. 225.

17. *EC*, p. 107.

18. *EC*, p. 316 sq.

19. *EC*, p. 232, 235.

20. *MM*, p. 182.

21. *PM*, p. 61.

22. *PM*, p. 208.

23. *PM*, p. 179.

24. *PM*, p. 199.

25. *MM*, p. 59.

26. *DI*, first chapter.

27. *DI*, p. 90.

28. *MM*, p. 219.

29. *PM*, p. 163, 167.

30. *EC*, p. 267, 270.

31. *PM*, p. 81.

32. *DS*, p. 67.

33. *EC*, chap. 1.

34. *EC*, p. 127.

35. *EC*, p. 86.

36. *EC*, p. 88.

37. *MR*, p. 313.

38. *EC*, p. 53 sq.

39. *PM*, p. 58.

40. *EC*, p. 54.

41. *MR*, p. 316.

42. *MR*, p. 314.

43. *MR*, pp. 313–315.

44. *ES*, p. 13.

45. *ES*, p. 11.

46. I do not believe, however, that Bergson was influenced by Plato on this point. Closer to him was Gabriel Tarde, who characterized his own philosophy as a philosophy of difference and distinguished it from philosophies of opposition. But Bergson's conception of essence and the process of difference is very different from Tarde's.

47. *MR*, p. 111.

48. *EC*, p. 88 sq.

49. *PM*, p. 198.

50. *PM*, p. 207.

51. *MR*, p. 317.

52. *PM*, pp. 259–260.

53. *MM*, p. 247.

54. *MM*, p. 249.

55. *MM*, p. 74.

56. *PM*, p. 210.

57. *ES*, p. 137.

58. *ES*, p. 137.

59. *MM*, pp. 172–173.

60. *PM*, pp. 183–184.

61. *ES*, p. 140.

62. *ES*, p. 140.

63. *EC*, p. 201.

64. *DI*, 3rd chapter.

65. *PM*, p. 214.

66. *PM*, p. 59.

67. *MM*, p. 83 sq.

68. *MM*, p. 115.

69. *MM*, p. 188.

70. *Ibid.*

71. *MM*, p. 272.

72. *PM*, pp. 169–170.

73. *MM*, p. 226.

74. *PM*, p. 208.

75. *PM*, p. 210.

76. *MM*, p. 188.

77. *MM*, p. 190.

78. *MM*, p. 173.

79. *MM*, p. 168.

80. *MM*, p. 180.

81. *ES*, p. 132.

82. *MM*, p. 180.

83. *MM*, p. 135.

84. *MM*, p. 83.

85. *MM*, p. 139.

86. *DI*, p. 180.

87. *MM*, p. 250.

88. *EC*, p. 220.

89. *EC*, p. 231.

90. *EC*, p. 319–326.

91. *MM*, p. 65.

92. *EC*, p. 255.

93. *DI*, p. 137.

Jean-Jacques Rousseau: Precursor of Kafka, Céline, and Ponge

1. Cf. *Arts*, no. 872, 6–12 juin 1962, p. 3 (On the occasion of Rousseau's 250th birthday). Attending the Sorbonne in 1959–1960, Deleuze devoted a year of coursework to Rousseau's political philosophy, of which there exits a typed summary, edited by *le Centre de Documentation de la Sorbonne*. [editor's note]

2. *Essai sur l'origine des langues*, IX, in *Oeuvres complètes*, vol. V (Paris: Gallimard Pléiade, 1995), p. 396.

3. *Les Confessions*, II, in *Oeuvres complètes*, vol. I (Paris: Gallimard Pléiade, 1959), p. 56.

4. *Les Confessions*, VII, ibid., p. 277.

5. T. de Quincey, *Les Derniers jours d'Emmanuel Kant* (Toulouse: Ombres, 1985).

6. *La Nouvelle Héloïse*, troisième partie, lettre XX, in *Oeuvres complètes*, vol. II (Paris: Gallimard Pléiade, 1961) 1558.

7. *La Nouvelle Héloïse*, quatrième partie, lettre XII, ibid., p. 496.

8. *La Nouvelle Héloïse*, quatrième partie, lettre XIV, ibid., p. 509.

9. *La Nouvelle Héloïse*, cinquième partie, lettre III, ibid., p. 571.

The Idea of Genesis in Kant's Esthetics

1. *Revue d'esthétique*, vol. XVI, no. 2, avril-juin (Paris: PUF, 1963), p. 113–136. That same year, Deleuze will publish *Kant's Critical Philosophy* also with PUF.

2. Cf. *Critique du judgment*, "Introduction, § 2, 3, 4, 5. Ed. note: All references to Kant in the article come from *Critique du jugement*, trans. Gibelin (Paris: Vrin, 1960).

3. § 35.

4. On this theory of proportions, cf. § 21.

5. § 14 and 51. In these two passages, Kant makes the following argument: colors and sounds would be genuine esthetic elements only if the imagination were able to reflect the vibrations that compose them; but this is unlikely, since the speed of vibrations produces divisions of time that escape us. However, § 51 does admit such a possibility for certain people.

6. § 40.

7. Ibid.

8. § 22.

9. § 20–22.

10. § 22.

11. § 26.

12. Ibid.

13. Remarque générale.

14. Ibid.

15. § 29.

16. § 30.

17. § 38: "What makes this deduction so easy is that it does not have to justify the objective reality of a concept…"

18. § 30.

19. § 58.

20. Ibid.

21. Ibid.

22. § 10. This paragraph launches the problem of the deduction all over again.

23. § 42.

24. Ibid.

25. § 58.

26. § 39.

27. § 42.

28. Ibid.

29. § 46.

30. § 47.

31. § 49.

32. § Remarque: de la Dialectique.

33. § 49.

34. § 48.

35. § 19.

36. § 50.

37. Introduction, § 3 and 9.

38. § 59.

39. Ibid.

40. § 49 and 57.

How Jarry's Pataphysics Opened the Way for Phenomenology

1. Alfred Jarry, *La Chandelle verte*, "La Passion considérée comme course de côte" in *Oeuvres complètes*, I (Paris: Gallimard Pléiade, 1987), p. 420–422.

2. *The Gay Science*, III, § 125; *Human, All Too Human*, II, 2nd part, § 84.

3. *Gestes et opinions du docteur Faustroll, pataphysicien*, livre II, viii, in *Oeuvres complètes* I (Paris: Gallimard Pléiade, 1972), p. 668.

4. Kostas Axelos, a Greek philosopher, headed the series "Arguments" published by Editions de Minuit, where Deleuze eventually published two books: *Présentation de Sacher Masoch* (1967) and *Spinoza et le problème de l'expression* (1968). Despite friendly ties, Deleuze stopped seeing Axelos after the publication in *Le Monde* (April 28, 1972, p. 9) of a brief article on *Anti-Oedipus* in which Axelos most notably wrote: "My loyal friend, honorable French professor, good husband, excellent father of two charming children, (...) would you like your students and your children in their 'effective life' to follow the example of your own life, or Artaud's life, which so many scribblers claim for themselves?" [Editor's note]

"He Was my Teacher"

1. *Arts*, 28 novembre 1964, pp. 8–9. One month earlier Sartre had refused the Nobel prize.

2. *Qu'est-ce que la littérature?* (Paris: Gallimard "Folio Essais") 162–163.

3. *Qu'est-ce que la littérature?*, ibid., 293.

The Philosophy of Crime Novels

1. *Arts et Loisirs*, no. 18, 26 janvier–1 février, 1966.

2. In 1945, the novelist Marcel Duhamel created "La Série Noire" at Gallimard; it is a series dedicated to the crime novel, which he headed till 1977.

3. Maurice Leblanc, *Arsène Lupin contre Sherlock Holmes*, 1908, reedited by Livre de Poche.

4. In 1952, a democratic senator issued a report on organized crime in America.

5. *M. le Président* (Paris: Flammarion, 1987).

On Gilbert Simondon

1. *Revue philosophique de la France et de l'étranger*, vol. CLVI, no. 1–3, janv-mars 1966, pp. 115–118. This work by G. Simondon (1924–1989) was published in 1964 at PUF, coll. 'Epiméthée.' It's a partial publication of his doctorat d'Etat: *L'individuation à la lumière des notions de forme et d'information*, which he defended in 1958. The second part was not published until 1989, at Aubier, under the title *L'individuation psychique et collective*.

Humans: A Dubious Existence

1. *Le Nouvel Observateur*, 1er juin 1966, pp. 32–34. On Michel Foucault's book, *The Order of Things: An archeology of the Human sciences,* trans. Alan Sheridan-Smith. New York: Random House, 1970.

2. *MC*, p. 321.

3. *MC*, p. 353.

The Method of Dramatization

1. *Bulletin de la Société française de Philosophie*, 61è année, no. 3, juillet-septembre 1967, pp. 89–118. (Reunion of the French Society of Philosophy on January 28, 1967; present are Ferdinand Alquié, Jean Beaufret, Georges Bouligand, Stanislas Breton, Maurice de Gandillac, Jacques Merleau-Ponty, Noël Mouloud, Alexis Philonenko, Lucy Prenant, Pierre-Maxime Schuhl, Michel Souriau, Jean Ullmo, Jean Wahl.) This talk takes up some of the themes from *Difference and Repetition* (Paris: PUF, 1969), Deleuze's dissertation for his *Doctorat d'Etat*, which he was finishing at the time, under the direction of Maurice de Gandillac, and which he would defend early in 1969. See especially chapters 4 and 5.

2. In *Difference and Repetition*, Deleuze refers to the work of R. Ruyer, *Eléments de psycho-biologie* (Paris: PUF, 1946) chap. iv.

3. Cf. *Le Temps retrouvé* in *A la Recherche du temps perdu* (Pléiade, 1989) 451.

4. Jean Wahl (1888–1974), philosopher, poet, known for his studies on American philosophy, Descartes, Plato, and existential philosophies (Kierkegaard, Sartre).

5. P.-M. Schuhl (1902–1984), specialist in ancient philosophy, worked extensively on the thought of Plato.

6. Noël Mouloud (1914–1984), philosopher, developed a structural approach to epistemology.

7. Ferdinand Alquié (1906–1985), philosopher, specialist of Descartes and Kant, and one of Deleuze's professors at the Sorbonne.

8. Maurice de Gandillac (b. 1906), philosopher, specialist in medieval thought, and translator of German philosophers from the eighteenth- and nineteenth-centuries. Deleuze pays him hommage in DRF, "Les plages d'imminance."

9. Michel Souriau, philosopher, has devoted studies to the philosophy of Kant and the question of time.

10. L. Prenant (1891–1978), philosopher, Leibniz specialist.

11. J. Ullmo (1906–1980), philosopher, epistemologist.

12. G. Bouligand (1899–1979), philosopher and mathematician.

13. J. Merleau-Ponty, born in 1916, philosopher and epistemologist, has also worked on cosmology.

14. Jean Beaufret (1907–1982), philosopher, authored numerous studies on Heidegger (whose work Beaufret is largely responsible for introducing into France) and on Greek thought.

15. S. Breton, born in 1912, theologian, philosopher, priest.

16. A. Philonenko, born in 1932, philosopher, Kant and Fichte specialist.

Conclusions on the Will to Power and the Eternal Return

1. *Cahiers de Royaumont no. VI: Nietzsche* (Editions de Minuit, 1967), pp. 275–287.

2. Deleuze organized a colloquium on Nietzsche which took place in the Abbey of Royaument, July 4–8, 1964. This is the only such event that he would ever organize. As is customary, Deleuze had to thank the participants and sum up their positions.

3. Cf. *Zarathoustra*, III, "De la vision de l'énigme" and "Le convalescent."

4. *Ibid.*

5. *Gai Savoir*, V, 346.

6. *Beyond Good and Evil*, 213: "Thinking and taking something seriously, taking on its burden, it's one and the same for them, they have no other experience.."

7. *Zarathoustra*, II, "Des hommes sublimes."

8. Cf. Charles Mugler, *Deux thèmes de la cosmologie grecque: devenir cyclique et pluralité des mondes* (Klincksieck, 1953).

9. *Zarathoustra*, III, "Le convalescent."

Nietzsche's Burst of Laughter

1. Taken from an interview by Guy Dumur, *Le Nouvel Observateur*, April 5, 1967, pp. 40–41.

2. I have reconstituted the question missing from the original text. It is about the edition of Nietzsche's *Oeuvres philosophiques complètes* (Paris: Gallimard, 1967), for which Deleuze and Foucault had written together a general introduction in *Gai Savoir: Fragments posthumes (1881–1882)*, vol V, pp.. i–iv. [editor's note]

Mysticism and Masochism

1. Interview by Madeleine Chapsal, *La Quinzaine littéraire*, 1–15 avril 1967, p. 13. The occasion is the publication of *Présentation de Sacher Masoch*, accompanied by one of Masoch's works, *La Vénus à la fourrure* (Editions de Minuit, 1967).

2. Sigmund Freud, *Oeuvres complètes*, vol. XV (PUF, 1996).

3. *La Mère de Dieu* and *Pêcheuses d'âmes* were newly edited by Champ Vallon in 1991.

On Nietzsche and the Image of Thought

1. Editor's title. "Interview with Gilbert Deleuze" [sic]. Conducted by Jean-Noël Vuarnet, *Les Lettres françaises*, no. 1223, 28 fév–5 mars 1968, pp. 5, 7, 9.

2. See footnote 2 for text no. 16.

3. Ludwig Feuerbach, *L'Essence du christianisme* (Paris: F. Maspero, 1968).

4. Arthur Rimbaud, letter to Paul Demeny, May 5, 1871, *Oeuvres complètes* (Pléiade, 1972) 252.

Gilles Deleuze Talks Philosophy

1. Interview conducted by Jeanette Colombel, *La Quinzaine littéraire*, no. 68, 1–15 mars 1969, pp18–19.

Gueroult's General Method for Spinoza

1. *Revue de métaphysique et de morale*, vol. LXXXIV, no. 4, octobre–décembre 1969, pp. 426–437. The article refers to M. Gueroult's *Spinoza, I, —Dieu, Ethique I* (Paris: Aubier-Montaigne, 1968).

2. *L' Evolution et la structure de la Doctrine de la Science chez Fichte* (Les Belles Lettres) vol. I, p. 174.

3. Cf. *Descartes selon l'ordre des raisons* (Aubier), vol. 1, avant-propos.

4. For examples of such nexuses or intersections in Descartes, cf. *Descartes* vol. 1, p. 237, 319.

5. L. Robinson, *Kommentar zu Spinosas Ethik* (Leipzig: F. Meiner, 1928). Gueroult cites and discusses this commentary several times.

6. For *Fichte*, Gueroult already shows how constructability is extended to transcendental concepts, despite their differences of nature with geometric concepts.

7. The inquiry into this is one of the more profound aspects of Gueroult's method: for example, pp. 178–185 (the organization of proposition 11: why is the existence of God demonstrated by his substantiality and not by the necessary existence of the constitutive attributes?), pp. 300–302 (why do the eternity and the immutability of God and his attributes appear in 19 and 20, in relation to causality and not divine essence?), pp. 361–363 (why isn't the status of will in 32, directly concluded from the status of understanding in 31, but results by a whole other path?). There are many other examples throughout the book.

8. *Malebranche*, 3 vol., (Paris: Aubier-Montaigne, 1955–1959).

9. Cf. *Fichte*, vol. II, p. 3.

10. Appendice no. 2 (pp. 426–428). Cf. also appendice no. 6 (pp. 471–488). A comparison with the *Short Treatise* makes a rigorous appearance in Chapter III.

11. On these two misreadings, see the definitive account in appendix no. 3 (especially the criticism of interpretaions by Brunschvicg and Eduard von Hartmann).

12. Gueroult, *Spinoza* p. 163, 167.

13. Ibid., pp. 149–150, 156–158, and especially appendix no. 17 (pp. 581–582).

14. Ibid., p. 153, 162.

15. Ibid., p. 158. Gueroult provides further proof that a theory of multiplicities is fully elaborated by Spinoza when Gueroult analyzes another type of multiplicity, one that is purely modal, but no less irreducible to number; see appendix no. 9, "explication de la Lettre sur l'Infini."

16. Ibid., p. 234, 447. Gueroult points out that the *Ethics* does not apply the terms *simplex* or *ens simplicissimum* to God.

17. Ibid., p. 202, 210.

18. Ibid., p. 33.

19. On the ambiguity of the notion of figure, see appendix no. 1 (p. 422).

20. Ibid., p. 161.

21. Ibid., p. 141: "Spinoza says: 'you will quickly see where I am headed provided you *simultaneously (simul)* keep in mind the definition of God.' Similarly, it is impossible to know the real nature of the triangle if the angles of which it is composed have not been considered and their properties not demonstrated; although we would not have been able to say anything about the nature of the triangle either, nor the properties which its nature imposes on the angles that compose it, if the true idea of its essence had not been simultaneously given to us, moreover, independently of them." And p. 164: "The attributes have a character such that they can be related to one same substance, as soon as there exists a substance so perfect that it demands that they be related to it as the unique substance. But insofar as the existence of such a substance has not been demonstrated by means of the idea of God, we are not obliged to relate them to it and the construction cannot be completed." Also, pp. 226–227: "The unicity proper to the infinitely infinite nature of God is the principle of unity in him of all the substances that compose him. However, the unsuspecting reader inclines toward the opposite reading, that Spinoza must prove the unicity of God by his unity... With unfailing consistency, Spinoza takes the opposite path: he proves the unity of substances not by virtue of their nature, but by virtue of the necessary unicity of divine substance... Whence we find confirmed once again that the generating principle of the unity of substances in divine substance is not as has been thought: it is not the concept of substance as deduced in the first eight *Propositions* that would lead to pluralism, but the notion of God."

22. Ibid., p. 204, pp. 191–193.

23. Ibid., p. 206.

24. Ibid., p. 238, 447.

25. Ibid., p. 239.

26. Ibid., pp. 379–380.

27. Ibid., p. 237: "*Infinitely different as to their essence*, they are thus *identical as to their cause*, an identical *thing* meaning identical cause," and p. 260.

28. Cf. p. 290 (and p. 285, where Gueroult clarifies: "The incommensurability of God with his understanding means only that God as cause is absolutely other than his understanding as effect, and precisely, it follows that the idea as idea must be absolutely other than its object. Thus, *incommensurability in this case does not at all mean the radical incompatibility of the conditions of knowledge with the thing to be known, but only the separation and the opposition of the subject and the object, of what knows from what is known*, of the thing from its idea, a separation and an opposition which, far from impeding knowledge, on the contrary make it possible...").

29. Ibid., p. 281: "Thus, paradoxically, the attribution to God of an understanding and a will which are incommensurable with our own, in fact conceals an inveterate anthropomorphism, all the more harmful that it presents itself as its supreme negation."

30. Ibid., p. 12 (and pp. 9–11, the confrontation with Descartes, Malebranche and Leibniz, who still preserve a perspective of eminence, analogy, or even symbolism in their conception of the understanding and power of God).

31. Ibid., see p. 267.

32. Ibid., see the two passages pp. 347–348, 381–386.

The Fissure of Anaxagoras and the Local Fires of Heraclitus

1. *Critique*, no. 275, avril 1970, pp. 344–351. This article is about three works by Kostas Axelos: *Vers la Pensée planétaire* (Editions de Minuit, 1964); *Arguments d'une recherche* (Editions de Minuit, 1969); *Le Jeu du monde* (Editions de Minuit, 1969), abridged respectively VPP, AR, JM. On the personal relations between Deleuze and Axelos, see note 4 in "How Jarry's Pataphysics opened the Way for Phenomenology.".

2. VPP, p. 46.

3. AR, p. 172.

4. VPP, pp. 100–102.

5. JM, 266.

6. JM, 254.

7. JM, p. 273.

8. VPP, p. 295. Herbert Marcuse, strangely enough, supports his critique of functional or unidimensional language by invoking a traditional conception of the judgment of existence and attribution (*L' Homme unidimensionel*, Ed de Minuit, p. 119 sq.). The use Axelos makes of Marcuse's notions 'unidimensional' and 'multidimensional' will become clear momentarily.

9. JM, p. 412.

10. VPP, p. 312.

11. AR, p. 160 sq.

12. Cf. André Glucksmann, *Le Discours de la guerre* (L'Herne), pp. 235–240.

13. On the question "Is there a universal conflagration according to Heraclitus?", see Axelos's commentary in *Héraclite et la philosophie* (Ed. de Minuit, 1962) pp. 104–105: "Universal conflagration, understod as total annihilation, provisional or definitive, is not a Heraclitean vision. Because the world is not created by fire, it cannot be reabsorbed by it… Fire cannot overcome and annihilate the other elements because justice resides in discord and harmony in strife. Would Heraclitus, after insulting Homer for wanting discord to cease, which would be the destruction of the Universe, himself commit the supreme contradiction of destroying the Universe either momentarily or forever? If the world is the fire in all things, how would it be possible for the world to be consumed by fire?

14. AR, pp. 20–22.

15. Cf. Axelos's preface to György Lukàcs, *Histoire et conscience de classe*.

16. Beside these two texts on Heraclitus and Anaxagoras in AR, see VPP, *La Pensée fragmentaire de la totalité chez Pascal*, and *Rimbaud et la poésie du monde planétaire*.

17. Cf. Jacques Ehrmann, "L'homme en jeu," *Critique*, no 266. Ehrmann's five theses at the end of his article correspond to Axelos's conception: 1) The game has no subject; 2) the game is communication; 3) the game is a space-time spiral; 4) the game is finite and unlimited, since it traces its own limits; 5) the game implies and explains what is beyond the game.

18. Eugen Fink, *Le Jeu comme symbole du monde*, Ed. de Minuit.

Hume

1. In François Châtelet, ed., *Histoire de la philosophie, t. IV: Les Lumières* (Paris: Hachette, 1972), pp. 65–78.

2. D. Hume, *Traité de la nature humaine*, trad. Leroy (Paris: Aubier, 1973), p. 552; *A Treatise of Human Nature*, II, Part 3, Sec.9. Either Deleuze or Hume's French translator mistakenly has "percussion instrument" for the original "string instrument" [Elie During's note].

3. Hume, *Treatise of Human Nature*, II, Part 1, Sec. 10.

4. Hume, *Treatise of Human Nature*, III, Part 2, Sec. 3 (footnote).

How do We Recognize Structuralism?

1. In François Châtelet, ed., *Histoire de la philosophie*, vol. VIII: *Le XXe Siècle* (Paris: Hachette, 1972), pp. 299–335.

2. Jacques Lacan, *Écrits* (Paris: Seuil, 1966), pp. 386–389 [in "Réponse au commentaire de Jean Hyppolite sur la 'Verneinung' de Freud"].

3. Lacan no doubt has gone the furthest in the original *analysis* of the distinction between imaginary and symbolic. But this distinction itself, in its diverse forms, is found in all the structuralists.

4. See Claude Lévi-Strauss, "Réponses à quelques questions," *Esprit*-33.11 (1963): pp. 636–637.

5. Trans: On the concept of a pure, unextended *spatium*, see Deleuze, *Différence et répétition* (Paris: PUF, 1968), pp. 296–297, *Difference and Repetition* (New York: Columbia University Press, 1994), pp. 229–231.

6. Louis Althusser, in *Lire le Capital*, 2 vol., (Paris: Maspero, 1965), 2: p. 157 [*Reading Capital*, trans. Ben Brewster (New York: Versom 1979), p. 180].

7. Michel Foucault, *Les Mots et les Choses* (Paris: Gallimard, 1966), pp. 329–333 [*The Order of Things* (No translator attributed) (New York: Vintage, 1970), pp. 318–322].

8. Jacques Lacan, *Écrits* p. 30 ["Seminar on 'The Purloined Letter'," trans. Jeffrey Mehlman, *Yale French Studies* 48 (1972), p. 60].

9. Claude Lévi-Strauss, "Réponses à quelques questions." *Esprit* 33.11 (1963), p. 637.

10. Trans: Althusser, *Pour Marx* (Paris: Maspero, 1965), pp. 87–128; *For Marx*, trans. Ben Brewster (New York: Pantheon, 1969), pp. 89–127.

11. Trans: See Deleuze, *Logique du sens* (Paris: Minuit, 1969), pp. 88–89, *Logic of Sense* (New York: Columbia University Press, 1990), p. 71.

12. Trans: Althusser, *Pour Marx* (Paris: Maspero, 1965), pp. 131–152; *For Marx*, trans. Ben Brewster (New York: Pantheon, 1969), pp. 131–151, "The 'Piccolo Teatro': Bertolazzi and Brecht."

13. Trans: *The coup de dés* metaphor is associated in French literature with Mallarmé's poem, "Un coup de dés jamais n'abolira le hasard...", *Oeuvres complètes*, Eds. Henri Mondor and G. Jean-Aubry (Paris: Gallimard, Pléiade, 1945), pp. 455–477, and Deleuze cites Nietzsche's *Zarathustra* in *Différence et répétition*, pp. 361–364 [*Difference and Repetition*, pp. 282–284]. See also *Différence et répétition*, pp. 255–260, 364 [*Difference and Repetition*, pp. 197–202]; *Nietzsche et la philosophie* (Paris: PUF 1962), pp. 29–31 [*Nietzsche and Philosophy*, trans. Hugh Tomlinson (New York: Columbia University Press, 1983), pp. 25–27]; *Logique du sens*, pp. 74–82 [*Logic of Sense*, pp.

58–65]; *Foucault* (Paris: Minuit, 1986), pp. 124–125 [*Foucault*, trans. Seán Hand (Minneapolis: University of Minnesota Press, 1988), p. 17].

14. Trans: Deleuze draws this example from the work of Raymond Roussel. See *Différence et répétition*, p. 159 [*Difference and Repetition*], p. 121.

15. Trans: On the three types of determination, see *Différence et répétition* pp. 221–224 [*Difference and Repetition*, pp. 170–173].

16. Trans: See *Différence et répétition*, p. 237 [*Difference and Repetition*, p. 183] for a definition of "structure" as multiplicity and the criteria following which an Idea emerges.

17. Claude Lévi-Strauss, *Anthropologie structurale* (Paris: Plon, 1958), vol. 1, pp. 235–242 [1963, *Structural Anthropology* I, Trans. Claire Jacobson and Brooke Grundfest Schoepf (New York: Basic Books), pp. 213–218].

18. Trans: It is clear from this and later arguments (cf. the fourth criterion below) that Deleuze establishes one correspondence represented by the "differential relations-species-variables" triad, and another represented by the "singularities-organic parts-function" triad. Hence, our translation of "les uns ... les autres" as "former" and "latter," rather than as "some species ... others"; this translation, i.e. as a random variation *between* species would miss the "double aspect," only one side of which bears on species as such, the other side expressing itself as the distribution of parts *within* a species. On the distinction species/parts, see *Différence et répétition*, pp. 318–327 [*Difference and Repetition*, pp. 247–254] (in fact, most of chapter 5 deals with this "organization" that happens at the moment of "actualization").

19. ClaudeLévi-Strauss, *Anthropologie structurale* 1, pp. 343–344 [*Structural Anthropology* 1, pp. 310–312].

20. Serge Leclaire, "Compter avec la psychanalyse," *Cahiers pour l'analyse* 8 (1967), pp. 97–105.

21. Louis Althusser, *Lire le Capital* (Paris: Maspero, 1965), pp. 152–157 [*Reading Capital*, trans. Ben Brewster (New York: Verso, 1979), pp. 177–180]. Cf. also Etienne Balibar in Althusser *Lire le Capital*, pp. 205–211 [*Reading Capital*, pp. 211–216]. Trans: See Deleuze's reformulation, *Différence et répétition,* pp. 240–241 [*Difference and Repetition*, pp. 186–187].

22. Roman Jakobson, *Essais de linguistique générale*, 1 (Paris: Minuit, 1963), ch. VI [pp. 103–149] [*Fundamentals of Language* (The Hague: Mouton, 1956), pp. 3–51].

23. Trans: This expression is drawn from Proust's *Le Temps retrouvé*, in *A la Recherche du temps perdu* (Paris: Gallimard, Pléiade, 1954), 3, p. 873; see *Marcel Proust et les signes* (Paris: PUF, 1964, 1970, 1971, 1976), pp. 71–73, *Proust and Signs*, trans. Richard Howard (New York: G. Braziller, 1972), pp. 56–59. On the concept of virtuality, see *Différence et répétition*, pp. 269–276 [*Difference and Repetition*, pp. 208–214].

24. Louis Althusser, *Lire le Capital* 1, p. 82, 2, p. 44 [*Reading Capital* 64, pp. 97–98].

25. Trans: On the distinction between differentiation [*différencier*] and differential [*différentier*], see *Différence et répétition,* pp. 270–271 [*Difference and Repetition*, pp. 209–211].

26. The book by Jules Vuillemin, *Philosophie de l'algèbre* (Paris: PUF, 1960, 1962), proposes a determination of structures in mathematics. He insists on the importance in this regard of a theory of problems (following the mathematician Abel), and of principles of determination (reciprocal, complete and progressive determination according to Galois). He shows how structures, in this sense, provide the only means of realizing the ambitions of a true genetic method.

27. Jean Pouillon, "L'oeuvre de Claude Lévi-Strauss," *Les Temps Modernes* 126 (1956), p. 155.

28. Edmond Ortigues, *Le Discours et le symbole* (Paris: Aubier, 1962), p. 197. Ortigues also marks the second difference between the imaginary and the symbolic: the "dual" or "specular" character of the imagination, in opposition to the Third, to the third term which belongs to the symbolic system.

29. Louis Althusser, *Lire le Capital* 2, pp. 169–177 [*Reading Capital*, pp. 187–193]. Trans: See J.-A. Miller, "La suture (éléments de la logique du signifiant)," *Cahiers pour l'analyse* 1/2 (1966), pp. 49–51 ["Suture (elements of the logic of the signifier)," Trans. Jacqueline Rose, *Screen* 18.4 (1977–78), pp. 32–34].

30. Claude Lévi-Strauss, *Anthropologie structurale*, p. 224 [*Structural Anthropology*, p. 203].

31. Serge Leclaire, "La mort dans la vie de l'obsédé," *La Psychanalyse* 2 (1956). Trans: Deleuze refers to Leclaire's analyses in discussing questions and problems as "living acts of the unconscious," *Différence et répétition*, pp. 140–141 [*Difference and Repetition*, pp. 106–107, 316–317 fn. 17].

32. Trans: In a translator's note in *What Is Philosophy?*, Hugh Tomlinson and Graham Burchell remark: "In her translation of Sartre's *Being and Nothingness* (New York: Philosophical Library, 1956), Hazel Barnes translates *objectité*, which she glosses as 'the quality or state of being an object' (p.632), as 'objectness' or, on occasion, as 'object-state.' We have preferred 'objectality' in line with Massumi's translation of *visagéité* as 'faciality' in *A Thousand Plateaus* (Deleuze and Guattari, *What Is Philosophy?* [New York: Columbia University Press, 1994], pp. 3–4). On the question/problem as objective instances, see *Différence et répétition*, pp. 219–221 & 359 [*Difference and Repetition*, pp. 169–170, 280–281].

33. Claude Lévi-Strauss, *Le Totémisme aujourd'hui* (Paris: PUF, 1962), p. 112 [*Totemism*, trans. Rodney Needham (Boston: Beacon Press, 1963), pp. 77–78]. Trans: On totemism and its structuralist interpretation, see *Mille plateaux* (Paris: Minuit, 1980), pp. 288–89 [*A Thousand Plateaus*, trans. Brian Massumi (Minneapolis: University of Minnesota Press, 1987), p. 236].

34. Trans: On serialization and its relation to Lacan's analysis, see *Logique du sens*, pp. 51–55 [*Logic of Sense*, pp. 37–40].

35. Jacques Lacan, *Écrits* 15 ["Seminar on 'The Purloined Letter,'" p. 44].

36. Jacques Lacan, *Le Mythe individuel du névrosé* (Paris: CDU, 1953) ["The Neurotic's Individual Myth," trans. Martha Noel Evans, *The Psychoanalytic Quarterly* 48 (1979), p. 405–425], reprinted in revised form in *Ornicar*, pp. 17–18, 1979.

37. Philippe Sollers, *Drame* (Paris: Seuil, 1965). Trans: Deleuze says that Sollers's novel "takes as its motto a formula by Leibniz: 'Suppose, for example, that someone draws a number of points on the paper at random. ... I say that it is possible to find a geometric line the notion of which is constant and uniform according to a certain rule such that his line passes through all the points...'," and adds: "The entire beginning of this book is constructed on the two formulae: 'Problem...' and 'Missed...'. Series are traced out in relation to the singular points of the body of the narrator, an ideal body which is 'thought rather than perceived'," *Différence et répétition*, pp. 257 [*Difference and Repetition*, p. 326 fn. 16].

38. Jean-Pierre Faye, *Analogues* (Paris: Seuil, 1964).

39. Sigmund Freud, *Oeuvres complètes*, vol. IX (Paris: PUF, 1998).

40. Claude Lévi-Strauss, *Le Totémisme aujourdh'hui* 115 [*Totemism*, pp. 79–81].

41. Trans: The allusion refers Arthur Rimbaud's enigmatic prose poem "H" and to the final line, "trouvez Hortense" [find Hortense]. See Rimbaud, *Oeuvres completes* (Paris: Gallimard, 1972) 151.

42. Trans: On the refrain, see *Différence et répétition* 161 [*Difference and Repetition*, pp. 122–123].

43. André Green, "L'objet (a) de J. Lacan," *Cahiers pour l'analyse* 3 (1966), p. 32.

44. Jacques Lacan, *Écrits*, p. 25 ["Seminar on 'The Purloined Letter,'" p. 55; translation modified]. Trans: See also *Différence et répétition*, p. 157 [*Difference and Repetition*, pp. 199–200].

45. Trans: On the simultaneously relative and absolute status of movements (as characterizing the concept), see *Qu'est-ce que la philosophie?* (Paris: Minuit, 1991) 26–27 [*What Is Philosophy?*, trans.

Hugh Tomlinson and Graham Burchell (New York: Columbia University Press, 1994), pp. 21–22].

46. Trans: See *Logique du sens*, pp. 55–56 [*Logic of Sense*, pp. 40–41].

47. Michel Foucault, *Les Mots et les choses*, pp.19–31 [*The Order of Things*, pp. 3–16].

48. Trans: Deleuze cites Sollers and Faye in his discussion of the "blind spot" in *Différence et répétition*, p. 257 [*Difference and Repetition*, p. 326].

49. J-A. Miller "La suture (éléments de la logique du signifiant)," pp. 44–49 ["Suture (elements of the logic of the signifier)," pp. 26–32].

50. Claude Lévi-Strauss, "Introduction à l'oeuvre de Marcel Mauss," pp. 49–59, in Marcel Mauss, *Sociologie et anthropologie*, Paris: PUF, 1950. Trans: See also *Logique du sens*, pp. 63–64 [*Logic of Sense*, pp. 48–50].

51. Trans: See *Logique du sens*, pp. 57–62 [*Logic of Sense*, pp. 44–47].

52. Trans: On the object = x and word = x, see *Différence et répétition*, pp. 156–163 [*Difference and Repetition*, pp. 118–125].

53. Michel Foucault, *Raymond Roussel* (Paris: Gallimard, 1963) [*Death and the Labyrinth: The World of Raymond Roussel*, trans. Charles Ruas (Garden City, NY: Doubleday, 1986)].

54. Trans: See *Logique du sens*, pp. 266–268 [*Logic of Sense*, pp. 228–230].

55. Trans: On the phallus as "object = x," see the thirty-second series in *Logic of Sense*.

56. Cf. Macherey in *Lire le Capital*, pp. 242–252, the analysis that Macherey carries out on the notion of value, showing that this notion is always staggered in relation to the exchange in which it appears.

57. Foucault *Les Mots et les choses*, 392 [*The Order of Things*, p. 380] Trans: On the status of different "orders" in relation to one another, see *Différence et répétition*, pp. 236–242 [*Difference and Repetition*, pp. 182–186].

58. Trans: See *Différence et répétition*, pp. 251–266 [*Difference and Repetition*, pp. 195–206] and *Logique du sens*, pp. 67–73 [*Logic of sense*, pp. 52–57].

59. Michel Foucault, *Les Mots et les choses*, p. 353 [*The Order of Things*, p. 342].

60. Trans: See *Différence et répétition*, pp. 316–319, pp. 354–357 (conclusion) [*Difference and Repetition*, pp. 246–248, pp. 276–279].

61. Claude Lévi-Strauss, *Le Cru et le Cuit* (Paris: Plon, 1964), p. 19 [*The Raw and the Cooked*, trans. John and Doreen Weightman (New York: Harper and Row, 1964), p. 11].

62. Cf. the schema proposed by Serge Leclaire, following Lacan, in "A la recherche des principes d'une psychothérapie des psychoses," *L'Évolution psychiatrique* 2 (1958).

63. On the Marxist notions of "contradiction" and "tendency," cf. the analyses of Etienne Balibar, in Althusser, *Lire le Capital*, pp. 296–303 [*Reading Capital*, pp. 283–293].

64. Cf. Michel Foucault, *Les Mots et les choses*, p. 230 [*The Order of Things*, p. 217]: structural mutation "[this profound breach in the expanse of continuities], though it must be analyzed, and minutely so, cannot be 'explained' or even summed up in a single word. It is a radical event that is distributed across the entire visible surface of knowledge, and whose signs, shocks, and effects, it is possible follow step by step."

Three Group-Related Problems

1. Preface to Félix Guattari, *Psychanalyse et transversalité* (Paris: François Maspero, 1972), pp. i-xi. Deleuze and Guattari will met in the summer of 1969, in Limousin, and very quickly decided to work together. In 1972, *Anti-Oedipus* signaled the beginning of their collective efforts, which would continue for twenty years: , *Kafka : For a Minor Literature* (1975), *Thousand Plateaus* (1980), *What Is Philosophy ?* (1991). Cf. DRF, the letter to Uno: "comment nous avons travaillé à deux."

2. Guattari was initially a militant connected with Trotskyism (which will get him thrown out of the French Communist Party), and then later agitated in several different groups (viz., *la Voie communiste, l'Opposition de Gauche, le mouvement du 22 mars*); at the same time, he joined the team of experts at the now famous La Borde clinic, when Dr. Jean Oury first opened it in 1953. It is in this clinic that the foundations of institutional psychotherapy would be defined in both practical and theoretical terms, following the pioneering work of Dr. Tosquelles (in which the psychotherapeutic cure is thought of as inseparable from the analysis of institutions). Guattari, as a member of the CERFI (the Center for Research and Institutional Formation), was a student of Lacan from the very beginnings of the Seminar and a member of the French Freudian school in Paris. The texts from *Psychanalyse et transversalité* retrace the steps of his entire development from a theoretical and practical standpoint.

3. Marcel Jaeger, "L'Underground de la folie," in "Folie pour folie," *Partisans*, février 1972.

4. *Cahiers de Vérité*, série "Sciences humaines et Lutte des classes," no. 1.

5. Deleuze has here added a note on a personal copy: "for example, political economy is decided at least decided at a European-wide level, whereas social politics remain the concern of the State."

6. Michel Foucault, *Madness and Civilization*. Random House, 1965, appendix I.

"What Our Prisoners Want From Us..."

1. *Le Nouvel Observateur*, 31 janvier 1972, p. 24. Early in 1971, Deleuze joined the GIP (The Group for Information on Prisons), which was established in 1970 with the guidance of Daniel Defert and Michel Foucault. Following the dissolution of the GIP in December 1972, the ADDD was formed (Association for the Defense of the Rights of Prisoners). Deleuze participated in the Association with Daniel Defert, Jean-Marie Domenach, Dominique Eluard, and Vercors. In June 1971, Deleuze wrote a brief press release on the Jaubert Affair, which appeared in the supplement to *La Cause du Peuple-J'accuse*. (The journalist Alain Jaubert, beaten up in a police van as he accompanied someone injured during a demonstration, had been indicted for assaulting a police officer.) For further documentation, see P. Artières, ed., *Le Groupe d'information sur les prisons: archives d'une lutte 1971–1972* (Paris: IMEC Editions, 2002).

2. In December 1971 and January 1972, more than thirty riots broke out in the prisons at Toul, Nancy, and Lille. On January 18, 1972, Deleuze participated with Jean-Paul Sartre, Claude Mauriac, Michèle Vian, Alain Jaubert, and many others in a sit-in organized by Michel Foucault, in the great hall of the Ministry of Justice.

3. Dr. Edith Rose, a psychiatrist for the Ney penitentiary at Toul, had conducted a report on the detention conditions of the prisoners: tortures, suicides, punishment, the use of tranquilizers, etc. Foucault read long passages from it during a press conference in Toul on December 16, 1971, and with his friends purchased a page of *Le Monde* to make public before its appearance the official inquiry of M. Schmelck. From Dr. Rose's report, Deleuze composed a brief notice, "A propos des psychiatres dans les prisons" in the APL bulletin on January 9, 1972, in which he called on psychiatrists and psychoanalysts, "damaging witnesses" in the prisons, to denounce "the penitentiary regime in France." Dr. Rose will be dismissed from the penitentiary administration.

4. The Pleven reforms, following the Schmelck report on the prison riots at Toul, aimed at the improvement of detention conditions, cafeterias, exercise, etc.

Intellectuals and Power

1. An interview with Michel Foucault on March 4, 1972, in *L'Arc*, no. 49: "Gilles Deleuze," 1972, pp. 3–30.

2. Cf. "What Our Prisoners Want From Us," note 1.

3. See "What Our Prisoners Want From Us," note 3.

4. Cf. "Sur la justice populaire. Débat avec les maos" (5 février 1972), *Les Temps modernes*, no. 310 *bis*, juin 1972, pp. 355–366. Repris in *Dits et Ecrits*, vol. II, no. 108 (Paris: Gallimard, 1994).

Remarks (on Jean-François Lyotard)

1. *La Quinzaine littéraire*, no. 140, 1–15 mai 1972, p. 19. These remarks are on Jean-François Lyotard's *Discours, Figure* (Paris: Klincksieck, 1971). *Discours, Figure* is Lyotard's doctoral thesis; Deleuze was one of the members on the defense committee.

Deleuze and Guattari Fight Back...

1. Cf. La *Quinzaine littéraire*, no. 143, 16–30 juin 1972, pp. 15–19. This is a round-table discussion with François Châtelet, Pierre Clastres, Roger Dadoun, Serge Leclaire, Maurice Nadeau, Raphaël Pividal, Pierre Rose, and Henri Torrubia. The director of the *Quinzaine*, Maurice Nadeau, in collaboration with the philosopher François Châtelet, wanted to confront the authors of *Anti-Oedipus* with specialists from several human sciences: psychoanalysis (Roger Dadoun, Serge Leclaire), psychiatry (Henri Torrubia), sociology (Raphaël Pividal), philosophy (François Châtelet), and ethnology (Pierre Clastres).

2. Cf. *Sexualité humaine* (Paris: Aubier, 1970).

Hélène Cixous, or Writing in Strobe

1. *Le Monde*, no. 8576, 11 août 1972, p. 10. (On the book by H. Cixous, *Neutre* (Paris: Grasset, 1972).

2. H. Cixous, *Dedans* (Paris: Grasset, 1969).

3. H. Cixous, *L'Exil de James Joyce ou l'art de remplacement* (Paris: Grasset, 1968).

4. Strobe or strobelight: the discountinuous lighting of a scene. The effect produced depends on the frequency of the flashes and movements in the scene.

Capitalism and Schizophrenia

1. The French text is a translation from the Italian, in an interview with Vittorio Marchetti, "Capitalismo e schizophrenia," *Tempi Moderni*, no. 12 (1972), pp. 47–64.

2. Arthur Rimbaud, *Une Saison en enfer*, "Mauvais sang," in *Oeuvres complètes* (Pléiade, 1972), p. 95.

H.M.'s Letters

1. *Suicides dans les prisons* en 1972 (Paris: Gallimard, coll. 'Intolérable,' 1973), pp. 38–40. This text is unsigned, the usual practice for GIP; it was written with Daniel Defert, a sociologist, Michel Foucault's partner and co-founder of GIP. See the introductory note to "What Our Prisoners Want From Us."

2. Pierre Arpaillanges, Director of Criminal Affairs and Pardons at the Justice Department since René Pleven had taken office in June 1969, published a report in 1972 severely criticizing the workings of the penitentiary system (prison dysfunction, overpopulation, etc.). Still secret when Gilles Deleuze and Michle Defert composed this text, the report would be made public by the minister in June 1973.

3. George Jackson, a militant African-American, was imprisoned in San Quentin and Soledad, where he was murdered on August 21, 1971. Gilles Deleuze and members of the GIP collaborated on a special edition: *L'Assassinat de George Jackson* (Paris: Gallimard, coll. 'Intolérable,' 1971).

4. See "What Our Prisoners Want From Us," note 4.

Hot and Cool

1. In *Fromanger, le peintre et le modèle* (Paris: Baudard Alvarez, 1973), exhibition catalogue. Born in 1939, Gérard Fromanger gets himself noticed in May '68 by exhibiting huge plastic spheres in the streets of Paris. But Deleuze is concerned here with the monochrome composition which Fromanger turned to early in the '70s.

2. M. McLuhan, *Pour Comprendre les médias* (Paris: Mame-Seuil, 1968), pp. 39–50.

3. D.H. Lawrence, *Eros et les chiens*, ed. Christian Bourgois (Paris, 1969) p. 195.

Nomadic Thought

1. *In Nietzsche aujourd'hui? tome 1: Intensités* (Paris: UGE, 10/18, 1973), pp. 159–174. For the discussion following, see pp. 185–187 and, pp. 189–190 (only those questions addressed to Deleuze have been retained). The conference "Nietzsche aujourd'hui?" took place in July 1972 at the International Cultural Center in Cerisy-la-Salle.

2. A high school student on the extreme left, injured by the police during a demonstration in 1971.

3. Maurice Blanchot, *L'Entretien infini* (Paris: Gallimard, 1969), p. 227 ff.

4. Franz Kafka, *La Muraille de Chine et autres récits* (Paris: Gallimard, 1950), pp. 96–96.

5. Leo Strauss, *De la Tyrannie*, followed by Kojève, *Tyrannie et sagesse* (Paris: Gallimard, 1997).

On Capitalism and Desire

1. Editor's title. "Gilles Deleuze, Félix Guattari" in *C'est Demain la veille*, ed. Michel-Antoine Burnier (Paris: Editions du Seuil, 1973), pp. 139–161. This interview was initially supposed to appear in the magazine *Actuel*, one of whose directors of publication was M.-A. Burnier.

2.Pierre Victor was the pseudonym of Benny Levy, the one-time leader of the Proletarian Left (Gauche prolétarienne), which was outlawed. Cf. *Les Temps modernes*, "Nouveau Fascisme, Nouvelle démocratie" no. 310 bis, juin 1972, pp. 355–366.

3. D. Guérin, *La Révolution française et nous* (Paris: F. Maspero, 1976). Cf. also, *Lutte des classes sous la Première République: 1793–1797* (Paris: Gallimard, 1968).

4. On George Jackson, see note 3 for "H.M.'s Letters."

Five Propositions on Psychoanalysis

1. Originally published in Italian. "Relazione di Gilles Deleuze" and discussions in Armando Verdiglione, ed., *Psicanalisi e Politica; Atti del Convegno di studi tenuto a Milano l'8–9 Maggio 1973*. Milan: Feltrinelli, 1973, pp. 7–11, 17–21, 37–40, 44–45, 169–172. Abridged and edited.

Faces and Surfaces

1. With Stefan Czerkinsky and J.-J. Passera, in *Faces et Surfaces* (Paris: Editions Galerie Karl Flinker, 1973). The occasion was the exhibition catalogue devoted to a young Polish artist whose work—monochrome compositions—remains unknown (the artist killed himself a little after the exhibit).
2. Six drawings by Deleuze, reproduced in *Chimères*, no. 21, were part of the exhibit.

3. Concepts are not in your head: they are things, peoples, zones, regions, thresholds, gradients, temperatures, speeds, etc.

4. The border-hole and the margin-border are the two units of painting, among other things. The one can be understood as the territorialization of the other, such that the other is then the deterritorialization of the one. But all of this is reversed when you walk around to the other side.

Preface to Hocquenghem's *L'Après-Mai des faunes*

1. "Preface" in Guy Hocquenghem, *L'Après-Mai des faunes* (Paris: Grasset, 1974) pp. 7–17. Guy Hocquenghem (1946–1988) was a writer and a member of FHAR (Front homosexuel d'action révolutionnaire / Homosexual Front of Revolutionary Action, created in 1970). He met Deleuze at the University of Vincennes, where Deleuze was teaching.

2. Guy Hocquenghem, *Le Désir homosexuel* (Paris: Editions Universitaires, coll. 'Psychothèque,' 1972).

3. The Arcadie Club (1954–1982) was a group that formed around André Baudry, who believed that homosexuals should unite with discretion, "courage," and "dignity." On the right of the political spectrum, Baudry's group was opposed to the "scandalous" public demonstrations of FHAR.

A Planter's Art

1. In *Deleuze, Faye, Roubaud, Touraine parlent de "Les Autres"—un film de Hugo Santiago, écrit en collaboration avec Adolfo Bioy Casares and Jorge Luis Borges* (Paris: Christian Bourgois, 1974). This is part of a brochure that was distributed at the door of the theatre Quartier Latin to defend and support Santiago's film, which had caused a scandal at the Cannes Film Festival in 1974.

List of Translators

Bergson, 1859–1941
Translated by Christopher Bush

How do We Recognize Structuralism?
Translated by Melissa McMahon and Charles J. Stivale

Hot and Cool
Translated by Teal Eich

Five Propositions on Psychoanalysis
Translated by Alexander Hickox

Index

Fatal Strategies Jean Baudrillard

Foucault Live: Collected Interviews of Michel Foucault Sylvère Lotringer, ed.

Hatred of Capitalism: a Semiotext(e) Reader Chris Kraus & Sylvère Lotringer, eds.

Lost Dimension Paul Virilio

SEMIOTEXT(E) • THE JOURNAL

Sylvère Lotringer, *Editor*

Flesh-Eating Technologies Sara Diamond & Sylvère Lotringer, eds.

Imported: A Reading Seminar Rainer Ganahl, ed.

Polysexuality Francois Péraldi, ed.

Autonomia: Post-Politics Politics Sylvère Lotringer & Christian Marazzi, Eds

SEMIOTEXT(E) • FOREIGN AGENTS SERIES

Sylvère Lotringer, *Editor*

The Accident of Art Sylvère Lotringer & Paul Virilio

Chaosophy Félix Guattari

Crepuscular Dawn Paul Virilio & Sylvère Lotringer

Driftworks Jean-François Lyotard

Ecstasy of Communication Jean Baudrillard

Fearless Speech Michel Foucault

Forget Foucault Jean Baudrillard

Germania Heiner Müller

A Grammar of the Multitude Paolo Virno

Inside & Out of Byzantium Nina Zivancevic

In the Shadow of the Silent Majorities Jean Baudrillard

Looking Back on the End of the World Jean Baudrillard, Paul Virilio, et al.

Nomadology: The War Machine Gilles Deleuze & Félix Guattari

On The Line Gilles Deleuze & Félix Guattari

Politics of the Very Worst Paul Virilio

The Politics of Truth Michel Foucault

Popular Defense and Ecological Struggles Paul Virilio

Pure War Paul Virilio & Sylvère Lotringer

Revolt, She Said Julia Kristeva

Sadness at Leaving Erje Ayden

Simulations Jean Baudrillard

69 Ways to Play the Blues Jurg Laederach

Soft Subversions Félix Guattari

Speed and Politics Paul Virilio

Why Different: Luce Irigaray

SEMIOTEXT(E) · ACTIVE AGENTS SERIES

Hedi El Kholti, Chris Kraus & Sylvère Lotringer, *Editors*

The Empire of Disorder Alain Joxe

Reporting from Ramallah: An Israeli Journalist in an Occupied Land Amira Hass

Still Black, Still Strong Dhoruba Bin Wahad, Mumia Abu-Jamal & Assata Shakur